Above it All

DENNIS BROOKS

DEDICATION

This book is of course first dedicated to the Vietnam Vet and the ones that have lost their lives while serving. And of course to A, B, C, Troops of the 1/9ᵗʰ Cavalry, some of the bravest men that anyone could have known or served with. Even though some of their fellow countrymen back home had turned their backs on them, this never stopped them from serving with honor and being there for each other.

This book could not have been written at all without my wife Veronica and her support and encouragement as well. She too faced her share of duress during these difficult years of waiting me to return home from combat, my continues P.T.S.D. mood swings, as well as the pain staking six years it took me to complete this book. Her love, understanding and her support has been the single most fact on me being able to bring my story to life.

My daughters Brandy and Jenny for putting those smiles on my face at times when things were hard for us all, as well as my brother Vodie for keeping it real for me and too always being there, my Son-in-laws Steve and Dave also giving me support and understanding.

ACKNOWLEDGMENTS

To April Redmon for the long hours she spent helping me.

To my Slaton High School fiends Kathy, Marlin, Jill, Janis, Benny, for being first outside family to read my book and giving me their honest opinion and advise which I respect.

Slaton Texas for inculcating in me the attributes that carried me through life and through the trials and tribulations I faced in front line combat.

Sherrell Wilson, for giving me that seed of motivation to start me writing it all down and soon after with help from my family "Above It All" started taking place.

To my friend Ernest Castillo, for his graphic designing of this book and patience to make it happen.

Last but not least my best friend Johnny Outlaw who was there in the beginning for me and will be there until the end, never judges me for my faults, sharing the highs in my life and being there during some of my lows. Single most used phrase I stole from him. "Free Your Mind, and Your Ass Will Follow"

PART I

INTRODUCTION

In the beginning, when I wrote my so-called book, I did not write down this early part of my life. I wrote the part about my combat experience first. My family wanted me to tell of my youth, and some very hard times I went through. They and many good friends think it is my childhood that helped me get through the combat I experienced in Vietnam. It is not that I think my life is all that interesting or even worthwhile documenting. It is only at the request of my girls Brandy, Jenny and my wife, Roni, and those friends that I added this part of my life. I also want people to realize I don't claim to be an author, just an average guy that has a story that needed to be told.

Let me share with you the true story of some very brave men, and a boy who thought he would be Above It All.

Chapter 1
We All Begin Somewhere

I'm not what one would call a smart man. Of, course, being smart can be defined in different ways. In my later years I am fortunate to have been blessed with a very good memory. I can remember life before I could walk. Now, I don't remember a whole lot from back then, but I do recall trying to *learn* how to walk. My mother said I started around nine months and she was always skeptical of my recollection reaching back that far. My short term memory is not as sharp as it once was, but I still remember pretty well the events in my life.

How much I can remember is not as important to me, as much as not forgetting the things I learned along the way. Without a doubt I am appreciative of the life I have lived, and the life I am living today.

When you are young you never really understand how the chain of events in your life can determine how you will live. Not that you don't have choices. I learned late in life that you do, and you also have a say as to the type of person you are and what kind of person you want to be or become. Sure, life can deal you some hard blows, but as you get older you have to come to the realization that you control some of your own destiny.

The rest is a flip of the coin. You have to play the hand you are dealt.

We also live by example to a certain degree, and my mother was that example for me. As I grew older I realized just how damn smart my mother really was, and it had nothing to do with book smarts. My mother lived by example and she tried her best to set a good one for her children. Oh, yes, and let's not forget common sense, for if you have no common sense, then there is no hope for you in today's world. I was not blessed with a whole lot of this great virtue; it took me longer than the average bear to acquire a little. These attributes, to me anyway, are all as equally important as the other. Setting a good example, I have found, can be harder than getting an education or trying to acquire common sense.

My mother had a great deal to do with me achieving the goals I set for myself. Her best advice was not to set my goals so high that I could not achieve them. By doing this I would not be disappointed by trying to achieve goals beyond my capability. My mother must have known something about me that I did not.

To achieve those goals, education was at the top of her list. Of course I did not listen, for one has to have common sense to follow the advice of one's parent, and like a lot of kids I was born without this great attribute. Only later in life did I acquire enough to see me through to what some refer to as the so called golden years. (I hate that term.)

My mother did not acquire an education for herself, and therefore she learned firsthand the importance of having one. But what my mother did have was a lot of common sense, and by setting a good example for us, she taught her children how to make it in this race called life.

My mother was a migrant worker. Where there was work, that's where we would live. Seventh grade is about as far in school as my mother went. Which underscores why she always talked about the importance of an education and tried her best to inoculate this into her children's minds. I know if she had it to do all over again she would have stayed in school. Before her death in 2002, we had talked about this subject many times.

My mother before she was married.

My mother had three children, Beverley, my older sister born in 1944, who is four years older than me, my younger brother Vodie, born in 1955, who is seven years younger than I, who was born in 1948.

My sister my brother and I. (Modesto California)

All of us are Texans by family and heart, but because of the transitional nature of my mother's work, we were born in the fruit belt of California.

Lubbock, Texas is where my grandfather and grandmother settled back in the 40s and when my mother wasn't following the fruit belt this is where we lived. After all, there was plenty of cotton to be pulled and picked in the fall and she was not one to pass up any work. My dad's family had land around Lubbock and my mother would make extra money pulling and picking cotton for them.

I remember when I was four years old and mother and I were in the cotton fields. She had been picking cotton all day long and I, well I didn't last an hour in the hot sun, and so mother laid me on the cotton sack and pulled me up and down the rolls. For me it was kind of fun, but as I got older and tried a little cotton picking myself I learned how hard I must have been on my mother that day. I never heard my mother complain. My mother's actions imbedded into my mind that everyone likes a hard worker and as long you are willing to work there will be people that will put you to work.

My father, on the other hand, who I don't really care to acknowledge and don't have a whole lot of good things to say about, was for the most part a bum. I never saw him do any physical labor at all. He was always trying to dream up some small scheme to make money. Hard work was not part of it and so he became a dreamer and amounted to nothing during his life. He eventually talked my mother into moving out to California to live and this is where we settled for a short time.

My so-called father was nothing short of a jerk. When he finally achieved the goal of getting my mother to move away from her family, he started cheating on her, drinking and being an all around horse's ass. He knew my grandfather wouldn't stand for this type of unruly conduct and would probably whip him good.

Now would be a good time to let you know about my grandfather. For it is from him that I believe my mother got her true grit. My grandfather was in a way forced out of his home by his father (my great grandfather) to fend for himself. There were a lot of kids at home and at the age of twelve my grandfather was expected to bring home some type of income. My grandfather's way of thinking, was if I bring home the money I might as well be living on my own. He, also not an educated man, made it through four years of school and I guess gave up on it. But he had a lot of common sense and this attribute along with hard work made him, my grandmother, and his eight children somewhat of a living.

My grandfather with his two best friends, he is the one standing in the middle. Picture was taken in Kansas right before Buffalo Bill Cody took his show to Europe

Buffalo Bill, Wild West Show

My Great Grandfather with my mother on the left and my aunt Gene on the right.

My grandfather's life is a book within itself. At the age of thirteen he joined the Buffalo Bill Wild West Show and was one of four horse trainers for the show. All my grandfather knew was horses and ranch life. He is what they call today a horse whisperer and did not believe in busting out horses. As a very young boy I learned a lot from him about horseflesh and dabbled in breaking and training horses using what he had taught me, or more of what I remember him doing.

Now that you have a little background on my grandfather you can probably imagine his response to my father's behavior. Even though my grandfather was an old man of eighty-five he was as tough as nails. If he couldn't have whipped my father with his hands, he would have picked up an equalizer, like a crow bar, and commence to give my father an attitude adjustment that he needed and deserved. My father knew this, so getting my mother off to California would allow my dad to pretty much do what he wanted. It was within these years that things were hardest for my mother.

My grandfather and grandmother, grandfather is in his early 80s and grandmother is in her late 70s. (Lubbock Texas)

Chapter 2
California Mike

It was during these hard times that I became very close to my mother. Later in life I came to realize how things truly were for her and admired her for her hard work just to keep us fed and to see we had a place to live. I remember living in a tent in the orchards of California and working there until the peaches, grapes, or whatever was picked or cut, before we would move into some house.

My sister, Beverley, was a teenager at this time, did well in school and spent her time in the fields herself. She knew the hard work my mother was committed to and I believe she had a hate for dad long before I was aware of what was going on. Beverley had a social life with her friends in school and mother knew the fields were no place for her. But my sister helped my mother by taking care of the house and watching after me while my mother worked. So although wishing she could hang out with her friends, Beverley was stuck with being a part time mom and housekeeper.

My brother hadn't been born at this time. I was seven years old and helping mother in the fields became something that was expected of me. I could tell mother hated the fact I worked along with her, but the money was needed and I was proud of being able to make any contribution to the welfare of the family. Besides, to a kid, working the fields was kind of fun. But after several hours of working in the orchards I grew tired and bored and reached a point where I was more of a burden than help. I don't think my contribution was all that much anyway, but mother encouraged me no matter how small the task, and taught me a valuable lesson to never give up.

It was at this time a good foreman, I believe his name was Ted, would come around and let me ride on the tractor and trailer. He would go around to all the different locations in the orchard and pick up the baskets of peaches or crates of grapes. I would just ride around on the flat bed trailer as the field hands would load the fruit on it. Everyone knew me and being the only white kid in the orchard everyone knew my gringo name. I was teased a lot, but it was all in fun and I never felt like I was segregated in any way. In fact, we shared a tent with a Mexican family and some of my happiest times in California were living with these kind, generous people. I know of the illegal migration problem we have today in the U.S., but at this time in my life I knew nothing, nor did I care, about such things. When you are a kid, you haven't lived long enough to have an opinion on such matters, and you just don't think much past tomorrow. Hot tamales, beans, and fried rice were our main source of food and I never felt like I was hungry. Besides, I had all the fruit I could eat.

Living with these people taught me what a family was supposed to be like. The Mexicans are indeed family oriented; everything was for the well-being of the family. After the fruit season was over, we always moved to the outskirts of town. I missed my friends, and in a way I envied their close family ties. I knew I would be headed back to town soon and living in hell with my father and mother always fighting.

School would be starting and even though I hated school, it was a break from home. When school was out, my father would hardly ever be there and my mother had to seek work at the Gallo Winery. My sister was the oldest and she took it upon herself to be the boss. She was actually cool and she let me do whatever I wanted as long as I stayed out of trouble (which was never) and was home before mother got home. Mother didn't get home until nine or so at night, so being home before mother was easy.

My mother was almost due with my brother, but she worked every day at the winery until it was time to deliver my brother. If the winery would have known she was pregnant they would have laid her off. So to disguise her condition, she wore extra clothing to cover up the fact she was pregnant. Her Mexican friends covered for her as often as they could, but eventually it became too obvious and she had to quit work to have a baby.

Dad, mother, Beverley and me, mother about due with Vodie.

Meanwhile, while my mother was working and trying to make some kind of a living for us, I spent my time on the outskirts of the neighborhood streets of Modesto. My best friend was a boy named Mike Dias. He was of half Mexican and half Italian decent. And what I couldn't think of to get into, he could.

The first words I heard from Mike when I first met him were "do you want to fight?" It wasn't a real fight like you were mad at each other; it was a test to gage how tough you were. I had it in my mind I was pretty tough, but after a bout with Mike I found out quickly what tough really was. This guy was amazing; he did things with his feet I had never seen. It didn't take me long to learn his technique and together we were the toughest kids around. His dad had been a boxer at one time and he also showed us some moves that I have used all my life. We weren't all that old, but even the older kids left us alone.

At school we had quite a reputation and we had a small group of kids we let into our tight little circle. In a way, Mike and I formed a little gang. I remember one day this fifth grader (I was in the third) came over and started picking on some of my friends. Having no fear whatsoever, which was the lack of common sense, I went up to him and busted him in the chops, moved around to his back grabbed him around the neck. After getting him in a neck hold I fell to the ground, I had him in a choke hold from the back and lay sideways with my head buried into his back so he could not reach me. After awhile a teacher came over and broke us apart. The kid told the teacher I started it and I admitted I hit him first. The other kids came to my defense and the teacher looked at the size of this guy and looked at my small frame in comparison, shook her head and told the bully to get back to his area. After all was said and done, I was a hero to the kids and relished in the popularity this fight brought me.

Mike and I decided then and there we could take advantage of the situation and together we formed a protection plan. The plan was simple. Lunch cost thirty-five cents and the parents would give most of the kids that and an extra six cents for ice cream. We would charge the kids six cents a day and in return we would give them protection from the older bullies anytime during school hours. After school hours, it would be extra if you needed protection from any of the other kids. We even had a plan that would take them all the way to their homes. We knew we couldn't protect them all of the time, but eventually the older kids found out if they hurt anyone under our protection, than we would look them up and deal with it. We gave all our clients these cards we drew up and each of them carried one, if a kid carried one of these so called badges, than they were under our protection.

Eventually it was not worth it to the older kids to mess with us so we became a little organization that had a little cash in our pockets. All together we had over fifty kids in our protection program and that amounted to about fifteen dollars a week. To put it in the perspective of that day an age, a large candy bar was five cents, a Coke was five cents, a movie was fifteen cents and a hamburger was about a quarter. There were six of us in our little gang and we always had a little money. Eventually we got into stealing hub caps and stealing soda pop bottles for extra income. Our best source of dough was stealing fruit and selling it door to door. With the extra money, we put together a little fruit stand and actually purchased fruit wholesale from the farmers and sold it. The purchased fruit was a cover up; most of the fruit we sold was stolen from the orchards that surrounded the area we lived in.

We built a little club house out of old lumber that we bought from an old Mexican man and we opened up a little 'Our Gang' type club. We stole fruit from the orchards and sold it on the side of the road as our own.

We had a lot of customers because not having that much invested in the fruit we were selling, we sold it cheap.

Eventually the police got wise to our little operation and we moved the club underground. When I say underground, I mean under the ground. All of us dug this huge hole in ground covered it with 2 X 8 and plywood. Then we covered it with dirt to hide the boards and we had ourselves a great cave. We used candles for light and we held all our top secret meetings underground. It was fun, but dangerous. One time a tractor rolled over our hideout and the roof almost gave way. The tractor operator must have thought he just hit some soft dirt because he never missed a stroke and just kept on driving.

We eventually gave up this hideout and made a tree house. That also was given up because it became too popular with all the kids in the area. You see, we lived on the outskirts of Modesto and the area we lived in was surrounded by orchards. So we decided to have our meetings in the middle of an orchard and from that day on we just met whenever we deemed it necessary. One thing for sure, we never ran out of fruit to eat.

Stealing became a way of life for me. I only got caught at it once and the man that caught me was kind and overlooked it. I was embarrassed and never went into his store again. Instead of appreciating this kind act I did the opposite. I perfected the art of being a thief and I never got caught again. I stole a pellet gun rifle in front of a store owner's eyes. I stole everything from jewelry to clothing, from animals to money. Mike and I became good thieves and we never got caught.

Growing up without adult supervision allowed us to do pretty much what we wanted. The other kids couldn't hang out as much as Mike and me. Mostly because we both had mothers that worked and Mike's father was kind of like my father and really didn't care much what his son was doing. If my mother knew half the things I was doing and was getting into, she would have worn my hide out with a belt.

My very best clothes, going to church, the bible was a good touch. People just knew I was a good boy.

Chapter 3

The Belt

The belt was the answer for everything in my family. My dad used to beat me with it to spark an argument with mother and by doing so it would give him an excuse to leave the house.

He knew mother wouldn't stand by and see any of us kids beaten for no good reason. I remember one time mother telling him to just go if he wanted to go, and not use the kids for his excuse. 'Kids' usually meant yours truly.

Beverley was the girl and Vodie, my brother was just an infant. So being Dad's target was something I got used to. I looked at it as paying dues for all the bad stuff I was involved in. I finally got to the point I fought with him. Of course, it did no good. He ended up hitting me with the buckle end of the belt until my back bled.

Sometimes when he had had too much to drink, he would swing the belt and where it landed made no difference to him.

I carried scars on my back where the loop tang on the buckle stuck in my shoulder all the way to the bone. I wore that scar with pride to remind me how much I hated him. Since crying didn't earn me any relief from these beatings, I tried my best not to cry. One time I didn't cry and he stopped beating me, and looked at me as if he was trying to figure out what was wrong. About the time I thought it had worked he started in on me again. Finally I would submit and the tears would come. I hated the fact that he could make me cry. And swore to myself someday I would take the pain.

The worst though is when dad would turn on mother. One time he hit her so hard it knocked her out. I started crying and went to my mother's side.

"Ah, she is all right," my dad said.

I was crying, but they were tears of hate and from that day forth I started hating my dad more than anyone imagined. I told him if he touched her again I would kill him. He slapped my face, picked me up off the floor and kicked me in the ass. I ended up standing in a corner looking at my mother starting to move. Her jaw was already bruised and swollen. As she picked herself up off of the floor, my dad muttered, "I told you she was ok."

My mother went into the kitchen and wet a rag and put it on her face. Then she slowly walked over to me, put her hand under my chin and asked if I was okay. If *I* was okay. She was bleeding from her mouth; her jaw had started swelling and was black and blue. Her eye was swollen shut and she asked *me* if *I* was ok.

She pulled my face against her stomach and told me not to worry, it was alright. My dad walked over to her, grabbed her arm and spun her around. As he did, my mother picked up an ashtray from a lamp stand and hit him across his forehead. Blood flew everywhere and as he backed up holding his head, he dropped down on one knee and kneeled, bleeding. Mother stood over him with this huge ashtray and told him if he ever laid another hand on her again it would be his last.

"Do you hear me you son-of-a-bitch?"

My dad just kneeled there, said not a word and bled all over the place.

I admired my mother for what she did that day. From then on my mother had had enough and never let him touch her again without some kind of retaliation. My dad received six stitches that day. It was a good day.

When school was out that summer, my mother went back to work in the fields, and my sister took on the chores of being a mother to my new brother. She was only fourteen but took this responsibility with no complaints. My sister and I fought like all siblings do, but when it came down to it she was always there for me if I ever needed her.

I was fairly independent and she didn't have that much to do with me, but it was nice to know she was there. She had things she wanted to do with her friends, but it seemed to me she always had to stay home with Vodie. Mother knew I was okay because I stayed mostly at Mike's. His mom was like a mom to me and she got home earlier than mother did. She didn't mind at all that I was always there. After all, Mike just lived next door.

Eventually Mike and I decided to break up our club to where it would be just him and I. This way we didn't have to split the profits with any of the other kids. Heck, we were doing most of the gutsy stuff anyway. In no time Mike and I had over a hundred dollars saved. We put it in an old coffee can and buried it in a place that only he and I knew.

This was a great deal of money in 1955, especially for a couple of kids. If any grown-ups would have found out about this money, we would have had no explanation for it. There was no way anyone would have believed we came by it honestly. So we made a pact never to reveal our secret to anyone. If either of us did, that one would lose his half of the money and trust between us would have been broken. Trust and each other in Mike's and my situation were all we had. I had no other friends like Mike and he had no other friend like me. We were loners and we poured our deepest secrets on each other. He knew my family situation in every detail and I knew his.

We kept our mouths shut and our ears tuned in and for a couple of kids we thought we had it wired. Except for both of our family's situation, life was not all that bad. I know my sister had to wonder about me always having a little money here and there, but she didn't approach me about the subject and as I think back, I believe she just didn't want to know. Mike and I didn't flaunt the money we had made. We knew some of the old gang members knew what we were doing to get it and it wasn't beyond them to drop the dime on us.

Stealing became a better source of income than the bodyguard thing and it was a lot easier on the body. In two years I had stitches to my head, I had a BB stuck in my finger from a BB gun fight, one broken finger from where a 2x4 hit me during a club fight with an older boy. I had a hole in my knee from a knife a boy stuck me with and Mike had at least twice the injuries I had.

Yep, stealing was a lot easier.

The stitches to my head, I told mother I fell out of a tree. The BB finally popped out on its own. The broken finger Mike and I set; it still has a pop in it to this day. And the hole in my knee healed in about two weeks. I told Mother I cut it on a piece of glass I'd fallen on.

I caught mother crying once on a Saturday during the summer of '56.

When I asked her what was wrong she told me it was nothing, and that she just wasn't feeling well. The 'nothing' was that we had our electricity turned off and Mother had no money to get it turned back on. Dad didn't care one way or the other, but when the old washer in the well house didn't work and his clothes got to where he couldn't wear them around his bitches, he decided to do something about it. Where he got the money, I don't know but in two days time we had electricity again. The bill was nineteen dollars. Nineteen stinking dollars. Hell, I had that much hidden in my room. I decided then to help with some of the bills.

But how could I do that, without exposing Mike and myself? I got this bright idea I would wrap up some money in a rubber band and drop it where mother would find it. I went to Mike with the idea; he tried to talk me out of it at first, but soon afterwards he decided to go along with my plan. We dug up our money and I will never forget to this day how much we counted. Two hundred and three dollars and fourteen cents. We took out a hundred dollars and split it.

I rolled my half of the money up in a big rubber band, and one day while mother and I walked to the store, I placed the money on the side of the road so she could find it. I had to almost point it out to her before she saw it. She screamed and picked the money up and held it tightly in her fist. Seeing her smile almost brought tears to my eyes.

The rest of the way to the store my mother spoke not a word. She kept putting her hand on my shoulder but I really didn't know what for. I imagined that she was thinking of the best places to spend the money. I was so proud of myself and I felt good about what I had done for my mother. I knew if she found out where the money came from it would break her heart. I wished I had of made the money in an honest way, but there just wasn't a lot of work for a boy my age.

When we got to the store my mother stopped, faced me and said, "Dennis, you know this money is not ours."

"What?" I said. "This money is not ours?"

My mother then said she bet someone lost it and is in a hurt for it right now. I couldn't say a word. You have to be kidding me, I thought as my mouth dropped open and I stood there with what must have been a stupid look.

My mother turned and went into the store; walked up to the counter and told Mr. Mitchell, the store owner that she had found fifty dollars and was wondering if anyone had reported losing any money. Mitchell told my mother no, but he would ask around. Well, guess what? Two days later a man claimed the money and gave my mother ten dollars for returning it to him.

Mother looked down and showed me the ten dollars. "You see Dennis, honesty *is* the best policy."

I was dumbstruck. Mother mistook my bewilderment for happy beyond words and told me she would buy us a little ice cream for tonight. I said nothing, lowered my head and went next door to tell Mike. When

I told Mike he started laughing and at first I did not see the humor, then after thinking about it, I started laughing and we both laughed until we could laugh no more.

Mike suggested we get pay back on the ass that took my mother for forty dollars.

"What?" I replied.

"I don't know," Mike said. "This guy will have something we can steal."

I thought for awhile and told Mike no. "I think I am going to try to be honest for awhile."

"Honesty is for suckers," Mike told me. "See what it got your mom?"

I told Mike it didn't cost Mom a thing, it cost me. "Heck, Mike, Mother made money on the deal. She believes in honesty and that's a good thing isn't it?"

Mike told me it seemed like a fairy tale to him. Something you would see on the Mickey Mouse show. You know, where the kids got together at the end of the show and talked about all those good virtues. Then he said if that is what I wanted to do, he would give it a try himself.

I loved my mother for what she had done. I knew then and there I could never measure up to her. She tried to set a good example for me and I didn't want to take it lightly. If anyone had the right to be bitter in life it should have been my mother, but she kept hacking away at life a day at a time. Along the way she always tried to set a good example for us. My mother did live by example. When my mother took time off from work, she spent it around her kids. She was a good mother and I owe some of the good qualities I have to her and my grandmother. Setting an example is important, but it is very hard to actually do.

Mike was great too. He didn't make some funny remark on the way I was feeling. Like the good friend he was, he supported me. That is what friends do, support each other. Mike was a good friend and even though Mother thought he was bad company for me, Mike was my *best* friend. Mike wasn't a bad influence on me, anymore than I was on him. Like I said before, what Mike couldn't think to get into, I could.

It wasn't long before Dad and Mom were at it again. Mother got to the point she wouldn't take anymore of Dad's crap and they were always fighting. Dad quit laying into me with the belt to try and get Mother mad. It seemed Mother was getting up in his face every time she got around him.

I remember once we were downtown and Dad and Mother got into a big argument. Dad knew he could get to Mother through us. They both screamed at each other so loud everyone was looking and pointing at us. Dad, trying to get the upper hand on Mother, told her he would just take us kids.

Wrong thing to say to Mother. She told us to run, but before I could Dad had me by the back of my neck and proceeded to manhandle me to the car. I dropped to the ground to break his grip, turned over on my back, kicked upward and landed my foot into his balls. He doubled up and went down on one knee.

Before I could get up though he grabbed my leg, picked me up and threw me in the rolled down window of the car. He told me to keep my goddamn ass in the car and then turned his attention to Mother, who at this time was coming at him, carrying Vodie in one hand and doubling up to make a fist with the other.

I jumped out the window, went to the trunk of the car and pulled out a lug wrench. I may not stop him from hitting Mother, but I knew if I landed it right the damage would be done. I was concentrating on hitting him right above the knee cap, but as luck had it a police officer came and stepped in-between Mother and Dad and diffused what was fixing to be a very bad situation. The policeman eventually told Mother to go to the court house and told Dad to be on his way. Dad cussed and raised a little hell with the cop, but the cop just let it roll off his back and kept stepping toward Dad until Dad had backed off far enough to allow Mom to get into the car with us. Mother went to the court house and after several hours filed for her divorce.

When we finally got home, Dad was there and he was mad. Bev took Vodie to our bedroom and I followed.

Mother and Dad ended up in their bedroom arguing. The bathroom we had in that house adjoined their room, as did our closet. I went through the bathroom to their door and listened as their voices got louder and louder. Suddenly, I heard Dad hit Mother. I opened the door and he was picking her up off of the bed. I ran toward him with my head down and butted him in the ass at a full run. It got him off balance and he fell to the ground, but in a split second he jumped up and came at me. I ran through the bathroom into our room, his footsteps close behind me. I ran into the closet to go through it back into their room. I heard him stop and run back through the bathroom to cut me off.

Mother was now on her feet and confronted him as he came back into the bedroom. He was out of control. I squatted down in the closet looked over in the corner and saw Dad's 410 shotgun. I grabbed a hold of it and pointed it at the door. Even though I had never shot this rifle, I knew how. I was always interested in guns and I had made it a point to know how to fire this one. We were at home alone a lot and the gun was there for burglars and it was loaded.

The door burst open and Dad started parting through the hanging clothes to get to me. When he finally did, he found himself looking down the barrel of this rifle. He called out my name and told me to put down the damn gun. I aimed the gun low and pulled the trigger. The buckshot grazed his left side and Dad screamed like a girl and backed out of the closet. I stepped out of the closet aimed the gun at his head and pulled the trigger again. Nothing. The gun didn't fire. I didn't know how to chamber another round in the damn thing.

I let the gun fall to the floor and ran to my mother. She was screaming out "Oh no!" over and over again as she held me close to her. My dad just lay on the floor holding his side; his shirt was covered in blood.

Soon after, an ambulance came and it seemed everyone we knew was outside our door. Mike made his way to my side and put his arm over my shoulder. I put my arms around his neck and started to cry. Mike didn't know what to say and I didn't either. We just stood amongst the grown-ups holding onto each other. I wasn't crying for Dad that was for sure. I didn't know what would become of it all and knew there was a world of hurt coming down on me. I had visions of prison, jail, and I knew I wouldn't see my mother again.

Nothing, I mean *nothing*, happened. The police didn't even question me. No one asked me about anything. To this day, I don't know what was ever said. If Mother or Dad told them it was an accident or what, all I know is I was never approached about the incident, and

I for one was relived. This event was never discussed or talked about among the family.

My mother died in 2002 and for forty-nine years I never heard another word about this event. The one thing I do remember is that my dad had to have skin grafted onto the place where he was shot. The buckshot didn't go into his body; it grazed him and peeled his skin back like a banana. I remember seeing him without a shirt one time and there was a big white patch on his right side. Being part Indian, his skin had a dark complexion and the white patch stood out like a beacon. Growing up, I once brought this subject up to everyone; they acted like it didn't happen and changed the subject. I finally gave up and came to realize it was and is something no one in my family wants to talk about.

One thing for sure, Dad never hit me or Mother again. He threatened to whip my ass now and then, but it was the last time he ever hit mother or any of us kids.

Eventually, for awhile, the state of California stepped in and I was put in a home for kids without parents and my sister and brother went to stay with an aunt for awhile. Oddly enough it was my dad's sister Lulu. She and Mother were good friends and Mother knew she would look after them. It was just until the divorce was final and then we would be back together again. Why I had to go to a home, I don't know. It probably had something to do with me being hard to handle and my aunts didn't want to deal with me or maybe they knew the story of what really happened to Dad and didn't want to take the chance of me shooting them in their sleep or something like that. I don't know. I only know I was treated different after the event of shooting my Dad. I was never mistreated by any of my aunts and uncles, but I could tell they were treating me different.

Chapter 4
The Home

The Home wasn't that bad and the food was even better. I did have one run-in at the Home and shortly afterward I was back with my family again.

The women that were in charge of the place didn't put up with any nonsense and as long as you were behaved or didn't get caught at anything, life at the Home was okay. The kids, for the most part, were nice but I felt sorry for some of them because they were orphans and always talked about having real parents. Having parents, to me, wasn't all that great. I missed my mother but never gave Dad a second thought.

All these kids wanted to talk about was having parents. I stayed to myself and didn't mingle with them all that much. Their interest was so different than mine. I missed Mike and wished I could see him. I thought at one time I would never see him again. This made me sad and I hated to even think about it.

At this Home there was one kid that in some ways I kind of liked, but he was a bully and liked everyone to know how tough he was. He was a lot older and bigger than the rest of us and I figured it would be to my best interest to stay clear of him. I knew if I was pushed I would push back and I didn't want to fight this guy. He was older and one on one he could whip my ass. But I left him alone and he seemed to do the same to me.

Every Friday some women in the area, a church group or someone, would make pies for the Home. It was the only day we got to eat a dessert and all the kids looked forward to Friday. This particular Friday we were having cherry pie and I was anticipating having that pie.

After supper the women that ran the Home started bringing out the pies and I want to tell you they were at least 3" thick and the slices were huge. You could see the excitement in our faces. This one little boy who was about four years old was bouncing up and down in his seat. I mean this kid was excited and in turn made everyone else just as excited as he was. We were all laughing and we were all anticipating that first bite. As the pies were set down in front of us the women would tell us we couldn't eat it until we cleaned our plates. Well, it would be a little while for me because we were having Brussels sprouts and I hated Brussels sprouts, but for pie I would force them down.

Just as I was about to finish my last sprout this hand came from around my back and grabbed my pie. I reached for it just to have a fist crack me across my left ear, the pain made my eyes water. It was the bully. He had taken my pie and was returning to his seat to finish it off. Anger crawled up my back. I could have called out to the ladies that ran the home, but to me that would not settle the issue at hand. It had nothing to do with the pie. This kid had no idea what he had done. He thought he could get away with anything because of his size. A calm feeling came over me. To me fighting was exciting. I didn't start fights, but I have to say I liked it once it started.

I took my napkin and wrapped it around the fork end of my fork exposing the handle, this particular fork came to a somewhat of a tapered, but blunt point. I let the kid take a bite of my pie then calmly walked over to him, he saw me coming and started to stand, but before he could get to his feet I buried the handle of the fork about three inches into his back right shoulder. He started screaming and fell to the floor. I knew enough about these women that ran the home to know I was in deep trouble. So I made the best of it and grabbed my pie with my bare hands and started stuffing it into my mouth.

The two women burst into the room trying to figure out what had happened. By the time the kids told her what had happened and they figured it all out, I ate my pie and the bully's pie too. The larger of the two women walked up and slapped my face. As she started to slap it a second time I stopped her. She yelled out for help and between her and the other woman and a man who helped out around the place, put me in a closet and locked the door. I didn't put up much resistance I knew I probably handled it all wrong, but the point was made and I couldn't wait to see this bully again, for I wanted to see where I stood from his point of view.

This closet had been used for punishment before, I could tell because there was a chair placed in there and a small blanket. I knew it would be awhile before I was out of there because of these items. I didn't mind the solitude, what I hated was my sticky hands. The sugar from the pie along with the pie filling was like glue. I licked my fingers as much as I could but I couldn't get the stickiness to completely go away. No one said a word to me all night. Early the next morning, one of the women brought me a wash rag and a pale to piss in. I washed my face and hands with the washrag and relived myself in the pot I was given. The lady came around and took the pot from me later on that morning and told me she would let me out if I thought I deserved to be let out. I didn't say anything, she repeated herself and I answered back with 'I guess.' She asked me what I meant with a statement like that. I told her I wasn't going to stand by and take any crap from that kid I stuck with the fork. She didn't say anything for the longest time, and then she made the comment that the other kids told her what happened, but I was way out of line to do what I had done. "You could have killed him if you would have placed that fork in his neck."

I told her I wasn't aiming for the neck and I wasn't trying to kill him. Heck it was just his back. She didn't see it my way and didn't let me out until supper that night.

When she let me out that evening she told me to take a shower, clean up and come down to the dining room. As I walked down the stairs to the dining room I couldn't hear any of the kids talking. Usually at this time all of them were talking at once and it was actually the nosiest part of the day. When I entered the room you could have heard a pin drop. Everyone turned as I walked in and watched me all the way to my chair. When I sat down everyone was still looking at me, and half of them were smiling ear to ear.

A smile came across my face and all the kids started talking to each other. I glanced down the table to where the bully was sitting and he wouldn't even look at me. He had his right arm in a sling like he was really hurt, and I thought to myself, *this guy is a sissy*. I kept looking his way hoping he would make eye contact with me. He never did and from this day, till the day I left, about two weeks in all he stayed clear of me.

Later that evening the lady that slapped me told me she was sorry. In turn, I told her I was too and tried to explain if I would have called them in than I would have looked like a sissy. She told me looking like a sissy and being a sissy is two different things and that there is no way she would have thought I was a sissy, if only I would have just told her about it. I told her I didn't care if she thought I was a sissy or not, that wasn't important to me. But what is important to me was what the other kids thought, and that this bully knew I wasn't going to take any crap off of him.

She asked me if that was really so important to me. I replied yes and she just shook her head. Not where I grew up, she replied. Then and there I knew the problem and didn't bother to explain, or try and make her understand. Where she grew up, that was the key.

I never really looked at my family as being poor, but we were and poor kids do grow up different. They have a whole different set of rules to go by. I knew a couple of rich kids and although they were fun to hang around and you seemed to get along with them, their parents were always trying to segregate us. That was fine with me, I was just a kid and things like that don't play on a kid's mind. I have always been proud of my roots and, most of all, proud of my mother.

Even though we were poor I never really felt that way. Of course, I was stealing everything that wasn't tied down and actually between Mike and me we had more money than some of the better off kids had. I know one thing for sure: Mike and I had a lot more fun than most kids. Evidently doing things the honest way didn't last and Mike and I returned to what we did best and that was to steal.

Chapter 5
The Wrist Rocket

Living in the fruit belt wasn't all that bad either. Name a fruit or a nut and we had it. Even in the so called winter months we had oranges and nuts of every kind. Actually, Mike and I would eat breakfast walking to school. School was about three miles away, which gave us plenty of time to pilfer the orchards and vineyards for breakfast. One thing was for sure if you were hungry you could always find something to eat. Of course, the farmers didn't appreciate you eating and taking fruit from their orchards and vineyards. If you got caught you paid the price and the price was a load of salt rock or pork rind loaded up in a shotgun and the farmers would not hesitate to shoot your ass with it.

One time I bent over to cut some grapes off of a vine and got splattered with salt rock from my knee, up my side and across the back of my neck. The impact hurt like you wouldn't believe as it penetrated my skin, but when the salt rock dissolved under my skin it set me afire. Mike was with me at the time but didn't get hit. The farmer fired two shots at us and I was the lucky one.

It was a known fact that if you carried the marks of salt rock on your skin the neighbors and everyone that saw the scars knew you got caught by a farmer for stealing fruit. I tried to cover up my marks by wearing paints and a shirt, but Mother soon found out from the scars on my neck and of course she was inquisitive of why I quit wearing shorts and started putting on a shirt.

It wasn't long before mother found out, but she was more upset with the farmer that shot me than the fact I was stealing grapes. Everyone thought taking a handful of grapes was permissible and you shouldn't get a load of salt rock for such an act. It wasn't like we were loading up crates of grapes. Plus, I had such an innocent look and way about me that no one thought I was close to being a thief. I played on the fact that I was just a boy wanting some grapes and got shot for it. Everyone in the neighborhood was sympathetic toward me and I played on it big time. I then wore my scars with pride and the neighbors let the farmer know in no uncertain terms that they didn't appreciate him shooting a small boy. It was great, but the farmer knew we were more than innocent little kids and he would shoot anyone of us that came onto his property. He knew it was more than just this time we had taken grapes from him. In the past we had stolen hundreds of pounds from this farmer to sell on the side of the road and he knew it. But I played on the premise that I just wanted some grapes and got shot for it.

Well, Mike and I couldn't let this incident pass. We had to get even. My uncle Burton (Dad's Brother) showed me how to make a so-called nigger shooter when I was five. Now days they are called sling shots, but anyone that knows anything knows these are two different weapons. I think Wrist Rockets is now the correct name. Believe it or not, I did not know the true meaning of the word nigger and actually thought it was just the name of a Wrist Rocket. Anyway, Mike and I decided to make this huge Wrist Rocket. When we were done, there was no way you could hold it with one hand.

We cut it out of an old almond tree. The fork was three feet across and it stood at least four feet high. We cut an old inner tube up to make the rubbers, each rubber was four inches wide and we doubled them up. We cut grooves in the top of each fork of the sling shot and folded the rubbers over the tops and secured them with leather boot lacing. We took the whole tongue from a high top boot to make the pocket that would hold the rock, or really any projectile we wanted to load it with. We then attached it to the rubbers with more leather lacing and we had one hell of a rock launcher.

The first time we test fired this contraption, Mike and I could not pull it back far enough to get the distance we wanted. Since you couldn't hold the thing in your hand, we just wedged it in between a T post of a clothes line and a fence, but both of us couldn't pull it back far enough to hit this farmer's house. His house set in the middle of his orchard and we wanted to hit his house with a rock far enough away we couldn't be detected. So we recruited a friend by the name of Eric. Eric was a new kid that moved into the neighborhood and we started liking him right off.

Eric's parents were well off and didn't want him associating with us, but we poured on the charm so she eventually accepted us as good kids. His father was a preacher in some church and he was always trying to talk to us about God and never gave up on trying getting us to go to his church.

Anyway, we recruited Eric to give us a hand. He was all for the idea, he might have been a preacher's son but he was as mischievous as Mike and I. The three of us had no problem pulling back the sling shot far enough to launch a huge rock as far as we needed. We took a pipe and buried it in the ground at the angle we needed to launch a rock to reach this farmer's house. It was set up on the outskirts of his property and we could yank the sling shot out of the pipe and run with it. The pipe did stick out of the ground, but no one ever figured out what it was for. We ended up setting a couple of these pipes around in various locations, that way the rock would come from a different direction almost every time we fired. We only hit his house a couple of times, but we pounded his barn a bunch. This guy had a couple of mules and these animals got so jumpy from the rocks bombarding them the old farmer couldn't touch them. We made it a practice never to fire more than a couple of stones at a time. The old farmer would come out of the house with his shotgun and look all over the place. One day, he finally had enough and called the police. We cooled it for awhile, but the police couldn't figure it out either and we never got caught.

One day it all came to an end. It came about when I was walking home from school and found a letter that had been opened and was lying on the ground. I found it near a mail box that I knew belonged to this old farmer. The paper looked important so I took it home to mother, she knew what it was, it was a social security check and it belonged to the old fart that had shot me with salt rock.

Mother instructed me on how I ought to return the check to the old man and by doing so it might make him think different about me. I told her no way, he would just think I took it just to see what was inside. No way was I going to go up to this old fart's house. I told her I didn't care what the old man thought about me. Mother told me she would go with me and eventually she harped on it long enough that I gave in.

I will never forget the walk down that long road that led up to this old man's house. I have to admit I was a little scared. As we approached the old farm, I could see how the house needed paint and how the bare wood was exposed to the elements. The old barn was in worse shape than the house and as we got closer to the house I could see the damage we had done with our rocks. We had hit his house a lot more than we thought and I was amazed that we hadn't broken one of the large windows. The house looked a hundred years old and now that I think back, I can see it probably was.

We didn't have to knock on the door; the old man came out of the house with that shotgun in his hands. "What do you want?"

My mother took her arm and moved me directly behind her. She said not a word, walked up to the old man and handed him his check. She turned and we both started walking away.

The old man hollered out, "Where did you get this?"

Mother turned to face him and told him that I had found it on the ground not too far from his mail box.

The old man had been looking for the check and wondered why it hadn't arrived. He leaned the gun against the house and walked toward mother and myself. I stepped out from behind mother as to get a better look at him.

"I know you," he roared, as he looked me over. "You are that boy I shot with salt aren't you?"

I nodded.

"Your name is?"

"Dennis," I replied.

"Dennis, why would you care if I got this check back or not?"

"I *don't* care," I said.

"Then why are you here?"

"This was my mother's idea, not mine. I didn't want to come."

He started laughing looked at mother and stuck out his hand and thanked her. He turned to walk back to the house, stopped turned back around and walked over to me and thanked me, too. He offered his hand and apologized for shooting me with salt.

I didn't know what to say, but I wanted to say something. "Do you have any pets?"

"I have lots of animals, Dennis, but I have only two animals I consider pets. My mules. But someone has gotten them so jumpy lately I can hardly put a hand on them anymore."

I turned my head downward and stared at the ground. By doing so the old man knew something was up. He then asked if I knew anything about that. I didn't say anything, but the old man by now probably figured out I was the one bombarding his house and barn with rocks. He turned to my mother and asked for her name.

"Vermadean Brooks," she answered.

"Mrs. Brooks, I think it is time Dennis and I sat down and had a talk. Would you please leave him here with me?"

Mother looked down at me and then at him. Then she said something I thought she would never say. "I think it is time you and Dennis settle your differences."

Oh no, I thought.

Mother told me to stay there and she would see me later. I watched her walk all the way down that road hoping she would change her mind. She never even looked back.

"Well, Dennis, do you know my name?"

"No," I replied.

"My name is Jenkins, Larry Jenkins." He stuck out his hand.

I did too, and this is the first handshake from a grownup I ever remember getting. His hands were rough and huge. His hair was all gray and he wore a hat that looked like my grandpa's hat back in Texas. He had on cover alls and of all things; he was in his house shoes.

I'm not going to talk much about Mr. Jenkins. His is another story that is a book within itself. He ended up being one of nicest people I have ever met and I was truly sorry for the things I'd done to him. I ended up over a period of time telling Mr. Jenkins what I had done. Mike and I hung out at his place all the time. He and I finally got his mules tamed back down and Mr. Jenkins was always glad to see us come for visits, which we did almost every day. He let Mike and me cut across his orchard on the way to school and because we helped him around his farm, he let us eat all the fruit we wanted. He also let us play in the irrigation ditches when he irrigated and they were full of water. He let us know, no other kids were allowed to come on his place and he wanted to keep it that way.

We never shared his place with any of our friends and we always felt special hanging around with Mr. Jenkins. We treated his place like it was our own, we never stole from him again and we made sure no other kids stole from him either. I thought of Mr. Jenkins as a grandfather, he treated me like a son. I loved that old man. I cried and he did too, the day I left California to come back to Texas.

Chapter 6
Back to Texas

My mother got word that her father had died, and broke down and cried. She hadn't seen him in three years and you could tell she regretted ever leaving Texas. Mother and I would be taking the train back to Texas for grandfather's funeral while Beverley and Vodie stayed with Aunt LuLu.

Kids rode the train free back then. Beverley was too old and would have to pay a fare. We lied about my age so we wouldn't have to pay a fair for me. Mother told me not to tell anyone how old I was. She gave me a talk about lying, but in this case it was necessary and we would not be making a habit of it. So it was just me and Mom that made the trip back to Texas. I hated thinking about my grandpa's death. I loved him so.

He was a big scary man, and most of the grandkids feared him. He barked out everything he said, but it was all a put-on that I saw through at a very young age. He always had a pocket full of pennies. He would pull out a handful of pennies and would ask me to take as many as I thought I was worth. I would always take only one, and then he would tell me I was worth more than one penny and before the game was over I had a pocket full of pennies.

Growing up I heard lots of stories about my grandfather, but the best stories was the ones he told. He had so many grandchildren over twenty and he only gave special time to the younger ones. When I was around, I was his sidekick. He took me everywhere and I loved going with him. He talked to me as if I was a grownup. He would talk about things I didn't understand, but I was so happy he was talking to me and I hung on every word that came out of his mouth. As I think back, I believe he liked talking to himself and I happened to always be with him. I don't remember everything about my grandfather, but I do remember every conversation I ever had with him.

I knew I was his favorite and if I wasn't, he sure made me feel that way. None of my cousins hung around him. They were all afraid of him and didn't like the smell of his cigar. One time, all of my Aunt Gene's kids (10 of them, I think) sat around and talked about how mean grandfather was. As I got older, I came to understand why. My cousins were assholes and grandfather had no quirks about letting you know if you were one. Kid or not, you acted like an ass around my grandfather, he treated you like an ass. I, too, was afraid of him, or at least I thought I was. Later, I realized it was just respect I had for the man. He never disciplined me, never once can I remember him talking in a disciplinary tone of voice to me. He was always called me 'Chigger' and I never knew what that meant. He never told me, but when I was fourteen, my grandmother told me he called me that because I got under his skin. He told her I was hard to ignore, just like a chigger bite. I liked that about my grandfather. Only he knew what he was talking about most of the time and he left it up to everyone else to figure it out. Only my grandmother fully understood the man, because my grandfather confided in her about everything. Only later, when we moved in with grandmother, did I really come to know my grandfather and come to love my grandmother as much as my own mother.

I hated that I was so young when my grandfather died. I would have loved to have known him as a young man. Even in my youth I appreciated the time I had with this great man. A lot of my grandfather' life is unknown. He never talked about it in detail with anyone but grandmother. My grandmother told me lots about the man, but they were mostly stories. In stories, the personal touch of a life and its true personality are lost. I know of my grandfather through the eyes of a young boy, but to know him through the eyes of a grown man would have been such a treasure.

We buried my grandfather in Canton, Oklahoma. He was buried next to his son, Lewis Hunt, that died of small pox when he was fourteen. My mother caught the pox at the same time, but she only lost an eye from the fever the pox gave her. My mother loved her baby brother that died, when they both were very young.

Being close in age, they shared personal experiences with each other. I never heard my mother complain about the loss of her eye. I never knew she was blind in that eye until I was at least fourteen myself. She told me once that she would have given up both eyes for her brother's life. My mother didn't mention Lewis too often. I could tell it brought back painful memories and she would grow quiet then change the subject. I never heard my grandfather talk about Lewis. My grandmother said Grandpa blamed himself for Lewis's death. It was something the man had no power over, but he blamed himself.

After my grandfather's funeral, we went back to Lubbock, Texas to my grandmother's house. I had three aunts living in Lubbock, but I was only close to one, Aunt Ylova. She was my mother's oldest sister and she always treated me like I was special. During this trip, I brought Ylova the biggest peach I had ever seen from Mr. Jenkins orchard. She gave me the largest boiled egg *I* had ever seen. I found out years later it was a goose egg. Anyway, it was a big old egg and I ate it on the trip back to California.

I recall going through Grandpa's stuff with mother and all her sisters, Ylova, Gene and Audrey. There were two brothers, Uncle Bill, and Uncle Ralph. The only ones I cared for were both of my uncles and Aunt Ylova. The rest of the family I wouldn't give a nickel for. My grandmother was so sweet it was hard for me envision her giving birth to these selfish, self-centered women.

My grandmother gave my grandfather's cameo ring to his youngest son and my favorite, Uncle Bill. This was the first and last time I ever saw my Uncle Bill cry. Ralph got a Silver dollar that had an indention in it from a bullet that Buffalo Bill had shot and given to my grandfather. My grandfather always carried this coin. My mother got grandfather's watch and gold chain, she also received a fork and a spoon that grandpa always used and his wooden box of ivory dominos. I don't know what the rest of the kids received, but you can bet they argued over it. I didn't care much for my aunts and as time marched on I came to despise them.

After a day at grandmother's house, Mother and I went over to Ylova's house. Ylova wanted to talk to Mother. What it boiled down to was Ylova and Uncle Fred (my aunt Ylova's husband) was going to make a trip out to California and bring all of us back. Mother's divorce would be final by then and Mother was coming back to Lubbock and we would live with Grandmother.

Chapter 7
Good-byes and New Beginnings

In a lot of ways, I was happy to be coming back to a place I thought of as home. At the same time, I hated leaving my best friend Mike. I dreaded telling Mike I would be leaving and moving back to Texas.

The day Mother and I arrived back home, I went over to Mike's. I told him it would not be long and I would be going back to Texas. I had known Mike for four years. I might have only been nine years old, but I knew I would never see my friend Mike again. Neither of us talked about it much. We made the best of the time we had left together and visited some of our favorite spots.

We both had learned to swim in the irrigation canals of Modesto and we spent almost every day around our favorite swimming hole. We talked how we were going to keep in touch and so on. Most of all we talked about how growing up apart from each other was going to be strange. We had bonded as close as any two friends could. We loved each other like brothers and we both knew growing up apart and so far away from each other would eventually sever our relationship. But we swore to each other not to let that happen and we made most of the time we had left, and didn't talk about me leaving anymore.

Both of us went to Mr. Jenkins for my final goodbye to him. I often wonder of what happened to him. He was an old man, and even though you don't think about people dying when you are young, I knew Mr. Jenkins didn't have that many years left. He helped me to get a grip on things that were more important than being a hoodlum. He got me interested in planting a garden and stuff like that. He was a fine gentleman and I like to think he played a part of me giving up the streets and finding out you could work hard and make money honestly, that you would appreciate it more than getting it by means of dishonesty. My mother tried to teach me these things, but it took a male perspective to drive the point home. He was a father-figure to me and a real father is what I needed.

He had old school ethics and principles. Traits I came to appreciate in his generation and I think he is why I always sought out the company of the older generation; they seemed so wise to me.

When I went to say goodbye to him, he picked me up off the ground and gave me a big hug. I had my arms around him and I felt the wet tears on his unshaven face. I loved his whiskers against my cheek and I loved the smell of pipe tobacco on his clothes. It is a warm feeling and in his long arms I felt the love he had for me. In somewhat of a squeaky voice, choked up from emotion, I told him I would never forget him. He put me down, pulled a rag from his back pocket, and as he wiped his eyes dry he told me he would never forget me either. I turned and walked away, turning around from time to time. He watched me walk down his long road until I was out of sight. Even though I never talk about Mr. Jenkins, I often go back in time and think about this great man that I came to respect and love so much, and how he influenced my life. One can count himself fortunate in life to have come to know such a man as Mr. Jenkins. As time marched on, I realized I had learned many things from him. More than I knew at the time.

The day came and I remember it so well. I often reminisce about this day. I am sixty four-years-old and that day seems like yesterday. Fifty-five years ago I said a final goodbye to my friend Mike. As the car backed out of the driveway I yelled out to Uncle Fred to stop the car. My Dad was there with tears flowing down his face and when I jumped out of the car he thought I was running to hug him goodbye. He lifted his arms to receive my hug, but my hug was not for him, it was for Mike. I put my arms around Mike's neck as he did mine. We stood there holding onto each other for the longest time. We both looked down on our arms where we had cut ourselves and bonded our wounds together as to become blood brothers. We had seen this done in the movies (Davy Crockett) and we did it thinking it was cool. We both smiled at each other and together said, "Blood brothers, forever." It was a kid thing, I know, but as I look down at the scar I still carry today, I think back to a special time in my life and a special friendship I had in my youth and it makes me smile.

I never said a word to my dad that day. I never even told him goodbye. Mother said she had never seen him cry until that day. *Good*, I thought to myself, *I hope he never stops*. As we drove away I never looked back and I never gave my dad a second thought.

As time passed the hate I had for him finally died, but I was a young man of twenty-four with two kids of my own before I put it behind me somewhat. I made a vow to myself to never become the man he was and to love my children more than myself. Whenever I felt like

I was taking on any of my dad's traits, I shoved it aside and did the opposite. If I lived my life doing everything opposite of him, I knew I was doing it right. I hated all that he ever was and all he ever stood for.

I was overseas in Saudi Arabia working for a company called Augusta Bell Helicopters when I got word from a cousin on my dad's side of the family that my dad was dying and wanted to see me. They gave him about a week to live. I told my cousin I wouldn't go to him if he was dying ten feet away from me, not to mention travel half way around the world.

A horse I used to use when I did ranch work for a man in Oklahoma died around that same time. I grieved more for the loss of that horse than I did my own father. My father died in 1984. I don't know when the feeling of hate for him subsisted, but it had been awhile that I even thought about him. When I received the word he was dying hate rekindled, but didn't stay long. His death was the final chapter of that part of my life.

Coming back to Texas was different now that grandpa had died. Grandmother's house didn't seem the same. How could it be? His death left a big void in all of our lives. Grandmother's house was small, but we made it work. Mother, Bev, and Vodie slept in one room with mother and Bev sharing a bed. Grandmother and I slept in her feather bed. In the winter the bed was great, but in the summer the bed was a little hot.

Mother got a job working at Texas Tech College cleaning restrooms and mopping floors. It was a nothing job but it put food on the table. Mother was Mother and she never complained. Between my grandmother's Social Security check of $105 a month and Mother bringing in a whopping $45 dollars a week, they made ends meet. It was a good thing my grandmother's house was paid for and we had our own water well. We did all right. I never felt like I needed anything. I *wanted* lots of stuff like any kid, but was happy to have whatever we had.

I remember being bored one summer day and grandmother, seeing the state of mind I was in, called me into the house. We went into the kitchen and sat at the table. She pointed to an apple barrel we kept in the corner of the kitchen and she asked me to get out all the apples that were soft and put them on the table. I found four of five that were not spoiled but a little soft. We hated soft apples and grandmother would usually make pies out of them. But pies are not what grandmother had planned for me.

She told me of a riding stable that was about two or three miles from the house and if I wanted I could go down to the stable and feed those old apples to the horses. Grandmother knew I loved horses and it would be something new for me to do. My grandfather had taught me all about horses and in the way he taught me about these animals, he sparked an interest I have always appreciated.

After visiting the stables on numerous occasions, I became known to the wranglers and owner. I figured that I knew enough about horses that I could ask the owner for a job. Cleaning out stables and feeding the horses would be fine with me. I simply liked being around them. Heck, I even love the way they smell. One day, I got the nerve to ask the owner, T. J., for a job. The first time I asked for the job he told me he didn't need anyone. I hung around the stables anyway. I liked being around the horses and it brought back good memories of my grandpa, so I hung around and worked the stables for nothing.

Every time T. J. saw me doing something like cleaning out stalls or feeding the horses he would yell out, "I'm not paying you, you know."

"I know," I replied.

After a couple of weeks he broke down and gave me a job feeding horses and cleaning out stalls. It was a horse stable on 50th street and in those days 50th street in Lubbock, Texas was out in the country. It was a couple of miles to the stables from grandma's house so it took me awhile each day to do the job. When school started I didn't get home until dark. T. J. knew I was having a hard time of it and called me into his office one day to talk to me. I just knew I was getting fired. I had showed up late a few times and I thought he was going to can me because of it. I was only making about two dollars a day, but that was fourteen dollars a week and to us that was a lot of money. Anyway, T. J. called me in and told me I was a good worker but needed to show up on time to do the work.

He liked to close down the stables around sundown and at sundown I was still doing my chores. All I could do was agree with a nod and tell him that I understood. He laughed and told me I wasn't fired and he had a remedy to my problem for showing up late. He put his hand on my shoulder and told me I didn't understand squat. He said if I could handle being a wrangler, he wanted me to take the job. By doing so, he would let me take a horse home each night. That way I could be at work on time.

He said I treated his horses like pets and they responded to me better than they did to his other two hands. I had a grin from ear to ear. I know I did because T. J. couldn't quit smiling at *me*. T. J. asked if I had a favorite horse. I told him I had several and he laughed and told me we were going to see what I knew about horseflesh. I knew what my grandfather had taught me. Grandpa taught me about the size of the horse's withers and to tell when they were too large, and therefore would not carry weight all day or even in some cases for short periods of time. He taught me about cannon bones and a horse having one too straight that would put extra strain on his pasterns. He taught me about girth, muscle and conformation. How to tell the age by the indentures that sunk in above a horse's eyes and by his teeth, looking first at the hook tooth that meant the animal at to be at least seven years old to have one and then go to the length and the wear of the teeth. Yes, I knew about horses at an early age. I was only ten, almost eleven and I thought about how my grandpa started making a living for himself at twelve. T. J. was impressed by what I did know about horses. He had no idea that I was so well-rounded when it came to them. I picked a horse named Long John.

A wrangler's pay was five dollars a day and he was allowed to be tipped by the customers. People would pay a dollar an hour and fifty cents for half an hour to ride T. J.'s horses. I would size people up according to their experience, and then match them to a horse that was suited for them and take them for a ride around the country side.

Some people paid T. J. to keep their horses at the stables. I groomed, fed and exercised their animals when they couldn't. I never asked for anything in return. Eventually, the customers started tipping me and because of the extra care their animals received word got around to a lot of horse owners and T. J. started getting more customers that wanted to stable their horses with him. He started making more money by stabling horses than renting them to ride.

Working at the stables was good for me. It kept me out of trouble and soon I was bringing home more pay than my mother. I gave all the money to Mother and she did with what was fit. I know she used some of it to fix up an old 1940 Ford that was left at my grandmother's place. It was left there by Uncle Bill (Mothers Brother) when he went into the Army during WW II. After the war he fooled around with it some and eventually abandoned the '40 Ford.

He had modified it a little and put a 1954 V-8 flat head Mercury engine in it at one time or another and the car, once fixed up, ran pretty well. Mother used the car to get her back and forth to and from work. We were a sight though, riding around in this hot rod. It only got about fourteen miles to a gallon, but back then gas only cost eighteen cents a gallon, so it was affordable. Except for Ylova, all of Mother's sisters teased her about the car and made what I thought were cruel remarks. Mother let it go and didn't pay any attention to them. My aunts knew when to back off, because when my mother got pissed off she would confront you head on. My aunts didn't want to get their asses whipped by their younger sister, so they knew just about how far to push it.

Chapter 8
Bullies and Squealers

In 1959 I was doing horrible in school. I failed the third grade when we first moved back to Texas in 1957. Texas had subjects I didn't have in California, so they held me back a grade. The teachers were willing to pass me, but mother being the type of person she was thought it would do me good to repeat the grade again. I hated seeing my classmates go on to a grade higher than me. However, I didn't have any friends at this time in my life and really didn't want any.

I guess we were still struggling to make it back then and I dressed the part. I wore old cowboy boots and jeans to school and didn't fit in with most of the kids. My grandmother made sure my clothes were always clean, but you could tell by the way I dressed that we were having a hard time of it. All my jeans had patches on the ass that my grandmother had sowed. Riding horses a couple hours a day and six hours Saturday and Sunday kept my jeans pretty well thin in the ass. I didn't mind the patched up jeans, they were comfortable, but I hated the little remarks I knew some of the kids were saying behind my back. My classmates going a grade higher didn't help matters either.

One time, a couple of the kids called me a dummy, and from a distance they would spit at me. They weren't too far from wrong, I know, but I had more street sense than they would ever have and if I knew one thing about anything, I knew I'd better put a stop to this situation or it would just escalate into a bigger problem for me.

One of the boys who made this remark was the toughest kid in school. Or so I was told. I learned early in life if you whip the toughest guy around you won't have to fight your way to the top. Starting at the top was a lot easier than working your way up the ranks of the pecking order. So I just walked up to this guy and popped him in the mouth. I was aiming for his nose, once you hit them there the eyes water to the point they can't see as well and after that you can pretty much have your way with them. But I missed my mark and I thought by doing so the fight was fixing to begin. This guy just put his hands over his mouth and bled. That was it. The fight was over before it began. *What a pussy*, I thought. Man, from the kids I use to hang with a busted lip was nothing. This kid was a puss for sure.

I knew there would be hell to pay, but I also knew from past experiences what I had done was the overall best thing for me. I recalled that home I was put in where I stuck the fork in that kid's back. Things hadn't changed for me, except now I did not have Mike to confide in.

I found out that day the kids in Stubbs Elementary were squealers. I bet three or more kids ran and got the teacher. We had a different code we lived by in California. Kids didn't squeal on one another. Fights were one on one and everyone else sat back and enjoyed the show. Not in this school. I had three or four teachers on me before I even had time to make up some excuse. Most of the teachers didn't like me. I could tell by the tone in their voice when they talked to me and how they treated me in general. They would give me scornful looks for doing nothing more than walking down the hall. If any of them had to speak to my mother they used a different tone of voice and it was always 'Dennis could do anything he wanted, if he would just apply himself.' So needless to say when it came to the teachers, Mother listened to their every word. As I think back, I believe that more than anything, Mother wanted her kids to succeed and get an education. And if teachers recommended something, Mother would abide.

Mother got called into school for me decking this kid and before long we were talking to the principal. He told Mother I went up and hit a kid for no reason.

Mother looked at me and man she was mad. "Did you?" she asked

"No, "I replied, "he called me a dummy."

"That is no reason to hit someone," the principal yelled.

"It is where I come from," I answered back.

"Well, Mr. Brooks, you are not where you come from now, are you?"

Where had I heard that before? Just like with that lady in the orphanage in California, I didn't say anything. I knew it would be falling on deaf ears anyway. He held all the cards and being a kid I knew I was no match for a verbal confrontation with this 'educated' man. I wasn't going to even try and explain to him the code of ethics that kids live by. It seemed most adults had forgotten them. But I knew I would achieve what I was looking for and that was respect. No one would call me a dummy or any other name from now on. This I knew for a fact and no amount of education could solve problems of this sort as fast as a fist. Well, this was what I believed anyway.

When all was said and done I got expelled for two days. Mother didn't say much to me once we left the school. I heard her murmur 'I was going to end up like my father' and for a short time it hurt my feelings. But I knew she didn't mean it. I could tell by the way she bit her lip when she made the comment and by the way she treated me afterwards. I made the time up so I wouldn't fail the fourth grade.

Even though some of the kids probably still talked behind my back, I had earned respect among some of the kids. I was asked to come over to some of their homes to play and what not. Play? What in heck did they want to *play*? Play to me was the stables, nothing could top that. They wanted to play stupid games that I thought was kid stuff. I thought about what Mike would say seeing me take part in some of these games. Playing, for Mike and me, was jumping in the canal and letting the water current take us down as far as we wanted to walk back. Or making sling shots, or trying to catch hornets out of a nest, pouring water down a ground squirrel's hole and catching it. Or seeing how high we could climb a tree. These kids wanted to play fictitious games and dress up like Superman. I quit doing that stuff after the age of five.

I did run with a couple of fourteen-year-old kids that were pretty cool, but the stables is where my heart was and that is where I wanted to hang out. It supplied me with all the entertainment I needed. I was a type of kid that did not fit in. I was a loaner and most of the kids that wanted to be my friends were just kids that were being picked on by others and figured I would be a good friend to have. No one really wanted to be my friend. Or that was the way it seemed to me. In a way I blame myself, because when I was around them, without knowing it I tried too hard to be accepted. It made me look and act like a know-it-all and this was a turn off. To this day I sometimes find myself trying to be accepted instead of letting it come naturally.

I told T. J. what had happened to me in school and asked him what he thought about it. "Do you like fighting, Dennis?" he asked.

"In a way I do," I replied. "I don't pick fights, but when I get into one I like it."

He laughed and told me he kind of figured I did. T. J. then said something I have never forgotten. He told me there are things that are worth fighting for. But things that you might think are important to fight for, others may not. He told me most fights to him are stupid, you just have to pick out the ones you feel are right.

"Now, the fight you were in Dennis was right, but the way you did it in my way of thinking was wrong. You see, you should have met the boy after school hours and confronted him with the situation and let him know if he didn't stop, that there would be consequences to pay and let him know what those consequences would be. Then if you two fight the teachers would not be evolved and no rules would have been broken. Just two guys settling a dispute and if it had to be settled by fighting, then the decision would have been his, not yours. You would have given him a peaceful way out and the ethics of right would have been on your side. When you fight for something that is right in the eyes of others then the fight is worth the cost and if it is worth the cost, then you will never loose in a fight. Son, do you understand what I am trying to say?"

"I do," I replied. And I really did understand.

Then he told me as far as all the other kids go, they would hear of what I did. News like that gets around fast around kids.

I liked it when T. J. called me 'son.' It made me feel good that a grown man would take such interest in trying to teach me something that to him must have seemed silly, but at the time it was important to me. It was this talk with T. J. that made me pick my fights and to make sure I was never fighting just to be a bully. I hated bullies anyway and would go out of my way to push any issue with one. But I always, if possible, gave them the choice. T. J. was right. I have lost few fights.

In a way, T. J. reminded me of Mr. Jenkins in California. Even though Mr. Jenkins was much older, these two men thought along the same lines. I haven't thought of Mr. Jenkins in a long time. It was now 1959 and it had been two years sense we left California. I heard from Mike through letters we wrote back and forth to each other. But the letters were getting further and further apart and I could tell we were both headed down different paths. Mike went back to a life of crime and I figured before long he would end up in prison. I never knew what became of him. One day the letters stopped and as the saying goes, 'time marches on.'

Chapter 9
New Dreams

I enjoyed working at the stables and T. J. had lots of request for my services from customers. The customers liked the way I treated their horses and I was kept pretty busy. I received a lot of tips and with tips I was making around fifty dollars a week and Grandmother and Mother were glad to have the extra money. I kept enough for myself to have a little spending money and for the first time in my life I felt a sense of accomplishment. I know it was a nothing job in the eyes of some people, but to me it was something I had achieved on my own and I was proud of myself.

Working at the stables gave me dreams. I dreamed being a cowboy like Grandfather. I dreamed of having my own ranch some day. Riding Long John to and from work gave me lots of time to think and dream. I looked forward to the ride everyday and work never was boring.

I hated school and everything about it. I didn't really have any friends my own age. I hung around T. J. in my spare time. Mother met T. J. and she approved of him being so much a part of my life. I know everything coming out of my mouth was about T. J. this and T. J. that. T. J. was a good friend to have and he had become a part of my life and somewhat of a father figure to me as well.

T. J. tried to get me interested in school and between him and mother I got sick of hearing about how important an education was. I was in the fourth grade and I didn't know squat. I had never applied myself and there was a lot of basic book knowledge I didn't have. I didn't know how to apply myself to obtain the knowledge that I, as an adult, know is important. I never bothered to learn. I didn't care. I was too embarrassed to ask for help. I feared people would find out how much I didn't know. So I faked my way through school. Which means I cheated on every test or assignment I ever had. It was the easy way out and I took it. I wasn't even smart enough to see that was the reason my mother had such crappie jobs. I felt like I was destined for the same type of life and I accepted that I would never have a good education. I would not apply myself. Somewhere down the line, I lost the will to put out any effort when it came to academics.

On the other hand, I knew I wasn't afraid of work and I figured a lot of people just needed someone who wasn't afraid to get his hands dirty. That fit me to a tee. I was blessed with a strong back and good health. Only a weak mind.

Around this time in my life, Mother started dating a guy she knew while growing up in Oklahoma. L. G. Myers, aka Barney. She hadn't seen him since they were both kids. His Uncle Joe married my Great Aunt Mary (Grandmother's sister) and it kind of connected the two families. I knew Uncle Joe and thought a lot of him. But he lived in Oklahoma and I didn't see him all that much. I hadn't seen him at all since Grandfather's funeral.

I was a little skeptical of Barney. At first he was so nice I thought there had to be an angle. Mother sure liked him though. Barney put a smile on her face and made her laugh again. As long as someone could make my mother laugh, they were okay by me. One night I caught them off guard, kissing on the back porch of my grandmother's house. It embarrassed them like they were a couple of kids. I think Mother didn't know I knew what was going on because she hadn't talked to me about Barney in that way.

Barney is one of the nicest men I have ever known. He was in his mid thirties and it felt strange for me to like any man close to my dad's age that wasn't an Uncle or something. I liked Barney though, and he liked all of kids. He had been married and divorced like my mother and by what I could figure out his wife sounded like she was just like my dad. I felt sorry for the man.

Barney was funny and he talked and joked with us. Beverley knew Mom and Barney were serious about each other, but didn't think about it one way or the other. As long as Mother was happy, I was happy. At first I was a skeptic, watched and waited for him to do something wrong to my mother. I was old enough now I could stand my own ground. So I waited for this man to slip up. No one could be that nice all the time. Well, I was wrong. This man was a gentleman in every aspect of the word. I never knew a man so nice. I started liking Barney more and more.

It wasn't long before Barney asked Mother to marry him. Mother accepted his proposal, but I will never forget Mother coming to me and asking me how I felt about her marring Barney. My sister had been told and kept informed all along of how Mother and Barney felt toward each other and it was no surprise to her.

When Mother approached me with the news, I was happy. I hadn't really had a father figure in my life and I looked forward to having one.

Barney worked in a little town by the name of Slaton, south of Lubbock. He worked for the Santa Fe Railroad, and when he and Mother married Slaton was where we would move.

This brought on a couple of problems for me. First of all, we would no longer be living with Grandmother. She had become like a mother to me and I wasn't ready to move away from her. We had been living with her for almost four years and she had become a big part of my life. The next big thing was telling T. J. I would be moving away and quitting my job. This was going to be hard to do, so I had planned to hold off telling him until Mother and Barney had married.

Well, that day came. I rode Long John for the last time to the stables. I hated giving up this job. I had worked for T. J. for several years and we had become close. I took off Long John's saddle and hung it by the horn from a rope that dangled from the rafters in the tack house. Everything I was doing I knew would be for the last time. I was going to miss being around all these horses and all the people I had gotten to know. But most of all I was going to miss T. J.

As I walked out of the tack room I met T. J. He told me he was waiting for me, had something he wanted to talk to me about, and asked me to meet him in his office. I didn't know what it was, but it didn't matter. I was feeling so down. I didn't want to tell him I was quitting and tried to figure out what and how I was going to tell him.

His office was nothing more than a back room that was used to be a seed room in an old barn. I opened the door and T. J. was sitting behind this old oak desk writing a check. As I approached him he tore the check from its binder and handed it to me. He told me it was my pay check for the rest of the week.

We always got paid on Friday and it was Wednesday. I looked at the check and it was almost twice the amount I usually received. I mentioned that my check was way too much and that he had made a mistake. I could tell something bothered him because he didn't want to look at me.

He told me the check included a bonus. He got up and came over to me and stuck out his hand. As I held out my hand he grasped it with both of his and explained to me how he was going to close the riding stable down. He had been thinking about it for a long time and now that Lubbock had extended its city limits past 50th street, there were certain ordnances passed and large animals in the city limits would not be allowed. So after some time of thinking about it he decided it was time to close the stables. He told me that he had a little ranch south of Lubbock that was close to the town of Slaton and that he and his wife had decided to retire there and raise a small herd of cattle to subsidize their income.

Man was I surprised. I interrupted him mid-sentence and told my news about moving to Slaton. He offered me a job and I accepted it without hesitation.

We talked about when my family would move down to Slaton and the date I could start working for him. He talked to Mother and Mother let me go with him down to Slaton to see the ranch and to start getting things ready for the move. I could tell Mother was happy for me. She kept telling me how things keep working out for the better.

T. J. and I had a lot of work to do. He wanted to keep five of twenty horses he had for the ranch and sell the rest. He kept two horses I really liked. The horse I was riding, Long John and another colt named Yellow Jacket. I was excited about being a ranch hand. I knew I would learn more than things about horses. I would learn about cattle and to some degree about a way of life of a rancher. I knew very little about raising cattle, but the things I learned on that ranch supported a way of life for me for a few years in times to come.

I knew my grandfather had been a cowboy when he was younger and had started his life away from home being a wrangler. He had worked around cattle in his youth, but made most of his living when he was young around horses. Like I said in the beginning, my grandfather was one of several horse trainers for the Buffalo Bill Traveling Show.

My grandfather talked to me about raising cattle and some of what he told me stuck, but mostly I had forgotten all the important stuff. T. J. was going to teach me what I didn't know. I have to say, working on the T. Js. Ranch was definitely a learning experience for me.

Chapter 10
My New Dad

Mother and 'Dad' got married and while they were gone on their honeymoon, Bev and I stayed with one of mother's sisters, Aunt Jean. I can't remember who Vodie stayed with. Aunt Jean had a bunch of kids so I had lots of cousins to play with. But the only one I liked was Bill, who was fourth down on the pecking order. He was three years older than me and I use to think he was something. He ended up being a thug like all of Jean's kids and was to some degree a bad influence on me. He smoked and acted like a thug from a James Dean movie. Heck, he thought he was James Dean. He was bigger than life to me at the time.

We had gotten into it a couple of times and I have to say he was tough. He could whip my ass, but I put up a good enough fight he didn't want to test those waters again. In a way, by standing my own with him he respected me and we got along fine. I had been around people like him all my life and to some degree felt like I had slipped back in time to Modesto, California. I never shared my past in California with Bill. I let him take the lead and made him think he was the man. He was older and I took my place in the pecking order.

Bill and I parted ways and never hung out together after I became a teenager. We got into a fight over a girl named Pat. I split his head with a Coke bottle and that was the end of our friendship, such as it was. I tried to talk to him when I got back from Vietnam in 1970, but he acted like he had something more important to do and that was the last time I have ever said a word to him.

Aunt Jean was a horrible woman and only a couple of her eight kids ever mounted to anything. I hate to even talk about the woman. As far as I am concerned, I have talked about her too much already.

I was glad when Mother and Barney got back from their honeymoon. Barney was my new dad and it felt strange having a father figure around again. I have nothing but good things to tell you about this man. Accepting him as a father and calling him 'father' became easy. Mother wanted me to start calling Barney 'Dad' because of Vodie. Vodie was five, almost six, I was twelve almost thirteen and Beverley was sixteen going on seventeen. Having a man in our lives was strange to us all. To have a man who acted like a father was indeed strange.

I loved having him in my life. When you hear or read about me talking about my father or Dad, I am referring to Barney. I think of him as my real father and he thinks of me as his son. He took me fishing and hunting and it is because of this man that I love quail hunting to this day. Barney was a real father to all of us and we loved it. Life was good for us now. Barney made good money and it seemed we had no wants. We were middle class and it felt good.

I did have a problem with discipline in the beginning, but learned and came to appreciate the importance of it. Dad talked to me and never once in my life did he ever beat me with a belt. Once I had done something bad and Mother told Barney to whip my ass. Dad told her he thought I had enough ass whippings in my life and told Mother that was not the answer for this boy. Dad then took me off to the side and gave me a talking to.

I will never forget this day as long as I live. Dad planned a fishing trip for just him and me to go down to a ranch near Gail, Texas, where a friend of his was foreman. The place had a lot of buffalo wallows (water tanks) on it and all of them were stocked with fish. Let me tell you, it was in the middle of nowhere.

One morning Dad and I were sitting on the bank of a water tank and out of the blue he started talking about life and how someone should live it. He talked about setting goals in life and all kinds of stuff that I never even considered. Back then I lived for the moment and took each day as it came. He told me that I was living the best years of my life right now. He called them my carefree years and I should appreciate them by living these days as a time to plan for my future.

Then he told me something that I have never forgotten. He told me I was headed down the wrong road in life. It seemed to him that I didn't care one way or the other about my future that sometimes I get off in left field and don't even know what is going on around me. Dad told me life was passing me by and I didn't seem to care.

No one had ever spoken to me in this fashion. I really didn't know what to think. We discussed matters for the longest time. Dad mused about life in general and how I had missed out on a lot of things up to this point. "But Son," he said, "you need to get a handle on your life now while you are young and head yourself down a road that can be a little less bumpy."

Even though I knew my pride would keep me from ever getting a good education, I appreciated the interest this fine man took in me. I have often thought, *if I would have had this man in my life growing up as a kid, I may have taken a better turn in life.* I listened to what Dad had to say, but I didn't act on his advice until later have been playing catch up ever since. When we got back home to Slaton, things were different between Dad and me. We bonded on that fishing trip and are very close this very day.

Chapter 11
Slaton

We moved to Slaton when I was entering into the 4th grade. I was having a hard time in school and my grades showed it. Slaton schools were so much different than Lubbock schools. The kids here were more to my liking and Slaton, being a small town, had that small town feeling. You know where people really know each other. Sometimes this is not always a good thing, but for the most part, I like small towns.

The first day of school I got into a fight before morning classes even started. All of the kids, including myself, were standing around waiting for the school doors to open. This tall red-headed boy named Paul went around to each of the boys and asked them if they wanted to fight. I thought it was funny. It reminded me of the time back in California when Mike approached me and out of the blue ask me if I wanted to fight. Mike was gauging me then and I wondered if this guy was doing the same. When he came around and ask me if I wanted to fight I just laughed.

Paul didn't see the humor of this and pushed me and told me to hit him, so I did. I split his lip and bloodied his nose. He, like most kids that think they are tough, stood there holding his hands across his face while trying to control the blood dripping down onto his shirt. The doors of school unlocked and out stepped Mrs.

Weeks. She saw Paul bleeding and asked him what happened. *Oh no,* I thought, *not a good way to start out on the first day of school.* I knew the first thing Paul would say: I started it all.

That didn't happen. Paul told the teacher he fell while riding his bike to school and he was waiting for the doors to open so he could go to the restroom and wash his face. Later on that day, I approached Paul and thanked him for not mentioning my name. "I asked for it," Paul said and I knew then and there Paul was a good guy.

Paul didn't last long in school. After junior high, Paul dropped out and I never saw him around Slaton after that. We remained friends from the fifth grade through the eighth grade, but never ran together. The only reason I mention him is because he was my first encounter in Slaton and in a lot of ways he reminded me of California. I had seen hundreds of Paul's kind, a hoodlum, and knew the path he would take. He reminded me of myself in some ways, so I understood what he was going through. Like me, somewhere down the road Paul ignored how important school was and felt like he had to prove himself. So he acted like a tough guy to get respect anyway he could. He smoked and hung out with thugs and most of the time acted like one. I had put that kind of life behind me and all Paul and I really had in common was our education, which was pretty lame to say the least.

Things were okay for a couple of months; I actually made friends with several kids. It had been awhile since I have had more than one friend and it was good. In some ways I felt like a little kid learning to be around other kids again. To me, having friends was a commitment. You never turn your back on a friend and whatever becomes your friend's problems become yours as well. This wasn't something I was taught, this was something I had learned and experienced for myself. I came to appreciate this at a very early age. So having this feeling of loyalty and commitment brought me a whole bunch of trouble. I took it upon myself to be the protector, in a manner of speaking, for what I deemed as my new friends.

There were a bunch of school bullies that loved letting everyone know they ruled the roost. Punching Paul in the face that first day of school earned their and therefore the bullies left me alone. This was not so true for my friends. All my friends up to this point in my life were tough. You see there was Mike, Mike and Mike.

Anyway, I felt it was up to me to protect my friends that didn't know how to fight or just didn't want to. That first two months I bet I had at least eight or nine scuffles. I established a name for myself and no one messed with me or my friends. The only problem about fighting someone's fights for them is that they expect it all the time. And, hell, I wasn't even getting paid for this protection program. But to top it all off, my so-called friends would start arguments just to see me finish them. They were using me to get back at all the vendettas they had stored up for some time. Before you knew it, I got tagged as a bully myself. Being a little short on the uptake, it took me awhile to figure it out, but not without the help from a teacher.

She, too, thought I was a bully. Mainly because I whipped a couple of her 'good' students. Well, she took it upon herself to stage a fight between me and another boy. This boy was much bigger than I and was supposed to teach me a lesson. She had acquired some boxing gloves from the gym and figured she would let me and this other kid settle our differences after a dispute this kid started. This teacher stepped in and said we needed to put on the gloves and settle it and that was fine with me.

Now, I love wrestling and using my feet, but boxing is no stranger to me either. Remember me telling you about Mike's dad who was a boxer, teaching Mike and me how to box? I am not good, I really only know enough to get me in trouble. In this case it was enough. I whipped this kid so bad the teacher stopped it when she saw blood coming from his nose. Later, the teacher and I talked and when she figured out what really was going on, she informed me about my so called friends. It seemed she had asked around got the insight on what was going down and filled me in.

I could tell she felt bad for me and kept looking for some kind of response from me. She asked if it bothered me that the other kids had used me. I laughed and told her not really. By protecting them, I built myself a pretty good rep and if I hadn't done it then, I most likely would have to prove myself later.

Then she said, "That kind of a reputation is important to you isn't it?"

Man, where had I heard that before? My mind flashed back to that home that I was put in in California. I guess it was still important to me to let certain people know that I won't take any crap. As I look back, I think it was because I didn't like people talking down to me. When you come from the poor side of the tracks, people can be cruel. Not being one with great communication skills, fighting was easier and it got the point across a lot faster and left no doubt in people's mind on what side of the fence you stood on.

Time went on and I limped my way through junior high and was let into high school on 'condition.'

The condition was I had to pass the first six weeks or they would put me back a grade. From cheating my ass off and with help from my friends I passed the first six weeks.

I had my own car, a 1962 Chevy Corvair. I bought it with the money I made working for T. J. I got my driver's license when I was fourteen and for the first time in my life I felt like I was going somewhere. Where, I did not know, but somewhere. The freedom of having your own car is indescribable. Owning your first car has to be one of them of the most memorable moments in your life. Working for T. J. was paying off.

Now a freshman in high school, I took FFA (Future Farmers of America.) I loved agriculture and because I took such an interest in it, I made good grades for the first time in my life. At one time I wanted to pursue a carrier in agriculture, but I was never college material and soon gave that idea up. Being a rancher has always been on my mind since I was a kid. At best, I would only achieve being a good ranch hand. That was okay with me, I was happy and life for the present seemed good.

T. J. would meet me at Teague's Drug Store Monday through Friday during the summer and he would work me part time during the winter. T. J. worked me all he could and for a boy of the early 1960s, fifty dollars a week was not bad pay.

In 1964 I was sixteen years old. T. J. gave me Long John and I took care of him until the horse died that same year. At fifteen years old. I had been riding him for six years. T. J. and I had him put down after he fell and broke a hip. He had been running with some younger horses and somehow he wandered or grazed too close to the canyon rim and fell off into a ravine. He was an older horse and it would have been cruel to keep him around with a hip that would never heal properly. Plus the fact that it would have cost way more for the vet bill than he was worth. I hated losing that horse. He had been my means of escape.

Chapter 12
A Great Escape

T. J.'s ranch was connected to a few other big ranches (Sparkman, Baysinger and Harrison's) they all ran cattle together during the summer down in the canyon and every fall we would gather them up separate our herds then sell or feed them out during the winter.

Every summer I used to take off and ride Long John through the canyon off the Caprock from Slaton almost all the way to Gail, Texas. I camped at all the good water tanks (buffalo wallows) fishing and trying to live off the land. I wasn't really. I had a pack horse and that carried about twenty five pounds of potatoes, ten pounds of beans, cooking oil, a Coleman lantern, a couple frying pans, beef jerky, salt, bacon, fishing pole, and some water. I did end up boiling tank water to drink and cook with. I also had a sleeping bag, a 22 rifle, several knives, and an old Higgins shotgun.

I would use the 22 to shoot old jack rabbits and cut them up to use as fish bait. Catfish love rabbit meat and they will hit on rabbit liver faster than anything. I use to leave the liver out in the sun and get it good and hard. That way I could use it several times before it finally gave way to the water softening it up and a fish would eventually get himself a free meal. But not before I had caught a few for myself. I used the shotgun to shoot blue quail. Even though it wasn't quail season, I still shot a few. Man, they were good cooked over an open fire. As I said, I wasn't really living off the land, but I liked to think I was.

One time, I told Dad I would be gone for awhile. I was going to go ahead and try to make it down to Gail on horseback from Slaton. This is about ninety miles if you go by car, about one hundred and twenty by horse. Dad had a lot of confidence in me and knew I would be okay. He knew I could take care of myself. Floating this idea past my mother would be another thing. He assured me he would talk to her and let her know that a good part of the trip I would be on ranch land I was familiar with and that should help some.

Dad told me once that in the wild I was in my own element. I have to admit, I am at ease when I am out in the so-called wild alone. I never made it down to Gail that summer, mainly because it was a hassle dealing with the road traffic once you got off all the ranchland. Plus a lot of times I had to hobble the horses and sleep beside the road. So mostly I just stayed on the ranches and pretended I was a cowboy traveling across Texas.

This trip took me four weeks and let me tell you, my mother liked to have had a cow. I had never seen her as mad as she was the day I got back home. After all there was no such thing as a cell phone in the 60s. During the time I was gone, Dad kept telling Mother I was fine, but she knew I had gotten hurt or bitten by a rattlesnake. Mother was a worry wart, but she wouldn't be a mother if she didn't worry. She finally got used to me going on these trips, but never stopped trying to talk me out of it every summer.

I quit going on these trips when my friend, T. J., died in 1964. He had cancer of the lungs and pancreas. One day T. J. was fine and another he was dead. My eyes stayed wet for a week. T. J.'s wife told me he had been sick for a long time and knew his days were numbered. I never knew. T. J. never let on, but then that was T. J. s way. I never heard him complain about anything but maybe politics the whole time I knew him. I loved this old man and when he died, I lost a family member. I was only acquainted with him for about six years, but it felt like all my days. He had shared some good stories with me about his life. I knew him as well as anyone could know anyone.

Before T. J. died, he gave me a horse named Dan. He knew I hated losing Long John and gave me this horse to take his place. He always told me I needed a younger horse and he made sure I had one.

T. J.'s wife sold the ranch, I think to the Sparkman's. T. J. was buried somewhere in New Mexico and his wife went to live with their daughter in Colorado. T. J. also had a boy, but they got into some big argument years before and they never talked. His son's name was Danny. I don't know if that had to do anything with the naming of my horse, but I kind of think it did. The horse was five-year-old gelding and he was as good a horse as anyone could ask for. Deep down inside I think T. J. loved his son, but probably didn't know how to settle their differences. I don't know, T. J. never talked about his son, so it would be nothing but speculation on my part to try and figure it out.

Back in 1960, I gave T. J. a silver tie clip that was my grandfather's. T. J. gave me a nickel he shot with a 22 at fifty yards, open sights. It was a bet he had made with some guy over a horse, he won a big Quarter Horse stud with that shot. T. J. told me it was a lucky shot, but the nickel became his lucky charm and he carried it everywhere. It reminded me of that silver dollar that Bill

Cody gave my grandfather. I used to think T. J. might still be alive if he would have kept it. But that is superstition and I have come not to believe in such things. I have that nickel to this day though. I keep it in my jewelry box. It has the 22 slug buried inside.

Chapter 13
The Four Sixes

The summer of 1965, I hired on at the 6666 Ranch (Four Sixes) to separate and bring in the cattle off the range. The Four Sixes Ranch is still a forerunner in the cattle industry today. Working on that ranch was an experience I will never forget. It taught me a lot about cattle and taught me just as much about hard working men.

At first I thought I had made a mistake hiring on. Right off the bat the hands tagged me with the name 'The Pup,' and that became my nickname for the three weeks I worked there. The ramrod of the group was always dogging me when I would do something a little different from the way they did things. He would tell me to go and find a tit to suck and leave the real work to the men. One night while we were eating around a camp fire, he made a statement to all the hands that next year he was going to make sure he had buttermilk in camp for all the new pups that show up. It just so happened I was the only so-called pup on this trip. All the guys laughed and making fun of me was a pastime for all the hands. Mostly it was for fun and I have to admit it made me try harder to try and stand up and meet every ones expectations.

After a couple of days, everyone saw I wasn't giving up and started to treat me as one of the hands. Of course, like cattle, I had my pecking order and that put me at the bottom of the pile. I was the last to get my food. I was a 'gofer' for all the older men. You know, go for this and go fetch that type of thing. I bet I hauled two cords of firewood to the camp during the three weeks I worked there.

Our cook was an old ranch hand that went by the nickname Sonny. Sonny was crippled by a bull when he was younger. As time went on he couldn't sit in the saddle four to six hours a day so he became a cook. He still had a string of nice horses and he worked with them every time he had a chance. Sonny and I stayed in touch all through my high school years and he taught me how to ride bulls, when a friend named Dale Harris and I decided to rodeo one summer.

Sitting around the fire one night, the subject of quail hunting came up. Quail hunting is something I know about and I figured I needed to contribute to this conversation. So I spoke up and made the comment that I loved eating quail so much, I could eat quail every day. Right away Sonny said, "Bet you can't eat just quail for one month. And being you are just a pup, I bet you can't eat quail everyday for the two weeks you have left, starting tomorrow."

Like a dummy, I said, "How much?"

Sonny told me to make it easy on myself. Thinking this would be a great way for me to make a little money, I told him fifty dollars. He walked over to me, spit in his hand then stuck it out and said, "It's a bet."

I spit in my hand and we shook on it. Everyone around the camp wanted to get in on the bet. But no one would bet on me. I should have known something was up. They all knew something I didn't and I heard a few of them say 'good luck' as they rolled over in their blankets.

Sonny had an old shotgun he carried for snakes. The bet was I had to shoot and eat at least four quail a day. I told him I could eat six. He laughed and said I could eat all I wanted but I had to at least eat four every day. I could eat whatever he cooked up for breakfast, but dinner and supper I had to eat a total of at least four quail.

The first day some of the men told me to shoot all the quail I wanted and they would have Sonny cook up a few for them. I told them there were a lot of quail and that would be glad to shoot as many as they wanted. That first evening I had eighteen quail and the guys were glad to see I had gotten so many.

Like a big shot, I told Sonny he better cook me up at least six. A few of us sat around eating quail and it became the norm every evening and soon some of the older men were encouraging me to bring in extra every day if I could. Before it was all said and done everyone got a taste of quail. Me? Well, I learned that the human body cannot stand quail every day. Oh, I did well the first four to five days, but before my two weeks were up I couldn't eat another quail. Quail meat is so rich that after a while the body doesn't want anymore, and if you try and force it down it will come right back up. Sonny knew this little bit of information and turned it on a green kid.

After my three weeks were up and we were all waiting to get paid, Sonny was there with his hand stuck out. I made three hundred dollars for about a month's work. Sonny made fifty dollars doing nothing but letting a loud-mouth boy dig his own grave. It was fun, though, and I was accepted by all the hands by the end of the summer and was asked to come back anytime I wanted work.

I perfected some roping skills that summer and learned a lot about running a ranch. There was a lot more to learn, but I loved ranch work. Each man I worked with knew enough to run a big ranch operation in their own right. I learned there is a lot more to running and working on a ranch than meets the eye.

I learned about fixed and variable cost of running a ranch and how important the stock market is to the rancher. That you needed to be somewhat of a veterinarian. You have to know how to stitch, de-horn and pull bleeders, deliver breach births in cattle and horses, know how to deal with bloat, blow flies, screw worms, and inoculate the types of vaccinations necessary to run a cattle operation. You need to know how to deal with blown out uteruses, mastitis, calving and breeding genetics, not to mention artificial insemination. If you can't learn this, then don't get into ranching. You won't succeed.

Chapter 14
Making the grades. Or not.

I started my freshman year with a bang. There were four of us that came over from junior high played football for the last three years. Dale Harris, Claude Strickland, Dole Etherege and me. The high school coach watched us through junior high and greeted us with a big pat on the back soon as we walked through the field house doors. Football, for me anyway, is the best game ever played. I loved it. We all did.

At Slaton the High School, Coach would pass down the team's plays to the junior high coach and by the time you got into high school, you knew the plays already. High school was hard for me academically. By being a fairly good football player and with my friends' help in cheating I kept alive until my junior year when it all caught up with me. I was failing a couple of classes and not doing too well in a couple of more. It didn't keep me from playing football because the school bent the rules for some players. They will let you keep playing and try to help you bring up your grades, even fudge you a few points if that is what you need to keep playing. I was to the point I had to make up some credits and my I dropped out of football my junior year.

On my report card, I changed my grades as not to let mother know I was failing in school. I would turn the Fs into Bs so she would think I was passed. But one day the school counselor called my mother and asked if she could come to school to talk about my grades.

I knew the gig was up and there would be hell to pay. I really don't know what I was thinking. I knew sooner or later it would all catch up with me. But I chose to take the easy way out and not deal with my problems. If I could put it off until tomorrow I would, I was that type. I would face anyone in a fight no matter their size, but when it came to being truthful with me, I was a coward. Not hurting Mother was my biggest concern. It was a stupid thing to do. The last person I wanted to hurt was my mother. She had been through enough in her life and she didn't need me adding to it.

I sat in the counselor's office watching tears flow down my mother's face as she was informed of my real grades. Neither one knew I had been changing my grades, and the truth was all brought out during this meeting. It tore at my very soul to see this strong woman brought to tears by me. I had seen my mother cry many times over the years, but this time she was crying over something I had caused. She didn't deserve this. I knew it would be awhile before this incident passed.

I had cheated my way through school since the fourth grade. I never learned the basic skills in school that is the foundation to all your learning and understanding in an academic world. I now felt I was too old, and my pride kept me from asking for help. It was always easy to blame my upbringing, but deep down inside I knew I had the same opportunity as everyone else to get an education and I simply didn't apply myself. I had pissed my education away.

I had a couple of teachers take a real interest in me and helped me bring my grades up. Mr. Myers in Science and Biology, Mrs. Lindsey in English. They could read me like a book, and they actually took the time and patience to explain and teach me these subjects. Math was a lost cause with me. The math teacher was a real peace of work, and there was no love lost between us.

The worst though was letting my mother down. She knew what life would be without an education, and she had her hopes and dreams set on me doing something with my life. Before she passed away in 2002, she got to see her oldest son make something of his life and had expressed to me many times how proud she was of me and the man I had become. I loved my mother for the sacrifices she made for us and the love that was always there. I miss her splendid nature as well as her pioneer spirit.

Chapter 15
True Love Ways --Shirley

Everyone has heard the expression, 'You never get over your first love.' There is a certain amount of truth in this saying.

I haven't talked about girls up to this point. Throughout my family life my girls wanted me to talk about someone other than their mother that I may have cared for when I was young. Shirley is the only one that really came to mind. I had a lot of girls that were friends, and I dated most of them. I really only had deep feelings for two: Shirley, and my wife, Veronica Kitten Brooks.

I had more than a few girlfriends growing up, but Shirley, I have to say, was my first real love. Even though I had deep feelings for her, Shirley may not have shared these same emotions for me. She was a grade ahead of me and I thought she would be the girl I would marry. The first time I noticed Shirley was at the end of the school year of 1966. I liked Shirley the first time I heard her wonderful laugh.

It is not the initial thing guys usually notice about girls, but her laugh did it for me. Of course, I liked Shirley's other features, but that came later. Her laugh was the hook. The first time I talked to her, I was more than nervous. I don't remember everything. I am sure I stuttered and hem-hawed around and looked like a complete idiot. Eventually I must have done or said something right, because not too long afterward we started dating and before long I fell head over heels in love.

Shirley was special and fun and she always made me laugh when she and I were together. I remember my friends Dale Harris and Johnny Outlaw once told me that I always had this stupid grin on my face when I was around her. I guess this was true because I always felt better about myself when I was with her.

It was not long after we started dating that I gave Shirley my grandmother's ring, which was nothing more than a small gold band with a couple of diamond chips in it. My grandmother passed before Shirley had a chance to know her, but I knew my grandmother would have liked her. The ring was not valuable; it was just a gesture of love. Since my grandmother and I were so close, I wanted Shirley to have something of hers. I can truly say I was in love with Shirley, but, like I expressed before, I guess Shirley was not all that in love with me.

The feelings that she had for me were more friend-like. I don't really know, when you are young you assume a lot and I guess I assumed she was in love with me as much as I was with her. We were both young and I had never been in love before. As we all know, things don't always work out to the way we would like, or even the way we might perceive things are going to happen. I guess Shirley and I weren't meant to be. Stupid little things can make a whole chain of events change. Something one might say, or do. When you are young, you don't grasp how important it is to cherish such things as forgiveness and understanding, or have the foresight to talk things out. Communication is a big factor in any relationship. I scored poorly in all these areas and it was due to my own shortcomings Shirley and I did not end up together.

The beginning of the end of our relationship, for me anyway, was that she started dating some guy from

Lubbock who had a Corvette, or so I was told. All I know is soon after she dated this guy, Shirley started treating me different. I don't even know who he was, but I was jealous. I would have done anything to have kept Shirley as my girl.

Her friends may have teased her about dating an under classmen. Peer pressure does play a part in such matters. Just speculation on my part. Once, while she was driving up and down the drag with some of her friends, she threw her chewing gum at me as I pulled up beside them in my truck. All of her friends laughed as if they thought it was funny. My feelings were hurt and instead of just letting it go I got mad. I know, sometimes I am a slow learner but it didn't take a whole lot of smarts to realize it was over between us. I could do nothing more than take it. I called Shirley a bitch, and as soon as the words came out of my mouth it felt like a knife had pierced my heart. Soon afterward, Shirley and her friends had me pull over on the town square. She got out of the car and asked me if I meant what I had called her. I told her no, and she turned and got back into the car with her friends. I knew then it was over between Shirley and me.

I have had some low points in my life that I dealt with, like my real dad and other stuff, but Shirley walking away from me that day broke my heart. I ended up getting a pint of Champion Bourbon, went out to what we all called the drinking tree in the canyon and downed the bottle in about an hour's time. Getting a little tight didn't help, but then it didn't hurt either. I tried to figure out where I blew it. I didn't talk about it with anyone but Johnny Outlaw, and even then not much was said. I didn't like thinking about Shirley, doing so put a knot in my stomach. Isn't it mind-boggling how something so insignificant and stupid as throwing gum can bring about events that can change one's life? I was immature not to laugh it off and try to find a way to win her back.

It would be hard to give Shirley up. She had me wrapped around her little finger, and she had done it so easily. She couldn't help but notice how much influence she had on me, but up to now she had never abused the power she had over me. She was never vindictive or mean. In fact, this was the first time I had ever been disappointed and upset with her. I figured I would lick my wounds, take my injured pride and move on. It was prevalent to me, by this gesture with the gum, that she was ready for something different from our relationship. I guess this, as minute and stupid as it was, was easier than talking to me, or maybe it was to demonstrate to her friends she could pretty much treat me like she wanted and I would take it. Anyway, that was my perception. What is ironic about the whole thing is that it was true. I was head over heels in love with Shirley, and I would have done pretty much whatever she wanted.

Her smile, personality, and charm held a spell on me that was intoxicating, and that she would even give me a second thought gave me pride in myself. Not too many people have given me the feeling of having pride, but Shirley did. Shirley was a free spirit, and in that sense I like to think that she and I were alike. We were both very young and probably had doubts about true love. Having these feelings for someone at such a young age was a little scary and confusing, for me anyway. Shirley probably knew what she wanted in a partner and at this time it was not me.

I will really never know the cause of our break up. As time passed I put my broken heart in check and went on. It took me awhile to put her behind me and get on with it. I was hurt, full of pride and bull-headed and I did not even try to mend our relationship. I made it plain how I felt about her while we were together and no other explanation was needed on my part. This was my reasoning back then. She acted like she did not want to further our relationship anyway and I had no say one way or the other on the matter. You cannot force someone to love you.

We did get together one night after a small rodeo on Western Day in 1967. She may have been reaching out to me for some kind of reconciliation. If this was her motive, I was stupid and did not seize the opportunity. I am not all that sure that reconciliation was even a part of the equation. I think for Shirley it was more of a final goodbye.

That night, as I was driving her home, she asked me to pull over on the side of the road to talk. This was the last time I was ever alone with Shirley. I told her I loved her that night, but the days that followed I did not pursue the relationship. Shirley was not in love with me, after all. She did not tell me that she loved me back; she did not say the words I wanted so much to hear. She didn't mind being with me, but wanted to keep her options open.

Shirley may have been at a crossroads in her life as well, and was just as confused about her future as I was about mine. I have come to see it was most likely my fault our relationship never really blossomed. And too, if I had that night back, I would have handled it so differently. Being as immature and small town as I was back then, and not knowing how to handle the situation, I let Shirley slip away.

Who knows how far our relationship might have taken us, if I would have known what to say. Shirley probably did not hear the words she wanted to hear from me that night either, and I was haunted by the fact I might have failed her as much as I failed myself. More was needed from me than just an 'I love you.' I was not the right person for Shirley. I had some growing up to do and I think Shirley knew this too. I think she knew it from the beginning.

I will always have a special place in my heart for her. As you get older you acquire a little more common sense, which allows you to have some kind of an understanding of your true feelings for people and also allows you to make better decisions. It also allows you to be truthful with yourself. I should have been a little more forgiving. I blame myself for not trying to patch up the feelings we had for each other. Even though we have not spoken to each other in over thirty-six years, I still think of her as an important part of who I am. She helped me grow up in some ways but for sure made me think twice about committing myself so whole-heartedly to someone else. Shirley was, and I am sure still is, a wonderful person with good values and morals. In all I am glad she came into my life. I wouldn't have missed our short dance together even if I could go back in time and do it all over again. Shirley and I never really got the chance to take our love to that next level. This of course was due to her morals and not mine. We never shared ourselves with each other to the degree that can really bond two people together.

I don't believe Shirley pondered over me too long. I could share with you many things we talked about while we were together, but there is no point in doing that. She and I have taken different roads and what was important to us then has nothing to do with today. Besides, the things we talked about are mine and mine alone. There are moments in one's life they may want to keep to them self. The memories and affection one may carry for someone over a period of forty years plays no part in reality today. That is why over many years they become your memories and yours alone. I am sure Shirley does not give me a second thought and if she even did it will not carry the same emotions from back then and that's okay. I know she is happy with the choices she has made. Shirley ended up marrying a great guy who I knew in high school. There is no doubt in the long run, she made the right decision by ending our relationship and getting on with her life. They, I know, have a great life together and still live in Slaton.

For me they are just great memories of a wonderful person that touched my life. So I can share my feelings for Shirley with just about anyone. She had more of an impact on my life than I did on hers, and I'm not the first that has happened to.

For me, life so far has been short and there is never be enough time to close some chapters. I have wasted the first part of my life thinking there was no time limit. Toward the backside of my life I became bitter after the war in Vietnam and kind of just dropped out of touch not only with myself, but with all my friends, with the exception of my best friend then in high school and my closest friend today, Johnny Outlaw.

Even though one may think fondly of someone of their past, it does not have a whole lot to do with what is true today. These are only parts of one's life, the entirety they have lived the course he or she has chosen. You live with these choices and make it the best life you can with the decisions you have made. I have made some bad decisions and believe me, I have paid dearly for them. But the friends and relationships I have had have been good ones, and have helped me stay the course in this race.

With Shirley I learned that a breaking heart isn't as loud as the sound of thunder, or even an exploding bomb in combat. Sometimes it can be as quiet as a feather falling, or even a baby's sigh, and the most painful thing is no one really heard it except me. A broken heart is a heart that has at least felt love, and I can say my heart did feel love, my first. For me, loving her came with two requirements: heartbreaking and healing. Without a doubt, healing takes the longest.

I have also learned over time that you can still carry a type of love for someone for nothing more than the person they were in that special place in time in your life. I have no resentment of my time with this wonderful person. I am a better man for knowing her, than not. Since then, we have traveled down different roads, and have our own families now. The affection I have for her is only special to me. It is an honest feeling with nothing to hide and nothing but the best intentions for the both of us. I could never disgrace my memory of her with words or actions that would bring grief to her or my families in this day and time. These are just memories of mine that I hold dear and cherish, but to others it is nothing more than what is now an old man's memories and a part of some ones past. Inner thoughts are ours alone, when it comes down to it; it plays no importance to anyone else.

Sure, I would like for her to know what an important person she was to me in my carefree years. And that the things I told her when we were both so young and full of life were heartfelt and true. She will always be special in a way known only to me. It is not important that she never thinks of me. It is only important that I can recall this special time in my life. I am not the only one that has been touched in such a way by their first love. After all, 'A heart that truly loves, never forgets.' (Proverb)

Chapter16
True Love Found

The other girl in my life was Veronica Kitten, who ended up being the biggest influence on me and is my wife today. Roni came from an old German family with unbelievable morals. I met Roni shortly after Shirley and I parted ways. I was drawn to Roni like a moth to a flame, and after Shirley, I wanted that feeling of love again. If I could find love again my heart could at least start to heal. I found love again, but this time I would take it slow, and not jump into the deep end of the pool. I would be more careful this time around.

Roni came over from the Catholic school to go to Slaton High for her freshman year. Her parents wanted her to go to Cooper, a small town close to Lubbock. There were ten kids in her family and she is was the only one that ever went to school in Slaton. Her parents were outraged that she wanted to go to school there but she enrolled without their permission anyway. I liked her spunk from the start.

I thought I was in love with her, but I was afraid. I knew I had to quit all this moping and move on. I also did not want to end up like my parents, in a divorce. My mother and real father had to be in love at one time and look what happened to them. I didn't want that kind of a relationship, and so far, with the exception of Shirley, I couldn't see myself staying with any of the girls I'd dated so far for life. I was a little gun-shy and was not all in that big of a hurry to get into another serious relationship. So Roni and I took our relationship slow and we dated each other four years before we married.

After I returned from Vietnam we tied the knot, and that is another story. Getting to know Roni was not all that easy. She was only fourteen and was very shy, even getting her to talk to me was like pulling teeth. She used to walk over from the Catholic school to Slaton High every morning. Her mother wouldn't drop her off at Slaton High. This was part of her punishment for enrolling in there and not going to Cooper. She had younger siblings that were going to the Catholic school and her mother would drop them off every morning. For me this was great, I would drive by and ask her if she wanted a ride. She would quietly reply yes and crawl up into my pickup. But trying to get her to talk to me wasn't easy. I only had a couple of blocks to give her a ride, not much time to think of something clever to woo her with.

Finally, after a few weeks, we were dating. We fell in love with each other from the very start. I believe we connected so well because we had some of the same background. Her father, in a lot of ways, was like my father. Her father was an alcoholic and she grew to hate the things her father was doing, like I hated my real father in general. I understood her feelings in every aspect and how it bothered her. Her family life reminded me a lot of mine. She came to realize she hated her father's drinking and not really the man himself.

One time I asked my mother how someone knew if he or she was in love. As it stood then, I felt like I loved all the girls I have been with. I was confused on this subject of true love. I didn't want it to be a one way street again. Mother had made the mistake in marriage with my real father and I figured if anyone would know, she would. I expected her to laugh, but to my surprise she did not. She smiled and told me when I found the right girl I would know.

"How will I know?" I asked.

She told me that I would feel for that person like no other person. Not a whole lot of information to go on, but I kept it in mind. I wanted more of a plain black and white explanation on true love and really, there's not one.

A special feeling was all I could pull out of her. I let one special relationship slip by with Shirley. I would do whatever it took this time, and try my best with Roni. I made a promise to myself not to be so selfish and unforgiving with Roni, and to maybe take things a lot slower and not make the same mistakes I made before. I told Roni of the feelings I had had with Shirley, and even though she was young, she understood.

After a year or so together, I knew Roni was the girl I wanted to share my life with. Her being so young did bother me; I was even the first boy she had really even kissed. She was fifteen, and I was nineteen. I felt like that in a couple of years, if everything was going well, I would ask her to marry me. She told me she loved me, as I did her. But she had never dated anyone but me. How does she know she is in love? This was something I would think about all the time. I had no wish to go through what I went through with Shirley, so I got this stupid idea to break up with Roni and give her a chance to date other boys, you know, to find out for herself if she really thought she was in love with me. I could hardly bear the thought of her dating another guy, but I felt this was the only way for her to find out for sure that she was in love with me. She told me over and over that she knew she was young, but she knew she was in love with me. Still, I thought there was no other way for us both to be for sure, so we broke up.

After only a couple of weeks Roni quit eating and ended up with an ulcer, I couldn't bear it anymore and we got back together, and except for Vietnam, Korea, Saudi Arabia, and some of my other travels we have remained together.

Slaton was like any other small town in America back in the 60s. Vietnam was on the news every night. My grades were horrible. I was now in my senior year of high school but I would still be short a credit and a half at the end of the year to graduate. The draft was in full force back then and I knew once out of school I would be prime meat. To top things off, my dad's work was moving to Emporia, Kansas and they would be moving. Mother tried to play the tough parent and tell me I was going with them, but I knew I would not. I could not leave Roni. Here was a girl that thought I was somebody, the only person in my life that loved me for being me. I know she was young and I didn't really know if she knew anymore about love than I did. But I was not moving off to another state and away from her. Mother let me know in no certain terms that I would be on my own, and I would find out how hard it was to make a living. Mother thought that would shock me into going with them. But those words just made me even more determined to stay. I was staying and that was that.

Graduation came and of course yours truly did not graduate. I only needed a credit and a half. I decided to go ahead and go to school the next year and try and at least get my diploma. It was hard for me to see all my friends move on. Some went to college and so on, all my class was gone except for three of us, (Rex Conner, Phil Brassfield, and me.) I knew Shirley had made the right move by ending our relationship. She was going to some trade school collage in Lubbock and was about to start her race in life. And I was still stuck in the starting blocks.

I was working nights at a Whiles Shamrock Truck Stop in Slaton, pumping gas and fixing truck flats. I worked nights because they let me keep all the truck flat money. I averaged about thirty dollars on a good night, and my check was around ninety dollars at the end of each week. It didn't take me long to find out this was not enough money, so I got a second job working a gas station on 50th street in Lubbock, fifteen miles away. I went to school from eight o-clock in the morning till twelve o-clock noon. Then I would drive my car to Lubbock start work at two; get off at eight that night. I would then drive back to Slaton start the night shift at nine o-clock, work till three in the morning, get a couple hours sleep and then do it all over again. I lived out of my car most of the time. On my time off I slept at my sister and her husband's house in Lubbock. Between gasoline, food, car payment and expenses I was going nowhere and getting there fast. I knew I had to do something so I dropped out of school to get a full time job. Soon after, the draft caught up with me and I went into the Army.

***

I often reflect on my life in Slaton, Texas. After Vietnam I considered my years there as my carefree years, and I wouldn't have traded them for anything. I sometimes envy my friends that have lived out their lives in this great West Texas town. Things never remain the same and I know things are different there now. When I revisit my hometown my mind is flooded with the great times I had there and the wonderful people I was fortunate enough to know. It is the values I learned and the friends I had in Slaton that carried me through the hard roads I traveled after leaving, that have carried me through my travels around the world. Nowhere I've lived compares. When things were rough for me in combat I let my mind take me back to those easy years in Slaton, and the burdens of combat and war a little easier to handle.

I fell in love for the first time in that small, dusty town, and I found my true love and life-long partner, my wife, Roni. I never knew how much Slaton would become such a big part of my life and have so much of an influence on me. If I had it to do all over again I would have never left, but then hindsight is always better than foresight and I didn't know what we had until it was too late.

Oscar Wilde, an Irish poet, once wrote, "Ordinary riches can be stolen, real riches cannot. In your soul are infinitely precious things that cannot be taken from you."

PART II

Introduction

It took me six years and many bottles of Scotch to write about the war. I lost some very good friends, along with my innocence, in Vietnam. I do not consider myself an author of any kind and if you read this so called book you will see why. I tried to write it for my family as one would write a diary, but I could not tell this story unless it was written down like it is branded into my mind. Some of the following text is very graphic in nature and the bad language is not meant to offend anyone. It is how it was.

My friends have encouraged me to write down these memories. I have tried several times over the years, but it has been very hard. Mostly due to the emotions which play on my mind for days afterward, and taking me back to what I fought so hard to put behind me over the years.

I'm getting older now, and I'm afraid people will forget who we all were and what we did, or didn't, do. Whichever it was, it was a sacrifice for us who fought in Vietnam, as well as all Americans. This book is about war, a war that in size may have been small. But the effects of what it did to us as a nation and what we did to ourselves are enormous.

It's a story, based on true events in my life and about men who fought and faced death every day. It is about their trials and tribulations in combat, men who shared love and respect for each other in a way that the average person will never come to understand.

I want to share with you this camaraderie that can only be experienced in combat, and how it bonded those of us who fought together for eternity. The bond that never has to be mentioned to be understood. For those on the first lines of defense in Vietnam it was an everyday war. Not some engagement, not some battle here or there to go down in some history book. It was an ongoing physical and mental battle, not only with the enemy, but with us and each other. All I really knew about the war in Vietnam was about as much as any kid knew, it was some little war on the other side of the globe and it was on the news every evening.

The book is also for my fallen brothers, to try and bring some understanding of their losses and what we went through on the front lines of Vietnam. I tried to put into words what a combat veteran experiences and the by-product left over from war that he will carry with him the rest of his life and the horrors one may face with combat itself. The infliction that man can bring upon man. I am not seeking any recognition for what I did in Vietnam. I am not proud of some of the things I did in combat and I am ashamed of some of the war crimes I may have committed. I only ask that if you read this part of my life, please do not judge me or soldiers in general for the things we did. Trust me when I tell you that we are harder on ourselves for the things we have done in war, than you could ever be on us.

I hope my story will bring you a little closer to people that sacrificed so much for all of you. It matters not to me what views you may have had about the war in Vietnam. This story is not about that. My goal is to bring to life a story of some brave young men who were forced to become men under great duress. A story told like it was and not some fictitious idea that lives in the minds of Hollywood. Maybe to let you come to know their true personalities so you can help keep their spirits alive. Do not let their legacy be just names on a wall. The names of the KIAs in the book have been changed to protect some of the families and honor their wishes. The true names of the KIAs are listed at the end of my story. This way the manner of their death will be spared, for it is only their sacrifice that need be honored and not the details on how it was given.

This chapter has been the hardest for me to write. When I returned from Vietnam I talked about the war with certain people. But I never brought up this single event once, until several years ago setting in a truck with my best friend, I opened up and told this story to him. It was hard to hold back the emotions and it is still hard for me to deal with today. I hate to dwell on these events long but I had to finish this chapter. This will be my last attempt to try and document this event. . This is my 5th attempt to record this tragedy. There is no Title, never could think of one that would fit the occasion. As you can tell I am not very good with titles anyway. The only people that have ever heard this story in its entirety is my wife Roni and my best friend Johnny Outlaw. (This is the short version)

Chapter 1
Paying Rent

I had not yet had my turn in Vietnam. But I knew it was only a matter of time. I was twenty-years-old, a drop out and the draft was going strong. The Lottery method had not been activated at this time and I knew it was only a matter of time. I had no idea how the next few years would change my life.

In November of 1968, I received that dreaded brown envelope containing 'greetings' and I knew it was my turn to pay rent on all the freedom that I had taken for granted all of my life. In high school we always talked about Vietnam, but hoped it would be over by the time we graduated. Besides, we told ourselves, we probably wouldn't go anyway.

My best friend in high school was Johnny Outlaw. He is still. He and I were going to join the service on the buddy plan. We went to Amarillo, Texas to do our physical and paper work. I knew that if I was drafted into the Armed Forces my lack of education would most likely put me into ground combat or wherever the military wanted me. On the other hand, if I joined voluntarily I could get the MOS (Job Scope) I wanted. I was smart enough, or at least I thought I was smart enough to know I didn't want to be a grunt and pound the ground. Even though it would mean an extra year, we would rather do that than have the Army put us in the field. This way, we felt we were somewhat in charge of our own destiny.

Anyway you looked at it, I was going into the Armed Services whether I liked it or not. If you were in college or going to go to college, you were not going to be drafted. I was a drop out, so I had no problems qualifying and really had no other choice but serve. I was A-1 prime meat and the only way out of going to 'Nam was to head out for Canada. At the time, I felt like I was obligated to serve. I owed something to my country, so Canada was not an option for me. It had come time for me to pay rent on all that freedom I had taken for granted. I just didn't know at the time how much that rent would be.

Helicopters were for us. Outlaw and I envisioned ourselves flying other people out to the battle or doing whatever those helicopters did. They were flying *above it all* and to us that seemed like a better road to take. I did not have enough education to qualify for pilot training, so I settled for the next best thing. I would be a door gunner and fly above, of what I thought was the real fighting on the ground. Well, Outlaw failed his physical and ended up staying home, while I passed and went to El Paso to Fort Bliss for my basic training and then off to Vietnam.

Outlaw still carries guilt because he did not get to go with me to Vietnam. After serving in Vietnam, I was glad my friend did not go with me. He and I have talked about it on several occasions, and I can tell it still bothers him no matter how much I assure him it was not his fault and there was nothing he could have done to make things different. Being helicopter gunners was originally Outlaw's idea, and he can't but help blame himself that I went into combat without him.

The first thing I had to contend with was going to school and learning about these aircraft. Then from there, if qualified, I could go to advanced courses in adjacent to door gunner school. At the time, it sure looked like a good idea to me.

I was sent to Fort Bliss, Texas for basic training. Don't really have much to say about basic training. Basic training is basic. At the time I thought it was cool, but after Vietnam basic training was what the title applies, basic. After basic I was sent to Fort Rucker, Alabama for helicopter training.

The school was really not all that bad. It was interesting learning about all the different aspects of the aircraft that I would be flying and working on in Vietnam. I went to school on the Bell 205, (UH-1D) known as a Huey. In 'Nam some models took on the titles Slicks, Dust Off, and other titles depending on how the aircraft were used.

For the first time in my life I really felt like I could amount to something. I never applied myself in school and by not doing so I built up this complex of being a loser. I blame myself for not getting the education that I needed. But here was this two million dollar aircraft I was going to be working and flying on, and for a kid from a small town in West Texas it was big stuff, for me anyway.

When I was a kid, there was this TV series I used to watch called Whirly Birds. These guys would fly around doing all kinds of missions in the, 'civilian world' with what is now an old Bell 47. I use to imagine being a part of the aviation world that included helicopters. At the time I thought it was only a dream.

Anyway, with this new training I cracked the books, paid attention in class, and studied every night, for the first time in my life. I applied myself. I wanted that flight training in door gunner school for sure. I didn't want to be stuck in maintenance working on these great aircrafts; I wanted to fly on them. I wanted to be a Crew Chief.

The hard worked paid off and I graduated ninth in my class of three hundred. Finally I had accomplished something in my life. A friend I hooked up with in A.I.T. helped me with some of my math and thanks to him I was on my way, but the best thing of all, I knew I would not be pounding the ground in the jungles of Vietnam. I would be flying above all that crap; I would be 'above it all.'

At this time I was going through door gunner training and having a little fun. For the most part that was true. Our main job was learning how to shoot an M-60 machine-gun from a helicopter at different speeds and angles. We worked on aviation terminology and mechanics of the aircraft, but mostly handling of the M-60 machine gun. The gun we used was a mounted M-60, but when I arrived in 'Nam and attached to a unit, I learned to use a cut down modified version of this gun, which some tag as a free style and without a gun mount. I also went through a jungle survival course.

After flying in 'Nam, I understood why they taught the course. The jungle can be as deadly as the enemy and just as unforgiving. We were learning to deal with both. But my mind was still on those helicopters.

The plan that Outlaw and I put together had worked so far. When I got to 'Nam I would not be pounding the ground, and I would not be dealing with that jungle crap. I thought of Outlaw often while I was going through gunner school. Outlaw would have loved that crap. I missed my friend. In school, if there was something exciting to do, he and I would most likely be doing it together. I couldn't help but think of what he would be doing right now. I depended on Outlaw's friendship more than I realized. He and I did not write each other because he was moving around a lot and didn't have a permanent address.

Chapter 2
Vietnam Bound

I remember all of us waiting to get our orders. We tried to act like Vietnam was no big deal. But deep inside we all hoped we would get some other assignment like Germany or even Korea. The orders came down and they were read to us all aloud. Out of a class of three hundred, only five went to Germany. How those lucky few were picked remains a mystery to me. Evidently, being in the top of the class had no bearing on the matter.

I arrived in Cam Ron Bay, Vietnam in June of 1969. I will never forget when they opened the door to the aircraft and the heat came down the ilea and hit me dead in the face. I hoped I had what it took to stand up to the commitment I made to myself and my homeland, to see this thing through. I was scared and hadn't even set foot in country yet. I didn't want to let anyone down and naturally, getting killed crossed my mind more than a few times. I was in Cam Ron only long enough to process through and get assigned to a unit.

Before long, I received my orders and was assigned to the Cavalry. Some of the Short Timers (A Short Timer is someone that doesn't have long in country and will be headed home) told me that I was headed right into the thick of the war. I thought they were just joking with the FNG (Fucking New Guy) but later I found out it was no joke. About sixty of us were loaded up on a C-130 cargo plane and flown down to Ben Hoa. (Saigon.) Once there we went through more jungle training and learned how to rappel from helicopters, re-qualify with an M-16 and those of us that had jungle training had to qualify with an M-79, known to the grunt as simply a Chunkier (Grenade Launcher.)

All this training lasted about a week then we were assigned to our units. I was assigned to Charlie Squadron 1st Division 9th Cavalry (1/9th Cav.) I first ended up in a place called Phu Phien with another FNG whose name I can't bring to mind. I do remember though about three months later he was shot to death by one of our own men. He was killed over a card game. A so-called point man from the Blues shot him in the stomach with a shotgun, all over a stupid card game. This all went down right before he was headed to Hawaii to be with his wife on R&R (Rest and Recuperation.) The fact I can't remember his name has bothered me over the years. He was a friendly sort of guy and we both comforted each other on that initial shock of arriving in Vietnam together.

I would like to clarify that the Blues were a great asset to our day to day operation. They were a team of Grunts that were used in our unit for aircraft recovery. They would be inserted into an area were a helicopter had been shot down and set up a P O D (Perimeter Of Defense) around the downed aircraft. Then a team would be inserted into the area to recover the downed helicopter and also serve as protection for the recovery team. The Blue Team was a great bunch of guys and we fought side by side for the year I was over there. You will hear me mention them from time to time. I have the highest regards for them, except for the individual that killed this friend of mine.

This friend and I looked out the window of a Chinook helicopter that transported us to our assigned unit and thought no way in hell is this the place where we were going to be assigned. Pheu Phien looked like the end of the world. We were dropped off, standing on the flight line in disbelief. We wondered what the hell we could do to get out of that hell-hole. We both thought end up in a place more like Saigon.

As he and I pondered how we were going to pull this off, an E-6 Sergeant approached us. Before he got close he blurted out, "I need two volunteers to go to a place called Quan Loi. I need one guy with a 67N2F (MOS) & an 11Bravo."

Could this be true? We looked at each other and I remember told him that it couldn't be any worse than this place. He agreed and like a couple of dummies we raised our hands. Remember that old saying about never volunteer? No matter what never, ever volunteer and when someone asks for replacements, you might want to ask yourself why people need to be replaced.

The Sergeant told us that a gun ship from Quan Loi was making a mail run and we could hop a ride to Quan Loi with them. But then he kind of laughed. It was that laugh that stuck in my craw. A gunship and it is coming here to pick up mail? If they have to pick up their mail here, what kind of hell-hole are they from?

I recall this grunt lying up against his duffel bag on the side of the flight line. He seemed to find great pleasure and humor about our situation. He was a thin man and although he must have been close to our age he looked older. We must have looked a sight to him. He picked himself off the ground and walked toward us. I don't remember his name, but he stuck out his hand introduced himself with a strange grin on his face.

"Look," he said, "the chopper that is going to pick you up will be coming from that direction." He pointed south. "You are going to one hell of an outfit. B Troop 1st and the 9th Cavalry, have you heard of them?"

I didn't say a word; I could tell he was fixing to let me know all about this subject. The whole time he spoke to us he had this shit eating grin on his face.

"Well, they lead the Cavalry Division in kills. They're headhunters for sure, and they just cruise those choppers around looking for action. They get high on it. You boys will have a lot of fun with the 1/9th Cav." Then he added an extra layer of sarcasm before walking away. "You boys ever heard of not volunteering?"

Not too much time had passed when we heard a chopper coming from the direction that the grunt had pointed out to us. A gunship was making a short final approach. Gunners were standing on the skids and they were holding M-60s in their hands. First time I have ever seen a gunship with non-mounted 60s. And they were cut down M-60s without a by-pod on the front of the barrel. These guys knew their shit and you could tell it. They had their flight helmets on with the sun visors pulled down so you could not see their eyes or their faces. You could tell that this display was for our benefit.

Upon landing, a big, red mail sack was thrown on board and the guy that brought out the bag talked to one of the gunners and then pointed to my friend and me. The gunner stepped off the skid of the chopper and started toward us. We picked up our duffel bags and met him half way.

"Are you the two FNGs that we are supposed to pick up?" he yelled above the rotor noise.

We nodded and followed him to the aircraft.

As I crawled inside the A/C I noticed that there were no seats except for two jump seats the gunners sat in. The A/C was stripped of its weight so it could carry more ammunition. This crew and A/C had seen battle and you knew it. By crawling into this aircraft I entered their domain and felt somewhat out of place.

The Crew Chief (Head Gunner) told us where he wanted us to sit and then turned to the pilot and co-pilot and said something into his mike. They laughed. As I looked around the aircraft and I noticed they had some Vietnamese tied up with a bar that ran behind his back and his hands tied up front. It hit me then and there that they had taken a prisoner. As I glanced into this man's eyes I saw nothing but loathing. I had never been looked upon by someone that really wanted to kill me. His hatred emanated from the tenseness of his muscles bearing against the ropes that bound him. You could *feel* it. The pilot lifted off and in no time we were low-leveling across the runway. The pilot pulled back on the stick and the aircraft shot straight up into the air. He nosed the aircraft over and in a second we were headed south.

The pilot turned toward us and looked at his crew chief. He then said something over the intercom and nodded his head as to give them the go ahead. The gunner grabbed this prisoner by the hair and pulled him backward and jumped into the middle of his chest. He pulled a knife from off his vest and rammed it into the man's mid-section. He held him down with his body weight as the knife sunk in all the way. At the same time, the prisoner was kicked and gasped for air and his foot kicked me in the knee. The shock sent me to my feet. I reached out to pull the gunner off of this man only to feel a gun barrel crack across my arm. The other gunner told me to back off and sit my ass down.

As I did, I saw a pool of blood on the floor of the helicopter where I was sitting. I moved my duffel bag over to cover up the pool of blood and sat on top of it. What was this all about? I looked over at my friend and he stared back at me. He searched for some kind of reassurance and I think I wanted the same. All we saw was fright. I turned back toward the man on the floor. He was no longer moving. He was dead.

The gunner then cut off the dead soldier's right ear, looked back at me and kissed the ear. He placed the ear on his flight helmet between a cover strap from some steal pot (helmet) that was stretched around his flight helmet. "Don't worry, my man, you will get your cherry busted soon. Real soon."

I noticed there was more than one ear in this band around his helmet. I counted eight.

The aircraft banked left with a jerk and came around 180 degrees. We were headed back toward Phou Phien. The gunner dragged the body over to the cargo door and stuffed a 1st/9th patch in the dead man's shirt pocket, along with what appeared to be a note. The pilot then low-leveled across the Phou Phien's airstrip and the gunner threw the body out.

As the aircraft did another180 degrees and came about, we saw some soldiers on the ground gathering around the body as it lay on the flight line. They were giving us the peace sign and laughing. Later, I found out the note said 'Compliments from B troop 1st and the 9th Cav.'

Chapter 3
Cowboy Up

Quan Loi was our next stop. This would be my home for the next year. I thought about Canada, and decided it did not seem like a bad place to be. Maybe the people that went to Canada knew something I did not. I put that out of my mind. I was there and I had better adjust fast or else this place would eat you alive. I had to adapt to a new way of thinking that was for sure. It seemed no one wanted to help you make that transition. No one wanted to let you into their circle. Later I would come to understand why.

When we arrived at Quan Loi, I was still in a state of shock. It took the flight from Phou Phien to Quan Loi for me to regain some of my composure. (That must have reeked with FNG!) I could not put out of my mind what seemed to me a murder.

As we approached Quan Loi, I saw it was nothing more than a firebase cut out of the jungle. As firebases go, it was big. Looked like at least One Division. Within the P.O.D. of Quan Loi there were artillery, tanks, infantry, armor, and a company of gunships. B Troop 1st/9th Air Cav. This would be my home and unit for the next 358 days. I had already started counting down my time for DEROS (Date Estimated Return Over Seas.)

As we made a final approach to Quan Loi, I noticed there were some soldiers standing next to the flight line; no doubt they were waiting for the mail. Mail was worth its weight in gold. It was the only touch that you had with the outside world and with civilization. The CO (Company Commander) knew the morale of the men depended on it. I also learned how important mail was. I lived to get it and when I didn't it was depressing. They were also waiting to see the new replacements, the new meat on the block. Us. This greeting party was going to have a little fun at our expense.

As the helicopter touched down, my friend jumped out first. I heard someone asked him what his MOS was, he told them 11Bravo (which is a grunt) and after hearing that they kind of brushed him aside and was headed straight for me.

I knew one thing. I wasn't taking anymore shit. I jumped out of the helicopter and turned around to get my bag. I saw the blood on my duffle bag from the man we just killed. Everything was coming to a boil in my head and I was not in any mood to be screwed with. "What is your MOS, dude?" someone asked.

"67N2F," I replied. I felt a pat on my back as someone took the bag from my hand.

"Hooten is my name. They call me Hooter. I fly gunner in Scouts. What do they call you man?"

"Brooks," I replied.

This guy Hooter winked and said, "Great, follow me and we will get you settled in."

As I walked along beside Hooter I heard someone else yell out, "Welcome aboard dude!"

Hooter shouted over the rotor noise. "You will like being a gunner Brooks. We take care of our own."

Finally, I thought. *A little respect. Maybe I found a home after all.*

Hooter took me to a tent that had sandbags piled up around the outside of it. "Get attacked often?" I asked.

"About four times a week we get mortared. We have had two ground attacks in the last three months. Trust me dude, you won't get bored around here."

Yeah, like that was what I was worried about.

"Have to report you in first, Brooks. The First Sergeant will want to welcome you himself. He does that with all the FNGs... I mean, new guys."

I could tell by his retraction Hooter wanted me to feel a little more accepted by not calling me a FNG. I appreciated the gesture and patted him on the back as in thanks.

The First Sergeant was a short man with a cigar sticking out of his mouth. He looked the part.

"Sergeant, we have a new man. Brooks is his name. He is a Door Gunner First Sergeant and he will be Babcock's replacement," said Hooter.

The Sergeant smiled and stuck out his hand. "Welcome aboard, Brooks. Welcome to the Scouts." He patted me on the back and spoke at the same time.

"Scouts?" I replied, "What is a Scout?"

"Hooter will explain it all to you later in greater detail, but you will have to fly Scouts for at least three months, then if you want to you can transition over into Slicks. Or you can fly gunner on Cobras, but everyone, and I mean everyone, has to pay their dues in Scouts first."

Sounded good to me. Just as long as I would be flying and not pounding the ground I would be one happy camper.

"It takes a certain type of man to fly gunships, Brooks. Welcome aboard and be proud you are a gunner. Put him with West, Hooter, and we will get him moved to the flight line after you have cleared out Babcock's stuff."

I thought that went well.

As we were leaving the tent, Hooter put his hand on my shoulder and told me that West was a nice guy and that he was a short timer that would be going home in about three months. "He is not all there, if you know what I mean, but in a good way, dude and you will like him. And his brother."

"A brother?" I replied.

"Yeah. James and his brother, John, came in on the buddy system so they could stay together. They had a younger brother, but he won't have to serve in combat because his older brothers volunteered."

As we entered the tent (hooch) I saw someone sitting over in a corner cleaning an M-60. He had his head down and seemed to be in his own world. The hooch smelled of marijuana and the room was lighted with candles.

"Heads up!" Hooter yelled out as we went through the door.

This guy raised his head and with a smile replied, "What's up Hooter!"

"Got you a newbie, West. (First time I wasn't called an FNG) Brooks meet West." West got up to shake my hand. He was tall and lean, and spoke with a nice voice that actually made you feel welcomed. That and his good firm handshake put me at ease. "Take that bunk," he pointed across the room to a corner of the hooch.

At last, a place to lay my head. I walked over to the bunk and fell upon it. I was so tired. I felt like I hadn't slept in days and that day's event didn't help much. The death of that soldier that gunner killed haunted me.

The silence was soon broken. "What is your MOS, Brooks?"

"67N2F," I replied.

West didn't say a thing. He kind of laughed and looked down at a rifle he was cleaning. That made twice someone had given me that kind of laugh. One that suggested there was something going on that everyone knew but you. One making you want to know the rest of the story.

Without further delay I asked, "Something wrong with that?"

"No, but do you know what the life expectancy of a door gunner in this unit?"

"No," I replied.

"Man, you have about a fifty-fifty chance of getting killed flying as door gunner with these nuts."

I was pondered what West had told me. I was never too lucky at coin tossing and a fifty-fifty chance of getting killed was not good odds anyway you looked at it. "Why are the odds of getting whacked so great?" I tried not to show fear. It didn't work. West knew I was more than concerned.

"They don't use these aircraft for transporting troops," he explained. "These are gunships. They spend all day looking for someone to fire at them so they can do what they love doing. Killing gooks and stirring up shit. These are headhunters, my man. And they take no prisoners unless ordered to."

I can't really explain what went through my mind at this moment. I believe it was something like, *I'm screwed I thought to myself,* s*o this is what I put it all on the line for as a gunner?* I had always thought along the terms of taking other people out to do the fighting and only using my gun on occasion. This is not what I had in mind at all. "How do they actually engage the enemy?" I asked West.

"Oh, just about every day," he replied. "At least one out of the eight LOH, seventeen Slicks and nine Cobras find someone to kill. About once or twice a week, we lose an aircraft to the gooks. The gooks hate us, man and they will do almost anything to get to those aircraft. You see, these choppers bring down a lot of hurt on the gooks and their operation. They are bringing supplies from the north down through Cambodia to support the war here in the south. Quan Loi is about three clicks from the Cambodia border. Our gunships put a big hurt in their operation and they do what they can do to rid themselves of their problem, which happens to be us. We are on the first line of defense, my man. Pheu Phen is the second and then Saigon."

I came from, Pheu Phen; it did not seem like to be that bad of a place to be stationed. The way I looked at it, the further away from Cambodia you were the better. I did not like what I was hearing. This was nothing like I had imagined it would be. My mind was totally lost in all the things that had happened to me that day. I was confused, scared and in a world where the rules were made up as you went along.

I think the door gunner kissing that ear and telling me I would get my cherry broke bothered me the most. I could not put this day's events out of my head. Could I adapt to this environment? Or was I totally screwed? If I could not adapt, my chances of coming out of this mess were not good.   West raised his voice and I was brought back to the present. "Brooks! It's cool dude. There is a way out of all this. And it will put you in a safer position."

At this point, I was open for any suggestion. "Okay, tell me how," I replied.

"Flying is strictly on a volunteer basis. They can't make you fly."

"Really?" I replied.

"Nope. Because flying in this outfit is a very dangerous job, it is strictly on a volunteer basis. Because you have a secondary MOS 67A10, you can do mechanic work on these helicopters and stay here on base instead of flying every day. These aircraft have to be worked on. You can work in maintenance and keep them flying. Nothing is wrong with that, and it will be a lot safer than flying gunner, especially flying Scouts.

"Look man, I have lost good friends that were gunners. I owe it to them to let you know what you are getting into. The gunners in Flight and Scouts are a great bunch of guys, but they are not going to tell you what is in store for you if you join them. They know you would quit before you even got off the ground. That is why they treat you so good. Man, don't you see? They are short on gunners. The guy you are replacing Babcock, bought it two days ago. They haven't even got his stuff cleared out of his hooch. That is why you are here with me instead of with them. They haven't made room for you yet.

I fell back in my bunk and told West I wanted to think for awhile. I was tired, needed sleep, and it seemed like a good way to escape, even if it was only for a short while. When I woke, it was dark. I must have slept for hours. I heard something that sounded like I was back home, you know, in the real world. It was a movie playing somewhere. I don't recall what movie it was. Anything to remind me and make me feel like I was home was welcome, especially now. I sure felt alone and I could not get my mind off of my girl, my family and my friends. I was lured to the sound of that movie like a moth to a light. I stopped someone and asked him what I was hearing.

"A movie," he replied with a laugh. "Yeah, FNG, it's a movie. We have them every night, if we can get them and if Charlie will leave us alone long enough to watch them." He walked off shaking his head. "FNG's" crack me up."

I could tell this F.N.G. crap was not going to go away anytime soon, and either the loneliness. I walked up to this tent and when I opened the flap everyone threw a beer can at me, yelling, 'Close the flap man!' 'Gooks are going to see the light and the next thing you will hear is a mortar on our asses.' I closed the flap fast and sat in a chair close to the wall. I believe it was a James Bond movie. All I know is that I felt safer in the company of other soldiers, even if I was the only FNG.

I bent over and put my face in between my hands and rested my elbows on my knees. I was still tired and going back to the hooch crossed my mind. A sudden, rocket-like sound shot over us and I hit the floor with my hands covering up my head. Next thing I know, everyone was laughing. *Oh shit,* I thought. *That wasn't incoming and I am on the ground like an idiot.*

A couple of hands grabbed me by my shoulders pulled me to my feet. "Welcome to Flight, Brooks."

Everyone started patting me on the back. They had set of a night flare and man, did it work. I just knew it was a mortar zeroing in on us because I opened the tent flap and allowed the light to shine outside. Boy was I green. I knew nothing of combat or what incoming would sound like if I heard it. This whole event was for their benefit and at my expense. But I didn't care, I was at least accepted. Among a few anyway.

The next day, I got up early and drank a little coffee. I thought about what West had told me the day before. About how I could get out of Flight. After all, I came over here not really wanting to see action. I just wanted to fly around and do my time, but it turned out flying was the most dangerous job. I wondered if that made me a coward, and to some degree that bothered me. Then again, to some degree it was true. I was not ready for combat. Maybe hanging out in maintenance for awhile would be the best thing for me. I tried to justify what I was about to do, but deep down I did feel guilty. Like I was bailing and there would be those that wouldn't understand.

I had to go to Top and let him know I did not want to fly Scouts, but wanted to work in maintenance instead. This was not going to set well with him. Not wanting to put it off any longer, I went over to headquarters to plead my case. Like I said before, Top was a short man with gray hair and had a look on his face that let you know he was in charge and had earned his stripes.

I approached him and let him know I did not want to fly Scouts. I thought he was going to shit a brick. His face turned red and he bit down on his cigar, looked me straight in the eye and let me know that I was something lower than whale shit.

"Don't want to fly, do you?" he grabbed a piece of paper and started writing something down. After a minute or two of writing, he signed it and threw it at me. "Report to Flight Line Maintenance in an hour and don't let the door hit you in the ass on the way out."

That sure was a different response than I got the day before. But at least I was out of Flight and maintenance bound. My objective had certainly changed since I left the states. All my big plans of flying crew chief and door gunner on my own ship had taken an entirely different rout. Hiding out in maintenance seemed to be about as safe as a job one could have over here, and I was going to take it.

It didn't take me long to realize that maintenance was not what I had trained for. The mechanics I came to know were all hard working people and took a lot of pride in their work. I just didn't feel like I fit. My dreams were about flying, not being stuck on the ground. Flight personnel had this special camaraderie that was not present anywhere else. One that was envied among other soldiers. They were treated differently, with a little more respect.

Each evening, when work at the flight hanger and flight line was completed, we all would walk back to our hooches, at least 500 yards from the flight line. The walk back usually was done with all of us walking in pairs about ten yards apart, in case we were mortar attacked. The causalities would be minimized. My thoughts while taking this stroll each day were always of home and whatever thought that allowed me to escape from this place. Suddenly was on the ground and knocked senseless. A 107 mortar had landed in front of me. The projection of the mortar and the blast sent all the shrapnel forward of where I was walking, not a piece hit me. Still, my ears felt like ice picks were stuck in them and I had a hard time trying to lift myself from the ground. People spoke to me but I could not hear a word, it was all a bunch of mumbled words coming out of their mouths.

They checked me over to make sure I hadn't been hit. I was good, nothing was really wrong except for my hearing and dizziness. Then they moved on to someone else. There were six of us knocked to the ground, but only four of us got to our feet. A couple of guys in front of me were not lucky. They were lying on the ground being attended to by a couple of medics. One caught several small pieces of shrapnel across his back. The other guy also caught it in the back, but with a piece as big as a banana. It split him almost in half, from his groin up to the bottom of his ribs. By the time the medics got to him he was in complete shock. They shoved great big wads of cotton up and into his lower body cavity to stop the gushing of blood, but it didn't stop it or even slow it down. His lower intestines were lying on the ground and the red, clay dirt clung to them like red flour. He died right there. I stood dumbfounded, partly from the explosion but mostly from what I'd just witnessed. This man's name was Phillip Harris. I remember him as a guy that always had a smile on his face and a dog that always followed him around. The dog was also killed.

Chapter 4
Back to Flight

I came to a decision that would change my life forever. I decided that I couldn't stand around seeing people I knew get cut down and do nothing about it. Phillip worked in maintenance and he got killed. I decided that if I was going to get killed, I was going to do it on my terms. I wanted to do more than work on these aircrafts. I wanted to be a part of Flight and hunt this enemy down. I believed I had what it took to do the job, but I was scared. I was nothing more than a confused kid that had come to a crossroads in his life. Crossroads can be a tricky business. When you are young you don't seem to stop and think about how decisions can affect that your life forever.

The next morning, I went back to see Top. I knew I was going to get an ass chewing about not making up my mind. To my surprise, he simply stuck out his hand and welcomed me back. He held on until I looked him in the eye, then told me how we are all scared and that I would do fine and that was about all he had to say on the subject. Short and to the point, that was Top.

The next day I reported to the flight line as instructed. Everyone was glad to see the so called FNG. I spent the next few days going over my duties concerning the aircraft that I would be flying and working on. There were three aircraft that we used to hunt down Charlie.

They were the LOH OH6A Hueys, Bell 205 C, D, H, models, and of course the Cobra AH1G.

These aircraft were configured with all kinds of armament designed to work in all kinds of ways to accommodate our needs. This is what my new friend, West, did. He installed armament on these aircraft so we could keep the edge on Charlie as best we could. He was a specialist and was very good at what he did.

There are several types of rockets we used. Rockets with ten and seventeen pound war heads. Some of the seventeen pounders we used were loaded up with flechette. A flechette, is a small dart that has a very sharp point and the fins are also sharp. When projected at high speeds they would penetrate clean through a body, if it didn't hit bone. These flechette rockets would explode fifty feet or so above the ground and cause all kinds of damage. Some of the seventeen ponders were also loaded up with white phosphorus that would stick to the skin and burn you beyond belief. All the aircraft, except for the LOH, were armed with rocket pods.

UH-1C Gun Ship, Slicks. In the nose of the Cobra we had an option of twin mini-gun or a mini-gun and a 40 mm cannon. On the Slicks, a mini-gun was hardly ever installed. Sometimes, on chase missions, one was installed on a gun mount in the back cargo area, but usually we flew with only two gunners with free style M-60s and rocket pods. Some were installed with 40 mm cannon, but not often. The Slicks had to watch their pay load, not knowing when they may have to extract a flight crew that may have been shot down. Two gunners and rockets were the order of the day for the Slicks.

The LOH, on the other hand, did not have these luxuries. Flying LOH, or Scouts, was an entirely a different deal. A pilot, observer, and a door gunner were all you had. The observer flew in the left front seat with an M-16. He may have a few clips of ammo, but his main job is to help the pilot and gunner hunt and locate the enemy. The gunner flew in the back right-hand side, sitting on the floor of the aircraft with his legs hanging out. When need be he would stand outside on the skid with his M-60. Let me expand on this. The objective of the LOH crew is to fly at tree top level and draw the fire of the enemy. Charlie would only fire at Scout aircraft if the gunner would expose himself by standing out on the skid. So a gunner would stand out on the skid most of the day. His position was right behind the pilot as to give the pilot as much protection as possible. Then, after taking fire, the gunner would return fire as the pilot got the aircraft out of there so the gunships could unload on the position of contact.

These gunships were usually a Cobra or a Slick that would come out of the blue and unload all they had on that position that was marked by a smoke grenade from the observer or the gunner, depending on the situation. Now, when a Cobra pulled out of his dive and started back up, Charlie took this opportunity to shoot up the aircraft's ass. This is when the gunships are most vulnerable.

It was the Scout crew's job to protect his ass when he came out of the dive. Sometimes, if you were in a hot area, they teamed you up with two Cobras. In those cases they could watch their own ass and we could get the hell out of Dodge. After the smoke cleared, we would go back in and see if we could draw fire again.

The flight crew that flew these missions called themselves Scouts. In my opinion, the most dangerous job in country was flying these missions. This is where the gunners got to be an endangered species and where the most casualties were taken. This is where you had only that fifty-fifty chance of making it past your three months, and hardly any chance at all of coming back if you did your whole tour in Scouts. But it does become an addiction for some and leaving Scouts never crosses their minds. At this stage of being a gunner, I just wanted to do my time in Scouts and go to Slicks. But first, like everyone in Flight, I had to pay my dues.

Learning to shoot the M-60 freestyle took a little getting used to. Back in the world we were taught to shoot from a mounted M-60. Here in real life, at least in the 1st / 9th , there were no mounted 60s. They were cut down versions with a pistol grip to fire the gun rather than butterfly grips that I was used to using. They were also equipped with what was called an aviation butt plate, made not to fit against your shoulder like the grunt version, but under or atop of your arm, depending on your style. Once you got used to shooting an M-60 this way, you would not go back to the conventional method. It gives you more freedom and with the cut down barrel it allows you to get on target faster. In some cases, as I found out, it can be the difference between life and death.

Chapter 5
The Hammer Head

Orientation was over and it was time to go take a real check ride and then eventually be looked upon as a gunner. I have to say, I was pretty nervous. This flight was going to see how easy they could make the FNG airsick, but still I was excited. There would be no observer on this flight so I knew this was going to be balls to the wall flight. I was introduced to a pilot named Charles Thunderbird, a medium-built man with a reddish tent to his hair. He shook my hand and gave me one of those shit-eating grins. He did not say anything to me except 'Let's do it.' This was going to be interesting. Getting me sick was not going to be easy for him to do, if that was on his agenda. I could probably take anything he could dish out, but had to admit that the anticipation of it all made my stomach churn.

As the aircraft cranked up, I sat down on the floor, placed both my feet on the skid and strapped myself in with enough slack so I could stand up if needed. I was told I would be doing most of my flying in this position. I had been given a wide strap from Hooter for my 60. I attached the strap to the 60 and hung it around my neck like a guitar. I was going to rock and roll with this baby and I was pumped. We took off and were airborne and over the green line in a flash.

Thunder wasted no time. He laid the aircraft over with the nose pointing straight at the ground and as our air speed went from 0 to 110 knots my adrenaline was kicked in at a max. I had never flown in a LOH and it was something. The aircraft was so maneuverable I couldn't believe it. The hair on my neck tingled and goose bumps crawled up and down my arm.

We started out doing a few spins at first. Then Thunderbird would pick out a few targets to see if I could hit them. I did well on some of the targets and on some I was way off. I was getting used to concentrating and dealing with all the G forces. This type of shooting was a whole different deal than sitting in a level aircraft with a mounted 60. The strap worked well and I don't think I could have done anything without it. Thunder did not say much, other than how I screwed up that shot' or 'that might work.' I was doing all I could to master firing the 60 this way. I liked it. The G-forces automatically made the gun harder to handle and to keep on target. Without a mount to support the gun, its weight would shift back and forth, up and down as you came out of a spin or a dive. After some time I got used to it and everything started working for me. The one thing that helped more than anything was the full tracers I was shooting. Unlike ground ammo, which one in four are tracers, all the rounds are tracers with aviation ammo. This allows you to get on target much faster and makes the difference in a life and death situation.

After about forty minutes of this kind of practice, Thunder told me we were going to do a maneuver that I probably hadn't seen or experienced. It is called a Hammer Head Stall.

We accelerated our air speed and started to climb. At about three thousand feet, Thunder pointed out a target on the ground which was an old rubber tree stump. He told me to start firing at it as we go into a dive and hold that line of fire on that stump, until he told me to stop. *Big deal*, I thought. *This doesn't sound all that hard. How did this maneuver get the name Hammer Head Stall?* As we started our dive I concentrated my line of fire on that stump. We were falling like a bag of rocks, but I did not let this break my concentration on that stump. Then as we started pulling up I felt the weight of my gun go from about fourteen pounds to about thirty pounds. I compensated for the weight change and kept my line of fire still on the target, *Great*, I thought, *I'm doing it.* The aircraft was now in a straight vertical climb. I shot almost straight backward and watched the target get smaller and smaller as we were gained altitude. Then everything came to a halt as our forward air speed stopped and we started to slip backward. We were in a position you don't want to put a helicopter in. We were about to flip over and go inverted. This I knew was a no-no and we were going to die. Helicopters do not fly upside down. I stopped firing my 60 and grabbed on to both sides of the door post to brace myself.

Thunderbird yelled, "Fire! Keep firing! Keep firing!"

I couldn't move. I was scared beyond words.

He gave the aircraft hard right pedal and the aircraft swapped ends, where the tail rotor was, was now the nose of the aircraft and we started back down at the target in another dive. I came out of the scared shitless mode and fired at the target.

"Good, good," Thunder said. "Good man," he repeated. After flying back over the target Thunder told me to stop firing and I did.

Shook up but exhilarated. I yelled out over the ICS, "Again! Let me try that again."

Thunder laughed as we started toward the clouds to repeat the Hammer Head Stall.

After a few more Hammer Heads, I finally got the hang of it and life was good in the 'Nam. The first time I felt good since I've been in country. It was time to go back to the LZ (landing zone) to refuel and call it a day. On the way back to the LZ, Thunder talked to me. He told me that I did well and that the first mistake on the Hammer Head was normal and that he had never seen a new gunner not shit his britches the first time they experienced that maneuver. Made me feel better because I was still embarrassed from freezing up on that first Hammer Head. For the first time he didn't refer to me as an FNG. We were starting to be friends. I did look down at my boots to see if there was crap running out of my pants. When we approached our flight line at Quan Loi, a few of the gunners looked up at us, and several gave us the thumbs-up. Thunder told me not to party to hard; we were going to do it again the next day. That was okay with me, that day was a good day.

Hooter approached me as we touched down, while I was still strapped in the aircraft. He grinned and patted me on the back. "Good job."

"How do you know?" I yelled above the rotor noise

"Your shit-eatin' grin," he said. "Now it's time to get down."

"Get down? What is getting down?"

"You know, dude, get high."

I acted like I knew all about it, but I did not. I had only smoked dope a couple of times in my life; I never called it getting down. I liked that phrase, I would remember it.

That night we all met in a large bunker that a couple of guys had built. It was huge and I thought they had the safest place on the compound to sleep. I had never seen so much dope. It cost about one dollar a pound and they smoked it like it did. You could get high just from the smoke in the bunker. And I have never been so high on dope in my life. The dope was so good that I thought it had been laced with opium.

We got high, drank beer, and talked of home. Listened to Grass Roots, Shawn Dells, Stones, Beatles, Kinks, and the Doors and so on all night. Come morning I was hurting and had another training flight.

I got sick flying that day and the more I would throw up the more Thunder would do spins and Hammer Heads. He did teach me a lesson and I never mixed too much partying and flying again. He understood the situation at hand, and let it pass without bringing the subject up again. Three more days of door gunning practice passed and I was considered ready for my first mission. If I had any say in the matter I would at the very least go on training flights for a couple of months, but it was time to cowboy up and get on with it. Anymore training would just be a waste. It was like a vacation, it was actually fun.

Chapter 6
Cherry Broken

Next morning I knew I would not get my first mission because I only finished training the day before. I helped out on the flight line humping rockets to the aircraft, hauling ammo, pulling dailies, and making myself helpful around the flight line. Tomorrow though, there were rumors that I would have my first mission. I was a little nervous. Actually, more than nervous. I was more on the scared side of nervous. Most of the crews had not really made contact with the enemy so far, either VC or NVA. In fact, the only reports of any action at all were of a crew that had blown up some ammo cart the VC used to haul food and ammo. I hope when I get a mission it is nothing more than doing battle with an ammo cart, that wouldn't bother me in the least. All the crews were depressed from not finding any signs of the enemy at all in the last several days. It didn't bother me. I really didn't like thinking about it anyway. I knew it wouldn't be long that I would have to face my fears, but I was in no hurry to do so.

Sure enough, that evening Thunderbird and I came up for a mission for the next morning. Part of me was saying 'Oh Crap!' and another part thinking 'YES at the same time. Kind of like watching a scary movie when you were a kid. You know, you may hide your face in your hands, but you had to look to see what was going to happen next.

Thunderbird came over that evening to explain how he does things and what was expected of me. If we made contact, he would keep me positioned facing the enemy no matter what. I was the crew's only defense and it would be up to me to protect all of us by using deadly force and deadly force only. He asked me if I was ready to do that. I looked down at the ground and thought about how I would feel. I looked back up and told him I thought I was ready. This is something I had contemplated many times.

He replied in a straight, stern voice, "No thinking about it, Brooks, are you ready to do just what I said and be ready to take another life?"

" I am," I replied.

"Okay. Remember what you have been taught and be ready for anything. I will tell you when and what to shoot if need be, you listen and pay attention to me. Okay?"

"Okay," I replied.

I could not sleep that night. My thoughts were of home some of the time, but mostly about the mission. I got up and sat beside my bed. West, who slept like a cat, heard me move around and asked if I was ok. I told him I was, and he returned my answer with 'bullshit.' He got up and opened his foot locker and pulled out a water buffalo horn that had been converted into a water pipe. He told me what I needed was something to take the edge off. For West, a little smoke was the answer for everything. Which really was not a bad way to look at things.

We fired up a bowl and right off West started talking about Harley Davidson motorcycles. It eased my mind and I felt better. We stayed up most the night, but eventually I gave it up and went to sleep. I woke up sitting in a chair beside my bed covered by a poncho liner that West put over me. I looked at my watch and it was 05:00. I went ahead and got all my stuff together and headed down to the flight line. When I arrived, no one was in sight. I went over to the aircraft that I was assigned to for the mission and pulled another Daily on it. We had pulled a Daily on the aircraft the day before, but I needed something to do. I broke down my M-60 and cleaned it again. I wanted everything to be right.

Thunder showed up around 07:00. He had been to a flight briefing and had the location for the mission. "Are you ready?" he asked.

"I am," I replied. "Let's do it. Where is the observer?"

He told me that he would be here in a minute, but didn't know who it was going to be. They always picked volunteers from maintenance fly observer. That way, if you got shot down the company would not lose two gunners. The same rule applied to flying two pilots in the Cobras. Sometimes observers were very hard to find. No one wants to go flying if there is a good chance of getting shot down. Sometimes they would use supply clerks. Anyone with a set of eyes qualified. On a day like today they probably thought it was safe. Their thinking was along the line that I was an FNG and the mission would probably be an easy one.

After several minutes passed, I saw a tall, lanky fellow walk toward our aircraft with a flight helmet under his arm and an M-16 slung over his shoulder. It was West. I couldn't believe my eyes. He never wanted to fly. He even tried to talk me out of doing so in the beginning. West walked up to me with a big grin on his face, patted me on the shoulder and told me if today was the day I was going to get my cherry busted, he wanted to be there for the event. He also told me that he only flew once in awhile and only with Thunderbird and another pilot named Knight, who I hadn't met yet. Either way, I felt better knowing West was going along on the mission. He was becoming a big brother figure to me, but most of all it would be nice to have a friend along. It is hard to explain the relief. West had seen combat, he pounded the ground with his brother a few times and had gotten into several fire fights. At least we had another person besides Thunder that had seen combat.

"Well, let's turn and burn," Thunder said, "Charlie is calling our names."

As I strapped myself in and fed the belt of ammo into my M-60, I noticed my hands shook. I took a deep breath, sat on floor with my legs hanging out of the aircraft and my feet placed lightly on the skid. I was ready. We came to a hover, backed out of the revetment, nosed the aircraft forward down the flight line and were off. I wasn't able to relax. My hands held the 60 so tight that within fifteen minutes they ached. I loosened my grip and settled down to the point I could actually see past my nose.

It was a hot day, but the wind blowing over my body from the air speed made it bearable. We flew fast at tree top level, diving in and out of valleys, sometimes barely clipping the trees. Once in awhile we would climb five hundred feet or so to take a mental note of our location, then down again. *Where are our high birds?* I thought. I pushed the button on the intercom I held in my hand and asked Thunder about our gunship support.

He laughed and told me we were going out just for a quick run, to verify an LZ for a grunt insertion later on. After the insertion we would support them by being their eyes until it got dark. "No action today, Brooks, just observation."

West laughed and made the comment that was one of reasons he volunteered for the day. That was okay with me. I settled down and started to enjoy the flight. Thunder said we would keep a low profile and stay at tree-top level. On the way back from the AO we would pick out some targets and I could get a little practice in. I felt a lot better and settled down to what looked like an easy day at the office.

Thunder told us we were headed close to an area where some gooks had been spotted and we were to look for an LZ where we could insert a ground team to operate and work the area. We would be in the AO in about ten minutes and should keep alert and our eyes open. You never knew, we might see something.

Our air speed was around 120 knots and the tops of the trees below my feet were nothing but a dark green blur. A beer would've been nice about then. Because of the location of Quan Loi, Chinook helicopters had to supply our AO with water. On top of that, everyone in Flight got to draw a six pack a day as part of his rations. Right now I had two six packs due me and tonight I thought I might get with West and down a few. Chinooks were also bringing down eight three hundred pound blocks of ice. They did this every Friday and tonight would be the first time in a long time we had any ice in the company.

I was jerked from my day dreaming by Thunder banking the aircraft a hard right as we went down into this little valley. He pulled back on the stick and the aircraft came to almost an instant stop. "There, Brooks!" He screamed over the mike. "There, against that tree."

"What?" My eyes focused on someone leaning against a big tree.

He was looking at us, but not moving. I think he hoped we hadn't seen him. Or we actually caught him sleeping. His hand was reaching for an AK-47 rifle to his right. He barely moved his hand toward it when I heard Thunder yell, "Make him bleed, Brooks! Make him bleed!"

I aimed the gun at him and froze.

"Damn it Brooks, fire! Fire! Shoot the son-of-a-bitch!"

I came to my senses and opened up on him. My rounds hit all around the area where he was sitting. His body jerked several times as my bullets penetrated his body. I could not let up off the trigger. All I could think about was keeping my line of fire on him. Thunder told me to cease fire. I did and the man lay motionless on his left side with his face turned downward. I had killed a man. All this took place so fast I didn't have time to digest it. I felt sick to my stomach. Thunder kept saying 'good job, Brooks.' But I was dumbfounded, incoherent and didn't really feel like patting myself on the back. I killed a man. I couldn't say a word. Thunder moved the aircraft closer to the body. All I could do was stare at this man I had killed with a hollow feeling in the pit of my stomach. I had done something that didn't feel justified at all.

I saw movement and a woman stepped out from behind the tree. She was dressed in black pajamas with a rice pan hat tied around her neck and laying on her back. I pointed the gun at her to let her know I had her covered. She moved forward, reached over and picked up the AK.

Thunderbird yelled again. "Make her bleed, Brooks! Make her bleed!"

I raised the gun up higher, lunged it forward as to let her know I meant business. All this time Thunder yelled at me to shoot her. I knew I had it under control. She went limp, holding the gun loosely pointed at the ground. Thunder kept yelling at me to shoot her, but I couldn't bring myself to drop the hammer on this woman. No matter how hard I tried, I could not bring myself to do it. I had just killed a man, probably her husband, and now Thunder wanted me to kill this woman, who I was sure was surrendering to us. Besides, above anything else, this was a woman.

She held up her left hand and lowered her head but Thunderbird kept yelling at me to shoot her. I still couldn't do it. All of a sudden this woman came to life, jerked the AK up and let go with a burst of rounds. She swept the gun from right to left. The first round hit next to my right shoulder, the rest walked down our tail boom. When she started firing I opened up with my 60. The aircraft began to vibrate so bad I could hardly see her. Thunder chopped the throttle and set the aircraft down hard. My finger was still frozen on the trigger. I remember the hard bounce made me shoot stray rounds straight down in front of her, almost all the way back to the aircraft. I concentrated and retuned the line of fire to her. I must have put three hundred rounds into this woman. I finally let up off the trigger as the aircraft rotors came to a stop. I unfastened my belt and walked over to her. Like checking a deer to see if it is dead, I put my foot under her arm rolled her over. Her body moved like a bowl of jelly. She was covered in blood and the left side of her head was almost gone. There were holes all over her body. The shock of her body lying there overwhelmed me and I felt bad, real bad.

I turned back toward the aircraft as it was still winding down. I looked at the damage. The line of holes down the tail boom. Some of the bullets entered the top side of the boom through the tail rotor driveshaft cover. No doubt bullets had penetrated our tail rotor drive shafts and that's why the aircraft vibrated so much.

I'd screwed up, really bad.

I turned around to assess the rest of the damage. The first rounds she fired went into the fuselage. Missed me by twelve inches. If she would have spanned from left to right she would have nailed me and Thunderbird.

A hand grabbed me and I spun around and a fist clobbered my left jaw. I hit the ground. I was conscious, but saw black with white spots everywhere.

Someone picked me up off the ground. "You stupid son-of-a-bitch." Thunderbird. He drew back to hit me again but West grabbed him from behind. He had Thunderbird by the neck and pulled him away from me.

"Back off, Thunder!" West yelled. "Just back off."

Thunderbird turned and walked back to the aircraft and called in on the VHF radio for help. "We have a downed aircraft," he blurted over the air in disgust.

West shuffled me over to the gunner's position on the aircraft. I put my ass on the floor and lay on my back. My jaw was already swollen and my head felt like it was going to split.

"Don't worry man, this isn't the first damn aircraft that has been shot down and it won't be the last. Ain't nothing! It ain't no thing," he repeated. "But what we better do," West looked back at Thunderbird, "is set up some kind of defense. These two may not be the only gouges on the block. Come on, Brooks."

I picked myself up off the floor of the aircraft, grabbed my 60, broke off about four hundred rounds from my ammo belt and walked off to get behind a berm with West.

Screw the gooks, I don't give a shit," said Thunderbird.

The rescue aircraft showed up as soon as we got behind a berm. West said there was a killer team working close to us that picked up on Thunders first M-Day. "Here comes the Cav to the rescue. We're protected now," West screamed out as he patted me on my shoulder. "My boys are here!"

Two Cobras gave us cover while a Slick came down and picked us up. I looked back at our downed aircraft as we went through transitional lift. West nudged me in the side and told me that the blues and a sling crew would come out and pick it up. "It will be flying tomorrow," he commented.

Two Scouts flew over my downed aircraft. They would watch and make sure that Charlie didn't get his hands on it.

What a day, I thought. *First mission and I got shot down, killed two people, and got the crap kicked out of me. I've most likely lost my job flying Scouts for sure. It didn't take long for this day to turn bad for me.* I looked around the aircraft and guess what? It was the same aircraft, same gunners, same pilots that I had come and picked my friend and me up at Phue Phien. I laughed and shook my head. I looked to see if a blood stain was on the floor. I was sitting in that same spot. I didn't see any stain. I glanced up at one of the gunners and he was staring at me. He pointed to one of the ears on his helmet. "Left yours back there, didn't you stupid?"

I looked at West and asked him what the heck that meant.

"You didn't cut the ears off those two, he said.

I shook my head, closed my eyes and thought of home.

When we landed at Quan Loi some of the gunners stood on the flight line in a group. When we landed, they patted me on the back then grabbed my gun, flight helmet and survival pack. "Take off the rest of the day, man. Everyone gets a day off that gets shot down. It's a rule we have and no one disputes it, *no* one. FNG or not, you get the day off, man, so enjoy it while you can." Two or three of them, along with West, walked us back to our hooch.

They placed my gear on my bunk and told me to take care of that jaw. I looked in a mirror, it was black and blue. The inside of my mouth was cut from my teeth. The impact from the punch really cut up the inside of my mouth. I stuck my tongue against the left inside of my jaw, there were three holes. The cuts burned when I took a sip of water. West went over and got our ration of ice. He combined his beer with mine, iced it down and then gave me a piece of ice for my jaw. He didn't say anything to me as I sat on my bunk, holding that ice pack on my jaw. I lay back on my bunk, and as the ice melted it ran down the back of my neck. I drifted off to sleep.

I awoke when I heard West opening the cooler. He grabbed a couple of beers, handed me one and then sat on the side of his bunk. "How you feeling, Brooks?"

"Rough," I replied. I took a sip of beer and the alcohol burned the inside of my mouth. I laughed and downed that beer and got another. "Sure wish I had something stronger."

West reached under his bunk pulled out old ammo can, opened it and pulled out a half bottle of Johnny Walker Black. The Scotch really made the inside of my mouth burn, but I needed something stronger than beer. West lit up a joint and we both got wasted in a matter of minutes. Eventually my jaw quit hurting. Hell, after awhile I couldn't even feel my toes.

We talked about anything and everything, but not a word about 'Nam or anything to do with war. Mostly about motorcycles and how he was going to ride his Harley to Woodstock and party down when he got back to the real world. West only had three months to go. I envied him. He was a short-timer, a two digit midget. That is what we called anyone who had less than a hundred days to go.

I had three hundred and thirty days and a wake up. I knew I would miss West when it came time for him to go back to the world. I hated to even think about him leaving. I had become very attached to West, he was a couple years older than me and I sort of looked up to him as a big brother. I would indeed miss his splendid nature.

We sat there in the candlelight, neither one of us saying much. West was dreaming of home and riding that new Harley to Woodstock. I also thought of home, a place I was beginning to think I would never see again. We both sat there zoned out and then out of nowhere a voice asked permission to enter our hooch. West jumped up from his stoop and sprayed some bug spray to try and hide the smell of marijuana. Then he went to the door of our hooch."Come in," he said and in stepped Thunderbird.

I jumped to my feet and started toward him with a doubled-up fist. "I took the hit before, but you will find it much harder to do it again."

Thunder put both his hands in the air palms open. "Hold up. I'm not here for anything other than to apologize to you. Can we sit down?"

I sat back down on my bunk and he planted his butt on my foot locker. West got up to leave and let us talk it out. Thunder told West he needed to hear this, too. West sat back down.

"Look, Brooks," Thunder said, "I was way out of line today. It was your first mission and we really didn't think we would run into any gooks today. This mission was not to put you in the heat of things. We wanted to break you in slow. And I'm sorry for the way today's events went down. It was supposed to be an easy, nothing mission. I could have flown on by and reported what I saw to the hunter and killer team that was in the same area. I didn't, so I am as much to blame as anyone for the way things went down. I wanted the kill and I put you, the new guy, in a bad situation."

I started to say something but was cut short. "Let me finish," Thunder said. "I was to blame as much as anyone. You are new, Brooks, you haven't been here but a couple of weeks and you have already seen combat to the point you received fire and returned it with two confirmed kills. No one I can remember had been broken in that fast. You did what anyone would have done under those circumstances. I just want to apologize to you. You are going to be a great gunner, Brooks, and I want you to continue to fly Scouts with me." He offered his hand.

I stood there with my mouth open, dumbfounded and shocked. We shook on it. I said nothing but 'okay.'

He told me that we were going to take it easy tomorrow and get the bird back up and flying. I could help out with the maintenance on the aircraft if I wanted.

"Other than that, you and West just hang out. I will inform your section leader." He stood and as he was about to walk out the door, turned to West and asked him for a joint. I laughed to myself and sat back down on the bunk.

After Thunder left the hooch, West looked over at me. "That went well." He laughed. "I knew he would probably do that. Thunder is a great guy. You just got off to a rough start with him. It's cool and you will see that everyone will be pulling for you. You are a part of the Scouts now and no one will give you any crap, especially now that you have gotten two kills under your belt."

Two kills, I thought. I didn't feel all that great about it. West then told me although they are confirmed kills, the other gunners only count the ones you take ears from. "It's a medieval thing they have going on amongst themselves. The more right ears you have, the more stature you have. At the end of each month they take an ear tally and whoever has the most kills for that month gets to choose his mission for one day."

"Don't the ears start rotting?" I asked.

West laughed and then explained to me that the guys would take the real ear and go up to a rubber tree and stick a knife in it. The rubber would ooze out and they then would fill the ear with rubber. Then after the rubber dried they would peal the rubber away from the real ear and then they would wear the rubber ear somewhere on their body for recognition.

They looked like real ears to me, I thought. At least I wouldn't have to put up with that 'cherry broke' bullshit anymore. From this day on, no one had to tell me when to fire my weapon again. I learned when and when not to fire my weapon and in doing so proved to myself and my crew they could depend on me.

Chapter 7
Initiation to Scouts

The next day I went down to the flight line to help get my aircraft back together and flight status ready. It didn't take that long. Everyone pitched in and even a couple of guys from maintenance came down to give us a hand. The bullet holes were repaired and Hooter and I finished putting the tail rotor driveshaft together. All that was needed was a test flight on the aircraft and I was back to flying. No one brought up the incident between Thunder and me. Everyone knew about it but treated me like I was a part of team and for the first time in country I felt like I was starting to fit in.

I took note on how everyone helped each other, doing whatever it took to get their aircraft ready for any mission that might come up. Thunder showed up the next day on the flight line. He came over to where I worked, patted me on the shoulder and continued on. By this display of friendship, everyone knew we had made amends. Thunder was letting everyone know it was over. I went back to what I was doing and noticed everyone had smiles on their faces.

About that time the scramble horn went off and everyone but me knew exactly what to do. I didn't even know what it was. Hooter yelled for me to grab my 60 and lots of ammo then jump into his aircraft. Hooter started it up, then crawled out and got himself ready. The pilot showed up, jumped in and we were off in a flash. I did not have my flight helmet so I screamed over the rotor noise. "What's going on?"

Hooter yelled back at me that someone had gotten themselves shot down and we were off to cover for them. I looked aft and I saw four more Scouts were also airborne, along with four Cobras and a couple of Slicks. "If you see anyone on the ground besides our people, shoot them," Hooter said.

If I knew one thing, I knew I would not repeat the same mistake I made the day before. It took us about fifteen minutes to get out to the downed aircraft. I saw red smoke and knew that was where the enemy had been spotted. I saw white smoke and that was where the downed bird would be. Being Scouts, we went right for the red smoke to lay down ground cover for the downed crew. Hooter told me to lay down fire all around the red smoke. We started firing our 60's. Four other Scouts joined in. A Cobra came right down in front of us, cutting loose with rockets and mini-gun fire. The Slicks joined in and we had what they call a hot LZ. Some rounds were fired back at the larger birds, we saw the tracers rising out of the jungle. We fired our 60s from where the tracers originated and the enemy quit firing. They knew they had been spotted. Everyone joined in and it looked like a bunch of bees swarming to protect their hive.

Meanwhile, two other Slicks extracted our downed crew. One went in to retrieve them while the other Slick gave them air cover. One of the LOH's went over to help them, but we kept laying down fire around the red smoke until we were told to pull out. We then escorted the Slicks with the downed Slick Crew back to our home base. As I looked back toward the hot LZ, I saw two Cobras setting up gun runs. Going back and forth, doing Hammer Heads over the location, while an LOH flew around the outside perimeter constantly laying down grazing fire.

Man, what a rush. We didn't know if we got any kills or not, but the sheer moment of it all was nothing but a big rush. Because I didn't have my flight helmet with me, I couldn't hear any of the radio transmissions. Regardless, I knew these guys had their shit wired tight. It was amazing to be a part of it all. To see everyone working together. What a team I was a part of. I looked over at the Slicks that had the downed crew onboard and they were giving us the thumbs up. Everyone was okay.

When we landed back at Quan Loi, a lot of the guys from maintenance went over to the downed flight crew to welcome them back. The gunners from the downed Slick came over and shook our hands and commented, like before, that they were off for the rest of the day and rubbed it in our faces. *Hope they enjoyed their time off more than I did,* I thought.

Hooter asked me if I was going to the Cross Rotors club that night.

"Cross Rotors?" I replied, "What is the Cross Rotors?"

"Oh, it's a little club we built out of scrap wood and ammo crates. Come on down, you will have fun."

The Crossed Rotors was a little homemade club where all of the flight crews met. It was mostly made up of guys that drank and didn't smoke dope. They didn't care if you did, but they were rednecks and proud of it. It was really quite a place. They had made a bar out of a main rotor blade off of a Slick and below in front of the bar they had LOH blades over lapped to look like tuck and roll leather. They went to great effort and took pride in making it look like a real bar. Behind the bar, made from sheet metal and fiberglass, they had a huge homemade ice chest, which was usually filled with Black Label beer and ice that was flown in from the rear. The ice only lasted a couple of days, so everyone made sure to show up on those days to have iced down cold beer.

The beer would cost you a quarter and this went toward buying meat back in Saigon to have a party with, when there was an occasion to do so. Believe me, there was always an occasion. Got shot down and lived. Good news from home. Going on R&R. Everything was an excuse for a party. I spent many good times at the Cross Rotors. The only drawback was it was Flight Crews Only. Many of my friends, especially in maintenance, never set foot inside the club.

It was when I told Hooter that I would get with West and maybe show up later that he let me know that this place was for Flight Crews Only. "We all have a lot of friends, Brooks, but we keep this place for our own. You will come to understand this arrangement as time goes on."

I was honored to be a part of flight, but I had real hard feelings about leaving West out of this. No sir, I didn't care for it at all.

That night I walked back from the flight line by myself. I opened the flap to the tent and there sat West smoking his joint. West asked me if I wanted a hit. I declined and told him I was headed over to the Cross Rotors, but only for short while. West grinned and told me all about the tight little group that built that place. "I know what is going to happen tonight, and you will be a big part of the entertainment."

"What?" I replied."

"I can't say anything else, but you will have fun." West told me the reasoning behind the club. "You guys need a club were you can build up your camaraderie. You guys keep the gooks off our asses. Flight is the backbone of this company, and every day they put their asses on the line for all of us. Guys in flight do two things that set you apart from everyone else. You guys face the enemy day in and day out. And you volunteer to lay your lives on the line day in and day out. Oh, of course we all can get killed at any given time. You never know when a mortar may hit and take you out. But you guy's volunteer to do this shit. You guys need something that sets you apart from everyone else, something that bonds you guys together. That's what it's all about, Brooks, bonding with your brothers. I promise, before you leave this hell hole, you will come to realize the things I am telling you. I'm high right now, but I know what I'm talking about."

I was not expecting that kind of a response. After I thought about it for awhile, I couldn't see West handling it any other way. West was a cool cat and I was coming to understand why everyone liked him so much. Not too many people were as well-rounded as West.

Hooter stopped by the hooch to grab another beer and walk with me to the Cross Rotors club. On the way to the Rotor club, we talked about the day's activities and how impressed I was with the way the operation was handled.

"Another day at the office," Hooter replied and we both laughed.

The sun was not quite down, but the sunset was going to be beautiful. I looked over to my left and saw there was a tent with the sides rolled up and the flaps pulled all the way back. There were some tables like I had never seen before and a couple of medics were washing them down. "What is that over there Hooter?" I asked.

"That's the dead shed."

"Dead shed? What is a dead shed?"

"Those tables are where they lay you out to gut you if you buy the big one. Bodies don't last long in this heat. They gut you and fill your inner cavity with salt to kind of preserve the body. When Charlie tries to overrun this base, sometimes we can't get anything in or out of here. Sometimes the dead can't be shipped out of here for three or four days. They gut you, tag you, and bag you in that tent."

I wished I hadn't of asked him. As we passed by, I smelled the stink of something rotting. I found out later that they threw all of the body innards into a hole and at end of each day cover it up. I saw that the tent was empty. That was a good thing.

We entered the club and everyone from flight was there. As we approached the bar, everyone had a shit-eating grin on their face and I knew it was at my expense. We sat around drinking beer and patting ourselves on the back from the day's events. They let enough time pass so I felt comfortable. Then I noticed a couple of guys covered the exit. An old sheet was pulled back and there stood three guys, one held up the 1st and the 9th Cav. Flag, one held the United States Flag, and the guy in the middle was carrying a tray with an skeleton head, upside down, resting on a base of some sort.

They came to a stop directly in front of me. Hooter then approached me with a beer in his hand. He poured the beer into the skull and told me, to be a member of the Scouts, I had to down all the beer in the skull's head. It was a tradition that had been started amongst the first Scout Gunners and has been honored down until present. He went on to let me know that no one had ever broken the chain and it would be up to me to carry on this tradition or break it. It was all in my hands. He then said he hoped I wouldn't be the first to break this tradition.

I had a big grin on my face and wanted to laugh, but no one even had a hint of a smile on their faces. These guys are serious about this shit. Everyone there waited for a response from me. I looked at the skull and it did look somewhat clean. You could tell that it had been used a lot. No big deal. I took hold of the skull with both hands, put my lips on the back base of the skull, it smelled like beer, yep it taste like beer and I started to drink.

I was doing okay until I felt something kind of lumpy. I looked down saw something white floating in the beer. I then closed my eyes and at the same time I was thinking whatever I saw it look like maggots. I tried filtering whatever was floating in the beer through my teeth. Something touched my lips and it felt like a maggot. I had to drink this entire beer nonstop. Then I opened my mouth far enough that something got through and it was now inside my mouth. It was a maggot. There was not a doubt in my mind what I had in my mouth was a big maggot. I kind of chocked on the thought and tried to push the maggot aside with my tongue, no use down it went. That was it, out of sheer reflexes my body would not swallow anymore and up it came.

Oh, CRAP! I thought. *I broke their tradition.*

Everyone was laughing, some even went to their knees. I looked down into the skull and there were huge maggots lying in the bottom, dead from the beer. I must have had another up chuck look on my face when Hooter took the skull from my hand and told me they weren't maggots, they were grub worms dug out of an old tree and placed in the skull. They couldn't stop laughing and it took me a brief second to realize the humor and I cracked up myself. I pointed to Hooter, and a few more guys, Walker, Scott, Morris, and told them I would get even. We all laughed then partied on, I was accepted, and I at last felt like I had friends again.

To top it all off, West was there joining in the fun. He was the only one in the company that was allowed to come into the Crossed Rotors club. He fixed all the aircraft up with their weapons. If someone needed a part for their 60, he got it. He would go out of his way to accommodate any configuration of armament and adapt it to the aircraft. He was as big a part of Flight and Scouts as anyone. And he was as big a part of this joke played on me. I laughed and told him he was at the top of the list. At that point everyone opened a beer and poured it on me. It was a good night.

Life was good again and the burden of being alone was gone. I had friends and I made a vow to myself that night that I would be there for these guys and I would do my best to never let them down.

Chapter 8
I'm Hit

One night, I was informed I had an early take off come morning. I showed up extra early to get the aircraft ready for that day's mission. We were going out on a head hunt mission and would have two high birds (Cobra's) with us. We were headed toward the Cambodian border and I knew, without being told, we were going to find Charlie. West came over to my aircraft and made sure I had plenty of everything. He went through my survival pack. He reminded me of some wife with her husband going out of town on a trip and checking the suitcase. He told me the area I was headed for was going to be hot. Hot, meaning we were going to make contact.

"Lots of VC?" I asked.

"No," he answered. "Lots of N.V.A. You keep your shit wired tight, okay?"

"Okay," I replied. NVA, I had been told since I had arrived in country, were the tough bullies on the block. I hoped we didn't see any. In fact, just to go out and burn fuel and come back would suit me just fine. The observer showed up, some dude from maintenance that I hadn't met yet. I walked up and asked his name.

"Steve," he replied. He told me that he had been in country for four months but hadn't flown observer yet.

He looked more nervous than I did. This guy wouldn't shut up. He was asking questions left and right, up and down. I just *thought* I was scared on my first mission. This guy is turning pale.

"Nervous?" I asked.

"Scared shitless," he replied.

"Why then, are you going?"

He told me everyone in maintenance was giving him a rash of shit about being scared to fly.

"Have any of them flown?" I asked.

"Everyone but me," he said.

I didn't say another word. Some things you just have to work out for yourself. Besides, I had my own crap to deal with.

We flew all day, stopping only to fuel up at different little fire bases. The whole crew was tired and we hadn't seen a thing all day. Close to sundown, it was time to start back to Quan Loi and I, for one, was glad the day was coming to an end. Thunder made the comment that he was surprised we didn't spot anything that day. We got a little altitude and along with the Cobras started back to Quan Loi. The Cobras both came up on my side of the aircraft and flew real close to us. *That's really cool*, I thought. The sun was setting behind the Cobras, off to our right side and a camera would have been nice to have. *That's exactly what I am going to do, buy a camera and get some great pictures.*

Steve screamed out in pain. I turned to look at him but saw nothing but his head. He was rocked back and forth and yelled as if he were in agony. Then my leg went straight out in front of me with such force it hurled me out the door. My belt kept me secure, but my knee and leg were in great pain. I had been shot. I threw out a red smoke, crawled back inside the aircraft and grabbed my leg. Steve kept yelling and Thunder went into a straight nose over dive to get us as low and fast as he could. We were a target at this altitude and had to get low fast.

"Are you hit, Brooks?"

"Yes!"

"Where?"

"In the leg."

"How bad?"

" I don't know. There's no blood, but I know I'm hit."

"Steve is hit, too," Thunder replied, "but I can't tell how bad it is. There is a lot of blood."

I looked up front and blood was all over the front window on the observer's side. Steve was only groaning.

The Cobras were making gun runs on that red smoked I popped. Thunder told me not to move and he would have us back in Quan Loi fast. I laid there and still noticed no blood. But I knew I was hit. When we landed, everyone ran up to us. They pulled Steve and me out of the aircraft, trying to be careful. I could hardly move my right leg. The throbbing pain was so great it took all I had not to moan.

"Where's the blood?" someone asked.

"There's not any," West replied.

"Look at his boot," Hooter yelled.

West grabbed my foot and I went through the roof. "You're okay, Brooks, the heel of your boot is shot off and your boot is split down the right side. I looked and sure enough the bullet had hit the back heel of my boot as my legs were hanging out of the aircraft. But I still could not walk. The impact from the round bruised my heel so bad that my right foot was swollen to the point they had to cut off my boot. For the most part, I limped around the next few days, with everyone laughing and saying 'I'm hit! I'm hit!' It was funny, but the bruised heel was still painful. Steve, on the other hand, took a hit across the top of the back. He was okay; the bullet grazed him and went out through the top of the aircraft and passing on through one of the rotor blades. He received a Purple Heart for wounds received in combat and was a hero in the eyes of all the maintenance personnel. Maintenance needed a hero and the recognition. Steve sure deserved the attention he was receiving, but he never flew again. I, on the other hand, got a pat on the back and a lot of jokes thrown at me. It was fun, I liked the attention, and it gave us something to laugh about.

Thunder never thought it was funny and never laughed at all. He did pat me on the back and told me that it was amazing that I remembered to pop the red smoke for the Cobras. "They never reported any kills over the incident, but you did well by keeping your wits about you, even though you were hurt."

To me, that was worth more than any medal I could have received, especially a Purple Heart. No one wants a Purple Heart. It made me respect Thunder even more. He was John Wayne in my eyes.

After my close call, I noticed that West's mood had changed. After a couple of days I confronted him about it. I wondered if it had been something that I might have said or done. He told me that he didn't like the idea that I took this incident so lightly.

"You have to laugh about it, right?" I remarked.

"You think it's funny?" he replied.

"I don't really think it's funny, West. But how do you expect me to act? I have to shuck it off, or I'm the kind of guy that will make a bigger deal out of than it really is."

"I know," said West. "Really, I do. It's just I have lost four friends, good friends, since I have been in country and I would hate to lose another. You and I have become close friends, don't you think?"

"Of course we have, West."

West then told me something I have never forgotten, and how right he was. "You will come to understand how I feel after you lose a friend, Brooks. You are going to lose a friend in this outfit. I can almost guarantee that you will. I hope that day never comes, but then and only then will you come to understand why you don't really want to make friends with New Guys. You and I share a hooch together and because we do, we share personal thoughts and dreams and that draws us closer together. But if you will look around, you will see a lot of the guys stay to themselves. They bunk in little holes with no one else. They don't socialize as much as others do.

"Now, these guys have friends, but they aren't really close to anyone. It really messes with you when you lose a friend. And you and I, Brooks, are becoming close and I'm afraid someday you're going to bite the big one. To the Army you will just be another statistic, but you will be another flashback for me. Another nightmare I don't want. Do you understand what I'm trying to say, Brooks?"

"I believe so" I replied.

"To top it all off, Brooks, my brother is a part of the Blues. He doesn't pound the ground every day, but he does go out and cover the aircraft that get shot down. Now he tells me he wants to fly door gunner just to get out of the field. I told him he had a better job where he was. He has the same amount of time to go as I do. I don't know why he wants to take the chance and fly door gunner."

I had met John a couple of times in the short period I had been here at Quan Loi. In a lot of ways he was like West. He wasn't as tall, and he didn't look like him in appearance. But he had that great personality. He didn't call anyone an FNG and he had a way to make you feel that you were a part of everything that was going on. A nice guy and he had a great dog named Tiger that wouldn't leave his side. The dog even went to the field with him.

Everyone liked Tiger, except Vietnamese. Tiger was raised by Americans and he hated gooks, no matter if they were on our side or not. They were quite a team, John and Tiger. Tiger had a personality of his own. He would make the rounds to everyone's hooch, begging for some c- rations each night. He had his favorite stops and a new guy to him was another sucker he would work. I liked Tiger and like everyone else, tried to coach him in to staying with me by giving him the best of my sea rations. Tiger would take the food of course. But always went back to sleep and be with John.

West made the comment that John thought Flight was the place to be because of all the war stories they talked about. He wanted to be a part of it all. West hung his head stared at the floor of the hooch and was silent for a long time. Once in awhile he would take a deep breath, sigh, and say, "I just don't know how to reach him."

Being the FNG, I usually kept my opinions to myself. But this time I wanted to confront West. I had to say something. After all, West had been there for me time after time in these first few weeks I had been in country. I took a big sip of beer. "Maybe John feels like he would be helping his friends better if he was in Flight. After all, everyone likes John. Everyone I know considers him a friend."

West looked up and stared right into my eyes. I could tell he was hurting because his eyes were all watery. "Brooks, if you had a close friend, would you want him to fly Scouts?"

West had a point, and at this moment I had no answers. I thought about my best friend in my home town of Slaton. Johnny Outlaw. I was glad Outlaw was not here with me. I couldn't take it if Outlaw was killed. I then realized what West was trying to tell me, and pondered on it for quite some time. After putting myself in his situation, I began to understand a little more of what West had been telling me over the last few weeks. "No, I would not want my best friend flying Scouts," I replied.

Hell, deep down inside I knew West was right. I was beginning to feel like I made a bad choice of coming back to fly gunner. But I was committed now and I was going to stick it out. I told West I would talk to John, but I figured he would probably not take the advice of an FNG.

The next day started early. I went down to the flight line extra early because I knew that John would be coming over to the crew chief's hut to drink a little coffee. I had seen him down there every morning since I had been in Scouts, so I figured I might get a chance to talk to him. Sure enough, there he was sitting on a wooden bench the gunners built to clean our 60s on, drinking coffee and visiting with people he liked. He was already in a conversation with a door gunner named

Lambert. Lambert and John were good friends; you would see them hanging out together like West and me. Lambert was in the Blues too, at one time, and like John wanted to get out because he hated pounding the ground. Lambert was a Scout gunner that I did not know very well, but he seemed to be a nice enough guy.

He was busy convincing John how great Flight was. Lambert had only been in Scouts a week longer than me. He also had not gotten as much as one single kill. Seemed to me he was more of a cherry than I was. I had at least seen a little action. I walked over and poured myself a cup of coffee. Both acknowledged me, hoping I would join them in their conversation. I shot the shit with them for awhile, wanting to get John alone so I could talk to him. Finally, I asked John if he would mind helping me carry a box of ammo out to my aircraft. I figured when we got alone he would start asking me questions about flight. He knew his brother and I were the best of friends and he asked me if West had even gotten out of bed yet.

I laughed. "You know West better than me. He will wait to the last minute and then hurry around to get down to the flight line on time." We both laughed.

Sure enough, as soon as we reached my aircraft John asked me how I liked Flight and then told me that he was thinking about transitioning out of the Blues.

"You don't like being in the Blues, John?"

"Not really. I would like to fly gunner the rest of my time here and when I go back to the world I would like to go through Flight School."

"Go to Flight School," I replied, "but I wouldn't fly Gunner here, John, if I were you."

"Why?" he asked.

I told him about all the reasons I could think of not to fly Scouts, but I noticed all I was doing was exciting him. He liked the danger of it all. What I hated most about flying gunner, he loved. *A truly brave man,* I thought. He seemed to me to have no fear of getting killed. I talked to him some more about the subject, but I could tell I was getting nowhere. I realized the frustration that West must have felt. Talking to John was like talking to a wall. He didn't want to hear about the negative aspects of being a gunner.

To some, bravery came so easy; to others like me it was nonexistent. John got me to wondering if I really had what it took to be a gunner in flight. When the time of need arose, could I for one be there for my brothers? To be there for them when it really counted was what it was all about. I knew by the way John talked and acted you could count on him. I believe that is the biggest reason everyone in flight wanted him. I knew John was twice the man I was when it came to combat and facing the enemy. I respected his dedication and commitment and thought of how easy it was for some to show no fear. Everything about flying gunner bothered me and played on my mind constantly.

Who wouldn't want someone of John's caliber? The more quality gunners you could recruit to flight, the better your odds were of making it back to the world. John had seen combat. He had been here for almost a year and I believe he knew what he was doing and he knew of the commitment. I marveled at his approach and views to wanting to be a gunner. For one, I was glad John was coming to Flight. John's presence would do nothing but better my situation. Deep down inside, I felt guilty. I felt like I was betraying West. West was concerned about his brother and I understood that totally.

I was stuck between a rock and a hard spot. That evening when I walked into the hooch, West was sitting on his bunk. When I opened the flap he looked up at me as if he was anticipating my arrival.

"Well, did you talk to John?"

"Yes, I did."

"Well, what did he say?"

I told West what was said between John and me and the hope that West had in his eyes when I first walked into the hooch faded away. I felt I had failed him and at the same time I felt guilty for wanting John in Scouts. I made it a point never to bring it up again.

Chapter 9
The Chase

John came to Scouts and we hit it off great. West hung out at the flight line more than usual and we three were inseparable. West was like an old mother hen. Every time John and I had a flight he was there. A lot of the time he would fly observer for us. Mostly he would fly with John. He hated to see John fly without him. But West had a job to do and most of time he could not go with us. John and I helped each other with our aircraft at the end of each flight day. Then before the sun went down we three would walk back to the hooch together. John got himself moved in with us and it seemed every night we would sit around and get high, drink beer and talk of home and what we all were going to do when we got back to the world. We talked about everything from girlfriends to grandmother's apple pie.

During these get-togethers I sometimes thought of the girlfriend I had back in high school, Shirley, and what she would be doing. Did she even know I was serving in 'Nam? I never got the chance for a proper final goodbye, and there were things that went unsaid between us. Most of all, my thoughts were of Roni and making it home. A lot of things plague your mind when you realize you might not be coming home ever again. The three of us, John, West, and I decided we were going to keep in touch with each other when we returned to the world. The three of us had chapters that were not closed in our lives and we wanted to make it back and have a second chance to set some things straight. We had all come to know how precious and important life and relationships were, and in some ways I guess we didn't want to take life and relationships for granted anymore.

The next day, John and I were teamed up to go on a chase mission.

A chase mission is where gooks have been spotted moving fast on the ground and gun ships are called in to do what they do best, head hunt. In fact, most of the other outfits at Quan Loi gave us the name Headhunters. Where we called ourselves hunter-killer teams of High Birds and Low Birds, the rest of Quan Loi called us Headhunters. They called us that because of the skull we drank from to become a member of the Flight team. And because of skulls that were mounted on some of the skids of the aircraft we flew. First and the ninth also lead the Cav. Division in kills.

Hooter would be flying # 2 gunner with me and John would be flying # 2 gunner with Lambert. Since they were using Lambert's and my aircraft for this mission we would be considered the crew chiefs. I walked up to Lambert and asked him if he felt we were in Slicks since we had the title of crew chief. We laughed. I liked flying with two gunners. Not only did you have the sense of security, but you had your ass covered on both sides of the aircraft. This made it easier on the pilot because either way he broke he had fire power.

By now I had been on several gun missions and had taken fire several times. I had been shot down once and had several bullets hit my aircraft on other occasions. But on this particular mission it sounded like we were going to see a lot of action. That was the consensus from the flight briefing we received. Thunderbird and Ryan were the pilots. I had met Ryan, he was a great pilot. To him everything was funny and he was bigger than life. Thunder, in my opinion, was better in a tight situation, but Ryan was the better pilot of the two. Both of them had been teamed up lots of times on chase missions. They had a system of how to execute them and worked well together.

'Saddle up' were the next words we heard from Thunder and in about two minutes we were airborne and on our way. We were paired with two Cobras and we were loaded and armed to the hilt. We flew side by side formation right off the tree tops. When Thunder made a cyclic move, Ryan would be right there with him. The two aircraft were mirrored to each other. The two Cobras were up in the clouds behind us. It was nice to have the extra cover. We were all excited and tried to anticipate the events ahead of us.

As we approached the AO, we noticed that red smoke had already been popped and a hunter-killer team flew the area. I turned the switch on my ICS control to block out all communications with all aircraft except Ryan and Lambert's ship. I put my mic switch in hot mic position to free up my hands and I was ready to rock. Hooter did the same and as we faced one another, we bumped fists and yelled out, "Rock and roll!" We were locked, cocked and ready to rock. We needed something to pump us up. I did anyway. I was feeling that yellow streak starting to crawl up my back.

The gunships that were already there took off. They were getting low on fuel and had to go back. They would eventually return to relieve us. We would keep this tactic up all day, trying to force the enemy into some kind of an engagement. It made for a long day of flying if you didn't find Charlie. We usually found them and by doing so all hell would break loose. I felt like today was going to be one of those days. Sure enough, Lambert's aircraft received ground fire and we came around to give them support. I stood up on the skid with both feet and leaned out as far as my strap let me, swung my gun forward and laid down fire where I saw tracers coming out of the jungle.

Hooter did the same. The gooks waited till Ryan turned his aircraft around and then started firing up his ass. Our return fire made them stop shooting at Ryan. Thunder nosed the aircraft over toward where we had seen the tracers and as we flew past I threw out a red smoke grenade and Hooter kept returning fire. Then Thunder banked the aircraft in a tight left turn and we got the hell out of Dodge. No sooner than we got clear, the Cobras dumped their rockets on the location where I dropped the smoke. Then Ryan passed over the area, again trying to draw their fire. Nothing happened but total silence. The only activity was the smoke rising out of the jungle. Thunder then made several passes over the area and still nothing. The Cobras either got them or they did not want to experience the wrath a second time.

We then split up the team. Ryan broke right and took one Cobra with him. We broke left and took the other one with us. We came around, making a heart-shaped pattern forward of the smoke about two hundred yards. If there were any survivors from the Cobras' rocket attack, they would most likely move away from that position. In this thick of a jungle they could hear us but could not see us, or make out our location. We had the advantage, unless there were a lot of them. We knew they would not want to deal with the Cobras again.

So what did Thunder do? He told the Cobras to pull out of the area. Thunder said that as long as they were around, we would not get them to fire at us. "We want them to think that we believe the rockets got them. So the only way to draw them out again is to get rid of you guys."

The Cobras took off. I did not like this plan. I looked at Hooter. "You ready Hooter?"

He shook his head. "Hell, let's do it," he shouted over the intercom, "let's do it!"

"Let's get it on then!" I yelled back.

I had loaded up a few WPs (white phosphorous grenades.) They weighed about eight pounds apiece. You can't throw WPs far enough to get away from them on the ground. But in the air they were great. They had a twenty second delay which allowed an aircraft to get clear. On the ground, you had twenty seconds to run as far away from it as possible. If just a piece of the phosphorous from the grenades landed on your skin it would burn a hole in you. We hoped that this might give us the response we wanted and get them to fire on us.

With the Cobras out of the picture, Charlie might take the bait. We made our first run over where we thought Charlie might be. Lambert and John had some WPs, too, and we decided to make our sweeps together, about fifty yards apart. Since the WPs had a twenty second delay, we could fly off into another direction and not to give our exact position away. As long as we moved in a circular motion it would be hard for them, especially down in the jungle, to pinpoint us at any given time. We completed our first run and nothing; we kept circling the area and still nothing. We moved off to the right about a hundred yards and were going to try it again when all hell broke loose. Tracers came up out of the jungle from every direction.

There was more than a platoon down there. It was at least a squadron and Lambert and John were right over the middle of it. We were being shot at, but not near as much as Lambert and John. Charlie concentrated their line of fire on them and fired at us just enough to keep us busy so we couldn't come to their aid. I had the WPs strung up through the pins on several wraps of safety wire. I started chunking them out as Hooter kept firing his 60. Most of the action took place on his side of the aircraft.

After the first WP went off, Thunder knew what I was doing, so he spun the aircraft around and I then threw out the last of the two WPs I had left. Thunder hoped that would make the gooks think we were making another pass and make them get their heads down. It worked. Thunder and Ryan took advantage of the situation and we got out of there. I didn't pop red smoke, because with all the WPs I threw out and all the rounds that were fired you couldn't tell where the action was. Thunder called the Cobras back and as they approached, Thunder and Ryan started for the clouds. We all knew that the Cobras were going to dump everything they had on that location. I flipped my ICS so I could hear all the transmissions that were taking place. Thunder called for more gunships and we had ourselves a hot LZ.

While the Cobras made their runs, we backed up to regroup. "That will wake you up," Ryan said.

"Are you guy's hit any where?" Thunder asked.

"I don't think so," Ryan replied.

Thunder told Ryan that after the Cobras made a few more runs, we would go back and check it out. Hooter said that he thought the WPs pissed them off. We laughed, mostly to hide our fear of what we knew was about to come. The Cobras finished their runs and headed for the clouds and it was our turn at bat. This time, one of us would make a gun run with both gunners firing. Then, as we came out of our dive and headed skyward, the other LOH would make their run to protect the other's ass.

We were going to use this tactic instead of pulling hammer head stalls to conserve ammo. We were the first to make our run. Hooter and I stood out on the skids, guns pointed forward and blazing. We weren't shooting at anything in particular, just strafing the area where all the smoke rose out of the jungle. As we finished our gun run, we received no return fire. Ryan started his run to protect our ass and to also strafe the area. He started his run too soon and we could not come around fast enough to protect his ass. At the time, I did not know what was going on. All I heard was Thunder yell out "Oh, shit!" and I knew something was up. Thunder pulled a hammer head and Hooter knew then what was going on. Before Thunder could tell us to lay down fire, Hooter was already doing so. The gooks started firing at Ryan, and as we came into view some of the fire was directed our way.

Tracers missed the aircraft, and me, by inches. I tucked myself close to the airframe to try and become as small of a target as possible. Most of the fire was directed at Ryan and over the comm. we heard "We're hit! We're hit!" They banked off into a hard right turn. We also broke right to let me strafe the area. As we got close to the trees, Thunder leveled off and we flew tree top level until we were clear and then popped up behind Ryan. Thunder asked him how bad and at first he did not respond.

How bad? Thunder repeated again.

"I have a gunner hit!" Ryan came back.

John, I thought. I prayed for the first time since I'd been in country. *Don't let it be John.* We pulled up on the right side of their aircraft. Blood streaked down that side and along the tail boom. It was Lambert's side of the aircraft. He lay backward on the floor as his legs hung outside the aircraft. Blood covered the whole lower part of his right leg. His left leg kept moving up and down, he was in great pain. But it looked like his right leg was moving also. I looked again and his right leg was spinning around and around. It would come to a stop and then slowly unwind the other direction. His leg had been severed at the knee and the airflow was spinning his leg until it could spin no more. I transmitted to John to pull him all the way into the aircraft. John pulled him in and blood continued to run down the right side of the aircraft and down the tail boom.

When we landed at Quan Loi, I ran over to Lambert and pulled him upward toward me. His face and hands were white. He opened his eyes, smiled at me and said, "I got that million-dollar wound, Brooks. I'm going home."

I looked down at his leg and all that was holding it on was a piece of muscle running down the right side of his knee. I removed the knife from Lambert's vest, touched the muscle with the edge of the blade and his leg fell to the ground. John and I held him until the medics showed up. John had given him three hits of morphine from the aircraft's first aid kit and Lambert didn't care one way or the other what was going on. We twisted down the tunicate that John had put above his knee until the blood flow stopped, and all the time Lambert kept saying, "I got that million-dollar wound, I got that million-dollar wound. Home, I'm going home."

The war was over for Lambert. I turned to look at John, but he would not look at us. Lambert was a close friend and John did not want Lambert to see the expression on his face and the water starting to form in his eyes. Lambert was out of it now and wouldn't notice anyway. But John would not render help of any kind, or even look in our direction. He came over to me later on and shook my hand. "Thanks, Brooks, for seeing to Lambert. I couldn't bring myself to even look at him."

"I know, John, I know."

Nothing else was said. Nothing else needed to be said. Hooter and I understood.

The flight line had a melancholy feeling the rest of that day. Cobras, Slicks and LOHs flew in and out to the hot LZ until the sunlight was almost gone. They reported over fifteen kills and it was estimated that there were at least fifty VC firing at us that day, but no NVA had been reported in the area.

Lambert made it back to the States. We never received one letter from him, not a word. I always thought Lambert might have blamed me for cutting the rest of his leg off.

A flight line Sergeant named Ken approached John and me and told John that he would be the gunner on Lambert's bird and asked if I could help him get familiar with the aircraft. We both acknowledged him and continued getting our aircraft ready for the next day. My aircraft had taken a couple of hits, one in the skid and one through the bottom half of the vertical fin. No big deal, it was nothing crucial and I had it fixed in a couple of hours. I left the hole in the skid though; it didn't need repair at this time. The other aircraft had taken several hits and it took us a little longer to fix it. We worked on it until dark and would finish it up early in the morning. John and I were tired and were ready for a beer and bed. Halfway back to our hooch we ran into West.

West had a worried look and when he saw us walking together, he slowed his pace, stopped in front of us and grabbed us both by the neck. "You guys really know how to screw up someone's day, don't you?"

I knew he was glad to see us, but I could tell by the tone in his voice that he was more than concerned. He was also pissed. When we got back to the hooch West and John got into it. West demanded that John quit flying and go back to the Blues. I understood why West wanted his brother to quit flying, but on the other hand, I understood why John would not.

I left the hooch, went out sat on an old bunker near the flight line and drank my hot beer and smoked some dope. I was starting to change the way I felt about my situation and hate was entering into the equation. I was starting to feel hate for the first time. I wouldn't quit Scouts now for anything. I was more committed now than ever, but I started to have thoughts about not making it back to the world. The odds weren't in my favor and it played on my mind day after day, until I got to the point I was certain that I would not be going back home, alive anyway.

In my letters home I tried not to reveal how I felt, but I know sometimes I let some stuff slip. Sometimes I wrote things to my fiancée to vent or to get it off my chest. She always wrote back with words of encouragement, hope and love. Her letters kept me from giving up as time went on.

I sat there for hours thinking. Sometimes the silence was broken by a flare, or by someone on bunker guard who thought they saw movement in the wire and cut loose with a few rounds. I didn't want to go back to the hooch. The tension was high and I wasn't in the mood to be in that kind of atmosphere. I didn't want to be put in a situation where I might have to choose sides. My thoughts turned back to home and my mind escaped for a little while. Sometimes a little while was enough. Most of the time, it was all I had. I had a long way to go and I wasn't ready to give up just yet. Tomorrow would be better. Dealing with this shit one day at a time was the best way to handle it.

OH-6A Loch
Close call but no one was hurt seriously.

I woke up the next morning with two months down and ten more to go. West and John only had one month and a wake up and they would be out of here. *Man, that must be a good feeling,* I thought.

I looked over at John's bunk and he was gone. He went down to the dispensary to see if Lambert had been flown out yet. They had to evacuate him that same day. John was ready to see him but it was too late. He never got to say goodbye to his friend. None of us did. All of us were friends, but to John, Lambert was like a brother. They had pounded the ground together and had been with each other for almost a year. It was hard for John and it took several days for him to get over it. I believe John pretended Lambert was in a sense no part of his life. That was the only way he could turn it loose.

Chapter 10
Getting Even

John started getting back to his old self. We had a few missions where we made contact, but nothing really happened and very few kills were reported. Intelligence reported a lot of activity in several areas and it was rumored that Charlie, along with the NVA, were planning something big. We flew mission's everyday and tensions were high. We could tell that Charlie was up to something because he kept such a low profile. We all needed a break and we got the Old Man (CO) to allow us to have a party. He agreed. He was proud of his men and knew how important it was to keep good morale.

It was a Thursday and we had received our ice and beer rations early. One of the guys got a hold of an ammo trailer we put six hundred pounds of ice in it and cooled down all the beer we could get a hold of. We had Black Label, Budweiser, Falstaff, Blue Ribbon and Pearl. Of course, the Budweiser went first. Then the Blue Ribbon and it was a toss-up over the others. It didn't matter after all the good beer was gone. A movie played, but most of us got high on grass and beer.

There was this guy we called Popp that always wanted to let everyone know he was a tough guy. He was, but that night we all had a little too much to drink and a challenge of any kind would be answered in a heartbeat. He made the remark that he would give a hundred dollars if anyone could throw him in the ammo cart. The ammo cart was full of ice and water and it would hurt your hand every time you pulled a beer out of it. He no sooner got those words out of his mouth when at least ten guys charged him, picked him up off the ground and slam-dunked him into the iced down beer.

To top it off, they held him there until he started screaming, "Enough, enough."

Someone screamed out, "Will you give us all a blow job?" Everyone laughed and chanted "Blow job, blow job." They were all joking, but made him say yes before they let him out. He was a humbled man and quite embarrassed. It was all in fun and after that everyone started throwing each other into the vat of ice. I hadn't witnessed them having this much fun since I had been here. It was great for the tension and morale. We all had a cold bath before the night was over and the tension that was once so dominant was gone, even if it was only for a little while.

After our cold bath, we all decided to play cards. West, Walker, Scott Hooter, and I started playing and West decided to break out the Johnny Walker Black. It was about eleven-o-clock and all of us were feeling the booze. All of a sudden a grenade was thrown in on us and rolled across the floor.

Grenade! West yelled and everyone hit the floor. West dove behind his bunk, Walker could not stop saying, "Oh, shit." Everyone else was on the ground with their hands over their heads. I got up and dove on top of the grenade as if to sacrifice my life for theirs. "Brooks!" West shouted. "Damn, Brooks!"

I rolled over and started laughing.

It was all a joke. I had John throw in a dummy that we had disarmed by inserting a spent fuse cap into the grenade. When everyone realized what had gone down they started beating the crap out of me. I couldn't stop laughing. I told you that I would get even. It was a good joke, but man I was sore from the beating. The next day, everyone had to admit that I had gotten them but good. I knew these guys wouldn't forget and I had better have my guard up at all times. I still had to get Morris and he knew it was only a matter of time.

Maintenance got to the point where they needed more support from flight line personnel. So when our twenty five, fifty, and one hundred hour inspections came due on the aircraft, we would follow them into maintenance, to help out with the work load. We were flying a lot of hours and maintenance had a lot of work to do. It was also going to be up to the flight crews to retrieve downed aircraft. We would be attached to the Blues, be inserted with them, prepare the aircraft to be sling loaded out by a Chinook. If the aircraft was beyond repair than we would destroy it so Charlie could not use any of the material or weapons against us. It would be up to the sling crew to make those decisions. By doing this extra assignment you would be granted a day off for each recovery, but could take no more than one day a month. Or, better yet, you could accrue these days for R&R in the rear.

A few of us volunteered and others would juggle their flights and take up the slack. It was a good way to get days off. Being on the ground with the Blues with gunships flying above you to keep Charlie off your ass didn't seem all that dangerous to me, or to several other gunners, so we volunteered. Since I had been trained to read a compass grid they put me in charge of the sling crew. I think the real reason they put me in charge was because all the other volunteers weren't mechanics. They wanted to make sure the aircraft could be retrieved without causing more damage than necessary.

Maintenance had a SP-5th class (Specialist 5, same as a hard 3 strip sergeant) named Kenny. Kenny and I became good friends and they would always assign me to him when my aircraft came in for these periodic inspections. He taught me a lot about aircraft. He was a hell of a mechanic and I never saw anything he could not do to keep these aircraft flying. He took great pride in his work and I learned a lot. He, too, was short, with four months to go and he let you know it. Every time someone called his name, the first thing out of his mouth would be, "Short!" and then and only then would he acknowledge that person. He hated the army or at least he wanted you to think he did.

He also ran the maintenance sling recovery crew. When it came to going after a downed bird he took it seriously, even though we had the Blues and gunships covering for us. He had been in a couple of fire fights during these operations and he hated it. He liked to go in, do his thing, and then take the first aircraft out. Sometimes this meant he would fly out on the sling bird. He wanted to go back to the world, and was doing everything he could to try and make that happen.

I liked him, I liked him a lot. He had this long nose and a thin face. He looked like a cartoon character called Biggie Rat that you would see in hot rod magazines. Once, jokingly, I called him Biggie Rat and it stuck. Everyone called him Biggie Rat after that day, Biggie for short. Even he liked the name.

Once, Biggie and I went out together to recover a downed aircraft. I was paired up with him to make sure

I knew how to rig the slings and the drag shoot to the downed aircraft. We flew out in a Slick and were inserted after the Blues went in and secured the area. The area was hot, Charlie was all around the perimeter, and we had a lot of air power. With all this firepower, the gooks really didn't want to give away their position. But our air cover had to leave. They got called away on a mission with a higher priority.

Once the air cover left, Charlie decided it would be worth the risk to set up an attack. They did and Biggie and I got caught up in a ground fire fight. I had my Car 16 (Cut down Assault Rifle) and Biggie had nothing but his 45 pistol. We got behind a berm in this rice patty and along with the Blues set up grazing fire. After awhile, the gunships returned and made gun runs on several enemy locations. That got their mind off of us and after awhile a Chinook helicopter was called in to sling out the downed Slick.

Chinooks are huge and picking up a Slick is nothing to them. They also give off a lot of static electricity. When you go to hook up the load to them to sling out, you slap the cargo hook and it will discharge the static electricity. If you do it fast, no big deal, but if you grab the hook you will get a shock that will knock you for a loop.

I was wet from lying in the rice patty, sitting on top of the rotor head of this downed aircraft waiting to hook it to the Chinook's cargo hook. The flight engineer on the Chinook looks down through the floor where the cargo hook is and guides the pilot down so I can hook up the load. The engineer brought him down so fast I thought he was going to squash me between his aircraft and the rotor head that I was setting on.

Out of sheer reflex I stuck my hand upward and it touched the bottom of the Chinook. A blue electric charge came off the Chinook and went through my body. I swear I thought I was electrocuted. It almost knocked me off the aircraft. I hooked the sling up to the cargo hook and after that was done I lost control of my arm. I finally got to the point I could move it, but the feeling didn't come back for days. Needless to say Biggie tagged me with the name Sparky, and that name stuck for some time until I picked up another nickname later on.

To top it off Biggie set me up for this job and somehow he and the Chinook crew chief made sure I got the full jolt. Biggie had a mean streak, but it was this mean streak I liked so much. It broke the monotony of day in day out combat and in Biggie's eyes it was a way he sized you up. You know, to see if you could take it. Yep, I have to say I liked Biggie, and he took care of his men. I never knew anyone that didn't like him.

I liked sling recovery missions a lot. Sometimes you would have to repel down into the jungle to recover the downed aircraft. I was really good at doing this job. I went on everyone I could, if I wasn't flying. It was a nice break from hunt and kill missions and wasn't as dangerous as flying the missions themselves. I got really good reading a map and shooting a grid to find our downed aircraft. The jungle was kind of nice if you weren't in any hurry. Sometimes it would take us all day to just cover three miles in triple canopy jungle. In triple canopy there is no other way to get to a downed aircraft other than rappelling down to it.

We never rappelled directly over a downed aircraft. This would give your position away. We usually rappelled two to three miles from its location and humped to it. Once on the jungle floor, you can hardly see daylight. You no longer have the luxury of being able to into a helicopter and fly back.

The helicopter has nowhere to land. Many times I have flown out on the end of a rappelling line. Once they pull you out of the jungle on the end of a line, you have to fly all the way back to the LZ that way. I always thought it was fun and really preferred it. This way of extracting could only be done if they could see you, most of the time they could not.

Popping smoke to pinpoint your position didn't always work, mainly because the smoke might travel under the jungle canopy and rise up in an opening somewhere else. So in order to get out you would have to hump to an area you could be extracted from by either the helicopter picking you up, or by rappel line. Sometimes we would have to spend several days humping to a location where we could be picked up.

You would get locations for extractions before you went into the jungle. Radio contact could be monitored by the enemy. So you had to prepare a back up grid on a map you could go to in order to be picked up. If you missed your pick up date or point, then and only then would you use your radio to make contact for pickup. I liked the assignments and I kept to myself a lot. The Blues didn't give us any flag. Probably due to the fact that the gunners had more kills than any of them. I don't really know. They just never gave us any grief. They stayed to their own and we did, too. Their platoon sergeant was in charge on the ground operations, but when we got to the downed aircraft we always made the calls. Most of the time, on these missions, we were only there to determine if the aircraft was worth saving and to rescue the crews. Or recover the bodies.

The sergeant and I had an agreement. If the aircraft was in good shape, but the operation to remove it would jeopardize any of our safety, we would destroy the aircraft and tell operations that it was beyond repair. The flight crews we picked up always agreed to this arrangement. After all, we were out in Charlie's backyard and none of us were going to end up POWs if we could help it. Get in, do our thing, get out and most of the time Charlie never knew we were there. Or they knew we were there, but didn't know exactly where. The aircraft had a locater beeper on it so we knew the location. Charlie, on the other hand, did not. Unless Charlie saw where the aircraft went down, we always beat him to it.

One time Charlie won the race, and it cost us all dearly.

Chapter 11
The Blood of a Brother

I had gone out on several recovery missions. Like I said before, I liked doing sling recovery. This particular time, I was put in charge of a sling crew of six well-trained individuals. I only took two at a time on these missions and rotated them as much as I could. I had made it a point to go out on seven of these missions in a row. I wanted some R&R in a couple of months, so I took the missions back to back.

But that day, we had a flight mission close to Cambodia. Thunder, me, and an observer whose name I cannot recall. He was from maintenance and wanted a little flight time. There were going to be some of our gunships working in the same area that we would be headhunting with. Some of our Slick gunships would be supporting ground troops with air cover. If we needed more help we could call them, but only if it was an emergency. You wouldn't want them to leave the troops they were supporting high and dry, especially if they were in a fire fight. We no sooner arrived at our AO (Area of Operations) when we took a strike in one of our rotor blades. The aircraft had such a bad vibration that we had to return to base. The Cobras that were assigned to us went ahead and stayed out in the AO to give the people on the ground fire support. When we got back, the skin on one of our rotors was peeled back like a banana. It would take a little while to install another blade and track it out, so the most of my day would be tied up.

The Cobras called back to operations and reported that they were getting some return fire and needed a LOH from Scouts to come out and do some recon for them. John was ready with his bird and I saw him throwing his survival pack on board. This would be his first mission without one of us along with him. He had seen plenty of action in Blues, so returning fire was not a problem for him. The only problem John had was not staying down on the trigger. Being a grunt, you don't fire your M-60 in a steady burst of fire. You fire off rounds with short burst as not to burn up your barrel. But when flying, you kept the trigger down, the cool air flowing over the barrel kept the barrel from getting too hot and jamming up. It was a habit John was getting over, no big deal. He was a great door gunner and we knew he would be fine.

What I needed to do was get that damn aircraft of mine back up and flying. John was standby until I took a round, now I would be on standby as soon as I got my aircraft flight ready. We put on another rotor blade from an aircraft that had been shot up so bad it would be out for maintenance for a few days. The blade hours were so far apart from mine that I really couldn't track the aircraft as well as I wanted. But it would do. I was back up, and that put us on standby.

I noticed that oil dripping from my engine cowling. I opened the cowling up and saw that a bullet had clipped my oil reservoir and opened it up enough that I was losing too much oil. I was grounded. *Shit*, I thought. I reported the damage to operations and they put a Slick in my place for standby. The only thing wrong with that is a Slick was too big to get down and do the job the LOHs could do. So the Cobras were informed that a LOH was going to their AO, but they really didn't have back up. Operations told them all they had was a Slick gunship in case they needed help with fire power. There was nothing more I could do except work on my aircraft. Hooter came over to give me a hand. His aircraft was into maintenance for a hundred hour inspection and my ship was now priority.

The flight line was hot and Hooter made the comment about some beer.

"Beer," I repeated and looked around. "You think we could get beer down and not get caught?"

"I know we can," he said, "we are the only two dudes around. Everyone else is flying or in maintenance. I'll be back." Off he went.

Before I knew it, Hooter returned with four ice-cold beers. "Where in hell did you find cold beers?" I asked.

"Man, I cooled them off with the CO_2 fire extinguisher from that standby Slick. You can't put shit out with those extinguishers anyway. Oh, maybe you could put out a burning body, or something like that, but a dead body don't care. And if it was any of our friends that were burning and already dead, they would rather us have the beer anyway. Now, are you going to drink, or think about it some more?"

"Drink," I said and we laughed, sat beside the aircraft on an ammo box and hammered our beers. We didn't have parts right then for the aircraft anyway. We felt justified in drinking those cold beers. We could justify any situation to drink a cold beer.

West showed up and we had a little private get together. I know he came down because he was concerned about John. After a the beers, it was time to get back to work. We had to fix the oil problem first, so we could do the flying we needed to track out the rotor system. The Cobras we were working with earlier were on short final, coming back for refuel. West was looking for John's aircraft. I told West that John wouldn't be back for fuel yet. West was worried, but you could tell he tried to take on the posture that he wasn't.

Hooter and I went over to help the Cobras refuel so the pilot and gunner could stay in the aircraft. As we were refueling, Mr. Knight opened up the cock-pit door and made the comment that there was a lot of movement out there and they wanted to hot refuel (not shut the aircraft down.) We refueled the aircraft and they took off. At this point, I wished my aircraft was flyable.

Mr. Thunderbird came down to the flight line and told us things were fixing to get hot on the AO and wished we had another aircraft. Being on the ground and not being able to help is the worst feeling. And if an aircraft gets shot down and you can't help, then it's ten times worse. If Thunderbird was worried, then we all had reason to be concerned. Thunder asked me if we could our aircraft up soon. I told him we hadn't even received the parts yet. You could tell he was worried more than he was letting on.

About fifteen minutes passed and the scramble horn blew. *Shit!* Hooter and I were stuck without a ship. We decided to jump on the standby Slick, but our 60s weren't near us. Hooter's M-60 was in his ship in maintenance and mine was back in my hooch. Not having an aircraft to fly, I didn't think I needed my 60 at the time. I had cleaned it and put it away under my bunk. Hooter got back just in time to jump aboard the standby Slick. I stood there shit out of luck and all I could do was wave at them as they took off. I hated being left behind. I got mad and threw my tools around. I shook with rage. Thunder came up and put his hand around my neck agreed that it really sucked being stuck on the ground. We sat on the revetment, staring in the direction of the AO and not saying a word.

After awhile, Thunder told me he was going to Operations to listen to the air transmissions. He asked me if I wanted to come. I told him no, my parts would be showing up soon and wanted to be here when they did. "Later, Brooks," he said as he walked off. West went to Operations as soon as the scramble horn blew. You can bet his ear was glued to the radios.

After awhile, I looked up and noticed a lot of personnel leaving Operations. Thunder walked toward me, so I dropped what I was doing. I could tell he wanted to talk. He told me that they were calling for a formation in front of HQ (Head Quarters) and needed everyone there. These type of formations usually meant trouble, so I hot-footed it toward HQ. Something was definitely up for the Old Man to call everyone to formation. We didn't do formations. It gave Charlie too good of an opportunity to drop a mortar on us and chalk up the causalities.

As I approached HQ, I saw that West was more than frantic. He had his M-16 with him along with his field pack. I knew then what had happened. John's aircraft had been shot down.

The CO didn't even let us get into formation, he just told us like it was. "Gentlemen, we have a problem. We have no aircraft available and we have a downed aircraft in the AO. The aircraft did not have the chance to get away from the area and went down right in the middle of where they received fire. The gunships on location cannot fire at the enemy in fear that they might hit our own people. The Blues are on another engagement with Charlie and can't be pulled out to help us."

Not being an infantry unit, we did not have people to pull and put into the field. The only infantry we had were the Blues, and they were tied up, so volunteers were needed.

"We need at least nine volunteers to rappel in and try to give our downed boys some support. All volunteers assemble at revetment #4. The standby slick is returning and will meet you there." The Old Man turned to West and told him he would not be going. West let him know in no certain terms that he *was* going and he would shoot the mother that tried to stop him. The Old Man understood. He didn't say another word to West, other than 'okay.'

I hated this shit, but there was no way I was staying out of this. West and John were my best friends and I guarantee they would be there for me if need be. I had to go back to the hooch and pick up my rappelling gear. All I needed was my D-Rings and my eight foot rope to rig up a monkey seat and my CAR 16, ammo, and water.

The Old Man called me aside and asked if I would go. He knew West and I were close and wanted someone there that West would listen to. I told the CO there was no way I would stay behind on this one. The Old Man gave me his Jeep and I drove back to my hooch, picked up my gear and returned to the flight line in no time. When I arrived, there were twenty or more volunteers. I didn't say a word. I stepped over behind the sergeant with West and everyone knew I was in. West kept looking toward the DMZ and mumbled, "Where is that damn bird?"

We had our volunteers. They were all experienced men and had seen combat in the air as well as on the ground. I was going to be the grid man (map man) behind point. Point was a guy named Jerry Lofton, a good point man. In fact, as I looked around, everyone was top notch in my book. We even had two from the Blues who were going on R&R that volunteered. This said a lot for them to miss their R&R to help. This type of response showed how much West was thought of in the company.

I went up to Lofton and ask him what he had heard.

"I don't know, Brooks," he said. "We are going to need you to get us to some clearing when we reach the downed crew. The pilots on the Slick coming in have the coordinates and location of where this place is located. They have it all worked up for you. Just exchange maps with them."

"Good," I said. This meant I didn't have to figure shit. All I had to do was to zero my map (orient it to the layout of the terrain) and shoot a line to the grid numbers on the borders.

Lofton told me that there had been a lot of movement on the ground reported and to expect trouble. I had a bunch of pin flares in my survival pack and I would let our gunships know our location all the time so they could give us fire support if we needed it. We would be using radio communication so we had a radio man with us.

The gooks knew where we were, so direct radio communication was no big deal. We were all pumped up and ready. I looked at West. He was getting antsy, eager to get on with it. I motioned him to come over by me. He put his hand on my arm and asked what I wanted. "I want you to stay with me and Lofton, okay?"

"Okay," he replied.

The aircraft came in and we hopped aboard. I looked over to see Hooter in the left hand transmission well. He motioned for me to put on one of the gunners helmets so I could talk to him on the intercom.

"What's up Hooter? How does it look?"

"Not good, Brooks. What the hell is West doing here?"

"How in the hell are you going to keep him away?" I barked.

"I know, but it isn't good Brooks. The ship took an RPG in the ass and the ship was on fire. There may be no survivors."

Shit. I never stopped to give it much thought. I only thought about how I would feel if my brother was down in the jungle, not the fact that he might be dead. *Not good*, I thought. *Not good at all.*

I gave the flight helmet back to the gunner. Looked around to find West looking at me. "What's up?" he screamed over the rotor noise.

"Nothing," I replied. "I was just getting information from Hooter that we might need later." I didn't want to alarm him any further.

As we approached the LZ I knew there was a lot going on. There were gunships in the area, but none of them were cutting loose. They didn't know where the downed flight crew was and they weren't taking a chance of hitting them with friendly fire. Charlie must have been enjoying himself by keeping us at bay like this. We approached the area where the aircraft had gone down into the jungle; there was a big hole in the top canopy of the trees. We hovered over the hole and we saw that the aircraft was still smoking. It had caught fire and there wasn't much left of it. When the pilot was ready for us to rappel, he gave us the go by nodding his head and we jumped.

We got to the floor of the jungle as fast as we could. We did not want to be targets hanging in the air for Charlie. Lofton and I were the first to hit the ground. We looked around. It was clear and we gave the thumbs up. The rest followed and when all of us were on the ground, we paired up and moved toward the downed aircraft. We found two bodies and West was frantic. We had identified the pilot and the observer, but not a sign of John. Because the vegetation in the jungle is so fragile, we could tell what had taken place. John had laid down his 60, pulled the bodies away from the aircraft and used the fire extinguisher on them. His gun was still lying on the ground next to the aircraft. As far as we could tell, Charlie moved in and abducted him. I don't know how many gooks there were, but we guessed around six to eight.

My mind was not on West. It was locked into combat mode and I had forgotten all about him. There was some blood on the ground and we followed it down the trail that Charlie made as he stomped through the jungle. The gooks had left the same way they approached. It was an easy enough trail to follow. If we hurried, we might be able to overtake them. John's life would depend on it. Being an enlisted man, they would most likely not take him as a POW. Everyone knew the only other reason they would take him and that was to use him for cover to keep the gunships off of them. Or they were going to execute him.

We could move much faster than they could because they had already chopped out a trail for us. All we had to do was follow it. We didn't care if they set up an ambush, we just wanted to stop them from getting away. If an ambush against us kept them from moving away, then so be it. We would welcome an ambush rather than going on wondering if we would see John again. *Please stop and fight,* I thought. I don't know how far we traveled, but it was some distance from the downed aircraft.

Finally, we came to a small clearing in the jungle where a small amount of light shone through the tops of the trees. We all got down, thinking this would be our point of contact if we were going to get ambushed, nothing, not a thing. Then we saw something in the middle of the clearing. It looked to be a body. We set up a cross fire position covering both sides of the body as Loftin and I approached. As we got closer, we saw the body covered in a massive amount of blood. And it was John.

They had skinned him like a catfish from his neck to his waist and had staked him to the ground with bamboo. They stuck bamboo through his eyelids and up through his eyebrows. They cut off his genitals and stuck them in his mouth. I could not move. I had never witnessed this kind of cruelty. Something you wouldn't have done to an animal, much less to a human. My heart sank and tears formed in my eyes.

Then I heard a moan. Loftin and I knelt beside the body. John was still alive. I pulled his genitals from his mouth and he gasped for air. He moaned again. He didn't have the strength to scream. His breathing was shallow. I couldn't bear it any more. I stood to walk away and hit West. He stared at his brother. Then he dropped his weapon and gear and let out a scream that sent a chill down my back. I grabbed onto West, and at the same time he struck out at me. I moved behind him and put my arms around his, holding both of his arms down by his sides. I pulled backward and tried to drag him away from John. He called John's name over and over. We fell to the ground with my face buried into his back and tears flowed down my face. I could not let go of West. We lay there until Loftin and two others pulled us apart. West was in shock. I couldn't bear to look at West. For some reason, I felt guilty, like I had failed my friends West and John.

Loftin put his hand on my shoulder and told me that John had died. I looked over at the body and they had covered it up. There was a body bag beside him and two of the guys were preparing to place the body into it. I looked over at West, who was still on the ground. He couldn't bear to look either. They radioed the choppers about our casualties. Three of us and West stayed where we were and waited while the others went to recover the other two bodies. We used this clearing where we found John as our pickup point. We could go no further. And we were not in any state of mind to fight. We were all in such a bad way that we could do nothing more but leave.

I shot off a couple of pin flares and it wasn't long before a Slick came to pull us out. They threw ropes and more body bags down. We rigged up slings for the bodies and the first Slick flew them away. West stood in the clearing, staring down to where John had been laying, staring at his brother's blood. Then, helmet off, he looked upward and watched the aircraft take John's body away.

We all sat and set up a POD (perimeter of defense) around the area. A little later another Slick came in dropped six ropes. Everyone was lifted out except Loftin and me. Later another Slick came and we were pulled out. The flight back to Quan Loi didn't take long. As we approached the flight line, there were at least a hundred men standing there to welcome us back. We were on the ends of two rappelling lines and as the helicopter lowered us down, our friends stood below us with their hands stretched upward to welcome us back. As we touched down, everyone patted us on the back and said 'good job, good job.'

It sure didn't feel that way. We failed, or that is the way I saw it. I felt so guilty for even thinking I liked John being in flight, or that maybe I had a part in encouraging him to join our ranks.

West was never the same. He went home with his brother's body. He returned about a month later, but not really.

After this tragedy, West and I were involved in two missions together but never really spoke to each other again. He never looked at me with any type of contempt; there were never any harsh words. He knew John's death devastated me. The only thing he ever did was give me the peace sign when I left country. I was getting on a helicopter that was taking me to Saigon to catch my flight back to the world. I looked out the door and there he was, standing at the end of the revetment watching me leave and giving me the peace sign. I did the same and that was the last time I ever saw my friend again.

West and me.

James Westland Sharp (West) was killed in action that same year. I was not in country when it happened. I ran into Lambert years later in Victoria, Texas and he told me about West. West will always have a special place in my heart as well in my memory. I never will forget his friendship. I had a special bond with West, but as the war brought us together, it also split us apart. I like to think that West severed our relationship because of the pain it would have caused him if I had gotten myself killed. Or maybe my presence reminded him too much of his brother. I will never know for sure. But the one thing that has brought me some piece of mind over the years was him giving me the peace sign and smiling at me as I lifted off that day, headed home. I knew in my heart then that our friendship was still there. His memory haunts me sometimes. I miss my friend, I miss him still.

Chapter 12
A Boy & His Dog

John's death hit the company hard. The pilots had all their get-togethers, but the enlisted men pretty much stayed to themselves to the point they were even isolated from each other.

Hooter, Biggie, Schultz, and a maintenance guy named Barney Barnet and I hung out together. At this time, I really didn't want to make any new friends. I finally understood what West tried to tell me that night back in our hooch several weeks ago. I lost two people that were close to me and I haven't been in country long enough not to be considered an FNG. I had witnessed and done a lot in that short period of time and though I was still considered a new guy, no one really called me a FNG anymore. In their eyes I was one of them now, and at this point I was treated equally in every way. We were all still friends, just didn't get personal with one and other like before. It did not affect our ability to fight together, or to have each other's back when needed.

Hooter told me that he had seen this kind of reaction before. "We will let our guard down," he said, "then someone will get killed and we all draw up unto our little cliques."

I totally got it and didn't even try to get too personal with anyone else. God help the new FNG that came into our little world. Everyone remembered what it was like, but it wasn't worth the cost to make new close friends. I confronted a new guy one time about this very subject.

His name was Irwin. We had bunker guard together one night and he started telling me all about himself. I stopped him short. I stuck out my hand for a handshake and I told him that I would be there for him in any situation when it came to a battle. I told him I would put my life on the line for his, but I did not want to get to know him. "I don't want to know anything about you or your family," I told him. "Please don't take this personal. I'm your friend, I just don't want to get friendly. Okay?"

"Okay," he replied.

I know I hurt his feelings and I hated to do it. But if I was going to keep my sanity, I couldn't go through again what I just went through with John and West. I turned my energy and thoughts into one thing: hate. I hated gooks, whether they were NVA or VC. Hell, I even hated the color. If I saw any gook, I had an instant hate for them. They all looked like a moving targets to me. It was the first time in my life I remember being prejudiced against any color or race.

The Vietnamese could care less who dictated to them, whether it was North Viet Nam or the U.S. They didn't give a shit one way or the other. They reminded me of little kids. If the North could give them ice cream they were for the North, if the U.S. could give them ice cream they were for the U.S.A. It was who could deliver the goods. They were like trees in the wind. Whichever way the wind would blow, was the way they would bend. It wasn't like we had battle lines drawn out. Like over here are the bad guys and over there are the good guys. Everywhere was a battle line. Even the ones we allowed to come into our compound to work for us weren't our friends. They would sell you out in a heartbeat. The only ones you could trust where the mountain people (Mountain Yards.) The Vietnamese treated these people like second class scum and the Mountain Yards resented them for it. I guess, in a sense, they were looked upon as the niggers of Vietnam.

We even had caught Vietnamese locals stepping off certain areas to give to Charlie, so he could drop mortars on us. I built up *such* a hate for the NVA and the VC. I even volunteered if it meant I might get to kill a gook. I knew I was becoming something I wasn't proud of. At one time I believed I would never become like those two that killed that prisoner the day I arrived. Now I was just like them, transformed into something less than human, a vampire.

I only had another couple of weeks to go and I would be out of Scouts and into Slicks. I looked forward to Slicks. I had already moved out of my hooch and closer to the flight line amongst the Slick gunners. As I said, I wasn't too sure how West would react to my presence. I still felt guilty about John. So I avoided the situation by moving out of our hooch and into the Slicks'. I really thought it would be best thing for both of us. I made up my mind that I would try and talk to him when he returned. But deep down I knew it would be in vain.

I had heard that West had reenlisted and volunteered to come back to Nam to his old outfit. I had also heard that he volunteered for Blues night patrol. These guys would get their information on Charlie from intelligence. Things like their movement and location and so on. Then they would go out and set up ambushes and the next day we would use chase birds to finish the job. These guys stayed to themselves a lot and really didn't have much to do with flight operations.

I knew why West volunteered to come back. He came back for revenge. For the sole purpose of killing gooks. I still thought of West as my best friend, but I knew it was going to be different. I was a reminder of what had taken place with his brother. On top of all that, I didn't need to be surrounded by that type of atmosphere. It was hard enough to deal with my shit much less the melancholy that would surround him.

The next day I was down on the flight line early. I wanted to be by myself and watch the sun come up. I had this bunker that I liked to climb up on and watch the sunrise. Everyone that knew me knew that's where I would be in the morning and sometimes at dusk. The guys on bunker watch left about the time I got down there and that meant I would have the bunker to myself. I went up and sat on top of the bunker and hung my legs off the side. I looked toward the east and the sun was just starting to come up. Something wet and cold touched my arm. I jumped and looked down. It was Tiger. I wondered what had happened to him.

He put his head in my lap and lay down beside me. I put my hand on his head and by doing so all the emotions I had experienced for the last couple of days hit me and I wept. Tiger adopted me that day. He would not leave my side and in some ways I felt like John was still present every time Tiger would do something human-like. Like that look they give you sometimes or they sense your mood and respond by trying to get your attention. Anyway, Tiger and I were a team now. I was now his choice and in some stupid way I felt honored. A dog has a way of making you feel like a kid and that is what I wanted to feel like more than anything else at this moment, a kid, a kid with a dog.

My thoughts took me home to Slaton, and instead of it bringing me joy like it usually did, I felt sad. I knew I could never go back to my carefree years, back amongst the friends I grew up with. Even if I could go back, I knew I would be different. In some ways, I still thought like a kid. I still had my childhood dreams wandering around in my head. The difference between then and now was I knew that they would never be anything more than just dreams. I was not growing into manhood at a slow natural pace; I was being forced into it by this stinking war. I was not ready to become a man. Not this way.

Slaton was always on my mind and I couldn't help but think that I would not see her again. I had to start dealing with death now. It was becoming a part of my life and there was nothing I could do to stop it. Vietnam was going to change the way I thought about things. I knew that morning that I was not only weeping for my friend John, I was grieving for a way of life I was losing. My carefree years, my childhood would eventually be lost forever. I wanted to hang on to some memory of my home town that would at least bring me piece of mind, so I thought about Shirley, the first girl I fell in love with, and Roni, the love of my life. There were things I wanted to tell them both. I wanted to smooth things over with Shirley, to make things right. And Roni. If only I could see and talk to her one more time. To tell her how much I loved her and to assure her I was coming home and we would be married. I would have given anything to see her again.

Then the silence of the morning and my deep thoughts were broken by Hooter calling for Tiger. Tiger looked back toward where Hooter's voice was coming from, but would not go to him. I got up and started toward Hooter. When Hooter saw Tiger, he called to him. Tiger ran over accepted the greeting and then returned to me. Hooter said that Tiger had made his choice. Hooter said there was a bet on who Tiger would adopt. "Brooks, your name never came up. Everyone thought he would choose someone that he had known for awhile. Go figure." He laughed.

Yeah, go figure, I thought.

A little later, Thunder showed up and asked me if I was ready to go.

"Yep! I'm ready, but I have a little request."

"What's that?" he asked.

"I want to take Tiger with us."

"No problem. He's the company's mascot. I couldn't say 'no' to the company's mascot. Has he taken up with you now Brooks?"

"I guess so," I replied.

"Great, it will be nice having him around."

"Thanks, Thunder."

"No problem." Thunder knew that this was John's dog and needed no explanation. Tiger would be good for both our morale,.

As we were flying out to our AO Thunder made the comment. "I hear you are going on R&R tomorrow."

"I am?" I replied. "I don't know anything about that, I haven't submitted a request."

"You got voted in, man."

"What does that mean?"

"Every quarter we pilots vote someone in to take an R&R and your name popped up more than anyone else's."

"For real?" I said. I was ready for a break. What was really good about it all, I didn't have to use the days I accrued going on all those sling missions. I would use those days later on.

"Yep, for real."

"How was it determined that I would be the one to go?"

"We choose by merits and attitude. You volunteering for all those sling missions and going after John - - " He mid-sentence, then continued. "Well It's just voted on amongst the pilots with the consent of the Old Man. You got the vote and that's all there was to it." Then he changed the subject and started talking about that day's mission.

I was grateful for the gesture, but I really didn't want to go on R&R under those circumstances. I didn't do anything that everyone else wasn't doing. I'm still considered to be a newbie and there may be some resentment there. I would settle this issue with the Old Man and Top when I got back from today's mission. The rest of the time flying out to the AO, Thunder and I talked about going to Slicks. He had been in Scouts going on six months now and he was also ready for the change. "You need a change of pace," he said. Then he asked me if I wanted to be his Crew Chief on a new UH-1C (Slick) that the company was going to receive.

We were also getting some new LOH for Scouts and two new Cobras. "Yes!" I replied. I was going from door gunner to my own Slick as Crew Chief. He told me I would be getting a stripe with the job and that was fine with me. More money is what came into my mind. I would be receiving the rank of SP-4 (Specialist 4th Class.) That would be equivalent to a Corporal if it was a hard stripe.

The day in the AO was uneventful and as we headed back to Quan Loi, I looked over at Tiger. He had crawled up onto my survival pack and slept. Flying was not new to Tiger and he was taking advantage of the cool air. As we made an approach to the flight line and slowed, Tiger jumped up walked over to the door and stuck his head out. He watched our approach to the flight line, which I bet he had seen at least a hundred times. He knew I would feed him, give him some water and then pull the daily on the aircraft. When the work was complete I'd hook up with Hooter and walk back to the hooch.

Tiger was becoming a good sidekick and friend for me. I was always concerned about taking him with us on missions, but he hated to be left behind. He was great on bunker guard, too. He knew what we were there for and stayed awake and alert the whole night. He alerted us a couple of times when there was movement in the wire. One time it was a tiger, and once it was actually some gooks trying to cut a hole in the wire. Yep, Tiger and I were becoming good friends. I could understand why John liked him so much. His presence alone put you in a good state of mind.

Tiger was not friends with everyone though. Tiger did not like this one WO (Warrant Officer, pilot) and every time this guy was around, Tiger would go crazy. If this officer would approach him, he would actually attack the guy. I never really understood why, until one day it was revealed to me. This asshole was taking his pistol from his hoister and pointing it at Tiger. Well, Tiger knew what a gun was for. He had been associated with weapons all his life. This asshole of an officer really thought it was funny and got some sick pleasure out of teasing him. I didn't confront the pompous ass at the time. I knew one day I would put him in his place, but didn't know how I was going to do that.

Hooter wanted to "frag the son-of-a-bitch," as he would say. I didn't think the guy deserved that, but I knew if I caught him doing it again, I would put a stop to it. That day wasn't long in coming. One day, back from a mission, I stood at my aircraft cleaning my M-60, using the floor of the aircraft as a table. Tiger zipped by and jumped into the aircraft like he was running from something. He turned and growled at something behind me. I looked around and saw that it was this WO walking up the flight line. Tiger growled louder and then he barked. I told him to quiet down and he did. But he continued growling in a low tone. Finally this officer came up and stood beside me. I didn't even look up; I continued cleaning my weapon.

He started making comments like, "You little shit. You don't like me do you?" He was enjoying himself and started laughing. I looked up and acknowledged his presence and then put my head down and continued cleaning my weapon. Then out of my side vision I could tell he was reaching for his gun. I knew what he was about to do. Tiger went crazy as this asshole reached for his pistol. When he un-holstered his weapon and pointed it in Tiger's face and said, "I ought to shoot your little ass."

I turned and grabbed the pistol with my left hand. With my right I drew back and hit him as hard as I could right on the nose. It cracked like a walnut. He let go of the pistol and hit the ground. He staggered to his feet, nose flat against his face and blood pouring from his mouth. I had broken his nose. The instant I hit this asshole, Tiger was all over him. Tiger only stood about eighteen inches high, not a big dog, but he was all muscle and teeth. He grabbed the WO by his left leg and the guy fell back to the ground. That was what Tiger wanted. This ass was now down to Tiger's height and Tiger didn't lose a second to grab him right on the chin and this asshole started screaming like a girl, trying to get this mouth full of teeth to let go of him. I waited a second or two before calling Tiger off. I figured Tiger had a little revenge coming and didn't want to deprive him. I called Tiger off right when more officers and Hooter arrived on the scene. I still had the pistol in my hand, I then turned, took the pistol and threw it over the green line (wire barricade) and then picked Tiger up and put him in the aircraft.

Thunder asked me what happened. I looked at him with this make believe scared look on my face and said, "I don't know. All I heard was someone telling me he was going to shoot my ass. I turned around and saw this gun drawn, grabbed it, and reacted as if my life was in danger. I don't know why he drew on me."

Then a voice hindered by blood screamed out, "I wasn't talking to you, I was talking to the goddamned dog!"

"How was I supposed to know that, asshole?"

He stood there bleeding, while I had this shit-eating grin on my face. I looked back at Thunder and he frowned, but his eyes smiled. He knew.

This asshole officer that Tiger and I clobbered filed an article fifteen on me and I lost a rank, not because I defended myself. Everyone that sat in on the board agreed about the right to defend myself. I got busted for calling him an asshole in front of about eighteen witnesses. I know the board knew that charge would carry a lesser penalty than striking an officer. I got the feeling they were looking out for me.

When Hooter was asked to tell what he heard, he told the truth, as he should have. But he finished his comment up with, "If it would have been me, I would have killed the son-of-a-bitch." He lost a rank as well. The WO had to go back to the rear and get his nose reconstructed and swore he would pay me back. I laughed. He got fined or some shit for drawing his weapon and was grounded for awhile, he also had to pull some behind the desk job. He was told by the Old Man to stay away from me and Tiger. If he was caught talking to me for anything other than business, he would be behind a desk for the rest of his career in the service.

After that day everyone called him Eagle Beak. Hooter and I felt good about the whole deal. We retrieved the pistol, bent the barrel and left it on his new desk for him to find. Hooter left a note on his desk, with the gun, that read. "Here is your bent gun, to go with your bent nose." What was really great, every FNG that arrived from that day forward was told this guy's name was Mr. Beak. So after a period of time a lot of the new guys were honestly calling him Warrant Officer Beak. It was priceless. Eventually he felt so humiliated that he put in for a transfer to the 273rd and the Old Man didn't hesitate to approve it. They took my rank and pulled the R&R I was awarded so I really didn't give anything up but one stripe. In the eyes of the company, mostly the enlisted men, Hooter, Tiger and I were heroes. I never had to confront the Old Man and Top about not wanting that R&R anyway. They took from me what I didn't want, so it all worked out in the end.

I was asked several times, if I had it to do again if I would do it the same way. My answer was always the same. "HELL YES!" It got a laugh or a smile from everyone that heard the story. It gave us all back the sense of humor that we all had lost since John's death.

Hooter and I got back our rank in no time. This was only one of many incidences that were humorous to us all. We were always looked for ways to make us laugh. Laughing was a great asset. Without it, we all would have gone insane. When everything around us seemed lost, we always had laughter in our back pockets.

Chapter 13
Monsoon Brings Trouble

One thing we hated more than the gooks was the monsoon rain. The rain would fall so heavy at times you couldn't see twenty yards in front of you. The ground around Quan Loi was a red soil. In the dry season the red soil would turn to a red-like flour. You stepped in it and it floated upward. It got into our skin and everything you owned. It was a part of our everyday life.

When the monsoons came, it was just the opposite. The ground turned to clay. It stuck to the bottom of your boots and before long you would be walking six inches taller than you were and carrying around an extra ten pounds of mud on your feet. It could rain for ten minutes and clear up. Then here it would come again and maybe it would rain for an hour or two then clear up again. Sometimes it would rain all day and night.

Charlie (Viet Cong) took advantage of the monsoons every chance he could. It was a good cover and he knew we could not see over twenty to thirty yards in front of us. This is the time he liked making his ground attacks. Charlie had tactics that worked very well for him. Whenever Charlie was out in force and we would attack him, he would retreat. When we stopped to set up a fire base for the night he would attack, when we fell back he would follow. For the Grunts in the jungle, this tactic was hard to deal with. Our gunships aided in this type of operation and this is when we got a lot of our kills. Whenever they engaged the infantry in force, we had a turkey shoot. Because we were so effective with our gunships Charlie hated us. We interfered with their operations and that would always piss them off. So the NVA (Northern Vietnamese Army) put a bounty on the 1/9th Cav. (A, B, OR C troop) we didn't at the time know this until we caught some prisoners during one of these ground attacks.

I remember one night we had flown all day and were so tired. We had put in eighteen hours and all we wanted was sleep. They had been a lot of movement in the area and we were making a lot of contact with mostly VC (Viet Cong.) No one could remember when they'd had so much contact with the enemy. We were shooting so much ammo a day that we carried two or three extra barrels with us because we would burn through them so quickly. By the time we got back to base it would almost be dark. When we pulled our dailies on the aircraft it was dark for sure. We didn't have time to clean our M-60s so we would carry them back to our hooch's to clean them and make repairs if needed for the next day's mission.

One night, during monsoon, the rain was coming down so hard that it was like a drug putting you to sleep. If you have ever heard rain on a tin roof you know what I mean. As the rain pounded the tin on our hooch its hypnotic effect was so strong all we wanted was sleep. We were all glad we weren't pulling bunker guard that night and life in that moment was good. We drank a little beer and ate some sea rations. I started talking about how a good chili would taste on a cold or rainy night that.

Hooter told me to shut the hell up, and that he hadn't had a good meal in so long that it almost hurt to think about a descent meal of any kind. We laughed and then gave it up for a goodnight's sleep. No one was in the mood for reminiscing about things that was out of our power to get a hold of, like real food, so we all drifted off into Ever Never Land.

About midnight Popp ran into our hooch and yelled out, "Ground attack!"

Hooter and I jumped out of bed put on some pants, no shirts, grabbed our 60s and wrapped a bunch of ammo around our waist and chest, with about a 200 round belt loaded into our 60s.

Popp said we had to be careful because we had gooks inside the wire. Oh shit, I thought to myself. Popp said that they had snuck into a hooch and had cut the guys' throats. They were detected coming out of the tent and were shot. It started a panic among some of the troops and they were shooting at anything that moved. In fact, they had shot some of our own men. I told Hooter, "Let's go grab some sand bags and set up a POD (Perimeter of Defense) between us and the green line."

Hooter mentioned that the VC had to have taken out a bunker or two to get this far inside our perimeter. We went out and set up some cover about fifty yards straight behind our hooch. Our hooch was about one hundred and fifty yards from the bunkers on the green line. Luckily, we both had M-60s. We set up a defense in both directions, in front and behind. Behind us, just in case some of the enemy had gotten into the compound and had the advantage of attacking us from the rear. Hooter was right; they had knocked out at least one bunker. We could tell because there was no return of fire coming from a bunker that was located directly in front of us. Either they were dead or had abandoned their position.

We heard enemy fire between us and the green line but could not see any tracers. This was a smart move on Charlie's part. By not using tracers he was not giving up his location. Hooter and I took turns making sure no one was approaching from our rear. Other gunners came out of their hooch's and approached us from the rear. At first, we thought they might be Charlie and we challenged them. After each group was identified we set up a horizontal line of defense pairing up two gunners each and then we spaced ourselves about twenty yards apart. That would give us two hundred yards of a defensive line.

We felt like all the gooks that had gotten into the area were killed and therefore didn't pay much attention to our rear anymore. Some of the guys that joined Hooter and me were smart enough to bring a bunch of hand flares. I counted over twenty gunners with their M-60s. We had the fire power. Hooter made a comment that the gooks screwed up when they chose to make their ground attack in the area of the gunners' hooch's.

There were nothing but gunners here and if the gooks approached our location they would be screwed. Everyone that was in position was experienced enough to know not to fire unless we knew it was Charlie, or of course we were being attacked. We were all shooting aviation ammo, which meant full tracers. This would give away our positions if any of us fired unnecessarily. And we were concerned about the guys down on the green line, on the bunkers. If we started firing they would receive our friendly fire. The bunkers weren't fortified from the back and it left them vulnerable to our line of fire.

We all agreed that if any of us fired, we all would lay down crazing fire in that direction. This way one location couldn't be singled out. Schultz showed up with a radio and we contacted the bunkers and told them we were directly behind them and to fortify their backs with sand bags in case we had to open up. We were going to keep our fire about fourteen inches off the ground, for at least the first two minutes. Then we would go to only one M-60 shooting in each location and use the others for backup only, if needed. That would give us around twenty M-60s putting out the initial crazing fire and ten firing at all times and ten in reserve after the first two minutes. I thought, *if Charlie breaks through this POD, he would have to have a lot of support*. If that was the case, tomorrow there would be a lot of casualties on both sides. The odds were in our favor, but you really never know for sure until the fighting is over.

We noticed that there was no firing, or any activity coming from the bunkers directly in front of us, so we knew there had to be gooks in between us and the green line. It would really be up to us to fill in this gap. Operations confirmed our suspicions: two bunkers had been knocked out. They informed us we were on our own, to stay put and hold the line. We passed it down. All the bunkers along the two hundred yards of defense we set up weren't knocked out and they let us know it immediately after we got through talking to operations. They knew who we were and knew that we all probably had 60s. They were as concerned as we were about being in our line of fire. We reminded them to reinforce their bunkers from the rear.

Most of the guys pulling bunker guard that night were from some artillery outfit, and had never got any face to face time with Charlie. They weren't looking forward to it. Their combat experience mostly consisted of pulling a string on a canon. We wanted to give them support but we had to stay put. We didn't want to go crawling around at night not knowing Charlie's numbers and strength.

Popp and his gunner were in a poison next to Hooter and me. He had detected some movement in front of his location. One of the guys had a starlight scope and yelled out that it was the cooks from the mess hall. I made out their location, about fifty yards in front of us. We had no way to tell them they were in the line of fire, so one of us was going to have to go down and urge them to get the hell out of there. Popp said he would do it since their location was directly in front of him. He went down and let them know what was about to happen, then came back to his cover and gave us the thumbs up. *Good,* I thought, but no sooner did that thought leave my head when those two cooks started firing off to their right.

We all yelled out, "Easy!" "Wait to you see something!" and everyone started laughing. They were probably scared shitless and fired at the first sound they heard.

"SCREW, you guys! We saw movement."

"Sure, sure they did," Hooter muttered.

A little later, the cooks came and took up a position between Popp & Scott, Hooter and myself. "Gook's man, "We saw gooks!"

Hooter and I looked at each other and smiled.

Then a guy named Paul and his gunner Bruce (A couple of Slick gunners) started firing. We all opened up as we had discussed. There were so many tracer rounds flying that you didn't need to pop a flare. It looked like daylight. There were gooks everywhere. It looked like all of them were Viet Cong and no NVA. Then rounds started hitting all around us. We kept our heads down and continued firing. After a couple of minutes, half of us let up and the other half kept firing, as we had planned. We kept this up for about half an hour.

The M-60s that continued firing were now getting so heated they jammed because of the warped barrels on the guns. At that time all of us that were holding back in reserve started firing. Some of the guys went back to their hooch's to get all the new, extra barrels they could muster. Then the gooks targeted our location with mortars. The first ones that hit were way off. Then they started walking them toward us. When the mortars got close we all stopped firing and got as low to the ground as we could. The enemy could not advance if mortars were going off. They wouldn't take the chance of hitting their own.

We hunkered down and held our position. The mortars came in so heavy that one of the gunners, Murray, got up and started running. He was going to get hit with shrapnel if he didn't get his ass down. We all yelled out for him to get down. He dove for a big hole and disappeared and we thought he would probably be ok. Then he starting yelling, Hooter and I looked back and he was trying to get out of the hole. *What the hell*, I thought. Hooter laughed and told me that Murray landed in a hole where they dump all the burnt shit from the shitters. It was hard to fire our weapons and laugh at the same time. Every time Murray would try to get out of the hole a mortar would hit close by and he would slide back into the hole. Between mortars you could hear him throwing-up. This went on for at least five minutes, until he finally got out of that hole.

You could smell him from fifty yards. When the mortars had let up we knew the attack would continue.

We turned to fire again but could see nothing. The gooks were retreating to what we called the kill zone, which was nothing more than open ground between us and the bunkers. The bunkers that had been knocked out were again occupied with American personnel. We had the enemy trapped between us and the bunkers and we did not let up.

We heard choppers running up and thought it might be our aircraft wanting us to go and load up. But it was Cobras taxiing down to the end of the flight line. One would position itself, fire all its rockets while still on the ground, move out of the way and go load up again while another Cobra would take its place. At the same time they fired their rockets they cut loose with the twin mini guns. It was an impressive display of firepower.

We kept firing until dawn. At first light we stopped and waited for awhile. Eventually we noticed hands rising up in the air. Gooks yelled, "Tôi đầu hàng, Tôi đầu hàng!" which means 'I surrender.'

We all got up and started toward them. There was a grunt unit that had moved over to where we were firing and they stood around a dead gook's body. Hooter and I and the two cooks went up to see what the big deal was. This dead gook had a cord tied to his arm that went under his body. This know-it-all sergeant told all of us to stay back. Hooter and I laughed and told him dead gooks aren't the ones you worry about.

"See that cord tied to his arm and running under his body?" he asked.

"Yes," I replied, "I see it."

"That is a booby trap."

"Bullshit," I said. "You think these guys had time to booby trap themselves?" I reached down to turn the body over and the sergeant grabbed my arm. Hooter stuck his 60 in the sergeant's face and told him not to put a hand on me. I looked back at Hooter and winked. I was reminded about that first day that gunner hit my arm and told me to back off. The sergeant let go of my arm. As I reached down to turn the body over, all the grunts from this other unit scattered and took cover. I turned the body over and there was this nice little automatic pistol tied to the end of a lanyard cord.

I asked Hooter for his knife, then cut the cord and held up the gun for that sergeant to see. He came over and told me that his men killed this gook and that pistol belonged to them. I told him bullshit for the second time. I pointed to the two cooks that had accompanied us. "You guys see these cooks? *They* killed this gook!" The body was directly in front of where the cooks first fired. We were all made fun of them and they ended up getting the first kill.

I threw my 60 to one of the two cooks, reached down and cut off the gook's right ear and gave it to the other. I took off the dead gook's sandals, trenching knife, pistol belt, and a red star Communist buckle and gave it to the cooks as well. I turned to the sergeant. "You can have the rest. After all, you said the body was your men's."

He gave me a dirty look and muttered something that I couldn't get him to repeat. Then Hooter, and I, and the two cooks walked off toward the flight line. On the way, we saw a lot more of the enemy surrendering. One gook with his hand blown off couldn't have been more than twelve years old. I glanced around. They all were very young. The oldest-looking was the one I just took the pistol from. There were a few older ones, but not many. Those were probably the squad leaders. They all had the red star buckles. I was told later they were field-commissioned officers. Yeah right. All they were to the NVA were suckers. The NVA needed some dopes to test our strength. They gave these kids some AK rifles and told them they had the best weapon in the world. Gave them some drugs and sent them in to get slaughtered.

The body count in the wire was over three hundred. I hadn't been up against the NVA in battle yet, but after this skirmish it was a matter of time. To be honest, I didn't give it a whole lot of thought. They were all gooks to me and at this time I felt like they were a bunch of cowards, letting someone else do their fighting for them. I found out later they weren't cowards and fighting was no stranger to them.

When we got back to the flight line, everyone was starting to show up. There were several dead gooks on the flight line. They were trying to destroy our ships and got caught. But so far we hadn't lost even one aircraft. The Old Man told us to get our ships ready. We were going to get these bastards while they were on the run and still in our backyard. He called us all together for a briefing and commenced to tell us how the gooks got past our bunkers and exactly what their objectives were.

The monsoon rain washed out huge trenches under the wire. They followed the trenches under the wire and knocked out a couple of bunkers quietly. The ones on top were supposed to be on watch while the ones on the bottom were sleeping. We would do this off and on at four hour intervals all night long. One of the guards on top fell asleep. They all ended up with their throats cut for their mistake. The other bunker got knocked out after the battle started and the gooks were then detected in our perimeter. They intended to try and kill as many of us as they could with a knife as not to alarm anyone.

We were told by a prisoner that they got a bounty of 500 pea (five American dollars or so, if I remember right) for every corner of poncho liner they brought back. Besides a GI's weapon, his poncho liner is the most valued item he owns. In order to get the piece of the liner that has the part number on it, the enemy soldier would have to kill the GI, because you can bet he was sleeping on it. Some of our prisoners had up to three of them tied to their belt. The count was nine that were killed that way. None of our guys were killed during the whole battle. We had about thirty wounded and that was it.

This time the canon cockers had all the causalities. Some other outfit across the post lost some men, but we didn't know any of them. We were informed later that day that they died protecting our aircraft. We were their main target because of our gunships, yet none of us were killed. That seemed unreal to us.

The Old Man wanted us ready in thirty minutes. None of us had gotten any sleep and we were all dead tired. We went back to the hooch to get our gear and grab a shower if there was any water left. When we got back to our hooch, Murray sat in a lawn chair right in the middle of it. He smelled like a shit pile.

"Take a shower asshole, you stink!" Hooter yelled.

"I can't, you assholes. The gooks hit the water point and showers with one of those mortars and there is not any water. And since you and Brooks think it is so funny, let's see you move me."

We grabbed our gear and scooted out the door. The chair later got tossed. We weren't about to even try and put a hand on him. Hooter and I reached the flight line in time to see a Slick and three Cobras take off. We knew we were going to be teamed up with the Cobras, so we figured we better hurry our asses up. When we got to our aircraft, Thunder was ready to go. Hooter's pilot, Mr. Knight, hadn't showed up yet.

"Well, I'll see you out in the AO, Hooter," I said.

"We'll be there," he replied. We fired up the aircraft and off we went.

Thunder did a PTO (Power Take Off.) Straight up and we were gone. Suddenly one of the Cobras blew up in mid-air. We thought it got hit with an RPG and went straight to the scene. I fired all around the area where the RPG could have come from but there was nothing. No one shot back at us. A Slick came over and joined in and punched off rockets as the two gunners strafed the area. We kept it up for at least twenty minutes.

Then we got an emergency radio call to return to base. We were in sight of the flight line and began our approach. They told us to park all the aircraft at the end of the flight line, shut it down and get away from it fast. There might be a bomb onboard. Thunder auto-rotated to the end of the flight line, told me to run as soon as we hit the ground. I did and as I turned around Thunder chopped the throttle, jumped out and ran.

We waited around for awhile and another aircraft located on the other end of the flight line exploded. No doubt about it, there would be no flying today. Not until we found all the bombs rigged to our aircraft. All we could do was stand around and watch to see if our aircraft would be the next to blow up. Intelligence questioned the prisoners and eventually found out there were no other bombs. What the gooks had done was pull the pin on an American grenade then put a rubber band around the lever to keep the fuse from striking. Then they opened up the fuel cap on the side of the aircraft and dropped it in. After awhile the fuel ate through the rubber band and then there was no more aircraft. The grenade would go off inside the fuel tank simple, but very effective.

So far we had lost four aircraft. Still, all we could do was wait and see if anymore aircraft exploded. The gooks had grounded every aircraft by using this simple method of booby trapping. They didn't have to put grenades in every gunship. They knew that if a few of them blew up it would ground us and they could continue their operation without any opposition. Smart, they were very smart. It took us two days of pulling the fuel cells to check for more grenades, but none were ever found. I did not know the pilot or the front seat gunner of the Cobra that blew up in mid-air, but I was told they were good men and would be highly missed by everyone that knew them. Their loss, the loss of any gunner and pilot, was felt by all. Not only our strength and fire power were cut, but losing our fellow flight personnel hit close to everyone that flew on a day to day basis. We all realized that it could have been us. Not only does it play on your mind, but it may hinder your performance. I thought about the incident and it bothered me a little, but I was grateful I didn't know them. Thunder, on the other hand, was close to the pilot and it affected him for some time, more than he let on.

Thunder was really a hard man to get to know. He was a great guy and had a way of making you feel important no matter what your job was. He liked the guys in maintenance and always made the comment to me that if you were tight with maintenance, you could bet your aircraft would always be taken care of when it was in their hands. "You, Brooks, fly on the aircraft, you are forced to do a good job because you are looking after yourself. But maintenance can screw your world if they have a hard on for you." He did have a point.

I knew Thunder liked a lot of guys in maintenance. He hung out with the maintenance officer and a lot of the mechanics. Probably for the same reason Hooter and I did. The gunner in the front seat of the Cobra that went down was in maintenance. The regular gunner got hit with a little shrapnel during the ground attack and was being attended to. A mechanic from maintenance filled in for him.

The enemy made it back to the Cambodian border without any pursuit from us. But they had been danced with and they knew it. In all, the VC lost over three hundred men and American casualties for Quan Loi amounted to about thirty killed and over a hundred wounded. In all, this was the biggest battle I ever witnessed. But it was not the worst. The worst to me were those battles fought head-hunting. Making an attack on a well-fortified position, like they tried to do in this attack, is shared by all. It seemed to me to be no big deal. Compared to head-hunting it was nothing. When you make contact in the field while head hunting, it's them against you and the fear and excitement is beyond any explanation. The excitement becomes an addiction and soon overwhelms the fear. When you mix the excitement with the hate, fear ends up taking the backseat and from that point on you just don't give a shit.

I was getting to the point where I really thought I would not make it back to the world. I decided that my days were numbered and there wasn't a whole lot I could do about it. I was caught up in the addiction and I lived for the kill.

Chapter 14
Next Stop: Slicks

In a couple of weeks, Thunder, Tiger and I would be going to Slicks. The company was going to send me to an L-13 Turbine Engine School for a couple of weeks. The school was located in the rear at a place called Vaung Tau. It was a place solders would go for R&R if they didn't want to go to Bangkok, Thailand, or some other place. Thunder told me that they were going to send me there to kind of gain back that R & R they took from me on that Article 15 I was hit with. In the mean time, I could go to the L-13 Engine course and it wouldn't be considered R&R. Sounded good to me, by this time I needed a break. Hooter said he wished he was going with me, but he had already had R&R and he was saving the rest of his leave to meet his wife in Hawaii in a couple of months.

He told me while I was gone he would look after Tiger. Tiger had a way of looking out for himself. But I felt relieved that Hooter would keep an extra eye out for him. I worried about the little shit. He was too independent and I thought that might get him in trouble someday. Murray would be taking over my ship while I was gone. I never let him forget about that night he jumped in the shit pit. He knew it was no use to fight it and laughed about the incident along with the rest of us. But he picked up the nick name Stinky and if you didn't want your chops busted you had better not call him that to his face. I never did. I could tell the nick name didn't sit well with him. Murray was a good mechanic and a good gunner. He was getting short and would be going home in about four months. He wasn't a two digit midget yet, but he was close. I still had so much time left I hated to think about it.

Thunder came down to the flight line the day I headed out for training. Before I jumped on the Slick, he came up and shook my hand. He had a great big smile on his face. First time he smiled so big that I could see his teeth through that big mustache. He shook my hand hard and put his arm around me. "Have fun Brooks, you earned it," he said as he put fifty dollars in my hand. "I know getting busted cost you, here's a little extra to help you out."

I was speechless and stood there looking at him.

"Well, get aboard, dummy, you don't want to miss this flight," he said. We both laughed and shook hands before I turned and boarded the aircraft.

As we lifted off, I saw Hooter holding Tiger and giving me the peace sign. Tiger just stared at me. I hoped he knew I was coming back and wouldn't take up with someone else.

It felt weird flying and not having my 60 in my hands. I looked up and there were my two old buddies again. They were the same gunners that had brought me to Quan Loi. I laughed to myself, they weren't as intimidating as before, and in fact I looked up and smiled at them. I had a headset on and we could talk back and forth. I didn't even recall their names. I am horrible with names, but good with faces. I figured I better remember their names soon, since I was about to become a part of

Slicks. I stuck out my hand and introduced myself to the one that popped me in the arm with his M-60.

He stuck out his hand and told me he knew who I was. "You have come a long way, newbie," he said. He then introduced himself as Todd and his gunner was Jack.

I didn't feel like a newbie and I really didn't have much to say to them. They were short timers and I let them ramble on. They were pretty proud of themselves and both had an ego that made you feel uneasy. They liked to intimidate people and make you feel that you could never stand up to their expectations. Their arrogance and their actions reminded me of that bully in high school. The funny part was, no one knew what was expected of them. They were in their own little world. They were killers, though and they wanted to let you know they were. I got tired of listening to their bullshit and took off my headset and hung it on a hook. Closed my eyes and acted like I was trying to get some sleep. It pissed them off, I could tell. But who gave a shit about what those two thought.

I never forgot what they did to that prisoner. It was not the act of killing the prisoner I was upset about, since I had experienced how cruel the VC could be to their captives. But I would always hold it against them for the way they tried to impress my friend and me, show us what big men they were. We were scared that day, they knew it and the whole thing was nothing more than some sick fun and entertainment for them.

Our unit was allowed to carry loaded weapons, even in the rear areas, so I brought along my 45 ACP pistol. I felt better carrying it. I had gotten to the point I had to have a weapon on me in order for me to even sleep at night. But when I got back to the rear at Vaung

Tau I felt stupid carrying it. This place was like back in the world. It had vintage American cars and the whole bit. Except for all the 'slants' & the smell of the market places, it was close to being back in civilization again.

The school would not start until Monday and this was Friday evening. I had two days to check in and figured I would stay off base and get a room downtown. I got a room in an old hotel built around the era of when the French occupied this country. It was old but nice and the rooms were clean. No air conditioning, of course, but a nice ceiling fan that I turned up all the way. I lay down on the bed and closed my eyes but could not sleep. It was too quiet. There was no outgoing fire, no helicopters flying around, no tracks (tanks) running around and the size of this room was unreal.

I had been in country almost four months and I had already adapted to another way of life. I guess what really bothered me is that I preferred my small hooch over this big room. As soon as I walked in I was analyzed my options. The bed is too close to the window. The window can't be covered with my back to it. The walls are too thin. I'm on the second floor. (*Good*, I thought) No other exit. The halls are narrow. *Stop!* I told myself. *This is stupid. I'm in the rear for heaven's sake.*

I glanced out my window and stepped out onto the balcony. I looked down on the street, and if I thought real hard about it, except for the smell, I could imagine I was back in the real world. I lay back down and tried to relax. I couldn't. Relaxing was something I had forgotten how to do. *Some dope would be nice,* I thought. On the streets was probably the only place I was going to find marijuana, so up I jumped, grabbed my pistol and out the door I went.

I had no idea where to go and really didn't care. I wandered the streets. I got the biggest kick out of all the hookers trying to proposition me. It had been a long time since I had been in the company of a woman. I had mixed feelings about it all. I couldn't see having these women at night and maybe having to kill them during the day. I really wasn't in the mood to deal with it all. So I smiled and kept walking.

Finally I saw a GI. I walked up to him and asked where I could buy some dope.

"What kind?" he asked.

"Some weed," I replied.

"Oh, I would say just about on every corner." He pointed to an old woman on the corner of the street. "How much do you pay for it in the field?"

"A dollar a pound."

"What," he said, "I can't believe it, one dollar?"

"We buy it from the mountain people, we call them Mountain Yards."

"They're darker skinned, aren't they?" he asked.

I laughed and asked him how he knew I was from the field. He told me my skin gave me away. My skin had a red tint to it from the red, flour-like dirt that I had been living in for four months.

"And, of course, your gun. No one but the Cav carries their weapons here, except MPs. I knew you weren't an MP."

"How much is the dope here in Vaung Tau?" I asked.

"A small bag will cost you three to five dollars, American." He walked over with me to the old lady and bought a bag for five dollars. He handed me the bag and I started to hand him the five dollars. He told me no and that it was on him. "But I would like to smoke some of it right now, how about you?"

"Sure," I replied, then we headed to a bar that he knew very well where we could get down. When, we arrived at this bar the mama-san that ran the joint came up to my new friend and gave him a kiss on the cheek. Evidently she knew him well. She gave me a hateful look, and then proceeded to take us to the back of the bar that led outside into this nice little garden patio area. We sat down at a table and in a little while she brought us some hot tea and some beers that were iced down in this old ammo can. I reached for the beer, looked at the label and it said Tiger Beer. As long as it wasn't Black Label or Blue Ribbon, it was OK with me. She brought us some rolling papers and a pipe. We sat there and smoked till we were high enough to start talking again. All of this was strange to me, but nice. I liked the atmosphere and it put me at ease at once.

"Your name," I said, "what is your name?"

"Ray," he replied.

I told him mine and we sat there and smoked until we both became at ease with each other.

"Brooks, I hope you don't mind if I ask you something."

Oh no he's gay, I thought. *No one is this friendly to a stranger in this country. Even mama-san gave me that hateful look.* "Go ahead," I replied.

"I'm stationed here in Vaung Tau. I have been here for six months. How is it out in the bush? Is it as bad as everyone says it is?" He hit me with more questions than I could answer.

"Why you want to know about the bush? You got it made here."

"I'm thinking of volunteering for combat," he commented, as if he was an excited pup looking for a treat or something.

"What the hell for?" I answered back. This guy was nuts and he was screwing up my high by even bringing the subject up.

"Because I feel like I'm not really serving my country so far away from the fight."

"To hell with the fight, trust me dude, you don't want to go and fight. Hell, I'll trade with you. You can take my place. You got it made here Ray. You don't want any part of the fight out there. It will warp your mind and it will callous your heart. It is a cruel place where men die every day. They do things to each other that are nothing less than medieval. Trust me, you don't want to go to the bush and I don't want to talk about it."

He dropped his head like he was disappointed or something. He kind of reminded me of John that morning down on the flight line. The more I talked to John about not flying Scouts the more he wanted to do just that. What is it with people? I never wanted combat and got it. People want combat and never get it. My high was gone I was as sober as could be.

I turned to Ray. "I have a short time here before I am thrown back into the heat of things. I don't want to talk war. You have this kind of an atmosphere every weekend. You got your women, you got your beach, you got your clubs, you got your women and you got your women and you want to give all this up for combat? You, my man, are screwed up. I don't know one of my friends that wouldn't give their right nut to be here for one year and go home a sane happy veteran. Ray, come on and give me a break."

"You're right Brooks," he said, "I know you're right. I just feel guilty that's all."

"Guilty? I would feel lucky, if I were you."

"You're right, Brooks. Let me show you the town. We will get a couple of girls and go to the beach, then go to the NCO club and eat a good meal, hit the bars and do whatever you want. Let me be your guide, I'll be the best goddamned guide you will have ever known."

"Now you're talking, my friend, now you're talking. Let's get our heads right and book." We sat back down and smoked some more dope and drank some beer and after a little while we headed out to have a little fun.

"First, Brooks, we got to get that dirt out of your skin."

"Ray, it won't come out."

"Oh, yes it will," he said.

We went to a bath house. First time I had ever been in such a place. We bathed in large tubs with soap and water, then you get out and sat in the sauna, then some women came in and had us lay ourselves on a bench. They bathed us from a bucket of hot water with soap again. Then when they decided we were clean they rinsed us down with clean water, and then we were ready for the bath house. We got down in this huge community tub. Women came over and massaged our bodies all over and stretched our muscles till they almost hurt. Then we were put on a table and massaged with oil until I almost fell asleep. I felt so good that I thought I had died and went to heaven. Then a young girl that was massaging me kept rubbing my chest. She would comb the hair on my chest with her fingers over and over. She had finished with the massage, but she didn't disturb me and kept stroking my chest. I heard Ray tell me she was fascinated with the hair on my chest. I wanted to lay there and let her keep grooming me. I opened my eyes and she smiled in a way that almost brought tears to my eyes.

I missed Roni. I laid there a while longer thinking of home and wondering if I would ever see Roni again. It had been forever since I had a woman touch me. I pretended it was Roni that touched me and drifted off into another world. A world where there was not a war and I home. A type of peace came over me and in my mind I was home. Then out of nowhere tears flowed from under my eye lids and I felt the young girl brush them away. I opened my eyes and the girl no longer smiled at me. Her smile turned to sadness and confusion. She looked over at Ray, who shook his head from side to side. She then put her hand on my neck said something to me in Vietnamese, turned and walked away.

After a while, Ray asked me if I was ready for the beach. I came out of my daze and answered him with a big 'yes.' I got dressed and reached for my billfold to pay, Ray told me to put it away. He would take care of the bill. "Come on Ray, you have done enough."

"You're my quest, Brooks. Trust me, it is not expensive at all. It only cost us three dollars apiece and that is high. It will cost you about a buck fifty anywhere else you go. But the girls are ugly, here they are beautiful."

He was right, they were beautiful. It was nice to have a woman touch my body again. I had really forgotten that feeling you get when a woman touches you. Humble in some ways and vulnerable in others. But most of all, it felt good for once to feel like you are alive again.

Ray had a steady girlfriend that was Vietnamese. He introduced her to me as Sandy. She was a hooker at one time and took on an American name. He told me he turned her into an 'honest woman,' as he put it and then he laughed. Ray asked me if I wanted a woman to be with or just someone to take along. I told him I would love to be with a woman, but I would pass on the offer at this time.

His girlfriend had a sister that was fifteen years old and she would be going with us to the beach. She was a pretty girl, thin and well-mannered. I was impressed with the way she handled herself in a traditional Vietnamese fashion. She would hold her head down and only look at me when I spoke to her. Her English was almost nonexistent. I was told to call her Lee, mainly because I could not say her Vietnamese name. Her older sister, being a prostitute at one time, spoke very good English. It went along with the trade. We all stepped out into the street and we caught a ride on a small bus to the beach. I hadn't been in the ocean since I was a freshman in high school. It was beautiful. We swam and lay out in the warm sun. As the warmth hit my skin, I faded in and out of sleep.

The NCO club was right on the beach; so we decided to get something to eat. I hadn't had a good meal since I had been in country. The girls were excited about going to the club. If you weren't in any of the armed forces you couldn't get in. Of course the soldiers could bring any of their so-called dates. Sandy had been with Ray on several occasions and it seemed she had told her sister all about it. They were both excited. I just wanted some good food for a change. I had dropped a lot of weight. I came over weighing 160 pounds and I was now down to around 145 pounds.

We asked to be seated out on the patio, and the hostess accommodated our wishes and seated us at a table that faced the beach. There was air conditioning in the club, but the air coming off the beach felt cool and the ocean smelled so fresh and clean. A waiter came out and took our order for drinks. I ordered Johnny Walker Black the girls had Cokes and Ray had a beer. The sun was starting to set and I couldn't wait to see how it looked on the water. Everyone probably thought I was acting like a kid. Ray told me the steaks were horrible but the seafood was great. Any good food would be ok with me. I ordered shrimp and shark steak. The sun was just above the water; I turned my chair so I could watch it fall behind the oceans horizon. I wanted to take it all in, I didn't know if I would ever have such a moment offered to me again. It is funny, when you live with death at your door how much you enjoy the little things. We all sat there with no one really talking. As I drank down my Johnny Walker Black, I thought of West. West got me to drinking Scotch and every time I drink it, I think of him. Then my thoughts would go to John. It was bringing me down so I switched my mind to the present.

There were some Aussie soldiers sitting at a table right across from ours. They kept making some comment and directing it toward us. I know I was hearing the word Yank a lot and knew by the tone in their voices they were trying to be smart. Aussies, when they have been drinking, are always loud. I think they lose their hearing when alcohol touches their lips. Ray noticed it bothered me and told me to ignore them. "What is their problem?" I asked.

Ray told me they like to come down and pick fights. "They are a bunch of assholes and don't deserve the attention they want."

I looked around and there were several American solders sitting around and ignoring these assholes. These are not the solders I know. Back in Quan

Loi they would love a situation like this. They defiantly wouldn't take this bull crap. Finally, one of them made a comment that used to cross my mind. He stood up and approached our table. "How can you yanks have anything to do with these women when your mates are in the bush dying? How can you even take these women when you know they would turn you over to the Communists, if they could make some money off of it?"

I looked up at him. "What the hell do you know about dying?" I stood. "What the hell do you know about killing, sitting back here in the rear with *your* buddies, putting me down while me and *my* buddies are out their keeping the gooks off your ass? You don't know me. You don't know what I've done or what I have experienced. But you will know what I am fixing to do if you don't get the hell out of my face and leave me and my friends alone."

I was wired. Even before I joined the military I was a pretty good fighter. I have always been good at it and now that I have lived and been in combat, fighting an asshole like this one seemed like nothing but child's play. But this was different, way different. This was not just a fight coming on. The muscles in my arm and back tightened. But I wasn't thinking about fighting, my thoughts were more on the line of killing this S.O.B. . He started to say something and I hit him as hard as I could. I hit him with a right upper cut that lifted him off the ground. He landed flat on his back and his head hit the floor so hard you couldn't help but hear it no matter where you were setting in the club. I'd snapped.

I was told that I grabbed a knife from the table, intent on burying it in this man's chest. Next thing I remember is a lot of people had a hold of me repeating, "Easy mate, easy." It was the Aussies along with some

American soldiers. Ray told them to ease up, I'd be fine.
I couldn't account for that last minute or so, and it kind
of freaked me out.

"You okay, mate?" one of the Aussies asked me.

"Yeah, I'm fine."

Several Aussies picked their friend up off the
ground and put him in a chair. I guess they could tell by
the look on my face that I felt disoriented. I really had a
hard time putting it all together for a minute or two. Then
I came out of it and was kind of embarrassed about the
whole deal. To this day I don't remember grabbing that
knife. But I was glad I left my 45 back at Ray's place. I
know I would have shot this soldier if I would have had
it. In one way, it bothered me. I knew I had to get my
temper under control. I was not the same person I was
before. I wasn't thinking about fighting this man, I was
thinking about killing him. I had been in a lot of fights in
my life, but never had killing ever been a part of the
equation or even entered my mind.

The girls were scared beyond concealment and
the mood had indeed changed. The Aussies wanted to
buy me a drink and talk, but I was still pumped and not
in the mood. I heard one of the Aussies say to the guy I
knocked out, "Messed with the wrong Yank, this time
mate."

My nemesis came over and shook my hand,
apologized and offered to buy me a drink. We sat down
at the bar and I ordered another scotch. I felt like I better
drink with this man, after all I might have taken his life.
He didn't know I was going to knife him, as he was
knocked cold. We all sat at the bar and talked about what
happened. When the Aussie found out I was going to put
a knife in him he got a little more nervous, and drank
more in five minutes than I could drink in an hour.

Aussies could indeed put down the booze. The MPs showed up but everyone said it was some other guys that just left the NCO club. One of the MPs asked the manager of the club was that true and he told them yes and they left. We parted company somewhat friends. Ray, me and the girls went to another place on the beach that was owned by another mama-san, smoked a little dope and the rest of night was about getting back to a good state of mind. Ray kept saying over and over, "You almost killed that guy; you should have seen his face when you hit him." And stuff like that.

The next morning was Saturday and I had two more days before I had to report for the engine course. I didn't know if I could take another day like the day before. I drank a little too much and my head didn't feel all that great. I spent the night at Ray's place. I got up, poured some water and went out to the patio and let the morning overtake me. I laid down in a hammock and fell back asleep. We all hung out together for the next couple of days and then it was time for me to report for school. I would be done with my classes every day around 14:00 hours. Ray said I could just hang out with him and Sandy. He told me that Lee was a little scared of me and wasn't sure if she wanted to be around me. She told her sister that I was dinky dowel (crazy) and I could not blame her at all.

A couple of weeks passed so fast. I wanted to stay, but at the same time I wanted to go back to Quan Loi. I missed my friends and my daily routine. Ray never let me pay for a thing so I left him a hundred dollars on my bed at his house. He went with me down to the flight line so I could catch one of our choppers. They were dropping off some grunts that were taking R&R and they would be picking me up for the return trip. When my chopper arrived I pointed it out to Ray. He looked at and made the comment that you could always tell a real gunship. I knew what he meant, they were different. I saw some guys get off and I started toward the aircraft.

I turned around and thanked Ray. "You will never realize what you have done for me, Ray. Thanks for being a friend and please stay away from the front."

"Take care of yourself, Brooks. See you back in the world."

I knew I would probably never see him again. I turned back around and walked toward the gunship. When I got close enough I could see that it was a couple of guys I knew from Slicks. One gunner was Paul and the other was Scott, he was flying R/H seat Crew Chief. I got on board and they wasted no time getting airborne. They both shook my hand and then patted me on the shoulder. I put on the headset so I could talk to them. I was glad to see it wasn't those two assholes that brought me here. Paul asked me if I had a good time on R&R. I answered him yes and he smiled at me. "How goes it back at Quan Loi."

They paused for a minute then answered, "Okay."

I could tell something was wrong because Scott didn't have much to say. You usually couldn't get him to shut up. I didn't want to know. If there was something going on I would just wait and find out what it was about when we got back to Quan Loi. The flight back was quiet. No one said a word except for the pilots talking to an ATC control tower when we passed by Pheu Phien. About an hour past that we were on a short final to our flight line at Quan Loi and I could see Hooter, Kenny, and a few of the guys standing around the revetment where we were going to park the aircraft. I positioned myself in the doorway with my feet hanging out. They all were waving to me and they were smiling. I was glad to see them smile. *Things are okay if they are smiling*, I thought. When we landed Hooter came up to me and grabbed my duffel bag and shook my hand. It reminded me the time when I first arrived. Everyone patted me on the back, I was among friends again, and we then started walking toward the hooch. As we walked into my hooch Tiger was on my bed, he got up, ran at me and jumped into my arms. He was licking me all over my face. Hooter said Tiger knew I would come back because all my clothes were here and he had that scent all around him. I was glad. Everyone came into my small hooch and was standing around. I knew something was up.

"What's going on guys?"

"Sit down, Brooks."

I sat on the bed.

"Brooks, Thunder and Murray are no longer with us. Your ship took a B-40 rocket in the ass and there were no survivors."

Everyone had their heads down staring at the ground. Tears came to my eyes and I couldn't speak, I tried and nothing came out. Out of respect and compassion, and probably not knowing what to say, no one would look at me. They knew how I felt and they did not want to witness my hurt. They one by one patted me on the back and left the room. Hooter told me that he would see me later and followed the rest of them out the door. I fell back on my bunk and stared at the sealing. Tiger came up and put his head on my stomach, I put my hand on his head while the tears rolled down my cheeks and to the back of my neck. After awhile I became angry, but saddened to the point I couldn't speak. I cleared my throat several times and tried to talk to Tiger.

Nothing, nothing would come out of my mouth but a squeak. *Thunder's gone*, I thought. *Murray, poor Murray he was taking my spot and died for it. It could have been me. It should have been me. I didn't want someone to take my place and lose their life in return.* I admitted to myself I was glad I was still alive, and this thought made me feel guilty and I was ashamed, but it was true, and the guilt would not leave me.

Some time had passed and I heard a voice asking to enter my hooch. It was the Old Man and Top. "Brooks, you want us to come back?"

"No, it's okay. What's up?" I asked.

"We know how you are feeling, believe me we do. But you just got to deal with it. It's hard I know, but time will heal you."

I told them that I couldn't fly anymore and to please put me in maintenance. Top put his hand on my shoulder and told me it was no problem and to take a day off then report to maintenance. "I have had a couple of weeks off, Top. I don't want any more time off. I don't want to lay around here thinking about this shit, you know?"

"I do," he said. The CO and Top both patted me on the back turned and walked out of my hooch.

I cursed God that day and from that day forward blamed him for what had happened to my friends. I was bitter. My friends became less and less until I had only Hooter, Biggie, Schultz and a new guy named Barney and, of course, Tiger. This time, though, the cut was not as deep. I dealt with Thunder's death better than John's. To some extent I was starting to callous and I thought I was getting somewhat used to death. Death was becoming a part of my life and I felt the transformation. Even though I didn't think of it at the time, my heart was toughening even more. Death became a way of life. I vowed to try and never shed another tear. My anger consumed me, but it brought me some kind of comfort as well. Anger became my friend. When you are angry, the hurt is minimized and you get on with it. It hurts to no end to lose a friend. That type of pain was something I had never experienced in my lifetime. That kind of pain is too hard to bear. My chest felt like it was going to split open and sleep did not find me for a couple of days.

Schultz & I working on my aircraft, Schultz is the handsome dude standing in front of the aircraft. He was a good friend with a smile always on his face.

Chapter 15
Back to the Beginning

Maintenance was okay this time around. It was a good place to get your head together and let your troubles kind of fall by the wayside. I was working with Biggie a lot and we went on several sling missions together. He was married and we spent a great deal of time talking about his wife and married life. I was to be married when I got back to the world and my pace had slowed down to where I would think about Roni more and more. Maintenance was giving me hope again. It gave the time to rekindle my dreams. Maybe I might make it home. The only thing I had trouble with was the scramble horn. Every time it blew I wanted to go and participate in the recovery. I was on the sling crew and I guess that was as close as I was going to get to helping, unless I decided I wanted to go back to flight again.

I kept my M-60 tucked away under my bunk just in case I ever decided I would go back. At this time, though, I was satisfied where I was. I got to put to use some of the things I learned from that turbine engine school I went to in Vaun Tau. I still dropped by the old club. I was still considered one of the flight crew, once in flight always in flight. That was the saying anyway.

I saw West a couple of times loading up on an aircraft and going to the field to set up night ambushes or doing long range recon patrol. I was told he had several kills to his record and was proud of everyone. I also heard that once in awhile he talked to himself and I started worrying about him. I had crossed his path several times in the last two months, but he did nothing but nod his head at me as if to say hello. He really never said anything to me other than that. I couldn't bring myself to speak to him. He withdrew our friendship not me. I felt like we were still friends, but he was so distant. I had my own shit to deal with and I was now into my sixth month. Most of the guys in maintenance stayed away from me and only worked around me if they had to. The people that knew me stayed my friends and the ones that didn't know me kept away. I distanced myself from everyone but my tight little circle.

Those two cooks from that night during the ground attack befriended me. Once in awhile we would have food actually cooked for us, and didn't have to eat stupid sea rations. This came about whenever the gooks decided to quit dropping mortars on our asses for any length of time. I knew by the good treatment I was getting from these two cooks was all because of me giving them that pistol and ear from that one dead gook on the night of that ground attack. That was the only reason I could think of that would justify them treating me so well. They treated me as if I was their best friend. They made it a point to take good care of me whenever they could. When it was time to eat they would always put aside something special or a little extra for me. They told me anytime I wanted something extra or had the munchies at night, just look them up and they would take care of me. It was nice having cooks for friends. Tiger loved it as well. They took care of Tiger like he was their own and Tiger played it for all it was worth. He could turn on the charm when it came to food.

The sling missions broke up the daily routine of maintenance and Biggie and I went on just about all of them. After awhile, they had to break us up and make two teams. I was in charge of one team and Biggie was in charge of the other. The reason they wanted two teams was they were afraid both of us might get killed and then they wouldn't have a team leader. That and the fact they wanted more men trained. Either way, Biggie and I were split up and hardly ever went on mission recoveries together again.

Me preparing a ship to be slung out after being shot down..

Hooking up a ship to be slung to the rear for repair.

The Hueys most always teamed up with Cobras and would sometimes fly night missions (Night Hawk) together close to the Cambodian border. One night, a Night Hawk Cobra got shot down inside Cambodia. They had flown off course and ended up getting themselves in a world of hurt across the border. At this time during the war we weren't supposed to be in Cambodia. Of course, if we had Charlie or the NVA on the move and they slipped across the border, we usually jumped the border until we got our satisfaction and then jumped back across before anyone who was anyone found out about it. And if they did we would say we misread the map.

Well, this time we had a bird down and the Old Man wanted them out of there before the higher ups found out about it. I didn't know the crew that got shot down and I was glad. Every time the scramble horn would blow I would usually crawl the walls until I found out who it was. On this occasion I didn't know this crew all that well and it was no big deal. That day I was attached to the Blue team to go in after this downed aircraft to recover the men, alive or dead, destroy the aircraft and get back across the border before detected.

We decided to hire a Mountain Yard for a guide. They hated the Vietnamese people because they treated them like shit. We paid them well and we knew most of them because we bought our dope from them. We were a means of an income for them and they liked Americans in general because we treated them so well. They looked at us as a way of getting rid of their problem, the VC. Hell, they would have done it for free if we would have asked them. We were only paying them about thirty American dollars but that would go a long way with them, and besides they were great to have along when you were in the jungle. They were masters at living off what the jungle had to offer. On occasions if we had too, we would eat monkey and some snakes. These people could come up with a whole menu of different foods to eat. And if they were in the jungle and did not want to be seen, they would not be seen.

Charlie hated them, probably due to the fact they couldn't catch them. They couldn't stamp them out, not in our sector anyway, mainly because they were under our protection. I really enjoyed spending time with these people and learned a lot from them about surviving in the jungle. I listened when they tried to teach you something and I respected these people for what they were.

There was this older Mountain Yard we called Little Bit and to anyone of us that he liked, when we called his name, he would stand in front of them and give a salute, and then yell out, "Number one!" Number one to them was the best and indeed he was the best tracker and hunter I have ever known. If he didn't like you for one reason or another he played stupid and ended up doing something in turn to make you feel the same. Then he would open up his mouth with no teeth and grin so big. He knew how to make an ass out of you, if you weren't on his list of friends. I made an effort to stay in his good graces. He had a sense of humor that I enjoyed and I always thought he was very smart. We tried to teach him how to use a gun so we could arm him when we went to the bush. But he preferred his bow, spear and a machete. After several attempts he finally got me to understand that bows, spears and a machete don't make noise and therefore don't give your position away. Where we confronted the enemy they avoided them. They would only kill if they had to. These people were so peaceful; I couldn't see how the Vietnamese hated them. Even the hooch maids that cleaned for us hated them. One day I noticed Little Bit was using a machete as a knife. I decided to give him a survival knife. When I gave the knife to him, he thought he had to give me something in return. I told him it was a gift and that he need not give me anything in return. He never forgot that small favor and kept me in dope for the longest time.

Well, this is the man we hired to take us into Cambodia. The village he was from was located on the border and he told us he would visit his people when the mission was done and he wouldn't be making the trip back to Quan Loi with us. We got the okay to use him from the CO, but some of the men didn't like the idea of using him because they thought he could not be trusted. They thought he might deliver us into the arms of the NVA, once we were across the border. I convinced the CO the guy was solid and I trusted him with my life. The CO didn't have a problem with the arrangement and allowed us to use Little Bit.

We were getting kind of a late start and the CO wanted us to get on with it. The aircraft went down that night and we didn't get on our way till 08:00 the next morning. We figured we would make it to the downed aircraft but would not make it back across the border in the same day. If we did it would be too late for the rescue aircraft to extract us. Night extractions were hard to do and we avoided them at all cost if we could. Using a big spot light at night at a hover made you a very big target for Charlie.

Little Bit had never flown in a helicopter and you could tell he was not looking forward to it. He kept pointing at the aircraft and blurting out, "Number ten, number ten!" Which in their logic, if number one was the best, than number ten was the worst. He wanted us to just meet him at the border, but we could not waste the time looking for him and letting the VC know our intent. I made a comment in front of him that I understood if he was scared. That did it. It now was a question of manhood and pride, there would be no way to keep him from going with us at that point.

We all had our gear and were ready to go, loaded up with plenty of ammo and a little food. Some of the Blue team members were loaded to the hilt. I looked over at Little and he had nothing but his weapons. This guy was something else. No shoes, no food, and the only weapons were his bow and a machete; he left his spear back at my hooch. I guess he figured he wouldn't need it. I had some LURPS (Dried Food) I would share with him if need be.

As I was making sure Little was getting situated, I looked up and noticed West was going on this mission. He was one of the Blues that was going to be a part of this operation. He looked over and acknowledged my presence, I nodded my head at him, but no such gesture came from him. He didn't even speak to me, not a word. I wondered why he was a part of this mission. We were to keep a low profile and there would be no contact with the enemy if it could be helped. The only time West wanted to go out was if there was a sighting of enemy movement. Or he was going out on an ambush patrol. He probably thought there was no way we were going into Cambodia without making contact. I wondered that myself, and his presence made me a little uncomfortable.

We finally got on our way, but there was one little problem we were going to have to take care of. We were going to have to fly over the border and let Little see where the crash site was located. This was the only way he would be able to take us in. After all, he could not read a map or ever knew what one was. The ones that knew Little knew he could take us to the exact location if he could see it first from the air. We flew over it, but did not hover as not to give the location away. In fact, we didn't even slow down. We acted like an aircraft that had flown off course and then headed back across the border. (DMZ)

The aircraft was about twelve miles inside Cambodia. It would take us at least the rest of the day and the next morning to get to the downed aircraft. The jungle was double and single canopy we could make fairly good time once we got on the ground. Little motioned to us and used hand signs like he knew where we could land the aircraft and be dropped s off. I took him up between the pilot's console and he pointed the way for them. Once we got close to the area the pilots could see a small rice patty and that is where Little wanted us to land.

Once on the ground, we un-assed the aircraft and took cover in the tree line. Little had us hold our position and he then disappeared. We waited for about forty minutes and he finally showed up. One of the guys held his gun up and almost opened up on Little. Little just shook his head and said "Dinky dowel, that man dinky dowel," which meant of course, he was crazy. He did not like the gun being pointed at him, and from that point on Little kept a close watch on that guy.

We got on the way. Little knew exactly where he was going. I had taken a reading on the downed aircraft when we flew over it. Little was headed straight for the aircraft as far as I could tell. He was our point man in a matter of speaking, and he had a whole different way of giving us hand signals. He would hold his hand straight up when he wanted us to stop. Pat his head when he wanted us to squat down. The only hand signal we all were familiar with was when he pointed to his eyes, which of course meant to keep your eyes open and alert. I was amazed how he maneuvered us through the jungle. It was great for me, I had to do nothing but follow him. I looked at my map and compass once in awhile but only to see if we were headed in the general direction. We were moving so fast and couldn't take the time to zero my map to my compass, but I knew we were headed the right way. As we moved through the jungle, Little would cut left or right, and whichever way he went we would find the rout easier to travel.

Little knew this area very well. His village was just over the border north of where we were dropped off. This area was his backyard. We moved at a good pace and once in awhile he would raise his hand for us to hold up. Then he would listen and stare for the longest time. Then he would move out like nothing was going on. One time he did this and I went up to where he was standing as he stared straight ahead. He squatted down and acted like he had seen something. I moved up slowly and when I got next to him I pointed to my eyes then to him as to ask what he was seeing. He then pointed to my eyes and to an area of thick jungle. He fanned his arm back and forth to indicate he wanted me to watch this area. I was down on one knee and I trained my eyes on this area that he had pointed out to me. I stared for awhile and I saw nothing, I looked over at Little and he was gone, vanished. I never heard him make a sound; he just disappeared right from under me. I trained my eyes back on the area Little wanted me to watch. Little's quick disappearance it made me feel like there may be something going on. The rest of the squad was about thirty yards behind me. I signaled for them to stand fast. We sat there for quite awhile. I turned to my right to see if there was any sign of Little. There he was standing right next to me. I jumped and must have looked like a seen a ghost because Little Bit starting laughing so loud that we all knew Charlie would hear him. But if Little wasn't worried about it then we should have known it was alright and the area was clear. Little moved through the jungle like a cat and after awhile it became kind of creepy, almost inhuman. It was something to behold.

After a little while, Little had us move out at a fast pace. The area was clear and you could tell it by the way Little carried himself without concern. The man was amazing and before we got to the downed aircraft he gained the respect and admiration of everyone. Everyone was glad he was along. If I had to use the map and a compass to get us to where we were at this time, it would have taken us a lot longer. Having Little along saved us a lot of time and sometimes that can mean the difference between a life and death situation. Little had the skills that Special Forces would give anything for. He had acquired these skills growing up and living in the jungle, skills that you can't teach others. You had to live it to be able to apply what he knew.

We got to the aircraft late in the afternoon. We approached with great caution. Little went in first and reported back that there were two American solders around the aircraft hiding. We were almost scared to move in, thinking they might shoot at us. But all they had were .38 specials and probably couldn't hit the broad side of a barn with them anyway.

We went toward the aircraft standing straight up and holding our rifles over our heads. They came running out, very happy to see us. One had a cut on his leg that he had received on impact; we treated it with some antiseptic powder and wrapped it tight. Little told us there was a worm already under his skin and it would grow fast, but would not eat much and he would be ok. Little offered to cut it out but the Warrant Officer wouldn't have it. He must have thought Little was a heathen or something. Myself, I believe I would have gotten rid of the worm or maggot and have Little cut it out. The worms or maggots are put there by blow flies and are similar to a screw worm back in the States. I had seen what a screw worm would do to cattle and such and I don't think I would want that worm crawling around under my flesh and eating away at my leg. *Oh well, it's his leg*, I thought.

Although the aircraft was in fairly good shape, we could not cross the border with another aircraft to recover it by slinging it out. We were going to have to destroy the downed aircraft. We didn't want to blow it up because of the noise factor and giving away our position. The pilots told us they flew about ten miles away from where they had taken fire, and they did not believe the enemy knew they had been shot down. We decided to disarm the rockets and bury them along with the ammo. Now I knew why West was along. He was our armament guy in flight and he would remove the mini guns and disable them and also bury them along with the ammo. They only had eight rockets, so this task of disarming the aircraft didn't take all that long. We took a brick of C-4 explosive placed it in the aircraft and lit it.

Now C-4 will burn a hot fire and will not explode, unless you stomp on it while it is on fire, or use a blasting cap. As the C-4 fire caught the magnesium in the aircraft on fire, we got out of the area. If there were gooks around they may smell it, but down in the jungle it would be almost impossible for them to tell which direction it was coming from. They would have to elevate themselves above the trees to see the smoke. The jungle was so green from the monsoon rains that the fire would not spread far.

We followed the trail that we came in on for miles. Then Little Bit varied us off to the north a little. We were going across the border and straight to his village. Once back across the border we made radio contact and scheduled a pick up. It was getting dark and Flight had one aircraft to extract five of us. It would be on the ends of repelling lines because there was not a clear area for the helicopter to land and pick us up. We would evacuate the two pilots, and three of the Blues. Five of us, including Little, would be spending the night in the bush. We were too far away from Little Bit's village to make it before nightfall.

After the extraction we decided to walk as far as we could before setting up a POD (Perimeter of Defense) for the night. We didn't know if there had been any gooks in the area that might have seen the aircraft. We figured it would be best to get as far away from this pick up point as possible. We made it about two miles and after Little doubled back and returned he assured us that no one was following. There was a chance we could have gooks in front of us yet, so we set up a POD and made camp. I broke out my 20 thousandths safety wire and rigged a couple of grenade booby traps to our rear. The three Blues that was left with us had eight claymores between them. They set them up around our POD and hunkered down for the night. We would change watch every two hours.

We broke off some C-4, and lit it to heat up some sea rations. West was with us, but he stayed to himself. I was hoping this would give us a chance to talk. But he spoke a little to the two grunts he was with, ate a little and then crawled up and went to sleep. Little Bit knew I had something for him to eat; I was always giving him food back at Quan Loi. He, like everyone else, liked the turkey loaf. I heated it up for him and gave it all to him. He deserved it. He had earned his keep today for sure. I ate some beef meat patties and some crackers. I gave Little Bit the chocolate bar, and then turned over and went to sleep.

It started raining and I noticed my body was wet, but felt no rain on my head. I opened my eyes and Little Bit was holding this huge leaf over my head. I went to get up and he said something in his native tongue and pushed my head to the ground as if he was telling me to lie still. I put my head back down and watched him watching over me until I fell back to sleep. I woke up again and he had himself and me covered up in those big leafs. But he was not asleep. He had remained awake all night. *When does this guy sleep?* I wondered. *I never have seen him sleep or take a rest.* When we would stop to rest, he would scout the area. When we slept, he would stay awake.

If you ever had an army made up of these people, you would have an army that could not be defeated. No wonder the VC and NVA hated them. These mountain people could humble anyone when it came to eluding you, and in combat I could only imagine their capability. They chose not to fight, but to elude and remain recluse. They knew they were no match against modern weapons and would not confront you one on one. But if they wanted to, they could get to you and there would be nothing you could do about it. Some of the guys I know felt a little uneasy with Little out in the bush. I felt a lot better with him along. I was glad he thought of me as a friend and not the enemy. After all, we were uninvited intruders in his land.

The next morning we got up early. No one slept all that well. West was sitting on his pack wringing out his socks. I had a fresh pair in my survival pack, but was saving them for when I was completely dry. We were headed for Little's village and would be there before sundown. As close as I could figure we were about eight to ten miles away and it would take us that long to get that far, especially going as slow as we were.

When we were getting close to Little's village, once in awhile he would stick his hand up and wave. We would look to where he was waving but saw nothing. He was waving to people he knew was from his village. Even though we never saw them, he did and he continued to wave every once in awhile and give out some call like a monkey. Later I found out this call was a call only his village would use to identify one and other. I think different villages used different calls and therefore one village could identify the other. Or in some cases no identifying call given usually meant something was wrong and to be cautious.

As we approached the village, once in awhile you would see movement in the bush along the trail. Little would say something to them and you would hear them giggle. We could tell they were women and children by their laugh. Laughing was welcomed and to hear this simple, friendly gesture put a smile on all our faces. Little took us right down the middle of his village, continually saying something to them in his native tongue. Before long, we had a bunch of people following us. You could tell many in the village had never seen a white man and we were the center of attention.

What seemed to be the head honcho of this village came up and greeted Little and made a gesture of smelling him. Little did the same then they embraced each other. Little then stepped back a couple of steps and bowed from the waist to this man. The man put his hand on Little's head, muttered something and everyone approached Little to greet him. This was the first time I had ever seen Little's family. He had a wife and two small children. One girl, that was the older of the two, was around six and a little boy that was around two. Although a lot of the people were shy and kept their distance, they all had large smiles on their faces which made us feel welcomed.

Little took us over to a pavilion with a roof and open on all sides. He motioned for us to rest there, to put down our equipment, remove our boots and take a rest under the shade provided. We were all tired from the walk and none of us got much sleep the night before, so this rest would be welcomed.

The helicopter that was going to pick us up that day was in the area. We heard it once in awhile. We radioed the helicopter and let them know it was getting too dark to even try to retrieve us and that we would be in contact with them tomorrow for an extraction. We wanted time to choose an area. We didn't want them to even come close to the village, we didn't want to give Charlie the idea that these people were helping us out.

We all hung out around the pavilion and relaxed. We all took turns sleeping and after awhile we all felt safe enough we all decided to get some sleep. The women brought us a large container of water and we filled our canteens and drank. Right before sundown, we were taken to a place where we could shower and clean up. As some of us were taking a shower we noticed the women were hauling water from a stream up to the shower and pouring it into a reservoir above our heads so we could continue to bathe. After we finished bathing, a couple of us picked up the containers these women were using to haul water and headed off toward the stream. The women came running after us and tried to take the containers from our hands, they didn't want us hauling water. To them that was women's work and men weren't allowed to carry the water. We laughed and hauled the water up the hill until the reservoir was full again. Little had no quirks about letting us know this work was not done by men. We just laughed and headed back toward the pavilion.

Later that evening we were invited to a meal that took place in a large hut. You could tell it was a place where once in awhile there would be large gatherings, tonight it was for us. The village prepared a large meal. We were all glad because we were running out of rations. There was lots of rice, chicken, pork all kinds of vegetables and all the food was a welcome sight. We were shown where to sit and as we sat the women brought in even more food, mostly fruit. As we all sat there we noticed they had this monkey strapped to small chair in the middle of the table. Once in awhile someone would give this monkey something to eat by putting a piece of fruit in its mouth. We didn't think much of it, we just thought it was an animal they were trying to tame and was more or less a pet.

In the middle of the meal, they opened up a slat in the table and the monkey that was strapped to this small chair was lowered below the table. Then the slat came together and the only part of the monkey that could be seen was his head sticking through the top of the table. Then one of men wrapped a steel cord around his head, stuck a small stick of some kind between his head and the wire and started twisting the wire until it cut into the monkey's head. The monkey's eyes went up into the top of his head as the monkey screamed, then in one pop, like opening a champagne bottle, the top of his head opened up, exposing the monkey's brain.

The Mountain Yard women dished out the brains to each one of their guests. I remember looking at Little and he put his fingers to his mouth, as in the gesture for me to eat it. It seemed it was some great honor to eat the warm brain that was being given to us. I stuck it in my mouth and started to chew it. It coated the top of my mouth with some waxy feeling and it tasted horrible. I mustered it down and was trying my best not to gag. After I got it down, I remember sitting there with this waxy foul taste in my mouth. The more I sat there the more I started to feel like I wanted to up chuck. I excused myself as if I had to go to relief myself, ran to the bushes down where the village set aside a place to relief themselves and started to throw up.

Afterward, I still had this waxy taste in my mouth and every time I thought about it I felt the urge to throw up. I went back to the hooch where the feast was taking place and acted like I just went out to take a piss. I sat there drinking some rice wine until I washed that taste out of my mouth. I looked over at West to see he had this shit eating grin on his face. I didn't think it bothered him, but a few of the guys afterward upchucked as well, and that made me feel like less of a pussy. The next day we all laughed about it, but all agreed it tasted like shit.

Later that day we hooked up with the helicopter that was to take us back to Quan Loi. Little went with us, but did not let us know he would not be going back to Quan Loi. He put his hand around the back of my head and pulled my head against his, we stood there with our heads together for a minute or two and then he cupped my right hand in his rough calloused hands and shook my hand hard. He turned and walked away from us never looking back. I never saw Little Bit again and I want to say I missed him then, I miss him still. He was a good friend and if I would have known I was never going to see him again, I would have seized the moment and maybe told him how much I admired his lifestyle and his skills. I would have said something more than what I did. I could not of course speak his native tongue, but I would have tried to let my gestures suit the occasion. Our parting ways have stayed on my mind all these years and I hope he had a long, good, and prosperous life. He was an older man back then so there is no doubt he has passed away by now.

In moments when I drink a little too much and when my mind drifts over the span of time and ends up back to Vietnam, I make it a point to think about Little, and it puts a smile on my face. He was a wonderful human being and a great man. I would have loved to have learned just a little of his skills.

Me, on the day we got back from Cambodia.

Chapter 16
Run Rabbit Run

One day Biggie and I were working on our sling equipment and rappelling gear when the scramble horn blew. We happened to be working close to operations, so we decided to pop in to see who was shot down. We would probably be going on the recovery anyway. It was my friend Hooter. Hooter's aircraft and his crew had been shot down. Mr. Knight, along with some observer that I didn't know. It sounded like they were down in the jungle and their mayday sounded like to me they were in a state of panic. They had been hit several times and were losing engine oil pressure and going down. I couldn't stand it. I turned to Biggie and told him to get someone else for this recovery mission.

I ran to the flight line and fired up the stand-by bird. I knew it would be one of the first to respond to this call. I figured I would have it running when the pilots showed up. Of course, the gunners on this ride had to be those two assholes Todd and Pete. Todd was shocked to see me and smirked out the remark, "I thought you were done with flight?"

"Not today," I replied. I jumped into the back as soon as the pilots showed up. Todd gave me a look that I was supposed to intimidate me. He then told me I couldn't go, and to get the hell out of his aircraft. I had my rappelling gear and my CAR rifle and four clips of ammo. I struck him on the shoulder with the butt of the rifle and told him "I'm going, and if you think you can stop me, then pop your whip, asshole."

He knew I was serious and I wasn't in the mood for his macho bullshit. He took up his position in his jump seat like a good little boy and didn't argue with me. I took up the position in the R/H transmission well and sat on the floor. One of the pilots was Mr. Ryan and he climbed into the pilot seat, looked at me, nodded his head and I knew it was okay that I was along. We took off. I put on a headset and listened to the radio transmissions. Hooter's aircraft was down in the trees and there were gooks everywhere. One of our Slicks and a LOH, Scout was at the location of the downed aircraft.

Hooter popped a smoke grenade, the color of the day was yellow and we had him spotted right off the bat. The LOH that had been shot down was piloted by a guy named Wendell and an observer named Webster. They transmitted back to us that the crew was oaky, but they had gooks coming in about two hundred yards north of their location the last they seen of them and they figured they were much closer by now. Then we heard Mr. Knight tell us that Hooter had lost his 60 on impact and they only weapons they had were the Observers M-16 and his 38.

Mr. Ryan punched rockets about two hundred yards out. He didn't see anything, he was just punching them off into the enemies reported location. The LOH flew over the gooks real fast and popped red smoke where the VC was spotted. We could tell by the location of where the smoked was dropped that the VC were moving in fast. They would be spread out by now and trying to right or left flank where the downed LOH was

located.   They were getting too close for us to use
rockets. I told Ryan I was rappelling in and to give me a
location so I could meet up with them later. He looked
back at me and told me to give him a second. I don't
remember who was flying co-pilot, but he took over the
controls of the aircraft, while Mr. Ryan pulled out a map.
It didn't take him long to give me a location. There was
really no clearing, we just decided I would just head
everyone south and when it was clear Ryan would come
to a hover, drop rappelling lines and pluck us out of
there. He gave me a map and told me to keep shooting
those pin flares of mine off. He gave me a general
direction to start heading, so there wouldn't be much
map reading. The map was in case we had to make our
way back to Quan Loi. We would just head out and I
would keep him posted of our location with flares. It was
simple, quick plan and we both agreed when he came to a
hover in front of our location at any given time, then and
only then should we be ready for him to sling us out.

He brought the aircraft back around to the
downed aircraft's location. I was already out on the skid.
I put about thirty feet of slack into my repelling line. I
wanted to freefall as far as I could as not to give the VC a
target to line up on, and if I was lucky I could get down
into the trees before they seen anyone rappelling at all. I
didn't want them to know how many of us would be on
the ground. The jungle was triple canopy and that was in
our favor. They couldn't make it to the downed aircraft
as fast as they would like, and along with the LOH and
Ryan's Slick pounding them, would give us a good
chance to out distance them. And in turn give us chance
to get to a place we could get picked up.

The VC were going to give it everything they
could to capture the crew. They knew an officer had gone

down with the aircraft and they would do just about anything to get him. They figured enlisted men didn't know shit and therefore Hooter and the observer would end up like John, or just shot in the head. I know Hooter and there would be no way the VC would take him alive. But also Hooter had no weapon; we had to get them out of there.

The radio in the downed LOH was not working and the downed crew had no idea what was going on. The only alternative was someone had to go in. That was going to be my excuse if I ever had to stand accounted for what I was about to do. After all, none of this was cleared through the Old Man or Operations, Ryan also was taking a chance by letting me go in on my own. Ryan and Knight were best friends and you could tell Ryan wanted Knight and his crew out of there. That made me feel better, because I knew Ryan would take that extra chance to get us. I thought of Mr. Knight as being my ace in the hole once I was on the ground.

We came back around and I saw Hooter on the ground looking up at me. I asked the gunner for his extra survival rifle for Hooter, he didn't have one. I rolled my eyes at him and jumped out. I was on the jungle floor in three seconds thanks to that extra slack in my rappelling line. When I got free of the line the Slick took off and resumed circling the area and giving us cover. Hooter came over with this big smile on his face. "What the hell are you doing here?"

"Come to save your bacon," I replied. He grabbed my survival pack and I handed him my 45 ACP and told him to try and hold on to this one and we both laughed. Mr. Knight came over and at that time, I told them of or plan to get us out of here. I looked at the observer and realized it was the supply clerk. I looked at Hooter and he said, "I know what you are going to say. Don't say it."

This guy was scared shitless. I walked over to him and asked him if he would give Hooter his rifle and he could use my .45 pistol. He wouldn't do it, he clutched onto that rifle like it was a security blanket. Knight came over ordered him to give his weapon to Hooter. He did but you could tell he sure didn't want to. Hooter gave him my .45. I only had four clips of ammo for my CAR 15 and the observer only had two clips for his M-16. I had two extra clips for my .45 and Knight had his .38 special with no extra rounds. I shook my head and thought to myself with a little luck we wouldn't need any more than what we had. "Let's get out of here," I said. We turned and started to move out. I didn't have to take a compass reading, the VC was approaching from the north and we were going to exit straight south, as Ryan and I had talked about.

The observer kept looking over his shoulder and every now and then you would hear him trip. I told him not to look back until we took cover. We would be doing that about every hundred yards or so. He was making a lot of noise and that bothered the shit out of all of us. Knight, Hooter, and I knew that the VC would try to flank us on both sides to keep us from losing them by doing a 90 degree exit. Flanking us would keep us on a straight course, by doing that they would be hoping to overtake us. We kept our eyes peeled left and right. After about a hundred yards I stopped and I shot up a pin flare into the air. We heard the VC more to our left than anywhere else. We went another hundred yards and I shot up another flare. The VC was still on our left. I believe we out-distanced the right flank and the ones coming straight for us, but the ones off to our left were traveling at the same pace. We needed to get rid of these guys. If we set up an ambush they would out-gun us and allow the rest to catch up. I had two grenades in my survival pack and Hooter had two in his. I had some twenty thousand safety wire I carried in my pack to make snares and booby traps with. We could rig up a couple of grenade booby traps with the wire but that would also take time. No, we decided our best chance was to try and lose them.

There was no movement or sound to our right, which was to the west. Hooter and I decided to shoot a south by southwest course and try and put distance between us and the VC. We hoped this would not allow them to advance on our right flank so we could out distance them. I changed course and after a hundred more yards I shot up another flare. I'm sure Ryan wondered what in the hell was I doing. I heard the gunships shooting and punching off rockets. I hoped it was our right flank they targeted and that was why we were now cleared that way. Ryan flew over us to let me know he had seen the flare, but he didn't come to a hover. It wasn't time to pick us up yet. There must be VC on our ass, or he would pluck us out of here. Knight looked like he couldn't go another step. The observer looked as bad, except you could tell he was about to lose it.

I asked Hooter and Knight what they wanted to do, fight or run? We decided to run. That was what I wanted to hear. I told Knight they would out-gun us if we had to confront them head-on and that our best bet was to keep moving, but it was up to him. He had a gash in his knee from the crash. I wanted him to make the call because I knew he knew his own situation better than anyone. We all go or no one goes, we all agreed to keep moving.

I had lost my bearing so I took out the compass and started our south by southwest exit again. Another hundred yards, another flare. Time was running out and so were my flares. I only had three left. I decided not to send up any more until we went at least twice the distance this time. I knew that would drive Ryan nuts but I had no choice. Without these flares our chances of Ryan locating us in this jungle were almost nil. I wasn't in panic mode, but I was getting close. If this is it then, so be it, at least I was with some good friends. Heck, we were all scared there was no denying that fact, but we were all in survival mode and would put up the best fight we could with what we had. I had the most firepower and the thought of me laying down grazing fire and letting the others go on did cross my mind. If there were no alternative I would do so. I would give them my flares but keep the map and compass in case I did get away.

Hooter shook his head and Knight glanced around like a deer hearing something, but nothing was there. The observer finally lost it. He lost my .45 as well and didn't want to say anything. Damn, I loved that gun. West gave it to me and I contemplated the idea of going back to see if I could find it. I looked at Hooter when I got the news of my weapon and he closed his eyes and shook his head, as if to say 'we are screwed.' Oh, well. So much for the .45 no gun was worth risking anyone's life, no matter how much sentimental value was attached.

We went two hundred yards or so and I sent up another flare. Ryan flew over, but again did not stop. We had to take a break. Hooter and I broke out the canned water from our survival packs and passed it around. The observer drank it so fast he started coughing. *Man, this guy is going to get us killed*, I thought. After a couple of minutes we moved out again. I shot up another flare and finally Ryan came to a hover above us. The ropes came down and everyone started tying off. The observer tied a slip loop and put it around his waist, this would cut him in half by the time we got back to Quan Loi. I had my D-ring and I never took off my monkey strap so I untied it and rigged it up on the observer. Then I tied a bowline knot in a loop for me and up we went. I believe the observer hit every branch on a tree coming out of the jungle. He had never rappelled and for sure had never been pulled out of the jungle on the end of a rope. I felt for the guy, he was so scared tears formed in his eyes.

"Use your feet to keep yourself away from the branches," I yelled. He never got it. His face looked like a mad hooker had got a hold of him by the time we cleared the trees. Hooter started laughing, and then Knight and I cracked up. We were all relieved and it felt good to release the tension.

The aircraft took some rounds in the tail boom when we cleared the trees, but we were all on our way and life was good again. As we were flying back to Quan Loi on the ends of those ropes, two Cobras and four LOH pulled up on each side. They were flying at our level as we were forty feet below the aircraft. On shorter lines above Hooter and me were Knight and that observer. Knight was above Hooter holding on to Hooter's line to keep himself from spinning around and around from the air flow. Above me was that observer, holding on to his line and not mine. He knew nothing about using the line of the other person, or using your legs to keep yourself from twirling. He spun like mad, getting so dizzy he started throwing up. I was glad our forward airspeed was such that his vomit went straight back behind us. I hung there anticipating a shower of vomit. I thought the guy was going to pass out.

The aircraft flying beside us gave us the thumbs up, their lips said, "Good job." Then they looked up at the observer and start laughing. When we approached Quan Loi, a lot of people stood on the flight line. We were shooting an approach to the middle of it. Ryan came to a hover and lowered us down. First me and Hooter, then Knight and that observer. The observer was so dizzy he couldn't stand up. I tried to tell him how to keep from spinning but he didn't hear me so I gave up. I thought it was justified punishment for him losing my .45 anyway.

Everyone patted us on the back and welcomed us home. This little adventure took all day and the sun was low in the sky. It was time for beer and a good war story that had come out in our favor, for once. That night they toasted Ryan and me to the point we were both embarrassed. I got plastered. I was put in for a Bronze Star for meritorious achievement, but I never received this medal and didn't really care one way or the other. My reward came from having my friend Hooter safe. And from the thanks I got from the whole crew. I know I slept well that night, something I hadn't done in a very long time. The flicks in my head shut down and I slept in total bliss.

The Old man did not chew Ryan's or my ass for taking the situation into our own hands. He congratulated our success, but hinted about not making a habit of it. Ryan and I talked about it some and decided we would do it all over again if the need ever arose. Our brothers meant more to us than an ass chewing or stripping of our rank. Hooter, Knight, and I, became best of friends. The observer never flew again. But he told this war story so many times that everyone started calling him Short Story. I could tell I wasn't going to be able to handle going back to maintenance again. Being stuck on the ground was more painful than flying. Every time the scramble horn blew it would drive me nuts and take a piece of me. Stuck in maintenance and on the ground while your friends are down in the bush didn't cut it for me, so off to Top I went. When Top saw me he knew what I wanted. He grabbed the paperwork and told me to report to Flight whenever I was ready.

Almost half my tour was over and my odds of making it back to the world were getting better. I knew going back to flight was not going to help those odds, but I just couldn't stay on the ground. I returned to Flight that day. Hooter was glad and also knew I would be going to Slicks, and he was not too happy about it. I tried to get Hooter to go with me, but he would not go. He had paid his dues in Scouts and could go, but he did not want to go anywhere else. He was getting short and did not want to do anything to upset what he called good karma. In my book Hooter was a very brave individual. His nerves were beyond reproach and no one questioned his bravery. I was proud to call him my friend.

Hooter was kind of superstitious that way, to some degree we all were. We all hung on to something to give us some kind of hope or to bring us good luck. I wasn't Catholic but wore a cross around my neck. At the time I really didn't believe in God. I didn't really know where to put the blame for the death of my friends, so I took it out on God and blamed Him. I received this cross from a ten-year-old girl that worked in the field with her father. We had seen them many times working in the rice patties around their village.

One day we happened to be flying by as some local VC were harassing them. As soon as the VC spotted our aircraft they took off running. There were eight of them and my gunner and I managed to kill two before they got to the tree line and to cover. We went back and landed the aircraft close to the two victims. The girl's father had been beaten and she of course had witnessed the whole event. They were either trying to recruit his services or trying to get food from him. After we made sure the two of them were okay, I turned to go back to the aircraft and continue the pursuit of these VC. She grabbed my arm and put a small golden cross and chain in my hand. Her family was Catholic, probably results of the French Occupancy. Anyway, I wore this cross around my neck for good luck the whole time I was in 'Nam. So I couldn't say anything about Hooter's superstition. I had my own, besides it worked for him. After all, he had been in country nine months now and still lived to talk about it.

As for me, I wanted to go to Slicks. I would still be going out to face Charlie, but after he had been found when the odds are on my side, not the initial first sighting when you usually took the casualties. I liked that idea better. Besides, Thunder was gone and it would be bad memories for me to stay in Scouts. Thunder and John's death played on my mind constantly and I could not put it to rest.

My first Charlie Model Gunship

When I got to Slicks I was offered Crew Chief (Chief) on a new C-model. I accepted the position. The aircraft was not new, but it was close. It had around five hundred hours in all on it, but considering the time the 1/9th put on these aircraft, this aircraft was considered a new one. As soon as I could stripped it down. I removed all the seats from the aircraft except for the two jump seats for the gunners. I removed the cargo doors but left the co-pilot's and pilot's door on. I looked over the aircraft and pulled a good inspection on it. I brought my M-60 down to the flight line to go over it to make sure it was still in good shape. I had it rolled up in a blanket that I had put in storage by sticking it under my bunk. I had it packed in LSA (grease) so I started cleaned it up and got it ready for service.

I had my head down cleaning my 60 when I felt a hand on my right shoulder. It was Ryan. He welcomed me back and told me he'd be the pilot of this aircraft and that we'd make a good team. He also paid me a compliment by letting me know that Knight, (who was also coming to Slicks) wanted me as his gunner too. He and Knight drew lots for me. They took the top three pilots that had been in country the longest and drew lots between them. I was honored. I told Ryan they wanted the new ship that was all.

He laughed and said, "That's also true."

It was nice of him to say what he did. It didn't take long for Ryan and me to become good friends. Almost everyone I knew considered Ryan and Knight the best of the pilots. They were both down to earth and I had a lot of respect for them. I was excited about my new assignment and the new aircraft.

After returning to the States, Ryan and I were stationed at Ft. Sill, Oklahoma for several years. After leaving the Army we worked together in Louisiana, flying people off shore for Chimerical Helicopters. We have lost touch over the years but we will always remain friends and brothers to the end. One of few, of the best, helicopter pilots I have ever known.

Chapter 17
The Transition

The transition to Slicks was no big deal. The atmosphere was kicked back. The Huey's were like three-quarter ton pickup trucks. In most cases you could carry all the ammo you wanted and had so much room you felt like you were at the Hilton. We still had to fly gun missions, but usually the enemy had already been spotted and therefore we gave up the element of surprise when you usually take the most casualties. You had time to decide how you would approach most every engagement.

The Scouts really had done all the hard work by finding them for you. I was glad I was in Slicks mostly because we had a lot more fire power. Rockets, two gunners, and sometimes you were rigged up with a 40 mm. That was always a nice edge. The 40 mm was a pain in the ass to maintain though and most of the time I was glad I didn't have to mess with them.

My gunner was a nice guy named Irwin. He had been in Slicks for about three weeks. He had worked in maintenance and was given this door gunner job without having to go to Scouts. I was told this was a new ship and because of the extra aircraft they had to pull someone out of maintenance to fly gunner. They could not afford to pull anymore away from Scouts since they had lost

Thunderbird and his crew, so they just appointed someone to fly gunner on the new aircraft. But you have heard that old saying, 'It's not who you know, it's who you blow.' And I believe this was the case. The way I looked at it he could have went to Scouts, then in turn someone in Scouts could have come to Slicks.

I would have loved to have had Hooter for my gunner. But Hooter was devoted to Scouts and I completely understood his reasoning. Irwin kind of resented me being the Crew Chief because he had been in Slicks longer than I, but he hadn't paid his dues in Scouts and he knew he was lucky to even be a gunner in Slicks. He was a very smart guy. A lot smarter than I and he got great pleasure of lording it over my head. He was always correcting my way of speaking and was a know it all. But I admit he did know a lot more than I did on about any and every subject. Despite of the inferiority I felt around him, I did enjoy his company from time to time, but he wore on someone fast.

I had experienced lots of combat at this time and the only way he could feel equality between us was to show me how smart he was. He could talk the leg off a jackass. It was like reading a book without really reading at all. All you had to do was listen. His talking had a calming effect on me in the beginning and as time went on he made me smile and helped me think about things besides death. I have to say, I liked him at the start, but I knew he would soon get on my nerves. He was someone I would not let into my tight little circle, but I did consider him a friend.

Tiger liked Irwin a lot more than I did, only because Tiger would drop by and get food off of him. Irwin felt like Tiger was his dog. He was always trying to get Tiger to sleep in his hooch.

He would do this by giving him extra food and petting him every chance he got. Tiger played him like a fine guitar. Tiger even laid down in his hooch and go to sleep. But I always woke with Tiger beside my bunk. Irwin never figured Tiger out. Tiger was Tiger and no one really owned him. He belonged to everyone; he just preferred to be with some more than others. Irwin, to Tiger, was just another food source and Tiger put him on his list as someone to butter up to for handouts. Tiger was getting so much food from everyone I stopped feeding him. He was eating better than me. Hell, he was eating better than everyone. As long as no one put a collar on him, or tried to tie him up, I had no problems with people trying to coach him into staying with them. Tiger was a free spirit. I believe that was what everyone liked about him.

Well, the peace and quiet never lasted long enough. Before we even had a chance to relax, we were out in the AO. At this time I had over nine confirmed kills to my credit and I began to wear ears on my flight helmet like a badge of honor. I had earned respect from everyone that mattered and except for the killing and putting up with mortar attacks life resumed to something you could deal with. The transition to Slicks from Scouts was a lot easier. Slick gunners were pretty much independent. They didn't depend on each other as much as the Scout gunners did, and their camaraderie wasn't as tight. I missed that about Scouts and coming up through the ranks I not only had the respect of the Scout gunners, I made great friends.

I came to understand a lot of things since the beginning. I gave up dwelling and worrying about who would be next. I took life in the 'Nam one day at a time and marked each and every day off my Julian calendar. I had around 195 days left in country. I was beginning to be known as an old timer and it felt good to have some time in country under my belt. We flew a lot of missions and it was on one of these missions I got humbled.

Once we flew out to retrieve some prisoners the Blues had captured on some ambush mission, and we came up with the bright idea that we would interrogate them ourselves on the way back to Quan Loi. We got one of the interpreters to fly out with us to retrieve these prisoners. We thought that we could do a better job of extracting information out of these gooks than intelligence. By doing so we would have the information first-hand to use to our advantage instead of waiting for intelligence to give us the news then have operations send us out on a mission they deemed important.

We loaded up these four prisoners on the right side of the aircraft, back in what we called the transmission well. This is the area where other company's gunners sat, but in the 9th this area on both sides of the transmission are clear. When you are sitting on the floor in this area you can see nothing of what is going on in the cargo area of the aircraft, especially on the opposite side of the aircraft. Anyway we put these four prisoners on the aircraft, crammed back in the transmission well. We would have our interpreter ask them a question and, of course, none of them responded. So we would put a sand bag over one of the prisoner's heads and drag him over and act like we threw him out of the right hand cargo door. What we actually did was put him back in the other transmission well on the other side of the aircraft where they couldn't see him. Then we would repeat the process with each one. Of course the last guy, thinking we had thrown out all of his buddies, spilled his guts and couldn't tell us information fast enough. Sometimes we would have to slow him down so the interpreter could get it all written down.

We had fun with this one. After he told us all he could, we put a sandbag over his head and acted like we were going to throw him out, regardless. The last thing he saw was we were at three thousand feet. Then we moved him up to the door and when he felt the wind hit him in the face he struggled. We acted like he was overpowering us and by doing so bought the pilot time to get us almost to the ground on the flight line at Quan Loi.

There, General Casey and a bunch of MPs waited to receive our prisoners. While the prisoner still thought we were at three thousand feet, we hovered over in front of the General and his staff and threw this guy out. The prisoner had no way of knowing we were just three feet off the ground. He screamed when we threw him out of the door and when he hit the ground the guy passed out. We thought we may have given this guy a heart attack. When we landed the aircraft Irwin and I picked the guy up. He was a mess. One of the MPs put some water on the man's face and he finally regained consciousness.

We thought it was funny and started laughing, but when we looked over at General Casey and his staff, I noticed they didn't see the humor in our little escapade. When the aircraft was shut down and the pilots climbed out of the aircraft, General Casey brought us to attention and let us know if he ever caught us doing something of this nature again he would see to it we were all put back in Ben Hoa jail so far we wouldn't see daylight for a year. He was pissed to the point he wouldn't let us speak.

Every time we tried to tell him we had debriefed them and had a lot of good information, he would tell us to keep our mouths shut. To top it off, he looked down on my skids and saw that I had a couple of skulls wired in place on the skid shoes. He went ballistic and told us to remove and get rid of those skulls right then. I removed the skulls and tossed them in a fifty-five gallon barrel we put our spent ammo in.

He turned and got in his jeep and had it take him to his helicopter.

After we knew he was gone, I retrieved the two skulls and put them back on the skids that evening. We wouldn't see him here again. Generals hardly ever came down to the front lines. In one way it was not a good day for us. But in another we had a bunch of information on the location and operations of the enemy in our sector and we would indeed put it to good use.

A week or two passed and we received word from intelligence of possible movement and location of enemy positions. We laughed it off, for we had already gathered this information from those prisoners we debriefed and it didn't take us two weeks to do it. We took the information we had gathered that day and along with eight other aircraft rained down a lot of hurt on our enemy and everyone reported numerous confirmed kills. Eventually we all got over the fact we got our asses chewed out by the Division Commander and the story of us doing what we did to those prisoners became a good topic over many beers and at least as many joints. But this would not be the last encounter I would have with General Casey and I came to find out he had a good side and really cared for the men in his command.

Some time passed and I had lost a lot of weight. I was down from 165 pounds, from when I first came into country, to 137 pounds. Even though I looked like shit, I was in the best shape of my life. Most of my weight loss could be contributed to the malaria pills I took every day. They kept your bowels clean out for sure. When you took a crap, you didn't know if you where pissing or shitting. You didn't wipe your ass; you just kind of blotted it. All in all, I felt good and I knew I would put the weight back on once I got back to a normal life style and good food again.

One time my aircraft was used to go and retrieve aircraft parts back in Saigon. A few of us guys decided that it would be a great opportunity to get some good food. The mess halls in the rear were noted for having good food. Better than what we, or anyone could get on the front.

We landed at the strip in Ben Hoa and decided to go to the mess hall and tank up. We went into the first mess hall we came to and walked over to a table and unloaded all our gear. I had brought in my 60 and my flight helmet (with the ears) I wasn't about to leave it all in the aircraft. We would come back and it would be gone. Anyway we unloaded our gear and started for the food. An E-7 sergeant halted our charge for the food. This guy thought his crap didn't stink. He told us we were too late for chow and to get the hell out of his mess hall. He then followed that up with the statement it would be a cold day in hell before he would allow anyone as dirty as us to eat in his mess. We did look a site. Our skin was red like we hadn't taken a bath in a month of Sundays and our no-max flight suits also had a red tint to them and looked dirty even though they weren't. We didn't think much on our appearance. Where we come from we looked normal, never had our cooks turned us out under any circumstances. Of course, we didn't really have a mess hall at Quan Loi.

My first inclination was to slap the hell out of this horses ass, but I restrained myself and turned, picked up my gear and headed for the door. We all started cussing him out and made an effort to bump into every table as we headed for the door. On the way out we had our heads down and were mumbling something. As we headed out the door someone else entered. It was General Casey and two of his staff. We dropped all our equipment and saluted.

He returned our salute and looked us over. "You boys have a problem with my mess hall?"

I guess he had seen us abuse the tables. "Well sir," I replied, "we just came in for some food and got a rash of shit from the mess sergeant."

"Concerning what?" he asked loudly as he looked me straight in the eye.

"Look sir, we were just trying to get something to eat."

"Do you know the mess hall hours?"

"No sir," I replied, "we really are not used to a certain time to eat and didn't know it was past serving hours. We just wanted to get some good food, that's all." At this time I really wanted to get back to the aircraft and leave. The pilots went to the officer's mess and I sure wish we had Mr. Ryan with us right now. General Casey looked at me and I knew he remembered the skull on the skid incident even though I did my best to conceal my face by looking down instead of at him. I had my flight helmet in one hand it had all those ear's on it. The one time I put those stupid ears on to freak out the soldiers in the rear and I run into a General, and one that I knew had it in for me if he recognized who I was.

"Don't I know you?" he asked.

"No sir."

"Where are you from?"

Oh no, I thought. "Quan Loi, Sir." I bit my lip, hoping he did not remember the skulls and us throwing out that prisoner as a joke. I hoped someone else would speak up and wished I hadn't.

"You troops come with me," he replied.

We turned back around and went back inside the mess. He pointed to the table and told us to put our gear against the wall and set our asses down. We did so, figuring we were in deep shit. He then called the mess sergeant over.

The sergeant saluted, "Yes, sir!"

Casey returned his salute and asked him what was going on. The sergeant commenced to tell the general what happened and when he finished Hooter spoke up. "Don't forget the part where you told us to get the hell out."

I liked to have crapped, but Hooter being Hooter did not falter and did not blink as he looked the mess sergeant straight in the eye. General Casey's face turned red. He then twisted, pointed at us. "See these men sergeant? You see them?"

"Yes, Sir!" the sergeant replied.

"These men may look a mess to you, but they look like and are heroes to me. They are the heart of our forces over here. They keep the gooks off your ass so you and your buddies can go down to the Ville at night and play around with your whores. They put their lives on the line everyday so you can sleep in peace in your air-conditioned quarters and enjoy life as if you where back in the world. You let these boys eat whatever they want and as much as they want. In fact, you wait on them personally."

"Yes, Sir!" the sergeant bellowed.

Man that was a shocker for us all. We must have looked dumbfounded. General Casey then swiveled and strode toward the door with his staff close on his heels. We all, at the same time, told him thanks. He then turned. "No, thank you," and walked out of the mess. That sure was a different encounter with the General than the last time I saw him.

That sergeant waited on us hand and foot. Once I looked up at the mess sergeant. "It must be a cold day in hell, huh?"

He gave me dirty look but said not a word. We made remarks to him like, 'Mary, could you get us some more of this or some more of that?' We treated him like a waitress and said things like, 'thank you, honey' and 'yes, sugar.' It was priceless. I drank so much milk that I got sick.

From that day on I thought of Generals in a different light. I sure thought different about Casey. Before it was all said and done, General Casey pinned two medals on me. He pinned one of my Bronze Stars with a V device (Valor) on me and a Purple Heart. General Casey was killed, I believe in 1970, when his helicopter flew into a mountain in Vietnam. I was back in the world at the time and heard about it on the news. Deep down he seemed to be a good man. I know he earned our respect that day, the day he stood up for the common soldier.

Chapter 18
Cobras

Flying Slicks was great. Although I had taken several hits with my aircraft, it was no big deal. All the Slicks had bullet hole-patches on them. It was a repair that became a badge of honor. It proved to everyone you were still in the fight. The aircraft was so big compared to the LOH it was only logical the Huey Slicks would take more hits. Bullet holes in their aircraft were the only thing the Slick Gunners could and would hold over the Scout gunners heads. It was an ongoing argument every time the Scout gunners and the Slick gunners got together. We would all argue on which saw the most action. In my opinion the Scouts saw more action. With them it was all up close and personal. In Scouts it was nothing to be looking down the barrel of an AK-47. Slicks usually took their hits from afar. Usually. This was not always the case. When it came down to it, everyone knew that the Scouts carried the most casualties. It was a subject no one liked to talk about, especially in this kind of debates or arguments. They weren't really heated arguments, it was more of camaraderie thing than anything else. It was just a way to rib each other.

Cobras, on the other hand, were another thing. No one really considered them apart of any of these debates and discussions. Gunners considered them assassins or ambushers. They would fly around at seven thousand feet and wait for you to call hell down on your enemy. They were like a hawk falling out of the sky after their prey. To a door gunner, there was no honor or combat skills in killing your enemy this way. But no doubt everyone was glad they were there. There fire power was unbelievable and no one really doubted their capability and their contribution to our day to day operations. A lot of us called them God when we really needed them. Sometimes we would call out over the radios 'Send down God's wrath' and everyone knew what that meant. (Pure Destruction.) And everyone would get the hell out of the way.

But to us they were arrogant and no one could stand them. They flew the greatest attack helicopter in the world at the time, and I believe that is what made them act so damn superior. I soon understood that it was pride, not arrogance. They were a tight knit group and deep down we all respected and appreciated what they did. I had a real boner for them because it was a Cobra pilot that pointed that gun at Tiger. After breaking Eagle Beak's nose, I wasn't the most popular gunner in the Cobra pilots' eyes. Regardless of what that ass was, he was one of their brothers and like us, they took up for each other's shortcomings. Our combat record didn't mean crap to them. It did not empress them at all. They didn't like us and I for the most part, didn't like them.

One evening while the Scout and Slick gunners were in one of these debates a few of the Cobra pilots walked by us. We couldn't see who they were but to most of us it didn't matter. Hooter was one that couldn't let this opportunity pass him by so he blurts out, "there goes the Thunder Chickens."

This did not sit well with any of them one of them walked toward us. It was Mr. Knight.

He was transitioning into Cobras and had just returned from a check flight. Even though I was not the one that made the remark, he walked straight over to me. "Having fun, Brooks?"

"Not really," I replied. I was embarrassed. Knight and I were good friends. Especially after I had went in and helped pull him and Hooter out of the bush. Hooter had to feel worse than I did. He used to fly with Knight. Hooter could do nothing but look at the ground. Hooter finally spoke and told Knight that he didn't know he was amongst the group. Knight told him it shouldn't matter. He was right. The Cobra team had lost four Pilots in the last six months and we knew they grieved their losses as much as we would have ours. Apologies were made and that was that.

Then one of the other Cobra pilots (FNG) started toward us. "Screw those guys, I'll kick their asses." As he approached he asked Knight if he needed any help. Knight told him no, that it was just a little ribbing amongst friends.

Hooter being Hooter couldn't leave well enough alone. "Screw you, asshole."

As it stood, no officer would mess with an enlisted man. If he did, he might find a grenade under his ass when he went to take a crap. Knight, being the kind of person he was, defused the situation and they both turned and walked away. Hooter, on the other hand, would not let go of it. He worked himself into such frenzy that it took several beers and a couple of joints to settle him back down.

Hooter was a good friend to have. He would lay his life on the line for you and had proven that time after time. On the other hand, he could be your worst nightmare. Demons danced around in Hooter's head and you never knew when one would come out to play. Hooter was the type you did not want to mess with. He had over thirty confirmed kills. His ears numbered the same. There were so many ears he no longer wore them, he hung them up in his helicopter. Everyone that knew Hooter knew what lines to cross and what lines not to. This poor Cobra pilot had no idea what he was getting into. We knew Knight would fill him in, or at least we hoped he would. Camaraderie was always present with all of us, but tempers would flare up in a heartbeat. No wonder, look how we were living. Cutting off ears and heads? No wonder Hooter had demons. Some things that I thought I would never be a part of in the beginning were now as easy as shaving.

I had changed, but the revenge I took out on the enemy made me feel better and in some ways I felt justified. I think Hooter felt the same. I had adapted to this kind of lifestyle, it all seemed normal to us. I no longer wanted to go on R&R. I just wanted to kill gooks. That was my goal and focus now. I wanted my revenge. I believe most of the guys felt that way. We never stopped and talked about what we were doing. We thought it was the norm and did it without question. What we were doing was war, but in some ways it felt like murder. I wasn't fighting this war for my country anymore. I was now in it for revenge, self-survival, and hate. I believe this is why I put that feeling of murder behind me. I knew this guilt would haunt me the rest of my life.

A week passed and one day Knight approached me and asked if I would like to fly front seat gunner in a Cobra. "Sure," I replied.

I always did want to fly gunner in a Cobra. To me this was the way to fight the enemy. Swoop down out of the blue, blow the shit out of your target and continue on. All in a day's work, plus the fact that you are flying around at such an altitude that it is cool and you don't sweat your ass off. It was almost like having air conditioning most of the day. Still, you can get shot down but compared to the rest of flight Cobras had it made.

Cobras usually fly with two pilots, but this increased the odds of losing two pilots instead of one. So they started letting enlisted men fly front seat as Cobra gunners. They had just started the program and they had a list of maintenance personal standing in line for the job.

I had worked on Cobra's in my short tour in maintenance so I was pretty familiar with the aircraft. The day of my first Cobra mission I got up and went down to the flight line, to check out the aircraft I would be flying in. I got a lot of ribbing from Scout gunners as well as the Slicks. My aircraft was in maintenance and I told them I would rather be flying instead of stuck on the ground. Hooter and Scott told me I could fly their aircraft. I laughed and declined the offer. Hooter asked me if I had lost my balls. I told him one maybe and we both laughed. The Cobra pilots had their fun as well. They looked at me and made the comment of becoming one of the Thunder Chickens. I laughed, but not as much as they did and with not as much enthusiasm.

I pulled the daily on the aircraft checked out the guns loaded up both sides with seventeen pound rockets and we were ready. Mr. Knight pulled his preflight and in no time we would be airborne. As Knight was pulling the preflight he kept reminding me to put on my chicken plate. Now a chicken plate is somebody armament that fits over your chest. When I first started flying Scouts I wore the damn thing, but in cretin maneuvers in the LOH it would bounce up and hit you in the chin and plus the fact it weighed about ten pounds. All in all, it was a pain in the ass. It got its name chicken plate because everyone or at least everyone in Scouts made the sound of a chicken when they caught you wearing one, of course to indicate you where chicken if you wore it. After awhile you get so used not wearing it you don't even think about it. It would not stop a direct hit with a bullet anyway. It would, on the other hand stop most shrapnel and a glancing hit from a bullet. But sense it was not a popular item with gunners I padded mine up and let Tiger lay on it for protection when we flew. Well, today Knight insisted that I wear the damn thing. He insisted to the point it was pissing me off but then he was wearing his, so I dug mine up and put it on to shut him up.

I didn't go to the flight briefing so I had no idea what our mission was. Whatever it was it would at least start out in the clouds where it was cool. I was plenty hot from loading all those rockets and I was a bit excited about flying front seat Cobra. I knew Knight would fill me in on the way out to the AO. In no time we were up and away. I sure missed my little buddy, Tiger, flying with me. He didn't care for it much either. When we lifted off the ground he followed the aircraft to the end of the flight line and stood there as we flew off and out of sight. I was told later he went back to my Slick, crawled up in it and lay under my jump seat where I flew gunner.

Flying Cobras was indeed different. You could not feel the massive air flow across your face and body. All you had was a couple of vents on both sides of the dash. I directed all the air across my face and body. At first it was pretty hot, but as we climbed up to altitude it got a lot cooler. In fact it felt like air-conditioning. I felt like I was in a jet fighter with the small cock-pit and all.

Knight told me we were going to make a few dives (gun runs) to get me used to using the gun turf and some G-forces that I hadn't experienced in Slicks or Scouts. He banked the aircraft to the right to the point I thought we were going to fly upside down, and dove out of the sky. We were at ten thousand feet when we first went into our dive and we were falling out of the sky like a rock. The ground was coming up so fast the thought of not being able to pull out of this dive crossed my mind. We were at 200 knots and we had lost six thousand feet in an instant. Knight told me to fire the guns at what looked like a small pond created by a bomb. I grabbed both gun handles put the pond in my sights and pulled the trigger. What fire power! There were two red straight lines right down into the pond. Knight told me to move my hands in a circular motion and keeping my window sight on the pond. I did and the two lines became a spiral of tracers to the point it literally looked like it was raining bullets. How could anything or anyone escape that kind of fire power? The gun turf was controlled with hydraulics and you didn't feel a thing.

Then I noticed that the ground was coming up fast when Knight pulled us out of the dive. The vibration from the G-force was so bad I could hardly see. I thought the aircraft was coming apart. And that chicken plate was bouncing off my chin. As we were pulling out of the dive I was pushed down into my seat. My flight helmet wanted to slip down over my eyes. I pushed it back up and tightened down the strap. By the time I did all of this we were coming out of the dive and the vibration tapered off. When I realized what had just taken place we were headed back up into the clouds. Man that was a different feeling. I had never experienced that in a helicopter. Knight told me I did fine and would get better as time went on. I told him everything was great except the for that chicken plate strapped to my chest, it about broke my jaw.

"Be sure to keep it on Brooks," he replied, "you never know."

This stupid thing is coming off as soon as I get back on the ground and I am not putting it back on. It's not bad enough dealing with all the vibrations and bullshit, but now I had this ten pound block of armor that would hit me in the chin every time we come out of a dive. *Nope, it's coming off.* If I had a place to put it, I would've taken it off then. In a Cobra you have a couple of small rear view mirrors you use to look back at the pilot. Knight was back there with a smirk on his face, when he looked and noticed I was looking at him he winked and told me I would get use to it. I told him there was no getting used to something that you weren't going to do anymore and I wasn't wearing that piece of crap the next time we went up. He shook his head and laughed. He bet I would change my mind if I stayed in Cobras.

"No way," I replied.

Knight briefed me on that day's mission. We were going to meet up with another Cobra from Alpha Company and they would show us where he took fire the day before. Eventually we hooked up with the Alpha Company's Cobra. He told us that he was shot at with a .50 caliber. Oh, how I hated .50s. They did so much damage to aircraft and I can promise if one hits you, you will not survive. At least the Cobra was a hard target to hit. That gave me some comfort, but not much. When we arrived at the area where he was spotted it was quiet. We weren't there long though, when the Alpha Cobra took fire. We were circling at ten thousand feet and were ready for the call. Knight rolled the aircraft over and down we went. I grabbed the mini gun handles and got ready for God knew what. On the first pass we spotted nothing. Then the Alpha Cobra came around and took fire again. This time we spotted the location where the rounds where coming from and we rolled in on it. As we got closer we saw a guy in something that looked like a coal car on rails. The kind old-time miners used in mines. It had a .50 caliber mounted on it, with two guys pushing him in and out of this cave. As a Cobra would come down to make a gun run the two guys would push him inside the cave. When the helicopter would start back toward the clouds they rolled him back out and he shot this .50 at the ass of the aircraft. This way you couldn't shoot back at him. We had seen this used before and knew how to deal with it, but this is the first time we ever saw a coal car used.

As the Alpha Cobra came around for another gun run we held back. Then when the Alpha Cobra made his move we got in position to come in behind him. Sure enough, as the Alpha Cobra made his run the car with the .50 was wheeled back inside the cave. As the Alpha Cobra came out of his run out came the car, except this time we made our dive and caught them with their pants down. When they saw us it looked like we caught a deer in our headlights. I opened fire and hit one of the gooks that pushed the cart, the other one took off. The guy in the cart must have pissed off people in high places because he was chained to this cart. He had no choice but to go for broke. He wheeled his .50 around and fired at us.

Those .50 caliber tracers looked like basketballs coming up at me. Each round looked like it was going to hit me between the eyes. I fired the minis and tried to hide behind the console, while trying to keep this guy in my sights. I wanted cover, as if the console would stop anything. I looked in the rearview and Knight was doing the same, except he was getting behind me. Every time I moved one way he moved the same. I was using the console for a shield and he was using me for one. No wonder Knight made a big deal of me having my chicken plate on. I was his body armor. I didn't finish the job and get the guy with the .50, but the Alpha Cobra got him with the next pass. I couldn't have been happier that he got the kill. I didn't want to make another run on that .50. Knight told me later that we would have used rockets from that point on. No use taking chances. Crapt, the first run was enough for me. We could have used rockets on the first run as far as I was concerned. Knight laughed and acted like it was just another day in the shop. I had been fired upon lots of times, but something about looking at those .50s shook me up. I saw them leave the barrel and head right for me. Even though they missed us by three to ten feet, they looked like they were headed right for my beak. I never flew Cobras again, not in battle anyway. Knight, as well as all the other Cobra pilots, took great delight in hounding me about this mission for the next few months.

I know one thing for sure, no one ever joked about calling them Thunder Chickens again, not with me around. That day I was the biggest Thunder Chicken of them all. When I asked Knight why he was using me for a shield and reminded him that my body and armor wouldn't stop a .50 cal, he laughed and said 'no, but it would slow it down a bit.' I never took offense because I would have done the same if the shoe had been on the other foot. But my Cobra days were over. Back to good old Slicks for me. I would rather go back to Scouts than fly Cobras. I never took part in calling them Thunder Chickens again. And I never thought of them as arrogant anymore. Knight was always a down to earth type guy and over the years we remained friends.

Mr. Knight and I were also stationed at Ft. Sill Oklahoma and served a tour in Korea together. In Korea he and I were body guards and the flight crew for a four star general. (General Knowles.) He was killed in a Cobra accident at Ft. Sill, I believe in 1974. I helped retrieve his body from the crash site. Ryan and I flew him back to Ft. Sill in my UH-1D helicopter. It was a final goodbye to a good friend. He was a great helicopter pilot and one of the bravest men I have ever known. He never forgot that day I helped him out of the jungle, it was the topic of conversation during many beers and a few joints we had together. I never forgot that day he and I made that gun run on that .50 cal. This was a topic brought up from time to time. I never got to talk to his wife, but I know he loved her dearly. He never stopped talking about her.

Chapter 19
The Final Transformation Completed

I was glad to be back in Slicks. My aircraft was out of maintenance and back on the line. Irwin spent half of my first day back telling me how hard he had worked on the aircraft while it was in maintenance and while I was out flying. I didn't even tell him of my experience. He would no doubt hear about it sooner or later. I simply thanked him for doing all the work while I was out having the time of my life. That kind of rubbed it in a bit but didn't shut him up. I don't know if he got the sarcasm or not. He was going to take an R&R and I was glad. I needed a break from this guy. Like I said, he was a very nice guy but a know it all. I thought about the first time I met him on bunker guard, the night I told him I really didn't want to get to know him. I actually think I hurt his feelings and maybe he told me about all this shit just to get back at me somehow. Who knows? I will just be glad when he's gone on R & R. Popp would be filling in for him as gunner.

Popp was also getting out of Scouts. He had more than paid his dues and was getting short. I believe he wanted to increase his odds of going home the same as I did. Whatever it was, I was glad to have him fly with me. Popp was a simple individual that liked everyone. He had his clique like all of us, but was more than willing to accept new friends. He had dealt with the same hurt as all of us. But he seemed to get over his grief better than the rest of us. Probably because he had so many friends, plus there is something to say about being simple-minded. I don't mean this in a cruel way. I'm pretty simple-minded myself. It's really hard to explain, but it's worth it if you can come to know Popp and his personality a little better.

Popp came from somewhere Alabama. He was a country boy from a long line of country folk. One time he wrote home and told his parents that he sure missed eating steak. Well, low and be hold in about two week's time, he got a package with a couple of steaks in it. It doesn't take a scholar to figure out that this meat would not take long to spoil and I mean *spoil*. Especially in the climate we lived in. It was December and I guess his parents thought the meat would keep long enough to make it to him, I don't know, but it was funny. Everyone laughed but not to the point that he didn't laugh too. He thought it was funny but everyone knew it kind of embarrassed him and therefore no one made a big deal out of it. They knew Popp and his family weren't the sharpest knife in the drawer. But then his parents made their living completely off the land and depended on no one for a living. How many people do you know that can do that? So you see, they were smart people, just not in the ways of the rest of the world. I, for one, like those kind of people and have always felt comfortable around them.

Anyway, I liked Popp and he liked me. He was one of those guys that never took part in calling people FNGs and he really didn't go in for teasing folks. I believe he had experienced this first hand in his life and didn't care for it. But Popp was indeed a team player and I know he liked having friends. I don't think he had many in his life but he had plenty here. Everyone liked Popp. He was one of those people that didn't have a lot to say but you just liked having them around. When he did talk about things people listened and if we where high it made everyone put the brakes on. Some of the time he commented on something that everyone else had already talked about and moved on. Everyone laughed in a friendly way and backed up to the topic we were discussing and brought him back into the conversation. Yes, I have to say everyone liked Popp. And he made our lives a little better by knowing him.

Popp was a good mechanic. Whenever I saw that he had a panel open or something off the aircraft I never questioned him. I knew he was looking out for all of our best of interests. He just liked to tinker with stuff. Besides, he had more experience working on aircraft than I. Popp was the first person to show me how to cut down my .60 so it would be more compact. This cut down version of the M-60 was his idea and every gunner and crew chief had their gun cut down to this version. For me, it showed he really shined when it came to something mechanical.

One time we were all sitting around high on smoke, and we all got into a debate of how hard it is to bring down a Slick or Cobra with small arms gun fire. Popp, being a true Scout gunner, defended the LOH (OH-6A) by telling us all about how hard it was to bring it down with ground fire. To top it off, reminded us how more crews survived a LOH crash more than any other aircraft. He was right. The aircraft had one of the best survival rates around. Upon impact the tail boom would pop off and because of the aircraft being shaped like an egg it would roll like a ball. I've seen many a crew survive a crash in this aircraft, were it a Slick or a Cobra you would be dead. But everyone was determined to defend their type of aircraft.

At this time a Cobra made an approach to the flight line. Popp jumped up, grabbed his M-16 and said, "I'll show you how easy it is to bring down a Cobra compared to a LOH." then started for the door. Everyone laughed and told him good luck. Popp stepped out of the hooch and the next thing we knew he was cutting loose on the Cobra that flew overhead. Everyone jumped up ran outside the tent, grabbed Popp and brought him back inside the hooch.

We couldn't believe what he just did. The tracers from the gun fire made it easy for the Cobra crew to see where the line of fire was coming from. Before long here came Top and the CO. They busted into the tent and wanted to know who fired that gun. No one was going to say a word. Popp stood up and told the CO that he was the guilty party. First time I had ever seen the Old Man so upset.

The CO looked at Popp. "What the *hell* did do you think you were doing?"

Popp stood there with this silly grin on his face. "Just showing them all how easy it would be to shoot down a Cobra."

"What?" The CO repeated. "What did you say?"

Popp started to repeat what he said, when Hooter jumped up. "Popp wasn't really shooting at the Cobra. He was just acting like he was as a joke to prove a point to us."

"As a joke?" the Old Man repeated.

"Yes sir, as a joke," Hooter said. That was the first time I ever heard Hooter say 'yes sir' to anyone. He always called the CO the Old Man. And if it had of been a different situation the CO would go along with it. But at the time the Old Man was dead serious and he was there to yank a knot in some body's ass. He was all business.

The CO started toward Popp, but Hooter stepped in-between the CO and Popp. "Could we just forget about the incident?"

The CO was there to make an example out of someone and at this point he wasn't there to be the enlisted man's friend. "Get out of my way."

Hooter stood there. "No, Sir!" He looked straight into the Old Man's eyes.

The Old Man turned to Top. "Get the MPs down here."

At that time we all jumped up and walked over to Hooter and Popp. We told the Old Man and Top that if they put Hooter and Popp under arrest, then they would have to take all of us.

The CO turned to Top again. "Get the MPs down here, I said."

Top turned and walked out of the tent. The Old Man stared at all of us. He really didn't know what to say. I believe he was trying to figure out what the hell he was going to do if we didn't back down. Well, I can tell you right now, no one was backing down and no one was going to arrest anyone.

When the MPs got there the Old Man pointed to Popp and told them that was the man he wanted arrested. The MPs started toward Popp as if he was the enemy or something. There was about twelve of us that were determined that this wasn't going to happen. As the MPs went for Popp, we got in between them told them to back off. One of the MPs reached up to grab a hold of Popp. Big mistake. In the blink of an eye someone struck the MP's arm with the spare barrel of an M-60. I heard his bone snap. The other MP went for his weapon and to his dismay, two gunners grabbed him and three or four other gunners pointed M-60s at their faces. The CO jumped in and diffused a real bad situation. He got the two MPs to back off and leave the hooch. The MP that went for his gun called for reinforcement.

The CO stepped out of the hooch behind the two MPs and after some discussion got him to cancel the call for backup. But in no time the MPs' CO showed up and as Our CO and theirs stood outside the tent talking, we all looked at each other as if to say 'what in the hell did we do?' Then everyone started laughing. Top, the two Company Commanders, and the two MPs must have thought we were crazy. You know, we were crazy. This little action we took against the system made more sense to us than anything else that was going on around there. Popp kept apologizing to us and the more he apologized the louder we laughed. The whole incident was stupid but so funny. We laughed until our ribs hurt. The whole time we were laughing the Old Man, Top, and the MPs Company Commander were in a hot debate.

By then the medics showed up and were taking care of the MPs broken arm. The Old Man was taking up for us and trying to smooth over the situation. The MPs' Commander and the two MPs reluctantly got into their jeeps and drove off. The one with the hurt arm left with the medics still holding his arm. It was indeed broken. I don't remember who took credit for breaking the man's arm and but it took awhile for us to settle back down.

The next day we were all told to report to the Old Man. He apologized and we apologized as well. The subject was never brought up again. It went to show how much the company needed their gunners and how much everyone thought of Popp. Besides, the Old Man did not want what went down that night to get outside Quan Loi. It would have been an embarrassing situation for the Old Man and a blemish on his record if the news of this ever got out to his peers. Without a doubt, no Commander would have handled it any different. What were they going to do to us? Send us to 'Nam? They knew we didn't give a crap. Jail in Ben Hoa and busted would be a better situation than what we were in anyway, and they knew we knew that for a fact.

From that day on Hooter was the Man and Popp relished the popularity the incident had given him. But Popp was kind of embarrassed about the situation. After that day no one ever got into a debate around Popp. He picked up the nickname Sniper (Snip for short) and preferred you call him by that. I still called him Popp, he will always be Popp to me. Popp and I had been on several missions together and he and I became good friends.

Tiger liked Popp and you could see them together at any given time. It seemed Tiger had claimed two masters. Everyone knew *no one* was Tiger's master. But Tiger did like Popp and Popp treated him like a kid instead of a dog. Tiger loved it. For the first time I found myself competing for Tiger's affection. Tiger liked Popp that much. I do believe Tiger learned he could get twice the attention if he played two masters against each other. Like I said, Tiger was smart. Too smart, the little shit.

The next day, while Popp and I were working on the helicopter, the scramble horn blew. One of the Scout's aircraft had been shot down and everyone that could was airborne and flying out to give the downed bird cover and yank the downed crew out if possible. It amazed me how Tiger knew what the scramble horn meant and would be in the aircraft ready to go. Now that we were in Slicks and had the room, it was easy for him to fly with us. To us, making him stay behind on the ground was cruel. Tiger liked flying. I believe it was the cool air he liked more than anything, and of course he didn't like being left behind.

After we were airborne we found out that Hamilton's (Scot's old Gunner) aircraft had been shot down. Everyone was reported to be okay and they were waiting for us to pluck them out of what was said to be a hot LZ. Because the crew was facing what could be a bad situation, we knew they would be ready to get the hell out of there. We all knew how it felt to be shot down in enemy territory, on the ground and surrounded by the enemy. We also knew that Charlie would be trying to get to them, so it became a race to see who would get to them first. There were a couple of Cobras already on the scene so we knew Charlie wouldn't be near as gutsy with them breathing down their necks. It was a typical extraction that we had done a hundred times.

Everyone knew what their assignment was and all the aircraft maneuvered into position to make the extraction. Our aircraft was selected to pick up the downed crew. I really didn't like going in on extractions. Mainly because as the aircraft slowed down to a hover it made you too easy a target. But with the Cobras on hand we knew Charlie would not be so willing to give up his position to them and fire at us. But still, you never really knew so for those few intense moments the hair on your neck would tingle and your shit would be wired tight until you were out of the LZ and had regained your air speed and altitude.

As we approached the LZ we saw the Cobras circling above the area where the LOH had been shot down. They were laying down fire with their mini guns around the POD that the downed crew had set up. We nosed the aircraft over and made a low pass over the downed crew. As we flew over we started laying down fire on the outer perimeter of the LZ. Then we circled and with our M-60s still laying down fire started setting up our approach. Even though Popp and I saw no enemy, we kept our .60s pumping out rounds to the last minute to let the crew jump onboard.

The aircraft never came to a stop and never touched the ground. The crew flung themselves onboard as we slowed down. In an instant we were going through transitional lift and we were out of there. Hamilton grabbed our shoulders and patted us on the back. He and his crew where happy campers. They were screaming 'all right' at the top of their lungs and we all laughed as we headed back to Quan Loi. I looked at the downed aircraft, the Blues where being inserted and were setting up a perimeter around the downed LOH. A Chinook would soon show up and sling the downed aircraft out of the LZ and back to Quan Loi.

All of a sudden we started taking fire and heard the rounds hitting the bottom of the aircraft. Bullets came up through the floor and red hydraulic fluid sprayed us all down. The rounds must have hit a hydraulic line. I yelled over the intercom that a hydraulic line had been hit. Knight responded, telling us we still had hydraulic control but he was still looking for places for us to land in case we lost our hydraulics completely. Everyone tried to take cover the best way they could, covering up their heads and curling up in a ball. I popped smoke to mark the spot as if I was back in Scouts and then started laying fire down aft of the aircraft. Although I didn't see muzzle flashes or tracers, I fired grazing fire to keep Charlie's head down. The Cobras started working the area where I had popped the smoke and I knew we would be okay from this point on.

I didn't hear Popp firing his gun. I turned to see if maybe his M-60 was jammed. Popp was drooped over sideways in his seat. He had taken a round to his head. His flight helmet had been blown off and the only thing left of Popp's head was his bottom jaw. I knew Popp was gone but in a state of shock I unbuckled my seat belt and maneuvered to his side as quickly as I could. Not thinking, I tried to stop all the blood running from what was left of his head. I tried to put together a piece of his head as if I could fix it and make it right. In the blink of an eye, Popp was gone. It all happened so fast my brain could not catch up to what my eyes were seeing. I couldn't stop looking at what was once my friend.

Popp's blood was all over the aircraft. What I thought was hydraulic fluid was Popp's blood. Hands grabbed me and pulled me away from him. I was covered in Popp's blood. Popp was gone. Tears fell down my face as grief and anger raged through my body. I broke free from the grips of the other crew, as they tried to pull me back down. I struck Hamilton. Hamilton fell backward, I then grabbed my .60, stuck it out the door and started screaming and shooting at the same time. I didn't have a target I was just firing crazy. I was mad, hurt and out of control.

Knight said something to me over the intercom but I don't remember what it was. My senses where blurred, I had lost it. I finally stopped firing my gun. I turned and reached into a cubby hole of the door beam of the aircraft and pulled out a rain poncho. I went over to Popp and wrapped it around what was left of his head.

The air flowing into the aircraft spread Popp's blood everywhere. I took the bungee cord that Popp used to support his .60 and stretched around the poncho to hold the poncho over the place where Popp's head should have been. I then took a spare bungee cord out and strapped Popp's body to the jump seat so he wouldn't slump over. I couldn't look at Popp anymore. I remember sitting back down in my jump seat and putting my head between my legs. The crew said something to me, but I couldn't talk. My throat had a swell in it and I couldn't speak, when I tried my voice cracked. I just couldn't say anything.

The next thing I remember was a hand at the back of my neck. I looked up and Knight was there. We had landed the aircraft back at Quan Loi. Knight asked me if I was okay.

"Yeah," I replied. I turned to see medics unloading Popp's body onto a stretcher. I stepped out of the aircraft and walked up to where Popp was lying. His head was still covered up with my poncho. I stuck out my hand and placed it on his knee. The round that took his life had entered up through his ass, traveled through his body cavity and exited out of the top of his head. Popp forgot to put the steel plate under the bottom of his jump seat. The plate may not have saved him, but then who knows.

I turned to walk away and heard one of the medics blurt out, "Holy crap look at this guy"!

The anger returned and before I knew it I was out of control. I grabbed a hold of that medic and whaled on him. I couldn't stop hitting the guy. Knight and Hamilton grabbed a hold of me and pinned me up against the aircraft. Knight said something to me, but it was a blur. I was out of it and if I hadn't been stopped, there is no telling what I might have done. I had pulled my knife out and was about to bury it in the other man's chest. I was taking my pain and anger out on a guy whose only crime was that he didn't think before he opened his mouth.

The medic cursed at me as he picked himself off the ground. Hooter and Biggie told the medic to get the hell out of there. That medic turned to the other then they bent over and picked up Popp on the stretcher, placed him on the hood of a jeep and drove off. It was only then that Knight and Hamilton turned loose of me. I turned looked into the aircraft and saw a very fine spray of blood all over the inside. Below and around the bottom of Popp's jump seat there was a pool of blood that ran down the outside of the fuselage. I removed my shirt and started soaking up the blood with it. Hamilton grabbed a hold of my arm and told me he would take care of it. Hooter and Biggie suggested that I go to my hooch and lay down.

I was numb and didn't know what to do next. I didn't argue the point. I picked up my .60 and started toward my hooch. I was drained. *Tiger! Where is Tiger?* I turned and there he was. He was right behind me, shaking with his ears laid straight back on the top of his head. He had blood all over him. I picked him up and headed for the shower house. I washed him off, got in the shower myself, clothes and all and tried to wash the day's events from my body and out of my mind. If only it was that easy. I went to my hooch, laid down on my bunk and drifted off to sleep.

I woke up when I heard someone enter into my hooch. It was Hooter and Hamilton. Everyone in the company was upset over the loss of Popp and I thought they were just seeking out company for the evening but they were there on my account. Hooter had a bottle of Scotch in his hand (J. W. Black) that his dad had sent him from the world. He was saving it for some special occasion, but he figured it would be put to better use that night.

We three sat there, not grieving over Popp's death, but hashing over the good times we all had together. Even though Popp was a quiet type of guy, his absence was felt throughout the company. We didn't want to think of his death. We wanted to remember how he lived. And how in his own special way, Popp touched everyone's heart. We talked about the time Popp shot at one of our own aircraft and how we all stood up to the MPs for him. And the time his parents sent him those steaks in the mail.

Our eyes welled up as we sat there looking at each other. Hooter held up a canteen cup full of Scotch, made a toast to Popp's splendid nature and how he would be missed and not soon forgotten. Hamilton, Hooter, and I clicked our cups together and downed the last of the Scotch. We sat there most of the night. Between the three of us we finished off the bottle and as Hooter and Hamilton rose to leave, I apologized to Hamilton for hitting him.

"No problem," he replied. "I probably would have done the same. Hooter and I were concerned about you. We've never seen anyone zone out like you did today. Between West and his brother, Thunderbird and Popp, we have all had a hard run of it. We are all brothers and will be till our time comes. We all have to continue to pull together from time to time. I was just glad you guys plucked us out of there today. I hate the fact that it cost us a good man to do so. Three lives saved today for the cost of one. That is the way I look at it. That is the only way I can deal with this shit."

Hooter put his hand on Hamilton's shoulder they both turned and walked out of the hooch. The loss of one of us affects us all in different ways. Everyone deals with things like this in their own way and goes on with it.

Hamilton and Hooter were the only close friends I had left in flight. I had distanced myself from everyone else. The rest of my friends where all in maintenance and I had lost no friends in maintenance so if I had to choose friends, maintenance is where they would come from.

I figured I better feed Tiger and hit the rack. But where was Tiger? I hadn't seen him since I washed the blood from him and myself. I walked out of the hooch and looked for him in several areas. Knowing he was probably begging for food, I started looking for him at his usual stops. I looked everywhere but I couldn't find him.

I went down to the flight line and found him on top of what I considered my bunker. Tiger and I have sat out there many times, thinking and watching the sun come up or go down. As I crawled up on top of the bunker, Tiger acknowledged my presence by raising his head and wiggled his tail just a little. Then he turned his head and stared out over the green line. I never knew a dog that was so human-like. He was missing Popp. He knew what had happened. He had seen combat more than any of us. He had been associated with war and death for at least seven years, which was Tigers age.

He knew Popp was gone and it bothered him. I know animals can't reason, or at least I don't think they can. But this dog sensed that he would not see Popp again. It bothered me to think that he might feel the way I felt, so I sat down beside him and put his head in my lap. We had both had been here many times before. Except this time, Tiger came out to this bunker all on his own. Usually he followed me out here. I never expected him, or even thought he really knew what this place was and why I came out here. We sat there for the longest time. I kept thinking about how Popp got out of Scouts to fly gunner in Slicks to increase his odds of going home. Finally I got up and walked toward the hooch. Tiger followed. I was glad he did. I would feed him a little extra tonight and that might help him sleep. He did not eat. He slept on Popp's bunk. It was a very hard night for us both.

The next morning I hated getting out of bed. Not only because my head still spun from the night's activities, it was all because I didn't want to be around the aircraft that day. I had to help with the repair and I didn't want to be there. But I gathered myself together and headed down to the flight line anyway. As I approached the maintenance area I saw several maintenance personal standing around my aircraft. As I approached them I heard them talking about the whole ordeal like they were there. They pointed at each bullet hole and shook their heads. The aircraft had taken nine hits.

One guy that had been in country for awhile was telling some new guys all about it. But he was telling the story with respect and consideration for Popp, so instead of interrupting I just turned to walk away. I didn't feel like talking to anyone about the event. Then, one of the guys spoke up in a low voice, "Hey there's Brooks." I turned around. He was embarrassed that I heard him and he turned his head downward.

Burnet and Biggie was among the group. Biggie spoke up and asked me to come over. I really didn't want to go over there. As I approached them they all started toward me. One of the guys I didn't know stuck out his hand to shake mine. I really didn't know what to do. I stuck out my hand. He shook it and told me, "Good job,

Brooks." I really didn't know what to say. In suit, they all started patting me on the back as they all passed bye, one at a time. The praise was appreciated but embarrassing. I had done other things that were more significant than what happened the day before.

To be truthful, I lost it that day. I went blank for at least half an hour. I don't even remember the aircraft landing. They all knew that, I think, and this was their way of trying to build my spirits, or maybe restore any confidence they might have thought I lost. Even though I did not feel like I deserved any praise, the gesture was appreciated and made me feel a little better. Biggie and Burnet patted me on the back and said something in the nature of 'hard day at the office yesterday?' and gave me a smile. I needed that. Burnet always had a way to make you feel better under any circumstance.

I needed a little humor and these two guys where full of it. They knew me well enough to know that they could make that statement and I would take it in stride. They were a part of my tight circle of friends. That's the good thing about close friends. They know how to bring up a touchy situation to break the ice, then make light of it to put it to rest and you at ease. In this case a touchy situation that we all needed to put behind us. But of course an event we all would never forget. Somehow I felt responsible for Popp and they both knew I felt that way. You can't help it. You always feel some type of responsibility for close friends you lose. You always think about if there was something you could have done or said to change the outcome. They knew and in their own way they were helping me get on with it.

We three spent the rest of day fixing my aircraft and talking about everything from grandma's cooking to the three of us going in together and buying a vacation resort when we got back to the world and running it in a three-way partnership. It took my mind off of the day before and off the fact that I was working not more than two feet from where Popp was killed. Because of the good company and conversation it turned out to be a good day. A day I have remembered, a day that I have jotted down in this book and a day that will stick in my mind forever. Not a day of sadness but a day where two friends were trying to make another friend feel better. It was appreciated more than they would ever know. But that was the way it was in 9th Cav. Friends supporting one another when the chips where down.

All of us, having an understanding that it could all be over in the blink of an eye. We made the most of what we had and that was each other's support and company. That's the sum of life in general, isn't it? That we should make the most out of everything while we are still alive? I had heard this phrase all my life but took it for granted. Vietnam was teaching me this fact for sure; we just don't know when it all may end for any of us. Being so young I had never given death much thought. When you are young you feel you will live forever. But Vietnam gave me a different perspective. It taught me a lot of things. One was life is short no matter how long you live and if I ever get back to the world I will never take it for granted again.

Finding someone to take Popp's place would not be easy. Irwin was due back from R&R and I didn't know if I could handle his mouth. I went to Top and asked him not to put Irwin with me as my gunner. Top told me that we were getting two new Slicks and they would give Irwin his own ship. But very few new recruits were coming into the company and finding me a regular gunner might take awhile. Things were like it was when I first arrived, when flight was so short on gunners. No one from maintenance wants to fly door gunner either. After what happened to Popp, no one will be knocking down Top's door to sign up for flight, or any type of flying as far as that goes.

I didn't think about it one way or the other. I was in flight and flight was where I was going to stay. If anything, I wanted revenge more than ever. The kill is what I was concentrating on. I pondered on that first day I arrived, the day when those gunners killed that gook in front of us and then threw him out of the aircraft. Somehow, it didn't seem wrong to me now. It seemed justified. Even though I hated to admit it, those two where right about how I would change. At the time I couldn't understand how someone could do such a thing. I understood now and I know that I had made that transformation, was capable of being just as cruel.

It wasn't about the war and doing my patriotic duty anymore. Truthfully, it never was. It had become a personal vendetta. There was nothing I liked better than killing one of those little bastards. I'm sure they felt the same way about me and I'm down with that. That's one of the things that made it so personal. I felt the metamorphosis one goes through during these times, like everyone else I too was changing.

I couldn't see much outside Vietnam. I still had hopes and dreams, but they weren't as important to me as they once were. I was consumed by this war and the friends I had lost, all, of us were.

I still had a little over six months to do. I was going to have to come to terms with the fact that more of us may be killed before my DEROS (Date Estimated Return Over Seas) date was up. I was starting to go back to thinking I wouldn't make it back home, but it was something I couldn't dwell on. If I did, it put me in a state of depression that I couldn't afford. My shit had to be wired tight if I want to give myself the best possible chance of making it back home.

I never was a believer in predestination but I was beginning to see how certain people did. Popp got into Slicks to give himself the best possible chance of going home and look what happened to him. I wondered if it was worth all the precautions one took and if life is predestined. Those childhood dreams seemed foolish to me. I still felt like a kid in a lot of ways, but I knew I had changed forever. There was no way I could ever return to the person I once was, there was no turning back. How could I? My conscience and heart had become calloused and killing had become so easy for me. In a way it had just become another way of life.

If there was a God, I would be condemned for the things I did. Not necessarily because of killing someone in a war, but by the way I felt about it. I knew it must be wrong, but I loved it. I never felt more satisfaction and it was such an adrenalin rush. At this time I had twelve confirmed kills to my record. It was an addiction worse than any drug. Our kills became like scores in a football game, the ears like trophies in a hunt and all of us kept count. For this, I felt like I would be condemned by God. I caught myself hoping there was no hell or God. This way of thinking tore at my soul. At times, I thought I was going crazy.

I sometimes felt I was even destined for destruction. I was lost with no map to help me find my way. At one time it really bothered me to kill. I wasn't a natural born killer, no one is, but I had become one. I was able to take a human life and not think twice about it.

Blaming God was a way I could make myself seem blameless and not responsible for my own actions. After all, if there was a God, why did He allow such slaughter? It has to be His fault. Were there others that felt the way I did? We all sat around talking about our kills with enthusiasm and how tough we were. But we never talked about our true feelings. I think we were afraid it would make us look weak. We were all so young and were playing the roles that were expected of us.

The CO and all the way down to our section sergeants knew what we were doing to the enemy. Everyone knew we were cutting off ears to wear around our necks or on our flight helmets, decapitating some, only to put their skulls upon the skids of the helicopters. It was medieval and we were all taking part in it one way or another. Although the officers and NCOs never physically took part in our rituals, they knew what we were doing. But as long as it made us better combatants and upped our morale they turned their heads to what was going on and in turn we all thought it must be okay. The way we looked at it, the enemy started this shit. They were the ones that started mutilating their captives. At least when we cut off their ears or heads they were dead. We didn't care one way or the other what anyone outside flight thought. The whole gig gave us stature in the company.

I remember one time after a kill, we brought the body back to Quan Loi and everyone started staking claims for its body parts. One would yell out, 'I need a skull, I'll take his head.' Another would say, 'I'll take that other ear.' A few of the maintenance personnel came over to look at the body. The looks on their faces at the things that were being said cracked me up, in a sick way it struck me as funny, at first. Then I got to thinking they are the normal ones and we are actually the ones that were screwed up.

One of the section sergeants made the comment how cruel and sick we all were. "You guys are sick in the heads he shouted out at us.

Hooter told the sergeant to take a flying leap and if he didn't like what was going on than get the hell out of there.

When Hooter asked me what I was laughing about, I shook my head. "You wouldn't believe it if I told you."

He looked at me. "We are pretty messed up, aren't we"?

We both started laughing as we walked off. It wasn't our kill, so we didn't care what they did with the body. On the way back to our hooch we talked about some of the sick crap that we were doing. Hooter made the comment he thought wearing the ears was kind of sick at first, but eventually got into it and went along with the ritual. He said he didn't think about it one way or the other anymore. I told him I was the same, but instead of wearing my ears around my neck I kept them hanging in the hooch and I only wore them when we all got together at the club, or to get down with a few of our friends. He pretty much did the same. Other than small talk, not much more was said between us. I think we were both just thinking it over.

As I mentioned before, we were all putting up a front on how tough we were, or how tough we thought we were. I felt lost and in a lot of ways all alone. But revenge was my justification for it all and I could live with that. It was easier than it was in the beginning, to do what I was doing and it was not only me, we were all playing out a roll we were cast in. I knew it would get even more so as time passed. I was not pressured to do these things. I did them of my own free will and by doing so knew one day I would have to answer for it. Not necessarily for the killing in a war. But from some kind of pleasure I got from it all. I knew when I returned home from war the demons would want to dance in my head and come out to play.

But I kept the hope of going home alive and returning to some normal way of life again. The norm here was so far apart from the way of life back in the world. I knew when it came time for me to go back to it that the transformation back, if even possible, would be a harder one to make. I come to realize that I could never put behind me some of the things we all had done. Guilt used to eat at my conscience, but after ignoring my conscience for so long, it became calloused to the point I had none.

Knight noticed that I was changing and came around to talk to me several times. He was a guy that hated to get right to the point. He always considered people's feelings and didn't want to confront certain issues head on. But on the other hand if there was any injustice being dealt out he would be the first to jump right in and assess the situation and make whatever was wrong, right.

One night he let me know he was concerned that I was becoming so quiet in my nature and staying to myself more and more. I assured him I was fine and that it wouldn't be long until I would be back in the saddle again. Knight smiled, shook my hand and walked away.

I stayed to myself more because I, like everyone else, didn't want to accept anyone into my tight little circle. Everyone was like that. None of us made new friends. It was too hard on you when you lost them. In fact, there were gunners in flight that I never became close with because of this.

Some of the gunners didn't want to draw me into their circle and I understood why. But it never meant they wouldn't be there for me if I ever needed them. They would lay down their lives for me or any one of their brothers. You could never ask more than that from anyone. We all took that oath to protect each other and if the need ever arose, we would put it all on the line to live up to that commitment.

The more I tried to analyze my feelings and the way I felt, the more I realized that I had completed the transformation from a normal boy in small-town America to a person that had become hardened and almost without compassion. I had gone through a type of transformation that was necessary in order for me, or anyone of us, to survive physically and mentally. Everyone I knew was going through, or had already gone through this transition. The one single thing that bothered me the most was how I lost my compassion for humanity. I became as cold-blooded as those two gunners from my first day. I wasn't so eager to pass judgment on them so quickly anymore.

Hate became the blanket that helped me sleep at night. It helped me put it to rest and kept me focused. Hate became a friend and I was dependent on its presence. I kept this hate in my pocket. Revenge is its brother and we became one.

Chapter 20
Back In the Saddle

It was hard to start flying again. Hooter could tell I wasn't eager to begin gunning again. I had a real hard time putting Popp's death behind me. I had never lost a gunner before, someone that I had spent day in and day out with. It was hard to put it in perspective and get on with it. Hooter volunteered to come over to Slicks and fly gunner with me for awhile. He never told me, but I knew he was coming over on my account. It made my day having a friend like Hooter with me, but I was bothered by the fact he might meet the same fate as Popp.

Hooter and I talked about it and after hashing it out we figured we were a lot better off with each other than without. In a way I was selfish, I wanted the best gunner in the company with me. It not only increased my chances of survival having such an experienced gunner, but I would have a good friend with me and not breaking in some new guy. Most of all, I loved his nature and good conversation. Our talks always consisted of things that had nothing to do with war. He helped me through that difficult time after losing Popp.

Isn't it funny how you are always concerned more about your friends than you are yourself? I never had this type of feeling toward anyone other than my family. It was this type of feeling that brought us all close together. That, which was our best asset, was also our biggest burden. The pain when you lost a brother was hard, but keeping ourselves isolated from each other was even harder. We stayed a tight knit group of brothers. We swore an allegiance to each other, our allegiance and friendship was our most valued assets and we treated them as such. The respect for one another grew to the point there were never disputes over trivial bullshit. We didn't have time for such stupid encounters. We all united into one killing unit and everyone from the CO down gave us respect.

We kept a low profile in the company and mostly stayed to ourselves. There were now six gunners in our groupAt one time there had been ten of us. Scott, Popp, John, and the guy I replaced, Babcock, had all been killed.
There were other gunners that took their places, but we never became close to them.

We had friends in maintenance like Biggie, Burnett, and Schultz and considered them apart of our group, but they weren't a part of flight. We didn't worry about these guys. These three were a big asset to our operation and life would have been a lot harder without their support and help. Kenny (Biggie) would be going home soon and this would be one less person to worry about. I would miss him, but I would be happy for him at the same time. He had a wife to go home to and as he got closer to his ETS (End Time Service) date, the more he would talk about her.

As Biggie got closer to his ETS date, I would take his recovery missions for him. It was a break in my routine and I actually liked the missions. The crew he had trained was a good group of guys. Every time I needed someone to go with me on a recovery sling mission I had no problems getting volunteers. The missions made them feel like they were making more of a contribution toward the war, than just working on the aircraft.

I knew I would miss Biggie and his sense of humor. Watching him trying to change the bad habits he had accrued over here before he went home got comical. He came up with the idea that every time we caught him saying a cuss word he would have to do pushups. Ten pushups for each cuss word was the punishment. He had to do over a hundred pushups before we even got down to the flight line. That idea didn't last long. His arms got to hurting so bad he could hardly even move them. But he at least gave it a try. Biggie getting close to his ETS date made me think about my own. I still had a long ways to go, in fact I didn't like thinking about it too much. After awhile it became depressing, so I would put it at the back of my mind. We all use to get a kick out of sitting around and thinking of ways to go home. One of the ways was, if you got wounded bad enough you would be sent back home, but most of the time you getting wounded would only buy you a little time in the rear.

I remember one time in a ground attack while the bullets were flying over our heads, this guy I didn't know very well would stick his legs into the air hoping he would get hit so he could either go home or get some time off in the rear. I thought about doing this one time or another, mostly when I was down and depressed. But then it would be my luck the bullet would probably travel through my leg and come out the top of my head. Bullets have a funny way of exiting the body once they get under the skin. So this kept me from ever trying it. Plus the fact I only knew one idiot that actually pulled it off.

Time off for me was no big deal anyway. I had lots of leave built up and I could have gone on R&R if I wanted to. But I hated leaving only to come back to hear the bad news of someone getting killed. So I never took any of my leave that I had earned while I was in 'Nam. I would always think back to the news I received about Thunderbird when I returned from L-13 engine school in Vaung Tal.

I knew I would be one of the last of our group to go home, but it didn't bother me as much as it did in the beginning. Half my tour was over and in a way staying to see the outcome of everyone's fate would be closure. At least I would know who made it home and who that didn't. Besides, if I stayed maybe I could be instrumental in preventing one of my friends from being killed or at least do my part. I wasn't the only one that felt this way. A few of the other guys never took vacation either. It was something that we didn't want to do. We were always there for each other and it was this bond that kept us strong and made us feel safe. We did sometimes party a little hard but it was all we had to blow the pain from out of our heads, for a little while anyway.

For a little while each night we treasured each other's company and we made the most of it, no matter how silly we got. One time Alger, who used to work with West in Armament, got some undergarments sent to him from his girl and he dressed up with nothing but a black bra he had stuffed with rags and matching panties that had too much stuffing. We all cracked up. He caught us by surprise, entering into the hooch dressed to kill. It had to be the funniest thing I had witnessed sense I had been in country. We all copped a feel of that stuffed bra and had our pictures taken with him. Alger was a good sport and kept us laughing. He refers to this event as the night he almost got raped. It was always a good topic for future get-togethers and as much as we begged for him to do it again he never would. It was a onetime thing, he vowed, and becoming some thug's girlfriend was not on his agenda. He let us know that he was defiantly a pitcher and not a catcher. He was a good sport and we knew it was all in fun.

Alger and me

The war was always knocking at our front door and no matter how much we tried to act like we were back in the real world, Charlie would give us a rude awakening and jerk us back to reality. We were always getting mortared by him. Sometimes we would get hit during the day, but mostly we got it at night when we all were bunched together and the chance of casualties was at its greatest.

I knew several that were killed by these mortar attacks, but they weren't from Flight. These attacks were one of the reasons why we all got together underground. We figured the night was our time and wished Charlie would give it up. It seemed Charlie and the NVA never rested. Instead of wearing us down it only pissed us off more. We could hardly wait to get even with them when daylight came.

Charlie hated us. It was our gunships that kept them at bay and they knew it. Other outfits hardly ever got hit. In our situation tanks and big guns were not a threat to the enemy. There was a lot of jungle the tanks couldn't operate in and Charlie and the NVA could out maneuver them. They could stay out of reach of the big guns. The big guns were only at fire bases anyway and unless you were getting attacked they didn't play much of role where we were located. Our gunships brought the war to their front door and they hated us for it. That is why the NVA put bounties on our heads with the local VC, and Charlie would almost do anything to try and collect it.

Biggie's time to go back to the world came and everyone that knew him missed him. He was the topic of a many conversations for a long time. I saw West once in awhile, but he still never did anything but nod his head at me.

The everyday drudgery of combat was always present and it seemed my DEROS would never come. I thought of home more and more and the possibility of going home became increasingly real to me. Some days I hated thinking about home. It took me away from whatever I was doing and in some cases it was dangerous not to keep my mind focused on the mission at hand. I had begun to think I would never go home, now it was within reach. I had a little over five months left in country and couldn't keep myself from hoping, even praying, that I would make it back home. As I noticed a lot of new faces around, I knew I was getting short. But those new faces reminded me of the friends we had lost. The one thing that remained constant was the War, Charlie and Death.

Fear was the only thing that changed. When I first arrived in country and experienced death first hand, it seemed I would never conquer my fear of it and I admit I haven't and never will, but I have learned to *accept* death, which is a lot easier to do. For me, being afraid and fearing something are two different things and in the beginning I confused the two.

I would like to think I received my medals for bravery, but I didn't. Hate and revenge was my main motive and I believe others mistook it for bravery. When it got right down to it, it didn't matter to me what anyone thought. If anything, I had learned why West was like he was. I understood his solitude, his hate, his revenge. I knew West didn't hold me responsible for his brother's death and I believed whenever we met and made eye contact that he knew I knew.

Chapter 21
Geronimo

I could ramble on about this battle or that battle, but they were all the same. One confrontation with Charlie was like the one before and the one before would be like the next to come. What really mattered to any of us gunners were the kills we racked up. The more kills we accumulated the higher up the ladder of popularity you climbed. We wore our kills (ears) like medals and everyone that thought we were sick were the ones we punned the most. We thought it brought us respect and I guess to some degree it did. Deep down we all knew it was some crazy shit, but in a sick way we liked it.

Two confirmed kills in one day was a lot for a gunner to get. Kill got you free beer and gave those ones a bit stature that everyone relished in.

Believe it or not I missed Scouts so I figured I would fly gunner in Scouts for a couple to break up the routine.

Any gunner is welcomed back to Scouts so I had no problem finding a ship. Heck, Hooter said I could even take his. He told me I had been away from being a real door gunner for so long I probably wouldn't be able to hit a gook if he stood still. But Hooter was glad to see me come back to Scouts, even if it was only for a couple of days.

The next day we got an early start. I loved flying in the morning. It was cool and the jungle smelled clean, before all the rotting decay rose. Early morning had always made me feel good, like everything is new again. I was in a good mood and I was going to fly with my old buddy Mr. Knight. His Cobra was broken down and he thought he would do his buddy a favor and fly his mission for him and give him a day off. That was fine with me. I liked Mr. Knight, he was only a couple years older than me and we always had something to talk about. In fact, calling him 'Mr.' always seemed funny to me. He had a good education but didn't lord it over you like most officers in the 9th. He was a down to earth guy and he and I looked forward to flying with each other that day.

We started by more or less playing around with the aircraft. We did some low flying map of the earth shit then we would pop up to a couple of thousand feet, do a hammerhead and then head back to earth, pulling out to a straight and level flight a foot or two above the trees. Goofing off and glad to just be alive. Then the fun was broken when Knight spotted what looked like a man with a gun and a pack riding a bicycle down a trail. Knight did a ninety degree bank to the right, lined up on the trail and flew barely above the trees. Sure enough, there was a gook riding down this trail, but he didn't even acknowledging our presence. He was VC, no doubt it. He had an AK-47 strapped to his back with at least fifty pounds of rice tied to the bike rack.

We flew over him low-level, thinking this would send him to the bushes. But this guy kept a steady course down the trail. Knight laughed and asked me how I wanted to handle this. I told him I was going to throw an eight pound WP at him to see if I still had the touch. Because of the twenty second fuse on the W. P. grenade, I was going to have to cook this one off around fifteen seconds. That meant I would hold the grenade ten seconds with pin pulled before I threw it.

Knight came back around and as we lined up on the target I pulled the pin and counted around fifteen seconds and then let go of the grenade. The grenade hit the guy dead square in the middle of his back, flew him up and over his handle bars, the grenade then bounced off into the bushes and nothing. The damn thing didn't even go off, a dud. Regardless of the grenade not going off, the guy didn't move. Knight came back around and we landed. The gook had an imprint of the grenade in the middle of his back, about eight inches deep. Part of his spinal cord and backbone had been driven into his lungs he was indeed dead. As Knight and I got back into the aircraft we both laughed.

"That is crazy," Knight said. "You killed him deader than shit without a bullet fired.

"That's one!" I yelled as I reached down and cut off his right ear. I wrapped the ear in a rag and placed it in my survival pack.

We didn't see anyone else the rest of day. We flew around the grid or sector we were given and shamed out the rest of the day. We didn't have a high bird with us or even an observer. Knight and I were merely getting used to our old jobs and the company gave us a couple of areas to check out. Knight asked me if I wanted a little stick time and I told him 'of course,' so he landed the aircraft and let me fly left seat. We had no gunner now so we kept the aircraft high to let me have a little fun at the controls. The LOH (OH-6A) was the first aircraft I had ever flown. I loved flying it. Knight let me fly back to Quan Loi. We refueled and headed right back out. We had completed our assignments we were going out for the hell of it. As we flew over the tree tops, Knight asked me if I wanted to smoke a joint. I was surprised but agreeable.

This was the first time Knight and I had smoked weed together. I heard he was cool with it but didn't expect that he and I would ever be doing the deed together, especially flying around in the AO. I took the aircraft into a steep climb to show my excitement and he laughed. I looked over at his smiling face and today I can still see his white teeth peering out from behind his large bushy moustache. It wasn't long before both of us were stoned to the max. You ever have that dope that makes you laugh and gives you that good aura about yourself and your surroundings? Well, that was it. That day was a good day and we told each other how everyone needs a day off from the job. It drew to an end but Knight and I knew the next day we would be back in the saddle. Then we would be working close to the Cambodian border. Movement had been reported and we knew that usually meant contact with the enemy and combat.

The next morning I was ready. I had the daily finished on the aircraft and was ready to find out who we would be teamed up with and where we were going. Knight told me we had a high bird, which meant we were going head hunting. We would be teamed up with Window and Hooter. Two Scouts usually meant lots of movement and we were most likely going to have an exciting day. Hooter came over to my aircraft to remind me that he still lead the company in kills and that after that day I wouldn't be able to catch up. I laughed and told him he was pretty cocky for a guy for leading me by one kill. He told me yesterday didn't count because I didn't use my gun. Knight laughed and told Hooter the gook was just as dead. He then told Hooter I didn't need bullets, that 'Brooks could kill gooks with rocks if he had them to throw.' Everyone around laughed at that, including Hooter. Hooter told me he wasn't worried, I would be buying the beers tonight.

It seems funny to me now looking back, we were more concerned about leading the unit in kills than we were about actually getting killed. War had become routine. We accepted combat like it was just another day at the office. It did no good to worry about it. While in combat, accepting death as a possibility becomes a part of your everyday life. You get to a point you are tired of worrying about it and in a way come to believe in predestination.

Quan Loi was three clicks from the border and we had plenty of time to have a little fun on the way. Knight and Window played cat and mouse with the aircraft by playing follow the leader. Hooter would come up on the radios and ask me if I could hit this target or that target. To conserve our ammo we only fired at a few targets to make sure our guns were good to go. By the time we got to the AO, movement had been spotted and some enemy fire reported. There was no need for all of us to jam up the AO with a lot of aircraft trying to talk at once, so our three aircraft (two OH-6A and one Cobra) set up a flight pattern on the outskirts of the perimeter of operations.

It wasn't long when Hamilton's LOH spotted the gooks and delivered fire. All hell broke loose and everyone started receiving fire while a couple of ships, including Hamilton's, took hits. Hamilton dropped smoke where he had received fire and it was a good marker for us. Hooter's aircraft was the first to go in. His ship would cover Hamilton's retreat to protect his blind side, the ass end of the aircraft.

Knight banked a hard right to make a circle to put some distance between Window and Hooter. I knew once the circle was complete we would head in to cover for them. Then the high bird (Cobra) would dive down to dump his rockets on the enemy's position. We had done this maneuver many times. We wouldn't go in if the Cobra was in position to make his dive. But the Cobra was not ready to commit at this time, so we were next up to engage. We were in good shape, Hooter and Window shut the door on those guys and they quit firing. By now Knight and I hoped the gooks were taking cover and too busy saving their own bacon to be concerned with us. We made our run and sure enough, Hooter and Window made those gooks take cover. As we came out of our gun run here came the Cobra. Knight got the hell out of Dodge and all was well.

The only thing was, Hooter got a kill and now I was behind by two again. We would be going in first on the next contact and I sure wanted those kills. I radioed to Hooter and told him it didn't count because he hadn't gotten the ear yet.

"I will," he replied and as he flew by me in the opposite direction I saw him give me the finger. I laughed and then he turned around and mooned me. Knight and I both cracked up. The observer thought we were all crazy and made a remark that he wasn't doing this again, but he was laughing as hard as we were. It would be a good time around the hooch tonight. But man, I had to at least get one kill. I better not come home empty-handed that night or there would be hell to pay. I didn't mind buying the beer, but if I didn't get at least a kill I would be hammered like you wouldn't believe.

Knight told me to sit tight. We were going to get some altitude and see if we could pick up on some other action. It seemed everyone was in some type of an engagement with the enemy but us. Hooter had his kill and Window was tailing us and kept taunting over the radio, saying "We got ours, where are yours?"

About that time it came over the radio Hamilton and his crew needed help. He was about a mile from where we were and we headed there fast. Hooter and Window quit goofing off and gave us the thumbs up and fell in behind us. We had the aircraft all out and as we flew over this rice patty I looked down. It was nothing but a big blur.

We started taking hits. A fifty cal in the tree line had zeroed in on us and we were taking hits all over the place. The aircraft vibrated so badly I could hardly see. I asked Knight if we were all right but he wouldn't answer me. I knew then that Knight must be hit. I couldn't see him but I looked across and saw the observer in left seat looking like he was about to shit his pants. I knew for sure Knight was hit and to top it off we were headed for some trees.

If a flight crew knows one thing about going down, that is you don't want to go into the trees at any kind of speed. You will leave body parts in the trees. Trees have the tendency to rip the aircraft apart and the aircraft with all that sharp metal will rip you apart, so right away I thought about jumping. It is something I contemplated many times, so I thought it was my only option. Our speed had dropped to about seventy knots, we were about thirty feet off the deck and to me the rice patty full of water was a lot better choice than the trees.

So I broke off a bunch of rounds that fed my M-60 and threw it out, then shortly afterward I bailed. I turned my back to the impact and from that point on, everything is a blank.

The next thing I remembered was feeling cold. I mean *cold*. My eyes opened and right above my head was a large window unit air conditioner, blowing full blast on me. I tried to make sense of it all. I thought I was back in the States. Then I started remembered the crash and jumping and I tried to move but I could not. I tried to turn my head and again I could not. I then I yelled out for help. A woman came to my side and explained to me that I was okay and that I was in The Vaun Tau hospital. I had been in a crash and hurt myself, but I was doing fine and not to worry.

I looked up into those beautiful round eyes and thought I was home. I didn't care that I was hurt, I was home. Then I remembered her saying 'Vaung Tau.' As I pieced everything together I realized I wasn't anywhere near home. They told me I had ruptured my kidneys and cracked a plate in my lower back. They had me strapped down so I couldn't move. The doctor checked the feeling in my legs and I could feel them. He told me I would be fine, I just needed to lay still.

The hospital was great. I got addicted to the air conditioner and hated to give it up when I was sent back to my unit. In total I was there in the hospital about two months and it was a great vacation. The nurse that took care of me was sweet and as I started getting better we became good friends. I had an affair with her which caused me to get sent back to my unit. It seems my doctor was wanting to date this nurse and when he found out about her sneaking me out of the hospital on several occasions and about our affair, he had me declared fit and I went right back into combat.

The nurse's name was Vicki and I really don't want to get into our relationship, out of respect for my wife. It meant nothing to either of us. We were two people caught up in the times and we took from each other what was desired and needed at the time. It had been a long time since I had had a woman in my arms. She was seven years older than I and gave me more than I am sure I gave to her. I hold the highest respect for her and I wish I could meet her today. I never really got the chance to say a proper goodbye and that has bothered me over the years. I am sure she knows I cared for her. How could I not have some affection for her? She gave back to me something I had lost, and that was a sense of compassion again.

Everyone knew I would be sent back to the States. But no, here I was back in the middle of things. Back in Quan Loi.

Hamilton had gotten killed while I was in the hospital. I thought about all the good times we had together. I will always remember that time after Popp's death when he and Hooter came to my hooch and we drank that bottle of Johnny Walker Black, the time I hit him when he tried to pull me off of Popp. He was always slow to anger and quick to apologize if he had thought he might have crossed a boundary with someone.

Hooter was gone. He made it back to the States and was one happy camper. He left me a letter that was written to boost my spirits, telling me to never give up on going home. Hamilton's death hurt Hooter more than anything. The night of his goodbye party he broke down and cried. I had missed the big party and everyone told me the only thing that brought Hooter out of his stupor was talking about me un-ass-en that aircraft and hitting the only damn tree in the rice patty.

You see, Knight and the observer didn't crash the aircraft. Knight overtook the aircraft, pulling in pitch (collective) to get them over the tree line I thought we were going to hit. Then he set the aircraft safely into a river. Knight and the Observer swam ashore and thought I had gone down with the ship. The ICS (intercom system) had been shot out by the gunfire and they had no way of telling me what their big plan was.

Anyway, I was the object of everyone's humor for what seemed like forever. It was Hooter and his crew that saw me jump and it was he and his crew that took me to the hospital. Hooter had given me three morphine shots by the time they gotten me to medical help. Hooter told a story about how when they landed the aircraft at the hospital I was overwhelmed that there were American nurses coming to the ship to take care of me. Hooter told everyone he knew then I would be all right. To this day I don't remember a thing. I only remember waking up under that air conditioner.

Hooter led the whole 9th Cav. in kills. He had thirty-seven by the time he went home. I had only thirty-three at this time. Hooter, to me, was a rock. Every gunner or soldier wished they could have been like him. But 'Nam broke him down like all of us. In the end we all faltered, we all suffer battle scars in one way or another. Hamilton was Hooter's breaking point. After Hamilton got killed that was it for Hooter. He did not fly his last couple of weeks. In his letter to me he expressed his grief. Tears stained the letter where he wrote about Hamilton. His letter gave me encouragement, telling me to never give up on going home. He topped it off with

'You will never lead me in kills.' In the letter he left me a big old joint to smoke on his behalf and then signed off.

I made a bold statement in front of everyone one night, after smoking that joint, that Hooter left me, and that I would have more kills than thirty-seven by the time I left country. I only had to get five more kills to my record. Deep down I knew I wouldn't. My heart was not in it. The time in the hospital gave me pause for reflection and Hooter being gone took the wind out of my sails. Plus being with Vicki had an effect on me. My way of thinking had been altered. Women do have a certain influence on you. Vicki sure did on me.

I only had two and half months to go. I was a two digit midget and it felt good. The Old Man even started calling me a short timer. I was on flight status but the Old Man wouldn't let me fly for awhile. I think he knew it even before I did that I'd lost heart in the missions. Going home was becoming more to me than a dream. It was a reality and I didn't want to do anything to screw it up. I went to the Old Man (Colonel Young) and tried to explain to him I didn't want to fight anymore and he understood. He told me he would let my aircraft do all the mail runs and wouldn't use me on missions unless they really needed me. He gave me the option of going back to maintenance, but I wanted to finish my time in Flight. It had become a personal vendetta for me to finish my time in Vietnam in Flight. So I told him that I wanted to stay where I was.

I asked Colonel Young if he thought I was afraid.

"Yes, you are afraid," he said. "Afraid you won't see home again, afraid you won't see your wife or girlfriend, or maybe your parents or brother or sister. Dennis, everyone is afraid of losing those things. But as a soldier? No. I don't believe you are afraid any more or less than anyone else. You are not afraid to commit yourself to your job, and that is all any of us can do. Do your job for your brothers, your duty and pledge to your country, and your individualism as a man will never fail you."

At the time I used to think it was just a bunch of military hoopla, but as time went on I realized there is a certain merit to those words. I haven't forgotten them.

Flying the mail runs was boring, but boring at this stage of the game was good. I didn't mind being bored. Every day we made the mail run we made sure to take a different route each time. We didn't want to give Charlie a chance to set up some kind of an ambush with a B-40 or RPG. We flew off the top of the trees when we knew there was a possible danger and then we would go up to altitudes of 4000 ft. when we were getting close to Pheau Phien. Flying high was nice because it was so cool and you could close your eyes and let the sound of the rotors put you to sleep.

All the friends that I had were gone now, except for Barnet and Schultz in maintenance. I knew a lot of the guys in Flight but didn't associate much with them. I hung out mostly with Schultz and Barnet. Barnet and I slept in the same hooch. We had our own cubes about 10 ft. by 8 ft. and they were next to each other. Every night Barnet, Schultz, and me would get together and talk about anything and everything. We tried to keep the war out of our conversations, but time to time we did touch upon the subject. How could we not?

I never went down to the Cross Rotor club anymore. It had the opposite effect on me than its intent. Besides, Barnet and Shultz wouldn't be welcomed there anyway. Murray and Holt still hung out there at night, but the brotherhood that joined the club now were not the brothers I fought with. Everyone I had associated and fought with was no longer around. Soon it would be my turn to leave and believe me, I was counting each day.

At one time Barnett wanted to fly gunner. He got hooked on flying mail runs with me. We would pick out targets to shoot and he got a kick out of it. We didn't need two gunners to pick up mail, so the guys in maintenance liked flying left gunner seat. We usually made the mail run in the evening and this allowed people in maintenance to have their work assignments completed so they could go on the run with me. It was their time and the Old Man didn't care if they wanted to fly mail runs. In fact, the Old Man thought it was a good way to coach people into flight. I enjoyed the mail runner job and I enjoyed Barnet's company. Barnet got a little door gunning practice at targets each day and I shot at a few targets myself. It was fun shooting for the fun of it and not in combat.

I did get punned a lot by some of the new FNGs. I had heard them say I had lost my nerve. I guess in a way I had. Flying and fighting the war was about over for me, and going home in one piece had become a much higher priority. Especially at this stage of the game. My thoughts were of home and trying to figure out what I was going to do with my life. I had no interest in war, Vietnam, or the Army. But first steps first and getting home was surely my biggest and most important first step.

Punning me became most of the FNGs' past time, but none of them had seen real combat, so it didn't bother me. They thought if they got shot at or took a hit in their aircraft, they were really fighting the war. It wasn't long afterward that they quit making little remarks and comments about me. In fact, they wouldn't even look my way when I headed out to the flight line each morning.

Knight was the reason they started keeping their comments to themselves. I was told by Barnet that Knight took them aside and let them know in no certain terms that I had paid my dues. It reminded me of the time he confronted me when I was taking part in calling the Cobra pilots Thunder Chickens. Knight had a way of putting things in their proper place. He told them of the time I went in after him and Hooter and got a Bronze Star for doing so and that I had been given another Bronze Star for Valor. He told them I had over thirty Air Medals and I had received the Purple Heart more than once. When he was through they didn't have a whole lot to say. It was okay by me. They would have their chance to step up to the plate and prove themselves, and if I knew anything I knew this was going to happen.

Barnet got a kick out of hearing Knight rake them over the coals. And he didn't waste any time letting me know. It felt good to know my contributions in Flight didn't pass without notice. It made me proud that I was respected by someone that I held in such high esteem. Knight and Hooter were my heroes and I tried to fashion myself after them. If I was okay in their eyes, then I didn't much care what anybody else thought of me. I missed having my friend Hooter around. He was the only one that I really had anything in common with.

Knight was around, but he was an officer and they had their thing going on. He came around time to time and visited me in my hooch. We would set around and drink Jim Beam and talk about all the funny things that had happened to us. We never talked about our fallen brothers, only about the good times. Our conversations would sometimes take us down that path where our experiences and stories mingled with our comrades, but we both made sure it didn't become the main topic of our discussion. We had faced a lot together, but the one incident that made him laugh the most was me jumping out of that aircraft. This was a subject I knew would be around the rest of my life.

I always felt special that someone of his education, stature and background wanted to spend time with me. He had a way of making me feel better about myself. I had this inferiority complex because of my lack of education and he made me feel smarter by the way he would talk to me. Knight was a good friend and helped me develop more confidence in myself.

I made a mistake one day by telling Knight I was just a mechanic and nothing more than a crew chief and a glorified door gunner. He let me have it with both barrels. He pointed a finger at me and told me I was not just a mechanic, I was an aircraft technician and it was up to me how good of a technician I would become. He told me he didn't want to hear me down grade myself again by calling myself 'just a mechanic.'

One of the things that shocked me was that Hooter supplied Knight with dope. When Knight told me that, I almost fell off my bunk. "Hooter never told me that," I said. Knight laughed. The more I thought about it though, the more it made sense why Hooter would not tell me. We would never break confidentiality with another brother. Knight being an officer made it even more of a touchy situation if anyone found out. I'm sure Knight asked Hooter to keep it under wraps. He asked me if I had a steady supplier.

I laughed. "Oh I see, you need a contact now that Hooter is gone." I pulled a bag from my survival pack. Knight opened his shirt and showed me a big bag of his own. Knight thought it was funny I kept my dope in my survival pack. I told him man cannot live off of food alone and we both laughed. He asked me if I wanted to get down. I had just the spot. I took Knight out to my bunker. We smoked dope from an old water buffalo horn that Knight had made into a water bowl. Like I said, Knight was one of the coolest persons I have ever known.

This and a couple of other times were the last times in Vietnam we smoked pot together, before he went home. In Vietnam anyway. I will always remember flying around that day higher than a kite and simply being kids again. Small and minute as this event was, it's times like those you treasure the most.

Head Hunter Killer Team

Chapter 22
Cambodia Campaign

Well, you might know I couldn't stay out of the war long. The CO called me and a couple of other guys that were short timers to his office. What was strange is that he called us in to talk to us all at the same time. There was me and a couple of guys in the Blues that I was familiar with but didn't know all that well that went to see the Old Man. He told us there was an operation that was coming up that in some way may involve us three.

He told us he would use us only if it was necessary and it would be in a low profile assignment if he even had to use us at all. He wanted to tell us first hand because he didn't want us to think he had gone back on his word to try and keep us out of the war until we went home. He told us that as of now that was all he could say and we would be briefed with everyone else tomorrow.

As we walked out of the Old Man's office I said, "That was interesting."

None of us were very happy. We knew it was too good to be true for us to shame out until our ETS or DEROS date. I didn't say much, but I wasn't looking forward to whatever the Army had in store for us.

The next morning the CO addressed all the troops. I don't remember the exact day but it was in the middle of the week late April, 1970. The CO told us all that we were about to invade Cambodia. He told us we were to hit strong points inside Cambodia and to prepare our aircraft today with everything we would need for a full day's mission on that Friday.

I walked to my aircraft with a few FNGs and listened to them talk about going on sick call Friday morning so they wouldn't have to fly. Of course I didn't want to go. Four months ago any of us would have given our left nut to go into Cambodia, but now I only had a couple of months and I would be out. But I couldn't pass up this opportunity to pay them all back for the punning I took from them in the past weeks. So I said, "Man, I hate to hear that shit. The gooks have radar controlled anti aircraft 20 mm cannons across the border." You could see the fear in their faces. I laughed to myself as I headed to my aircraft to get it ready.

I zoned out thinking about this Cambodia campaign, while at the same time getting things in order on my aircraft. I had made a check list and I was double-checking it to make sure I hadn't forgotten anything. Then I heard, "Are you locked, cocked and ready to rock?"

I turned around and I felt better seeing my friend Knight walk toward me. He had a big grin on his face and two cold beers in his hands. "Want a cold one?" he asked.

"Sure! Not going to turn that down." We crawled up into the aircraft and started drinking our beers.

About half way through he asked me if I would be his gunner the next day.

"Tomorrow?" I asked. "I thought it was Friday?"

"Well, all the enlisted men think it is Friday. They don't know it, but for a fact tomorrow morning the Old Man is going to tell them different. He doesn't want any of the hooch maids to know for fear of them telling the local VC for money. Plus the Old Man doesn't want the whole company on sick call Friday. Leave it to Colonel Young to figure all the angles." Knight asked me if I wanted to fly with him. He could tell by my hesitation that I didn't really want to fly. He told me he understood and that the Old Man was going to let me fly gunner on the standby aircraft. So I may not even leave the ground if no one got shot down. I told Knight I would fly gunner with him. I was probably going to fly anyway. What were the odds that no one would get shot down? I would as soon fly gunner with him as to fly gunner with some other pilot.

That made Knight's day, he told me not to tell anyone we were all hitting Cambodia a day early. I wouldn't say a word. I wanted to see the expression on their faces when the Old Man dropped the news on them. I told Knight I had to tell a couple of people in maintenance and that Schultz and Barnet could keep their mouths shut. He didn't seem to care and we both laughed as we finished our beers.

That night I wrote a long letter to Roni that I never mailed. I wrote her a letter telling her if I didn't make it home to go on with her life. I wrote her the sweetest words I could think of telling her how much I loved her and how I could have never in a thousand years have found a girl as wonderful as her. I said my goodbyes in a letter to the only person in the world that really knew me. I sealed the letter, put it in my personal belongings and boxed up everything I owned. It was to be shipped out to her address if anything happened to me.

I had an insurance policy I'd taken out for $20,000.00 naming her as the beneficiary and I made sure the policy was also with my belongings.

I knew my chances of not going home had increased and sleep did not come at all. I spent the whole night mentally preparing myself. I was really fortunate in one aspect because none of the other guys knew what was in store for them when morning came. At least I had a chance to put things in order in my mind if death was going to knock at my door. I had come to terms with death before. This was not the first time I went through this ritual. Sleep never comes the night before, if you know you are going into battle. But this was so different, for once during my tour I had hope that I was going home. The hope now turned back into doubt and I had to give up the thought of actually making it back to the world. It was hard but before daylight I had put it out of my mind. I closed my eyes lowered my breathing, but sleep still did not find me.

I was up before sunrise and went out to my aircraft and drank a cup of coffee. I went over my list several times. I had double of everything. I didn't know who my gunner would be and at this point I didn't really care. I made sure I had my survival pack with extra water and food (LURPS.) I loaded up an AK-47 in case we got shot down inside Cambodia. I only had two clips (60 rounds) but I would only use the gun for hunting my food. Using an AK would not alert the NVA or VC of anything out of the ordinary. An M-16 or M-60, on the other hand, would draw attention to me if I had to use it behind enemy lines. Besides, humping an M-60 and all that ammo was out of the question. I thought about taking an SKS, but not enough fire power if you need it. I had my compass, maps, knife, and machete. I had pin flares, smoke grenades, and two hand grenades. I had my .45 ACP pistol and ammo, small first aid kit, and poncho. I brought a stick of C-4 along to cook with. I brought some cord to set up booby traps, some salt tablets and malaria pills and of course extra water in cans. I wasn't taking any chances of another ship not being able to pick me up. If I had to walk my way back to Quan Loi I would and I would be as prepared as I could to complete the trip.

Cambodia was mostly triple canopy jungle and getting rescued may be difficult. But I was also bringing along my rappelling D-Ring and strap. I know Knight didn't pack a survival pack. None of the officers did which I always thought was stupid. I think Knight was depending on me to get him back if it came down to it and that would be no problem, I had enough for us both. Of course the co-pilot would be screwed. I only really knew Window, Knight and Ryan and they all would be flying their own birds with FNGs for co-pilots. So anyone outside of my friends would be on their own. Besides, they were all officers and if captured they were treated better than enlisted men. Officers may get imprisoned but enlisted men get dead. So if it came down to it, before I got captured I would be a long gone pecan one way or the other.

It wasn't long before I heard some of the officers and Top going around and waking everyone up. I gave them awhile and decided to make it to the formation because I had to see the faces of the ones that had no idea we were hitting Cambodia that day.

When the Old Man told the company we were hitting Cambodia you could have heard a pin drop. Some of the new guys turned white as a sheet. All the older troops like Murray & Holt just shook their heads and after awhile grinned at the FNGs. I walked up to Murray and asked him what he thought. He made the comment we were too short for this shit. Then he smiled and made another comment about he wondered why the Old Man wanted us to get our aircraft ready two days ahead of time. We had those shit-eating grins on our faces as we looked at each other and then turned toward our ships. The three of us walking together to the flight line was like a gunfight scene in an old western movie. We were the old timers and walked side by side down the middle of the flight line. It struck us funny. Holt made some remark and we laughed then shook hands and headed for our aircraft.

When I got to my aircraft there were several people standing around it and they had cameras in their hands. As I got closer I noticed they were news people. As I got even closer, one of FNG gunners pointed at me and told one guy I was the one he was looking for. The reporter approached and asked me if I was Brooks. I acknowledged that I was and he started to interview me. He told me that he was going to do a small article on me and he would make sure it got posted in the paper in my home town of Slaton, Texas. He wanted me to get my M-60 and pose for a shot, so I picked up my .60 turned around and there was Knight standing behind another one of these reporters with his knife held close to this guy's ear acting like he was going to cut it off. Well, how could I keep a straight face after that gesture? I cracked up and as I did this photographer took the picture.

So, when it was all said and done and the story was posted in my hometown paper, I had this dumb-looking laugh across my face making me look like I was having the time of my life and looking forward to battle. I enjoyed the recognition and if anything it was a testament for my friends back home that I was still alive and kicking. I told Knight he had one coming. He just chuckled.

Knight then introduced me to a new gunner who was a grunt that had volunteered to fly with me. I looked at Knight in disbelief and as we stepped off to the side I asked him what the *hell* was going on. He told me this was all there was that every ship that could fly was flying and we were short on gunners. I told Knight they could have least given us a day or two with the guy. Knight acknowledged I was right but we would have to make the best of it.

I have nothing bad to say about grunts (infantry,) they have indeed pulled their weight in this war. But firing a free gun (not mounted) M-60 from a flying aircraft and at a moving target takes a little getting used to. His gun alone was a joke and he didn't take lightly to me dogging him about his gun. His .60 had a bipod barrel and a grunt shoulder stock on it. As soon as you stuck this gun out the door of a moving aircraft the bipod on the barrel would act like wings on an airplane and you would never get on target with it.

I handed him one of my spare modified barrels and told him to install it on his .60. I then went to supply and checked out an aviation butt plate and also had him install this modification to his gun. He didn't go for the modification to his M-60 and bitched the whole time we were modifying the weapon. There were no sights on the barrel and this bothered the guy to no end. I told him we shot aviation ammo which was full tracers and he would have to get used to walking his line of fire to the target and that the faster he could get on target the better for us all.

I explained not to lead his target like on the ground, even though the target may be running. That because of our airspeed there would be a huge power curve likened to a curve ball in baseball and that you fired behind your target and walk the power curve until it connected. And one of the worst habits that a grunt has when he flies gunner is he wants to shoot his gun in burst of ten rounds at a time. They do this in order not to burn up their gun barrels during a fire fight. But as I have mentioned before, in the air the wind flowing over the barrel keeps it cool so you can rock and roll and not worry about burning up your gun barrel.

I thought that any gunner at all is better than none at all, and if we have the time to practice a little before we get to our AO, the better off we will be.

As I continued to give this guy a little instruction, I looked at Knight and he would have his shit-eating grin on his face. He approached me and said, "Now you know why I wanted you to be my gunner."

I smiled and shook my head and told him I owed him two and was going to get payback. All he did was show me those teeth from behind that thick mustache. Nothing bothered this guy. Knight took everything with a grain of salt.

As soon as the sun came up troops arrived from everywhere. I saw people that I had not seen since AIT and some I haven't seen since jungle training and rappelling school. It seemed all of us had been stationed up and down the Cambodian border and now the Army was using Quan Loi as one of their base of operations for this campaign.

It was nice talking to some of my friends that I had trained with back in Ft. Rucker. While the pilots and squad leaders all went for the flight briefing we got caught up on all that had happened to us while in country. I didn't say much, I really didn't have anything to tell them that they hadn't heard a thousand times. I wanted to tell them about John and Popp and Thunder, but they didn't know them, it would just be another name. Everyone had lost friends. We all had that in common for sure.. We figured out that out of the four hundred of us that had come over here together, over half of us were still alive. No one wanted to ponder on the death count too long, for we all knew there would be more to fall before this so-called Cambodia Campaign was done. The war wasn't over for us yet, everyone was a two digit midget and we were counting down the days until we could get the hell out.

All of us had changed, the old personalities were gone. We started this war as kids and all that we thought was so important to us back then seemed funny to us now. Some of my friends changed to the point it was hard to recognize them. Everyone had lost weight and looked different, but it was more than that. It was a melancholy feeling where we morphed from kids back on the block to men. We laughed and exchanged stories, but it was small talk to be friendly and it was nice for us all to see familiar faces and friends we had made back in training.

The flight briefing didn't take too long. The pilots knew the sectors that had been given to them. They have known for some time and today's briefing was to go over all of it one more time. Knight and I had talked about where we would be going. It was a place over the border by what we call the Fish Hook on the map. Intelligence had spotted movement in this area and we and three other gunships would be head hunting in this area. It wasn't long and we fired up and headed out. Window and

Knight were teamed up in the same aircraft. It was strange having two pilots with almost the same flying skills in the same aircraft. Knight had been on a lot more combat missions and if it was left up to me he would be my choice of pilot.

They flipped a coin to see who would be flying right seat (pilot) and who would be flying left seat (co-pilot.) Knight won the toss I was relieved. I felt more comfortable with Knight in charge of the mission. Window was a good pilot and under normal circumstances I wouldn't mind at all flying on a mission with him. But Knight, if anyone at all, could get us back home safe. The only other pilot I would feel comfortable with would be Ryan. Ryan and Knight in my opinion were the best. Ryan was Hooter's pilot and I knew he hated flying with a new gunner on a mission were we all knew there could be a lot of action.

Everyone was tight. The chit chat we usually made going out on a mission was nonexistent. This mission was serious. We had all been across the border into Cambodia illegally on one mission or another and we all knew we most probably would be facing fortified positions of NVA. I figured after today combat with the VC would be a welcomed sight. No one liked going up against the NVA. They were very well trained and they did not know the word quit. The only time they would give up a battle was if it was not advantageous to continue the fight. As much as we hated them, we respected them just as much.

I didn't have a lot of faith in my new door gunner. I could tell he was scared, but I don't think he was as scared of the enemy as he was of the unknown. I unbuckled my seat belt and positioned myself behind him. I put my hand on his left shoulder and as he turned to face me I gave him the thumbs up, he returned the gesture. I didn't want to talk to him over the ICS because I didn't want anyone to know this guy was about to shit a brick. Besides, this guy's fear would be gone as soon as we got into the thick of things. I know this to be true. I had been in his shoes many times. I knew how he felt and I couldn't help but try and comfort him by letting him know I understood and I was just as concerned as he.

I went back to my seat and strapped myself in and allowed myself to take a minute to free my mind. I thought if this was going to be my last day on earth that I wanted to think of something that had nothing to do with war. I let my mind drift back to my hometown. I thought about Roni and the time we slipped off to the canyon and swam nude in a small pond that was fed by a waterfall. The waterfall was only a small stream of water falling from about a thirty foot drop. I climbed up to the fall and dove into the water below to show off. I swam over to her and we lay by the water's edge and made love. I got so caught up in my thoughts of home and Roni that I wasn't aware of anything, even the sounds of the rotor as it beat the air into submission and made that all so familiar whap, whap sound.

My thoughts of home and Roni were interrupted by Knight's voice over the intercom asking if we wanted a few minutes to burst off a few rounds for practice. I needed no practice but I sure wanted to see how this new gunner handled his M-60 while in flight. The guy did fine, he had been using an M-60 his whole time in 'Nam and after a few pointers I showed him it was no time and he was finding his target without using gun sights. He would do fine. He wasn't as good as other gunners that had been flying awhile, but I had a feeling after today he would probably be a pro.

Before I even got strapped in again we got a call from the Scouts that they had taken fire. Hell, we hadn't even got to our AO and we had already made contact with the enemy. Knight banked the aircraft right and we descended from about 5000 feet to our target. The Scout gunner popped smoke and we made a gun run. Knight fired rockets and as they hit my gunner and I strafed the area. We didn't see anything; we laid down fire so the Scout could get out without taking fire up his ass.   We had a Cobra following us and he had twice the firepower. It felt great having a Cobra covering our ass. After we made our run I looked back and the Cobra was unleashing hell on the enemy's position. As we were leaving, the Scout started taking fire again. There had to be a lot of enemy troops, mainly because the Scout was at least five hundred yards away from his first point of contact. Knight immediately called in for more aircraft and as I looked off in the distance I saw other gunships changing their course toward our location.

While Knight and Window communicated with the other aircraft to coordinate a gun run, the gunner and I searched for movement. I saw some, but we flew over them so fast I couldn't get a shot off. I popped smoke and told Knight to come about. He pulled back on the stick and the aircraft shot straight up. He then kicked in pedal as the aircraft stalled and we did a hammer head and started back down to where I had popped the smoke. He fired off a couple sets of rockets and I fired toward the area I thought the enemy would be. As we came out of our dive and leveled out I saw a gook run for cover. I fired and he dropped, but we flew over so fast I couldn't tell if I got him or not. Suddenly we took hits to our aircraft. A couple of rounds came through the floor. I turned and looked at my gunner, expecting to find him with no head. A flashback about Popp. For a second I was stunned and it took me a little while to get back to what was going on. "We're hit, we're hit!" I didn't have to tell Knight and Window that, but it came out anyway.

Knight dropped the aircraft until it skimmed the deck. We flew low and long enough that we figured we were out of the enemy's area and popped up high enough in case we lost our engine, so we needed altitude to auto rotate. He radioed the others that we were headed back to Quan Loi. I couldn't take my eyes off of the instrument panel. Oil pressure. Fuel. Engine power. Transmission pressure. Hydraulics. It all looked good. Knight also scanned the instruments and looked back at me. We laughed.

"Brooks, we are too short for this shit," Knight said.

"No shit," I replied.

Window and the gunner didn't see the humor and looked pissed. Window said that we were both screwed up and the gunner just shook his head.

It wasn't long and until we made an approach to the flight line at Quan Loi. I took a breath of relief as the aircraft was on short final. We slipped into our revetment, shut down the aircraft and I crawled out looking it over for all the places we had taken a hits. We took four in the tail boom and two in the belly. I hoped we were hit bad enough that I would be working on the aircraft the rest of the day. I really wasn't that anxious to get back into the thick of things and Knight wasn't either. After assessing the damage, I noted the aircraft took hits through some bell cranks and spars in the tail boom and the rounds that went through the belly of the aircraft damaged some control tubes, so I would indeed be down the rest of the day.

Knight told me he would go get us a couple of beers and we would make the most of what was a good situation. A couple of guys came down from maintenance and we started repairing the aircraft. I told them to not be in such a hurry and they understood what I meant. The Old Man came down, patted us all on the shoulder and told us what a good job we did and then hurried back to the control room to listen to what was going on in the field. I thought about those guys but I was glad not to be a part of it all. Knight came back and we sat in the aircraft and hammered the first beer down, the second we sipped and enjoyed our 'Miller time,' even though it was a Bud.

I taking those rounds put Knight into the state of mind I had been in all along. He realized that we were too short to fly those missions and I know he thought more about going home. Knight had seen as much action as I had, even more. I wondered several times if I would ever see Knight concerned about not making it home. That day was the day. I believe he always felt like he had to be an example for the rest of us and could never let his true feelings surface.

I was honored that he wanted to spend this time with me. He knew he could tell me anything and I would not let it go any further than the two of us. I never once heard him bring up our fallen brothers, but he poured his heart out about Popp, Thunderbird and others. It is these moments that are in your mind and heart forever, thoughts that are shared with someone but are never intended to be shared with anyone else. Almost like sacred vows of silence, a mutual understanding of one's most private thoughts. You can tell others about the events that have happened in your life and even admit the hurt you feel about the loss of a friend. It's the damage to your soul and spirit that you usually keep to yourself. You fear people will not fully understand and tag you for something more than just weird. You try to project a certain image, but when memory of combat creeps into your mind the façade you present is something way different than who you really are or what you truly think. All things were shared that day between us two and for one it was a comfort to know I wasn't alone.

We both sat there on the floor of the aircraft, drinking our beer and hashing out our times in 'Nam, revealing our deepest thoughts.

We both had had enough of this war and it was time to think of home. A place where all our troubles would fade away. We both knew it would be a long time before we would ever feel half-way normal again. Home was the common denominator that gave us all hope for some type of normalcy in our lives. A hope we desperately needed, but were not really fully aware of just how much.

The solitude was broken by the Old Man coming out to the aircraft. He saw us sitting around drinking a beer and asked if that was all we had to do. Knight stood and saluted, but I sat on my dead tired ass and replied, "Pretty much, Sir."

He pulled a bottle of Scotch from behind him, smiled as he handed Knight the bottle and told us we better do it up right. As he walked away he turned and told me he wanted to talk to me later on that evening. I asked Knight what that was all about. He had no idea.

I asked some of the maintenance guys if they needed help and they told me they had it under control, they would work all night and have the aircraft ready in the morning. I was hoping it would be down for longer, say one month and I would be in the clear. I had only a couple of months to go and I would be out. As I walked back to my hooch I remembered the Old Man wanted to talk to me. I headed for the CO's office, wondering all the way what he could possibly want to talk to me about.

When I reached his office the door was open. I heard the radio transmissions and all our aircraft were inbound to Quan Loi. The Old Man motioned for me to come in. He was on the land line and talking to someone about receiving some spare aircraft. He pointed to a chair. I started thinking maybe it was bad news from home. The Old Man must have seen the frustration in my face because he cut his conversation short, put down the phone and told me I was through flying missions and that I was going to be on standby recovery from now until the time my DEROS. He was going to put me with a couple of new pilots and I would only fly gun ship recovery if one of our aircraft got shot down. I had played this game before with new pilots and I wasn't too anxious to do the gig again. I told the Old Man thanks, but no thanks, I would just stay with Knight and continue to fly gunner.

He told me Knight had one more mission and he was going to ground him in order to give him the opportunity to make it home. Knight had more than pulled his weight. After talking to Knight that day, I knew this news would be welcomed. I couldn't fly with Knight, I would just as soon be put on standby recovery so I told the Old Man that being on standby would be okay with me. He had Top take me out to the flight line and introduce me to the two new pilots I would fly with. Hopefully there would be *no* flying with these two, but you never knew.

These two had been together since flight school and were good friends. Both of them had that new guy look. They were amazed at everything around them.

They had never seen gunships like these back in the States. They had only been in country a couple of days but they acted like they knew everything about everything. They didn't know crap from shyola.

Top took them over to the aircraft that would be assigned to us. I was familiar with it, it was Hamilton's old gun ship. It had his signature all over it. Hamilton's old poncho was stuffed in the cubby hole behind the pilot's seat. I stuck my hand in the hole and pulled out an old box of .45 shells. Hamilton must have put them there, they had been there for awhile. I put them back and took a mental note of where those extra rounds were. There were a lot of little things like this that made me think of Hamilton. For the most part it made me sad but in a weird way it brought me a little comfort, like Hamilton was with me somehow. His survival pack was tied to the back of his jump seat and for now I left it there. I would replace it with mine later.

Top left the new pilots with me and told them that Knight would be down later to finish their walk through and give them some more information on our operation procedures. It was getting dark and Knight and I were going to hit that bottle of scotch, so I was hoped Knight wouldn't spend too much time with these two newbies, but I understood if he did. Knight always felt an obligation to help everyone.

Knight showed up shortly after Top left and commenced to give them a quick briefing and some pointers. Then he pointed me out to these two guys and told them it would be in their best interest if they would listen to me tomorrow. They looked surprised and I think I probably looked the same. They didn't take much stock in that comment. After all, I was just an enlisted man and they hadn't lived in 'Nam long enough to know that the officer-enlisted men segregation shit didn't hunt over here, but they would learn.

Then he asked them if they had any questions and neither one of them said a thing. "Okay then," Knight said. "Brooks and I have a date with this bottle." He pulled that bottle of scotch out from behind him, flipped it in the air and caught it by the neck, put his arm around my shoulders and we walked toward my old bunker. Those two didn't know what to think. Actually, it stumped me just as much as it did them.

As we got out of hearing range, I told Knight he wasn't going to be the most popular person on their list.

"Who gives a shit?" He laughed, not caring if the new guys heard. As we headed for my bunker he reached into the pocket of his flight suit and pulled out a bag of dope.

Yep, it was going to be a good night for two people I knew.

As we sat upon that bunker getting stoked, we continued the conversation from earlier in the day. We talked about people we served with and some of the roads we walked down together. Our paths crisscrossed each other from time to time. Knight and I had become good friends and it brought me great comfort to listen to him talk about home. He told me he had gotten his DEROS papers and would be headed back to the States in a couple of days.

I knew Knight was going home soon, but I had put his leaving to the back of my mind for so long I believed he would be here for me until my time was up. I hated to see him go, but I was really happy for him. I could tell his leaving pulled at him. I assured him that I would be fine. Knight and I didn't say much after that, we drank that Johnny Walker Black until the whole bottle was gone and smoked weed until we looked like we were looking through peep holes in a piss pot. After awhile we stumbled toward our hooches. We fell to the ground holding onto each other, laughing, and then laid there talking about something and that was it.

The next morning he and I were still in that same spot. Barnet found us, woke us up and handed us both some water. Man, did my head hurt. Knight and I looked at each other and laughed—painfully. Barnet asked who the pitcher was and who was the catcher, and again we painfully chuckled and pointed at each other. "Catcher."

By the time I cleaned up and got back down to the flight line everyone stood around like they were waiting for me. When I asked them what was up the two newbie pilots rolled their eyes and muttered some sarcastic remark about the war was waiting on me, or some shit like that. I didn't even acknowledge their existence. I put my .60 in the aircraft, turned around and planted my ass on the floor with my legs hanging out.

One of the officers asked me if I knew how to greet an officer with a salute. Hell, I couldn't even think of the last time I saluted an officer. The Old Man was the only one anyone ever saluted. I wasn't in the mood for FNG bullshit so I told him to piss off. He got up in my face and told me to come to attention. I stood up, threw my .60 over my shoulder and headed back to my hooch. Boy, were these guys full of their own egotistical bullshit. But they would learn, they had a long row to hoe and I found their arrogant attitude humorous to the point I laughed and shook my head as I walked passed them.

I knew they wouldn't leave it alone. I turned see one of them headed to the CO, most likely to put me on report or something like that. I didn't fret about it. What could they do, send me to 'Nam? I went to my hooch and waited for the Old Man to get in contact with me. I knew it wouldn't be long and he would send someone to fetch me. After about twenty minutes Barnet showed up and told me the Old Man wanted to see me. He laughed and said the two new officers sure didn't have anything good to say about me. "Pricks," he muttered.

Barnet told me the Old Man was taking up for me by letting those two assholes know they better get over it. The Old Man told them he would talk to me and then sent Barnet to let me know he wanted to see me in his office. Barnet and I sat there for a little while and talked. I wasn't in any hurry to get my ass chewed if that was the case, but all in all I really didn't give a shit one way or the other. I wasn't that upset with the two new Warrants' (Warrant Officers,) they were FNGs and like any new guy, they would learn things were different in the 'Nam.

I finally made it over to see the Old Man and as I walked into his office I saluted him and told him I was reporting as ordered. He put his head back and laughed, which took me by surprise. He told me to sit down and then talked about fishing and hunting. After several minutes of him mainly talking about nothing, he jumped up from his chair and told me to consider that an ass chewing and go ahead and go back to the aircraft. Then he walked from behind his desk got close to me and asked me if I had a good night's sleep then grinned from ear to ear. He had heard about Knight and me spending the night lying on the ground. As we walked out of his office, he said, "And I don't want to see you in my office again!" He winked at me then turned and went back into his office.

That went well, I thought. Colonel Young (The Old Man) was one in a million. I liked him from day one.

He could read men like a book. No wonder he had everyone's respect.

I went back to my hooch and picked up my .60 and survival pack then headed toward the flight line. As I got closer I saw both the WOs standing outside the aircraft talking to that grunt gunner that I flew the mission with the day before. I thought he was going to be my gunner today as well. As I approached one of the WOs told me that this guy was going to be the Crew Chief and I was going to be his gunner. I knew then and there we were going to get the pecking order straightened out before it went any further. I put my .60 and survival pack in the aircraft, collected my thoughts, turned and let them have it.

"First off, *Sir,* you don't have the authority or right to change anything. I am certified on this type of aircraft, I carry a 67N20 certification and because of my combat record I have been awarded a 67N2F (Flight Status) for as long as I stay in the military. This grunt that you are trying to replace me with is carrying a 11B MOS and doesn't know one thing about this aircraft. To put him in charge will be one of the biggest mistakes of your short career in this so-called man's Army. And if you want to go to the Old Man and talk about this stupid ass decision of yours, be my guest."

The expressions on their faces looked like that of a deer caught in the headlights of some car. One of them looked at the grunt and asked him if that was true. The grunt grinned and told them he wasn't even too sure where you refueled the aircraft.

"Oh! Well, we didn't know that," one of them replied.

I told them there was a lot they didn't know and if they didn't get on board and try to acquire a little knowledge of the way things are done, they might not even make it through their first week. "Has anyone talked to you about what we are doing in this company?"

They didn't say much because they did not know what was true about what people had told them and what was bullshit. From what I came to understand, they had been fed so much crap they didn't know what to think and that got me to worrying that I might have to fly with those two idiots.

Well then and there I knew from that point on it would be up to me to try and bring these two up to speed. I went over to the map case and noticed they didn't have but a couple of area maps. I told them to go to Operations and pick up all the maps for 3 Core Area of Operations and come back here as soon as they could. Man, I could not believe someone didn't brief these guys at all. As they took off for Operations I went to find Knight. I needed his help because I knew these two weren't going to listen to everything I had to tell them and even though I could fly the aircraft there was a lot of that pilot shit I did not know.

I found Knight in his bunk. He knew he didn't have to fly so he was nursing his head and taking advantage of his down time for the next couple of weeks before going home. When I told him of my ordeal he jumped out of bed and we headed for the flight line.

The two idiots saw Knight and looked relived. They were glad to see a fellow officer like Knight coming to their rescue. I know I felt better. I wondered if these two guys even knew how to fly. When Knight approached them they started in with all kinds of questions. Knight took the maps they had acquired from Operations and wrote in all of the headings and different

Fire Bases' radio frequencies they would need in each sector.

While Knight filled them in I picked up my .60 and headed for the firing pit to check out my weapon and to let out some frustration. I told the gunner to bring his gun along as well. When we got to the pit I fired off about fifty rounds, the gunner did the same and then we both walked back to the aircraft. When we returned Knight told me he was going to take those two out and see how much they knew and familiarize them with the AO I told Knight to take the gunner and let him get some practice in as well.

"Sure," he said, "you are not going with us?"

"Nope. I am going to talk to the Old Man."

Knight laughed. "I bet I know about what."

As soon as the aircraft got transitional lift I turned and went to see the Old Man. After talking to him for awhile he assured me he would let Knight get them fully briefed and trained on how we made gun runs and so on. It made me feel a little better, but not completely at ease with the situation. The shorter I got to my DEROS the more nervous I became. I could hardly sleep at night.

A couple of weeks passed and my new crew and I had gone out a few times to get Mutt and Jeff familiar with the area and to make a few practice gun runs. My gunner was doing better and we were actually starting to get pretty good. Good enough that I was a little more at ease with the whole situation. Tiger liked all the flying we were doing, but I wasn't going to take him on anymore real missions.

Time clicked off and I had one month and two weeks to go. But I was so worried about making it back to the world that my weight dropped to 135 lbs. I felt great, but I didn't feel like eating. I would take one bite of something and I was full. Nerves.

The missions into Cambodia were still in full swing and a lot of caches of weapons in hidden bunkers were being found and captured. The Old Man decided to have my aircraft fly him and a staff from Saigon out to take a look at one of the huge ones that was found. He wanted my aircraft to haul enough weapons (SKS rifles) back to Quan Loi to let everyone take one home for a war souvenir. More or less a morale booster for the men, this sounded like a good idea to me and it was sure enough going to be a good safe mission. Usually the caches were taken from the enemy and it would be a secured area.

Loading everyone was a riot. We had no seats in the aircraft except for the gunners' seats, so the staff that had flown up from Saigon would have to sit on the floor. The Old Man was going to fly co- pilot and he was excited because he hadn't flown in awhile. You could tell that he wanted to fly on missions but being the commander he usually had other duties, like coordinating attacks when we would all be out in the field on gun runs and in the heat of things. It was strange having him with us. I knew this was going to be a bullshit mission, but it would most likely be a safe one.

It wasn't long and we were airborne and across the border into Cambodia. All in all we had only lost about four aircraft and no casualties in the Cambodia campaign. The company had racked up a lot of kills and hauled tons of weapons and munitions from Cambodia back into South Vietnam and we all knew after this campaign the mortar and ground attacks against us would be cut back for some time.

As we approached our LZ there was only a platoon securing the underground cache of weapons. We had to land the aircraft about a hundred yards away. As we shut the aircraft down I told the Old Man I would stay with the aircraft while they scoped out the weapons. He keyed his mic twice as to acknowledge my comment.

After the aircraft was shutdown he came around to where I stood and asked, "Why don't you get your gunner to stay with the aircraft and come along with us?"

"No," I replied. "I have no interest in seeing a hole in the ground with a bunch of weapons in it."

He laughed slapped me on my flight helmet then he and everyone including my gunner walked off toward the bunker.

To take advantage of the shutdown time I started looking over the aircraft. I had a couple of things I wanted to check out. My pitch change links were starting to get some wear on them so I wanted to crawl up and give them a quick check. After checking the PC links I pulled a rag from my pocket and started wiping the grease off my swash plate, rotor head and such. I guess I had been fiddling around for about fifteen minutes when all hell broke loose.

The Old Man and the platoon were under attack. I could tell by the gun fire that there was a lot more enemy fire than our own. I jumped off the aircraft, grabbed my M-60 and as many rounds as I could wrap around my body and started toward the gunfire. I only got a few steps and decided I better call in gunship support. The grunts probably had a radio but I decided not to take a chance. I hit the battery switch on the aircraft and pushed the radio button.

"Triple nickel, blue team leader you copy."

"Go ahead triple nickel."

"I need air support now! Old Man on ground, under attack do you know our local?"

"Roger, Brooks, on our way pop red for location ident."

"Popping red, but this is my local, not the Old Man's and it's his group that is under attack."

Then across the radio the grunt unit confirmed our transmission and said they would pop color red and this would be their local. I popped the smoke and then ran for the location where I heard gun fire. I didn't get forty yards and ran into an NVA soldier looking down at his weapon trying to load it. He had an SKS and was throwing ammo into it. He looked up and saw me then closed the clip hinge and slapped the bottom of his weapon and raised his gun at me. I opened up with my .60 and he hit the ground hard as the impact of the rounds strafed across his chest and neck. I didn't even look to see if he was dead as I jumped over his body in a run.

When I got close to where the battle, I could tell the gooks had the Old Man and his team pinned down in a cross fire. I was too far away to be effective. The gooks must have heard my .60 because four of them moved toward my location. I had not been spotted so I hit the deck with my .60 pointed toward a spot I figured they would appear. I raised my head to see if I could spot them. Wouldn't you know it? They split up to flank me.

Damn I thought, *I hate this crap!*

I decided to move forward and deal with whatever came down. At best I hoped to get into position where I could line up on both groups. If I could get into the position I wanted I would have the enemy on my left, flanked to their right and the other group of gooks I would have directly in front of me and I would have their backs. But now I had to deal with the shitheads in front of me, or wherever they were. I lost sight of them and I couldn't hear worth a shit from all the gun fire that was going down.

Every ten or fifteen yards I would stop and watch for movement. I was also afraid when our gunships showed up I would be right in line of fire. I had my pin flares with me and I hoped if I did get the chance to use them our gunships would know it was me, or at least know I wasn't the enemy. I had been out of touch with the new gunners and I didn't know if they even knew what a pin flare looked like. My mind tried to cover all aspects of what was about to go down but when it came down to it, the outcomes of these situations were usually the draw of the card anyway. I figured my best bet was to stick to the plan and ride it out. I wished I had more time to think of a better plan, because I felt trapped and checkmated.

First things first. The gooks in front of me were my first priority and my biggest threat. It wasn't long before I saw movement. It was a gook and he was being as cautious as I was. I let him get close enough that I knew there was no way I would miss and let loose with a short burst. He fell to the ground. I couldn't waste any time, the burst of fire would maybe make the other two or three take cover and now would be the best and only opportunity for me to move forward. If luck was on my side maybe the gooks wouldn't believe I would advance. I thought this plan of mine was stupid, but I was committed and there wasn't any time to think of another one. Or to turn back. The Old Man and his group were getting hammered by automatic fire and every second I spent hunkered down and not moving, seemed like eternity to me.

I finally made it to where the Old Man was pinned down and I was in position with both groups of gooks in my sights. I counted five in the group to my left and four in the in the group in front of me. The group to my left was the biggest threat. Once I fired my .60 all they had to do was shift their line of fire to their right. But the group in front of me would have to turn completely around to line up on me and I had the high ground.

I wasted no time laying out my ammo and connecting the rounds from around my body into one long belt, there were at least five hundred rounds. I kept looking over my shoulder for the gooks behind me and saw nothing. I considered them the least threatening at this time, but as soon as I started firing this .60 I knew it wouldn't take them long to respond and I would become a sitting duck. I needed to take out as many as I could with the first long burst of fire because the ones I didn't kill would turn their guns on me and I would be fighting a battle from three sides. I just hoped when I started firing the Old Man and his group would start an offensive move and give me a hand. I had no real cover except for bushes and that made my position as a defensive fortification nonexistent.

I had no sights on my .60 and no shoulder butt plate. I would have to shoot my weapon as if I were in the aircraft and I had to keep in mind there was no air flow cooling my barrel so I would have to fire my .60 in short bursts as not to burn up my barrel. I felt like a grunt. I wished I was in the air and had these assholes in my sights.

I took a deep breath, held it and cut loose. I swept the gun from left to right. I hit one right off in the first group and clipped another before he could take cover. As

I swept my line of fire to the second group they had already started getting in position to return fire. I hit one again right off and I thought I saw another fall but wasn't for sure. They all took cover and the Old Man and his group did exactly what I hoped and started laying down fire. They split into two groups and advanced toward the two locations. I swung my .60 back to my left to line up on any gooks I could see but they were all on the run. I aimed my gun to my rear and saw movement and heard voices coming at me. I popped another smoke grenade way over to my left, about twenty yards. I hoped they would think that was my location and not even look my way, but mostly it was for the gun ships that I heard coming in for a gun run. The gooks diverted to their left and were headed in the same direction as the first group. I shot up a pin flare and turned and trained my .60 back to the group of gooks that were in front of me. They started running and broke to the right but the grunts that were with the Old Man followed for a little ways, stopped and popped red smoke because they had figured they better let the gunships know of their location.

After popping several pin flares the gunships set up a circle of protection around us and two other gunships fired their weapons in pursuit of the fleeing enemy.

I rolled over onto my back and took several deep gulps of air to get my breath back. I must have held my breath the whole time because I was gasping for air and wasn't too sure I hadn't shit my pants. My stomach was in knots, but as I heard the Old Man call out to me not to shoot, I tried to compose myself and act like it was just another day at the office.

The Old Man thought I was hit when he saw me lying on my back. As he ran to my side he called out for a medic. I looked up at him knowing I must have been as white as a ghost. When the medic showed up the Old Man and me were both laughing, the medic didn't seemed confused at first and had this look that made the whole event even funnier.

When everyone on the ground regrouped, everyone talked at once. DuPont and Tim, a couple of grunts from the Blues, came over and thanked me and offered me some water. The Old Man got on the radio and started coordinating an extraction. I picked up my .60 and headed back toward my aircraft. My gunner came up to me patted me on the back and told me that would be the last time he was caught without a weapon (He'd left his on the aircraft.) On the way back I came across a pool of blood. It was in the location of the second gook I downed. I must have wounded him, but I wasn't going looking for him to find out.

About thirty yards further I came across the first gook I killed that had that SKS. I bent over and picked up the rifle. It still had packing grease all over it. It was brand new and he must have just gotten it from that cache of weapons. I thought the gun would be a good souvenir for my brother back home. He was now fourteen years old. Yep, the rifle would be for him. I thought about cutting off the ear of that gook but decided not to. I didn't care anymore about such things. Hooter was gone and there was no one to brag about it too. A couple of other short timers and I were the only ones that even still had ears. It was just as well this medieval ritual was put to rest. I did take his trenching knife and a pair of sandals off his feet, the sandals were made from old tires. I also cut off his buckle; it had a red star on it. This soldier must have been an officer.

When I got back to the aircraft with my booty I secured it and straightened out the ammo in my can. I grabbed the ammo in such haste I had a belt hanging down to the ground. I bent over to pick it up and noticed my hands shook. The whole event was sinking in and for the first time in a long while fear crept up my back. I turned around to reach for my .60 that I had leaned against the aircraft and there stood the pilot looking at me, bewildered. He didn't say anything, he was embarrassed he had caught me in one of those private moments not shared or talked about amongst others. I think he came up to thank me or something like that, I don't know. I didn't even hear him approach. I had lost my hearing in my right ear from an explosion some time back and it was easy for someone to approach and me not even be aware of it.

I got the water out of my survival pack, took a long drink and poured some over my head then crawled up into the aircraft and lay on my back. I heard the gun ships circling above and I knew we were all safe, so I closed my eyes and tried to regain back my composure.

The Old Man came up and grabbed my knee. I jumped and he laughed. "A little jumpy, Brooks?"

"Yep, just a little." I was embarrassed he had walked upon me so easily.

The Old Man motioned for everyone to gather around. I sat up, but since everyone was around the aircraft I stayed sitting on my ass. The Old Man turned and pointed at me. "See this man? We all owe him big time and I will be putting him in for a citation."

"Fuckin' A!" someone said.

"You got that right," said another. A few others made comments of approval and gratitude, but I was still trying to gather up my composure and hide my fear from the others. I wanted to act like it was no big deal but I couldn't get control of myself. I had been in many battles but this one I couldn't shake. I have only engaged the enemy on his turf four times on the ground and I didn't like it. I was out of my element confronting the enemy on the ground. While in the air and engaging the enemy I always had an advantage. Ground combat sucks and it was on this day I came to respect the grunt's job in Vietnam a lot more.

The fact that I was so close to going home bothered me as well. It all could have ended today. Usually I would have something smart to say and the grunts that were in the Blues knew I wasn't myself. Of all the people standing around I think they understood. Every time I looked at one of them they smiled at me, clenched a fist and held it shoulder high then say something like 'Good job mother fucker' or 'Fukien' A.' I smiled back at them. They could tell I was shaken, they had seen it many times I'm sure.

We finally got airborne and circled the area until everyone was extracted. The Old Man had fresh troops put on the ground to protect the cache and radioed the other gunships to start bringing the weapons captured back to Quan Loi. When we landed everyone unloaded. The Blues had been in the field for a couple of days and wanted to get cleaned up, grab a few beers and kick back. The Old Man jumped out of the aircraft before it was even shutdown and started toward HQ. He had to go and do that Commanding Officer shit and left me with the new pilot and the gunner to get things ready for the next day. The pilot didn't hang around long, which was fine with me and I told the gunner to go ahead and party with his grunt friends. He had come from the Blues and had a couple of friends he wanted to get down with. I was glad; I didn't want him around anyway.

Barnet and Schultz came over from maintenance to give me a hand and they brought a couple of beers. My buddies from maintenance were a welcome sight. Barnet had a big grin on his face and he made a comment about the day's event. He could tell by the way I responded I didn't want to talk about it, so he changed the subject. They knew in time I would get around to telling them the whole story. Talking with them was easy and even though they had not seen a lot of combat they understood how each event can trigger things in your mind that change your mood and outlook.

Left to Right, Alger, Kenny (Biggie) Schultz and me on the floor.

After we finished up with the aircraft we went back to my hooch and took the private party a little further. I was ready for a big fat joint. Schultz and Barnet didn't smoke dope but they knew I did. They told me to fire up, they didn't care. I pulled out a bowl and sat on my bunk getting my head right while they sat there drinking some scotch that I had acquired, and chasing it with beer. I went over to my cooler to see if there was some ice and had found someone had filled it up for me. I asked them if they did it and they both said they did not. Huh, I thought to myself, grabbed me a handful of ice, threw it in a canteen cup and poured me a nice shot of Old Johnny Black.

I knew they wanted to hear what happened so I told them a short version and summed it up fairly fast. They both told me I did a good job or something of that nature. They said they would have shit. I told them I did, and we laughed and continued the little private party. They thought I was joking. I never told them how scared I was and let them to continue to think I was some kind of a hero. It actually felt kind of good.

Barnet and Schultz came in country together and they were four months behind me. We sat there talking about home and buying that vacation resort that we were going to run together. We knew we most likely would end up going our separate ways, but it was a nice dream and it took our minds off the war. After they left I thought that even though I'd had enough of door gunning, I was not going to quit. I didn't want it to look like I was a coward. I didn't want to quit on those terms. I wanted to make it home and that made me want to quit flying. Two weeks left and I was still dealing with this shit. Then I got to thinking, Scotty flew up to the time he left country. What made me so special? I was going to suck it up and do the best I could to get it out of my head. I needed to be sharp if I was going to have to fly with this new crew.

I know the Old Man was trying to do me a favor by putting me on standby, but I'd rather fly with Ryan on combat missions than get stuck with any kind of a mission with this new crew. I had two new pilots that didn't know squat and a gunner that didn't have it together. You couldn't tell the new gunner anything. For instance, he had this habit of wanting to tuck himself back in the transmission well on the left side of the aircraft. I told him a hundred times if we crash and the aircraft rolls over, the transmission would crush him. His reply was that a bullet would have a hard time going through that transmission and he felt like his back was protected. Besides, he'd seen most gunners in other companies fly back there. The odds, to him, were better that he would get shot before a transmission would fall on him. Other companies and gunners weren't head hunters like the 1/9th. They were mostly troop transporters and used for extractions. The two new pilots didn't have any input in the matter; they were only concerned about themselves. To them we were just enlisted men. They hadn't lived enough in the 'Nam to know one way or the other about any of this shit. They hadn't come to realization that the gunners protected their asses, but they'd learn. This gunner was a hard head and you couldn't tell him anything, I gave up trying, I had my own shit to deal with. I finished up the night cleaning my .60 and soon after I drifted off to sleep.

The next morning I thought about going to Ryan and asking him if he needed a gunner but decided not to when I seen how well his crew got along. In some ways I felt like I was brushed aside and was no longer apart of the equation. I liked Ryan's new crew and was jealous of their camaraderie. I walked with them down to the flight line. They didn't know what their mission was for the day, but they were optimistic. Yep, I have to say that Ryan had a great crew.

Knight was leaving in a couple of days. He invited me to hang out with him and his pilot friends but I declined. The only pilots left that I really knew were Knight, Ryan, and Window. Knight told me we would get together on his last night in country and hit the Johnny Walker Black.

"Great!" I replied. I had never seen him so happy. He walked around with a smile on his face all the time. He congratulated me for a job well done regarding the other day in the field. I appreciated that, especially coming from him. Like I said before, Knight and Hooter were my heroes and any compliment from them made me feel honored and was appreciated.

The last night that Knight was in country we got hammered. He couldn't sleep knowing he was leaving the next morning, so we stayed up all night talking about old times. That night was the first time we ever brought up the subject of our fallen brothers. I told him about West, his brother, and myself. He knew West had changed but didn't know him all that well so it didn't affect him one way or the other. John, on the other hand, he knew very well and hated what had happened to him. Knight knew I had been involved on the recovery crew but didn't know how I got mixed up in it all.

Knight brought up the time I went in after him and Hooter and that observer that lost my .45 and threw up on the end of that rope all the way back to Quan Loi. He told me that was one event he would never forget. He asked me how scared I was that day and urged me to be honest. I told him I was plenty scared once I hit the ground, but I felt a lot better running from Charlie than fighting him. We both laughed, sat there, drank more than what should be legal and let the late night hours pass until it was time for us to get a couple hours sleep.

I got up the next morning and walked Knight to the flight line. One of our choppers always took the honor in flying the short timers to Saigon to catch their freedom bird back to the States. As I walked Knight up to the aircraft, he told me to watch my ass. We hugged each other, said our goodbyes and in an instant he was gone. I watched his helicopter fly away until I couldn't see it anymore. I reminded myself that I was leaving in a couple of weeks. I wished it was that day.

I went back to my hooch retrieved my .60 and headed back to the flight line to be on stand-by, I hoped we would stay on the ground all day. Sitting around the flight line all day was boring, but at this stage of the game, boring still looked good to me. I didn't have anything to say to the crew. The pilots went back to their hooches while the gunner and I stayed down at the flight line ready to have the ship running and ready to launch if need be. I got my hammock out of the aircraft tied it to the stinger then to one of the revetment panels. I took off my shirt and crawled into the hammock, closed my eyes and drifted off to sleep. The gunner crawled up into the aircraft and did the same. I had a headache from the previous night and I only caught a couple of hours sleep, the rest was welcome and badly needed.

I hadn't been sleeping long when the scramble horn blew. *Oh shit!* I thought. I jumped up, stowed my hammock, slid into the front seat of the aircraft and fired it up. When it got to flight idle I locked down the collective and scrambled out, grabbed my .60 then buckled myself into the jump seat and looked around for the pilots. It didn't take them long to show up and settle into the aircraft, but when we should have been airborne we just sat there. I looked over to the pilot and he pulled up on the collective with the lock still engaged. I laughed to myself, unbuckled my belt, reached up and disengaged the lockdown strap. He looked at me as if it were my fault. My laughing out loud didn't help matters. When we finally got airborne he was still irritated and even more so when the gunner laughed too.

The coordinates came over the radio. We were going to cover for a downed bird twenty miles inside Cambodia. The aircraft was not ours, it belonged to the A-Troop 1/9th Calvary, but we were the closest cover for them and would extract them if at all possible. I no longer laughed. We were a single gunship headed into enemy fire. The only thing I thought about was being stuck with these two idiots and a lame gunner while going into a hot crash site.

I turned to my gunner and told him to keep his extra barrel within reach and to keep his eyes open. I then told him to come up on hot mic so he wouldn't have to push the button to talk, he didn't know how so I reached over and switched his radio for him. *Stuck with these FNGs and on their first gun run.* The pilots were getting nervous, they repeated themselves and the pilot gripped the cyclic stick so hard the aircraft responded in jerky movements. I hated this shit.

As we approached the area where the aircraft was reported down we saw smoke up ahead. It was from a crash and not a smoke grenade; it was bellowing black smoke. This was not good and I told them so. I told the pilot to approach the LZ with caution and to make a fast pass over the aircraft before taking any aggressive action and then make a circle around the area. I needed to drop as many red smoke grenades as I could so the other aircraft that responded would have no problem finding the LZ.

The pilot told me to do my gunner shit and leave flying the aircraft to him and his co-pilot.

"Look asshole," have you ever done this before? No you haven't. I have spent my whole time over here doing just this kind of shit so listen to what the hell I am telling you."

He took his ICS box and turned it to ISO (Isolation) and cut me off.

I lost it. I picked up my spare gun barrel and busted it across the left side of his flight helmet. It didn't hurt him, but it got his attention. I then reached up and turned the intercom between us back on. "Look, dickhead, I don't care if you hate my ass. You better listen to what I am telling you. We are the only mother ones out here and you better approach this hot LZ with the utmost caution. We know for a fact we are going to receive enemy fire and we all stand a good chance of getting shot down. If we don't get our shit together and get it together fast we all will stand a good chance of getting screwed over but hard. So listen to what I am telling you and we will hope for the best."

After that he didn't say much, but at least made that fast pass over the crash site. The aircraft that was shot down ended up in a rice patty. I had the gunner throw out all of his smoke grenades as we surveyed the downed aircraft. No one could have survived that crash. The aircraft was so badly damaged that if it hadn't been for the rotor head and blade assembly lying off to one side you wouldn't have been able to tell it was a helicopter. We saw no life at all and no bodies, so the crew must have been in the aircraft. I was glad I didn't know any of them.

After reaching the other side of the patty I suggested we make a wide circle and wait for back up. There was no need to subject ourselves to gunfire if there were no survivors. If there had been they would have made it to the tree line and signaled us. We needed to circle the outskirts of this patty, but would take fire if we flew over any of the enemy's positions.

For a minute I thought he would take the advice, but I should have known this hotshot knew it all. He completely ignored what I told him. He wanted to show everyone he was calling the shots and took the aircraft to four thousand feet and nosed it over like we were going to make a gun run and punch off some rockets. He was making a gun run like we would do if we were covering for a downed aircraft with known survivors. I don't know what he thought he was doing. We couldn't shoot off any rockets or even shoot our .60s for fear that if there *were* any survivors hiding in the tree line, we might hit them with friendly fire.

I didn't say another word. I turned and stuck my .60 out the door hoping to cover our asses if need be. I know one thing for sure; when or if we got back to Quan Loi I would not fly with this asshole again.

Without warning I heard a loud explosion and the aircraft yawed sideways, nose to the right and the tail end trying to come up on our left. We had lost a tail rotor. I don't know what hit it but as I looked out the ninety degree tail rotor and gear box were gone, with half of the vertical fin gone with it. The pilot panicked, pulled in pitch to slow our speed for landing and our tail swept around so fast we flew sideways, spinning around and around. I threw my .60 to my side and grabbed the back of the pilot's seat with my left hand and the bottom of my seat with the right to brace for a crash. My ears were overwhelmed with the noise when we hit the ground. Water and mud flew everywhere as the aircraft rolled over and the rotors struck the ground. My heart felt like it was going to explode. I thought I was going to die right then and there.

When the aircraft finally quit rolling it came to rest on its left side. My jump seat had been ripped from the hard point and I ended up on the other side of the aircraft looking upward to where my seat had been mounted on the opposite side. I was laying in the water and mud of the rice patty. I unbuckled my seatbelt, found my survival pack, AK-47 (survival gun), my .60 with about a hundred round belt and threw them up and out of what used to be my door. I crawled up and out of the cargo door and fell to the ground. My left hand had a hole in it from the base of my thumb clean through to the inside and as I hit the ground I knew I had a hurt rib or two. I didn't think they were broken, maybe cracked. I had broken ribs before and I knew they weren't broken.

The pilot started to crawl out of the former windshield. He only had a scratch on his lower chin. The co-pilot was not so lucky. The aircraft hit on his side (left side) first and he and the gunner took the brunt of the impact. He had hurt his leg badly and his arm appeared to be broken. As I moved around to the gunner's side of the aircraft I found him beneath the main transmission with only his arm sticking out. I felt for a pulse. He was dead. I thought about how many times I'd told him not to sit back in that transmission well. I was glad I hadn't made friends with this guy, but at the same time I felt sorry for him.

I turned my attention to the pilots. We had to find cover and find it fast. The gooks would be on us in no time. The pilot and I pulled the co-pilot out through the windshield. He screamed in pain from his left leg. That let the gooks know we had an injured man and that would make them pretty confident they had us. I slung the AK and my survival pack over my left shoulder. I had a homemade sling on my .60 and I slung it over my right with the belt of about a hundred round hanging from its breach. Then the pilot and I helped the co-pilot over to the tree line and took up a defensive position behind a large fallen tree. My ribs hurt so bad I could hardly catch my breath.

I dropped all my gear, reached into my survival pack and pulled out a first aid kit. I had to bandage my hand and I took out a shot of morphine stuck it into my leg. In a minute or two the pain in my ribs was gone. I gave the kit to the pilot and told him to give a shot or two to his buddy. Then I set up a defensive position with my .60 resting over the fallen tree and aimed it across the rice patty in the direction I thought they would approach. I told the pilot to keep watch to our rear, and gave him my survival gun and two full clips (60 rounds.) I only had a hundred rounds or so of M-60 ammo and knew that it wouldn't last long in a fire fight. I figured Charlie knew I didn't have much ammo. They knew our situation and would attack us as soon as they could. They knew they had to take us before our gunships arrived. We didn't get off a May Day, but we did call for reinforcement beforehand. *If I could just hold them* off *till they arrived,* I thought.

I was right. The gooks approached us from the far side of the rice patty. They didn't want to waste time following the outskirts of the patty to get to us. I let them commit themselves halfway across the patty before I opened fire. I think I dropped one, maybe two, at the most before they took cover behind a berm. That was stupid on my part. I should have waited until there wasn't cover for them to hide behind. They flanked me left and right. I fired short bursts until I ran out of ammo. They knew I was out because I had good targets to shoot at and didn't. They stood straight up and started toward us. There were at least fifteen and they all fired at once. I could do nothing but take cover behind the log. I took the AK from the pilot's hands and fired a few rounds to make them take cover again behind the next berm. I knelt and took my survival pack, opened it, retrieved my compass and took a reading.

The pilot asked me what I was doing. I told him I was taking a reading and was going to get the hell out. Quan Loi was toward the east and I would have to head south to out flank those assholes before I could head back to Quan Loi.

"What? You are not leaving us. I'm giving you a direct order to stay here and continue firing at the enemy."

"Look, I am an enlisted man, you are an officer. The gooks, if I am captured, are going to have a good time torturing me before I die. You two are officers and you will become POWs. They don't think an enlisted man knows shit so they don't keep us alive, you dumbass. And even if they did, I would still rather take the chance I could make it back to Quan Loi than spend the rest of my days in a prison camp."

He repeated his 'direct order' and put his hand on his .38 as if he was going to pull it on me. I pointed the AK at him and told him not to be stupid. The thought of killing him then and there crossed my mind and I came close to pulling the trigger. I would have, but then I would have to shoot the co-pilot too and that didn't sit too well with me. He was in a lot of pain and didn't know what was going on. But I know without a doubt, if it had been only me and that pilot I would have killed him then and there and continued on my way.

I took another reading off my compass. I told the pilot, "Look, I understand if it was my buddy injured I would stay with him, but I don't know either of you that well and basically I don't give a shit one way or the other. The only thing I care about is staying alive and making it back home." As I turned to leave the pilot stood up and started to go with me. He was going to leave his buddy. *What an asshole,* I thought. *He is willing to leave his buddy and save his own neck.*

I couldn't take this asshole with me even if I wanted to. I couldn't go sixty miles with another person tagging along. I didn't have enough water or food for two. Oh, maybe if it was Hooter or Knight, because we would work together. But not this asshole. I could just see him giving orders the whole way. I would have probably shot him before the first day was over.

During this moment of debate two Cobra gunships popped over the trees and caught Charlie with his pants down. Both the aircraft opened up on the enemy with mini guns and when they were through there wasn't a gook standing. One of the Cobras came back around and gave out another short burst of fire to put the icing on the cake. I reached into my survival pack and pulled out a smoke grenade and threw it out to the edge of the rice patty where we were hidden. Another Cobra showed up and after all three of them circled for a short time to make sure it was all clear. Two of them landed close to where we were. The other flew cover for us. I ran out to one of the Cobras to let them know we had an injured man. The Cobra pilot told me there were no Hueys in the area to pick us up. I popped the ammo doors and on one of the Cobras I positioned the injured pilot and on the other door let the other pilot lie down and secure himself. I ran over to the other Cobra popped the R/H door and positioned myself and we all flew out of the LZ on the ammo doors of those Cobras. It might not have been the safest way to fly, but it was damn sure one of the most exciting and most welcomed. I had to leave my AK behind but tucked away my .60 to the inboard side of the ammo door where I lay and strapped on my survival pack.

On short final to the flight line at Qun Loi, like always in these types of situations, a bunch of the guys waited for us to land. When the aircraft touched down they ran up to us and helped us off those doors. The pilot that was injured had such a tight grip on the ammo door support cable that it took two guys to pry his good arm and hand loose. Everyone was laughed and kept slapping us all on the back. The Old Man shook all of our hands. It felt good to be back, but when I saw my gunner's two close friends looking my way the good feeling turned to sad.

Their friend would not be with them tonight. They had that look in their eyes when you know you have lost one of your own. I approached them and told them how sorry I was about their friend. I told them he was the best gunner I had ever had. Even though he was the worst, I felt like I had to say something nice about the guy. They shook my hand and told me that Jay really liked me as well. Jay. I didn't even know this guy's name until now. I had known his last name but I had never heard his first name. I always referred to him as my gunner. Jay. I will remember his name and refer to him as such if ever I have to talk about him again.

Jay.

I never even knew the guy liked me at all. I was always riding him about something. I felt bad that I had treated him disrespectfully. I didn't want to have friends and being an asshole and keeping distant from others had become an easy habit. Even though I was saddened by this guy's death, I was still glad he was not a close friend. It was better this way and easier to deal with. *Better him than me*, I thought, *better him than me*.

Barnet and Schultz helped carry my gear back to my hooch. The only thing I had in my hand was a canteen of water someone had handed me. When we got to my hooch I stripped off the clothes that were covered in dried mud and then opened up three beers and handed Barnet and Schultz one each. I plopped down in my chair naked. "That's it. I'm through with flying." I turned up my beer and killed it.

Barnet said that it was about time and both he and Schultz laughed. I told them what had taken place in the field and how the pilot and I got into it to the point I thought I was going to have to shoot the bastard. They both sided with me. But we all knew I had not heard the last of it. I didn't give a shit. I was safe now and as far as I was concerned I was through with flying, especially with idiots like those two.

It wasn't long before someone had word sent to let me know the Old Man wanted to talk to me. When I walked into his office he didn't waste any time about asking me what happened. So I told him from the beginning. I knew the pilot had filled the Old Man's ears with a lot of bullshit, so I didn't hold anything back. I told him how he wouldn't wait for support from the gunships to ignoring everything I told him.

"Did you strike him with a gun barrel?" the Old Man asked.

"Yes I did, Sir!" I was angry. I went a step further and told him at one time while we under attack on the ground, I thought about shooting the son of a bitch and if it hadn't of been for having to shoot the co-pilot too, I most likely would have.

"Don't tell me this crap," the Old Man responded.

"Then don't ask me if you don't want to hear the truth, Sir."

After spending the next hour with the Old Man he knew this pilot was going to be a handful and was afraid no one would fly with him after this shit got around. This so called asshole of a pilot wanted to bring me up on charges of insubordination, striking an officer and disobeying a direct order.

As I told the Old Man the whole story, he understood my situation and seemed to be sympathetic toward me. He told me not to bring the subject up again around anyone. I told him I had already told Barnet and Schultz. He put his head between his hands told me not to bring it up again and he would talk to Barnet and Schultz. Of course he knew I would give them a heads up on what was coming down.

I turned and started to walk out of the office but the Old Man stopped me. "Brooks. You are too short to be doing this shit, consider yourself grounded. I want to see you make it home. You have done your share and I know you will not quit flying if I don't ground you." He stood and stuck out his hand and told me he was proud to have known me and hoped he would see me back in the States. If only he'd known I was going to tell him the next day that I was done with flying. It worked out for the best, and I believe he still would have still shaken my hand. It was a pleasure serving under Colonel Young. Major Jolly, the CO when I first arrived in country, was an ass. Colonel Young had the respect of all his troops and was indeed a leader of men.

The first thing I did was give Barnet and Schultz a heads up on the Old Man wanting to talk to them and I told them what it was all about, so they would not be in the dark. Keeping this quiet was not going to happen. Schultz and Barnet had already told several people in maintenance what had gone down between the pilot and me. A man had lost his life and there is always a story that follows.

It wasn't long before everyone knew what had happened and to top it off the Blues blamed the pilot for the loss of their friend. They knew our procedures when it came to air cover and they knew that Ray had unnecessarily subjected his crew to a situation that could have been avoided. He could have waited for air support, but instead he wasted a man's life, lost an aircraft and injured his crew. He was not a popular man and the Old Man had to transfer him for fear someone would even the score. Even his fellow pilots severed their relationship with him. Either because they didn't approve of his actions, or because they wanted to stay clear of him knowing they could be caught up in the crossfire that would come about if the man stayed in the company.

For me, every time I look down at my left hand and see the scar left by the crash, I think of that day in Cambodia. A day when I came so close of taking a fellow soldier's life then dealing with it for the rest of mine. I was glad I did not. As for the pilot, I don't think of him much at all. He had an ego that was unmatched by anyone I have ever known. He made a fatal mistake that I know might haunt him to the end of his days. We all did things we were not proud of in 'Nam, but at least I can say I was never instrumental in the loss of an American's life.

Chapter 23
Homeward Bound

Now that I had no ship, I had no job. I could have gone to maintenance and spent the ten days left of my time working on aircraft, but the Old Man let me hang out and do pretty much what I wanted. Sometimes I would go down to the flight line and help out by loading up the rocket pods, or humping ammo for the gunners. A lot of the time I made the rounds and said my goodbyes to all the people I had been associated with over the past year.

Mostly I lay around my hooch or in the sun. I drank a lot of beer and smoked more weed than I normally would have. It felt great to know I was going home and I allowed myself to dream again. It was a time of reflection for me. I knew I had changed. I was no longer that kid from West Texas. Part of me still thought like a kid, but the other part battle-scarred. It was this part that put fear in the kid that was still present in some parts of my mind. There was a battle I fought in my head and I stayed confused more often than not. A new fear was brewed in my spirit. I was waging war against myself and just like 'Nam, there were no battle lines. Physically fighting a war was easier than battling the one that haunted my dreams.

The only thing that put my restless spirit at ease was thinking of home. I realized there would be complications. I knew I would not adjust to what people consider a normal way of life. Hardly anything in my life now was normal. I was going to be married as soon as I got home and wondered if it would be fair to Roni to load her down with my burden of Vietnam. I hated putting her through all that bullshit but I was selfish and didn't want to lose her and I would follow through with the marriage.

We had grown up together and if anyone knew me it would be her. We shared our love and our innermost thoughts. If our marriage didn't work out, I vowed, the fault would be mine. But I was willing to try and put the war behind me. I couldn't fathom how. I was bringing a bad deal to the table for her, but she was my only hope for some type of sanity in my life. I wouldn't blame her for wanting and trying to find a life that may be easier with someone else. *First things first*, I thought. Getting home was the first step.

The end of those ten days and a wakeup took forever coming. Tiger, seeing his previous masters leave, knew my mood and anxiety. I started packing my duffle bag a few days before and Tiger sensed that soon I would no longer be a part of his world. He quit sleeping on the floor and slept at the foot of my bed. I would have him come up to where I could pet his head and we would both fall asleep. He was my little buddy and I had confided in him like I would a human being. In fact I told him things I have never told a human. I wished I could have taken him home, but because of some disease dogs contract in Vietnam they could never be brought to the United States. Even the tracker dogs that were trained in the States would be left behind, never to return home. I knew Tiger would be taken good care of though. Everyone wanted him for a pet and when I left he would no doubt choose someone else.

Finally my day arrived. I would leave Quan Loi the next day back to Saigon to process out of country. Barnet, Schultz and a few other guys I knew gave me a farewell party the last night I was in country. Barnet had his father send him a bottle of twenty year. old Johnny Walker Black from the States for the occasion. West had introduced to me to it and it had become my favorite drink. I thought about West and hoped he would show up for the occasion. I didn't know what to say to him but felt like I wanted to at least say goodbye. But West was West and we would understand if he didn't show.

Everyone hit the smoke and booze hard and the party was over before it really got started. I was glad. I wanted to spend my last night with my dog. Tiger and I went down to our old bunker. I took what was left of the Johnny Walker and stopped by my hooch to pick up a joint on my way down to the flight line. Tiger and I sat there on that bunker for a couple of hours, me thinking of home and Tiger lying there with his head in my lap while I scratched him behind his ears.

The next morning I was up way before sunup. I couldn't wait to get on that chopper that had taken so many before me back to Saigon to catch that Freedom Bird back home. Mr. Ryan would be flying me for my last flight in country. The Old Man knew I would enjoy his company. Ryan had asked if he could do the honors. Ryan showed up early too and we sat down on the side of the aircraft and talked about old times.

"Where are you going to be stationed when you get back to the States?"

"I think a place called Ft. Sill, Oklahoma."

"Well guess what, Brooks? You will be with Knight, he got stationed there."

"No joke, really?"

"Yep, I think most of us will be going there."

He couldn't have given me any better news. I would have an old buddy with me when I got back home, to serve with for the rest of my time in the military. It wouldn't be long and we would be airborne and on our way. I left Tiger with Schultz. I didn't want him down at the flight line when I left. I really didn't want anybody to see me off. It was hard leaving, a love-hate situation. Part of me wanted to stay, but a lot more of me wanted to go. Quan Loi had been my home for a year, every revetment, every mortar hole; everything about Quan Loi was and always will be branded into my mind. In some ways I became a man there in the heart of war and in other ways I was still just a kid. I was twenty-one years old now, but felt much older. I was wiser in some areas, but felt so separated from people and alone. I could not see a future. I had learned and programmed myself in the last year not to plan too far ahead and to take life a day at a time. Back in world it was totally different. Planning ahead was expected of you if you wanted to make it in life. I could tell dealing with Vietnam and the byproduct it left embedded in my mind was going to take awhile to get over. I thought that all I had to do was make it home and things would fall into place. Deep down I knew I was just lying to myself. I got good at doing that. Lying to myself that is.

When the gunners showed up we cranked up the aircraft and brought it to a hover. The revetment the aircraft was parked in was down at the far end of the flight line. Ryan said he would make a long run down the runway and I could wave at everyone as we pulled pitch.

Ryan made a slow run down the flight line and as we pulled pitch to gain altitude and clear the green line, I looked down and there was West holding Tiger and giving me the peace sign. I gave him the peace sign back and he grinned at me and I read his lips as he said, "Good luck." Tiger jumped out of his arms and ran down the flight line after us. He ran until he got to the green line, stopped and watched me until I could see him no more.

I knew then that West held no animosity toward me and that was a relief. I knew also why he distanced himself, just as I had distanced myself from everyone. It's just the way of war and front line combat. We all knew this, but I was glad he said his goodbye to me in the end.

Tiger down on the flight line. This was taken the day I left and sent to me years later.

I sat in the aircraft with the wind blowing across my face. Thoughts flooded into my mind as if a dam had broken and released all its waters. I had done and seen a lot in a year's time. I brushed away my thoughts of 'Nam and tried to concentrate on the life ahead of me, but I could not, I knew a part of me would stay in 'Nam forever. Almost everything I was associated with gave me flashbacks and as they say in West Texas, I knew I had a long row to hoe in front of me.

The gunners that escorted me back to the rear that day asked me if I wanted one last dance with the M-60. I told them sure. I put the door gunner's flight helmet on so I could talk to Ryan and then crawled into the gunner's jump seat. Ryan asked me what I wanted to do. I told him I wanted to do one more hammer head stall and fire the M-60 the whole time and I would pick the targets.

"You got it," he replied and rolled the aircraft over into a steep dive. I hung out the door and rock and rolled that .60 until the barrel was smoking. I kept on the trigger all the way through the hammer head and didn't let up until we were at altitude again. Ryan asked me what I was shooting at, everything and anything, but mostly I was just relieving a little tension. Deep down I was shooting at the demons that danced in my head and hoping I could leave them here, where they belonged.

Ryan told me he had something better than shooting any gun, and motioned me up front with him. There was no co-pilot on these trips, usually the person leaving for home would get to ride left seat so I gave the gunner back his .60 and flight helmet and crawled up front. I put on the spare flight helmet that hung above the co-pilot's seat and asked Ryan what he meant. Both the gunners laughed as Ryan pulled out a bag of dope. It didn't surprise me much. He and Knight were close friends and I kind of figured Ryan got down, at least once in awhile.

No one smoked dope on missions, but this was relaxation time for the crew and they were going to make the most of it. Of course they wouldn't get hammered, just enough to take the edge off and enjoy the day. Me, I was going to get so hammered. Ryan asked me to fly while he rolled a few joints. I took the controls and Ryan told me to have fun. I made a few steep turns and then took the aircraft to 8,000 feet to enjoy the cool air and to get ready to kick back and get hammered.

By the time we got to Saigon and to the out of country processing station I felt no pain. Ryan and the two gunners shook my hand and Ryan told me he would catch me back in the States. Then he reached into his flight bag and pulled out a bottle of Johnny Walker Black. "You will need this tonight," he said and shook my hand for the last time. I guess everyone knew my drink. Ryan and his crew made my last flight a memorable one. Ryan had a great crew and I wished them the best of luck.

Chapter 24
The California Experience

Processing out of country was a pain in the ass. What should have been an easy procedure ended up getting a lot of us upset. I turned in my paperwork and was told to go to a holding area. The area consisted of a Quonset hut with a bunch of bunks with rolled up mattresses on them. I noticed there were about thirty of us waiting to process out of country. The closer I got to them I realized they were some of my old buddies from AIT. Most of us had come into country together and were now going to DEROS together. Some of the guys were going to ETS (End Time Service) but we were all put here in the hut together. We all wanted to leave country as soon as we could, but for some reason they were letting troops go in front of us. After two days there were over two hundred of us ready to go home. Most of us had come over together, had seen combat and now wanted to get the hell out.

About the time we had had enough, the Commanding Officer of the out processing center came over to give us the reason behind holding us back. He said everyone in this building were all front line combat veterans and since there were protests of the war going on in the States, the Army felt like it would be better for us and the public if they had us all together.

This did not sit well with any of us. But to calm us all down he said they had enough of us for one plane load and we would leave in the morning and that night the Army would furnish us with free beer. That made the medicine a little easier to take and the next morning was good for everyone. As long as we had a day and time that we were going to board that Freedom Bird, we were happy. Here in the rear we wouldn't have to worry about getting attacked. The only weapons we had were the ones we took off the enemy and were taking home as war souvenirs. The Army told us all the weapons that didn't have the proper paperwork could not leave country. I had the proper paperwork and I was going to give my weapon (SKS) to my brother. But a lot of the guys did not have the proper paperwork, so they sold them to the guys that were stationed there in Saigon. They took the money and paid for some strippers to come in and entertain us. This station in the rear had its perks.

Hardly anyone really paid much attention to the strippers. Well, maybe some of us did. I remember taking a look or two. Hell, I wasn't dead. Everyone had leaving country on their minds and were numb to the fact we were actually going home. Most of us visited with each other but didn't' talk about 'Nam. We sat around getting reacquainted and we paired up with the guy we got along with the most. I hooked up with a guy I knew back in AIT at Ft. Rucker, Alabama. I can't remember his last name but his first name was Rick. We had arrived in country together, he had given me this wide leather wristwatch band and I was still wore it. He was amazed I still had it on. He was a head and had some dope on him so we snuck off and smoked a little weed and mostly stayed to ourselves.

The next morning we were all up and ready to go. I felt sorry for anyone that told us we had to spend another day in country. We all filed up in a double line and walked toward our Freedom Bird. All the flights were commercial airlines and we knew it would be nothing but a big party all the way home. Rick and I took a seat on the right hand side of the aircraft in front of the wing. I told Rick if he wanted the window seat he could have it. I needed the aisle seat so I could stretch out my left leg when my back began to hurt. I never really got over my back injury but as long as I could stretch out my left leg I was fine. After the plane was loaded and everyone was seated the stewardesses introduced themselves and you could have heard a pin drop. These women could have been the ugliest girls in the world but because they were round-eyes they were beautiful to us. They were all good looking gals though and they had a sense of humor that was great.

They knew what we had been through and they made us feel welcome. We all were so polite to them they didn't know what to think. Most of the troops in Vietnam had not seen front line combat. Most of them had been stationed in the rear and chasing split tails was nothing to them. And the combat troops they had come in contact with were mixed among non-combatant troops and therefore each flight these girls had someone mess with them one way or the other. We were just happy to look at them. Talking to women was something we had not done in awhile. We felt like fish out of water and sat there staring at these beautiful women.

We all were quiet until the aircraft broke the ground. All of us at once screamed with joy. We were happy to get off the ground and leave Vietnam, never to look back.

After the first hour in flight passed the head stewardess stood in the middle of the isle and said she couldn't stand all this quiet. She rolled out this cart and it had every kind of booze you could imagine. All big fifth bottles and not those small bottles you could down in one swallow. But no Johnny Walker Black. I grinned and reached into my briefcase and pulled out the bottle that Ryan had given me. I was saving it for this occasion. The flight home would be a good one. One of the stewardesses saw me pull out this bottle of scotch and asked me if that was my favorite drink. I told her I didn't know if it was my favorite or not, but it had become a good friend and good friends never let you down. A corny line I know, but it got a laugh out of her. She turned to walk away and my eyes went directly to her ass.

She turned around to catch me staring at her. She took great humor seeing my face turn red. "You might have been out of action for awhile, but you're damn sure not dead."

I was a little rusty on my ass-looking skills and got caught. She didn't care, but I made it a point not to get caught staring at her ass again.

Later on as we all were feeling our liquor she caught another guy looking at her ass. She turned to him and winked then stuck her ass at him. "Come on, I know you want to touch it." He did and we all laughed. Yep, those girls were good sports and as the hours passed they seemed like friends we had known forever.

We stopped in Japan, but they wouldn't let us off the plane. They didn't want a bunch of combat troops storming the terminal. We didn't want off the plane anyway. The people didn't look much different than the ones in Vietnam. We waited for our plane to refill and we were off again. We were on our last leg of our flight and we would set down in San Diego, California. You could have cut the tension with a knife.

We all knew of the protests taking place in California. We had heard back in Japan that the plane in front of us had things thrown at them and people spit on the troops as they marched by them. We decided to get a plan together and approach this situation where we would have some control. When we got off the plane we would break off into groups of ten, and each group would act as its own pod or platoon. Each man that had a weapon would group up and they would lead everyone else past the crowds with ten guys with weapons bringing up the rear. Out of two hundred and seventeen of us we had a total of forty or so weapons. The weapons were checked in the baggage compartment of the plane. We asked a stewardess if we would be able to claim our baggage before we ran into the protest. She assured us we would, but she had no idea the baggage we were most concerned about were our weapons. We had no ammo and it was a good thing we didn't, but all the weapons had bayonets (tri sticker or knife) on the ends of them.

About one hour out of San Diego the pilot kept counted off the minutes and as we were seconds to setting down the whole plane of troops counted down, 10, 9, 8, 7, 6, 5, 4, 3, 2, 1 and the plane erupted shouts, tears rolled down the faces of some and looks of 'thank you, God' on the faces of others. I was caught up in the moment, lowered my head. *I'm home, I'm home* I thought as tears fell from my eyes. Before the plane came to a stop we regained our composure and stood to get off the plane. The pilot told us there was a little trouble at the airport and that there was a war protest going on. He told us to please be seated and when the situation was under control we could leave the plane.

As fast as tears came to my eyes, hate now dried them up. I could see hate in everyone's eyes. We had all spent a year laying our lives on the line everyday and now we have to come home and deal with this shit. We had figured as much and had our teams already made up. Finally the pilot told us we could start to unload. As we unloaded we each gave the stewardesses ten dollars. They had treated us so nice we wanted to show them our appreciation. They made over two thousand dollars. As we left the plane I looked back. The stewardesses all had tears in their eyes.

At least someone cares, I thought.

When we got to our baggage we formed into the groups we assigned ourselves. All of us with weapons took our positions in front and in the rear of the troops. Of course we would not click the bayonets into place unless we deemed it necessary. We didn't want to provoke any trouble but we weren't taking any shit. We didn't disserve this ridicule.

Rick had no weapon so he carried my duffle bag. For everyone that carried a weapon, someone else carried his duffle bag. As we got closer to the crowd we heard their chants. 'Baby killers,' 'war mongers' and 'government puppets' were among the ones I heard the most. They were cursing at us in anger, but as long as they kept their distance we didn't care.

There were a lot of police controlling the crowd. They had their arms linked together to keep the crowd back. We did not carry our weapons in a defensive or in an aggressive manner. Most of us fixed the slings on the weapons loosely so they would slide off our shoulders with the least effort as possible and use the vertical or horizontal butt stroke for our first defensive move and use the bayonets only if we felt we would be harmed, or in a life threatening situation. These protests were new to us and we didn't know what to expect.

As we walked by the crowd we saw the anger in their eyes. Why were they so mad? They were trying to intimidate us, but when we were not intimidated by their righteous anger and threats they started throwing, of all things, Frito Chip bags at us. We thought this was funny until one bag hit a soldier in the back. The bags were filled with shit and this made us furious. One soldier said, "Hell, let's give them what they want."

Half of us were ready and the other half, including myself, just wanted out of there. I was intimidated and allowed myself to get upset and too tight. All of a sudden some people broke the barricade and my side vision caught several people approaching me and screaming. I saw what I thought was a club coming at me. I turned my back toward the attack and while turning I slipped my weapon from my shoulder, whirled it around and gave this guy with the club a horizontal butt stroke right across the chops.

What I thought was a club was only a sign and a small one at that. I laid this guy out cold. His jaw was obviously broken and blood flowed out his nose and mouth. The crowd stopped dead in their tracks. I bent to check out this guy I clobbered and was jumped by four police officers. One of them took my weapon one put some kind of strap around my neck. My hands were cuffed behind my back and to this neck strap that choked me every time I tried to move my arms. I didn't resist because I knew they were police officers. I didn't feel like I did anything but protect myself. They had other plans and started reading me my rights, but the police officer didn't hardly get 'you have the right to remain silent' out of his mouth before one of the troops approached this police officer and told him he wasn't arresting shit. "Arrest that asshole lying on the ground, arrest this crowed for unruly conduct and disturbing the peace, you can even arrest the ones throwing those bags of shit at us, but you are not arresting this man."

Then a police corporal approached my rescuer and told him to back off and pushed him. Big mistake. He jumped up into that police officer's face and screamed at the top of his voice. "You want a war SON-OF-BITCHES? We will give you a DAMN war!" About twenty of my fellow brothers surrounded these four cops and their bayonets clicked into position. One soldier faced inward and one faced outward and so on, until half faced the crowd and the other half faced the police officers. The crowd liked to have shit their pants. They had never seen anyone like us get off the plane. They had over two hundred frontline combat seasoned vets ready to unleash hell upon them and the law and they all knew it.

The troops facing outward moved forward and the crowd moved backward in panic. The troops facing inward, toward me, took a side step to their right to line up directly with the outer circle as to protect each other's back. Then my rescuer looked at that police officer."Make your move, mother fucker. Let's get this party started."

None of the cops that held the crowd back or the ones held me knew what to do. They had never experienced this type of retaliation. The ten or so officers that came to the aid of the four in the inner circle stopped dead in their tracks when they ran into at least that many bayonets pointed in their faces. When the situation was about to erupt, a police sergeant that was trapped in the circle approached his loud-mouthed buddy and told him he would handle things. Then that sergeant turned to my rescuer (whose name I can't recall) and told him they weren't going to arrest me.

"You goddamn right you're not," he yelled in the sergeant's face.

"We are going to take him to a room," he pointed to a door about twenty yards away, "and we will release him there and from there we can take him around this crowd."

"That's fine," my friend told him, "but me and three or four of us will accompany you just to make sure your not bullshitting us."

The police sergeant was irritated by that remark but reluctantly agreed.

As we walked away from the crowd I noticed several things. The crowd was not near as boastful and shouting at us. They had retreated as far away from us as they could get and the police had no trouble of getting control of the crowd now that they were in shock. Another thing was that guy I cold-cocked was still on the ground but trying to stand, with some girl crying at his side. Blood still ran from his mouth and nose and he was counting his teeth. I must have loosened a few. He was trying to talk but the words were garbled because he couldn't move his jaw.

Yep, I would say his jaw was broken. I felt a grin on my face.

When we got to this small room, I was released and given back my weapon. The police were a lot nicer now that they were out of the eyes of the public, but I felt more like they were embarrassed by the whole ordeal and wanted us out of their hair. When we came out on the other side of that room we were in the lobby. It wasn't long before Rick showed up with my duffle bag. We laughed about but wondered if this was what we were going to be faced with all the way across country to get back home. He was headed to Salt Lake City, Utah and I was headed to Lubbock, Texas. Our paths split, we wished each other the best, and went to re-check our bags and catch our flights home. What bothered me is I never got to thank my rescuer, or even get his name. I turned around he was gone. Everyone simply wanted to get the hell out of Dodge and we all went our separate ways.

It was strange not having military around me all the time. I felt like a foreigner in my own country, alienated, and I didn't like it. I saw several military personnel at the airport and when possible we stood together and visited. I finally got on the plane headed east to Texas and was the only soldier on that plane. My next stop was Phoenix, Arizona. In Phoenix I had to get my bags again and every time I got my bags I had to carry this rifle around with me. Talk about getting stares. I wanted to get out of my military uniform and try to blend in, but carrying this weapon and duffle bag was a dead giveaway so I stayed in uniform. I walked a straight line to wherever I was going and I didn't look up, look at people. I didn't want any trouble. I just wanted to get back home.

I had a two hour layover in Phoenix and after checking my bags I decided the best place for me to wait for my flight would be the airport bar. I entered and sought out a dark corner at the end of the bar and ordered of all things, a whiskey sour. I wanted something different and as a kid I had one and it was pretty good. Then I stopped. *A kid.* I had one of these drinks at Fort Rucker, Alabama a year ago at the NCO club before I went to Vietnam. *A kid.* Man, that seemed like long ago but it had been only a year.

My thoughts turned to home and Roni. I thought of my friends back in 'Nam and I sat there not wanting to look up for fear my eyes would connect with someone who wanted to make an issue out of the Vietnam and the war. I knew one thing for sure. I didn't want another whiskey sour. I had lost my taste for sweet drinks. My next drink would be Johnny Walker Black on the rocks. *Ice. Ice anytime I want it.* I thought how nice it was to use the restrooms at the airport and flushing. Running water to wash your hands, paper towels, and to flip on the light anytime. Water to drink that wasn't red with soil mixed in it. Air-conditioning, perfume smells from women, women in general everywhere, the list went on and on and I relished in the small pleasures that I had been away from for a year. Little things that at one time thought I would never see again. It is funny how you take these simple pleasures for granted. I wouldn't be so fast to take them for granted again.

Before I knew it, it was time to catch my plane. I got up to pay my bill and the bartender told me it had been taken care of. When I asked, he pointed to an older man sitting at the bar a little ways from me. I was shocked. I walked over and thanked him for the drink.

"No, thank *you* for what you have done for us all," he said.

It caught me off guard and I got a little choked and didn't know what to say. This was the first time anyone had thanked me for serving my country. I shook his hand with a firm grip to show my appreciation for those simple but kind and much appreciated words. I couldn't talk. I turned and walked toward my gate. This kind gesture from this man made me hold my head a little higher and as I did, I saw faces looking at me not in anger, but with compassion and eyes were served up with a smile. These people were not California liberals. They were my kind of people and for the first time it felt like I had made it home. I didn't feel ashamed or embarrassed that I was in uniform. It made me proud but at the same time humble.

I had judged America wrong. These are the people we as soldiers had laid our lives on the line for and though a smile may be a small gesture of thanks, it was never appreciated more than that moment when my spirits were down and I was so low. I wore my medals with pride and my chest felt a little bigger.

Because my flight was paid for by the government, my plane ticket was not a direct flight. My next stop was Albuquerque, New Mexico. I still had to claim my baggage and re-check it and that meant carrying that SKS rifle around, but things were different now. People asked me about the weapon and how I got it. I didn't tell them anything other than it was a war souvenir for my brother. They didn't push for any more information than that and I was glad. If there was a long line, people would step aside and ask me to please, come to the front of the line. I was showered with welcome homes and words like 'good to have you back' and they really meant it, and like they really knew me. Even though they were strangers I felt welcomed, but every time someone would pat me on the back I jumped. I couldn't get used to people touching me as I walked by them. I started to feel uncomfortable, but not to the point I wanted them to stop. It did feel good to know there were people that truly welcomed me home and for as long as it lasted I relished in the kind gestures.

When I left Albuquerque I hadn't had any sleep
for two days and my body had to get some rest. As soon
as the plane was airborne I fell to sleep and the next thing
I knew the pilot was announcing we were landing in
Lubbock. My heart almost jumped out of my chest.
Home, I am home at last. I still had to get down to
Slaton, but that was only fifteen miles from Lubbock.
Lubbock was my backyard and being there felt like I was
home at last. Lubbock people were even friendlier than
all the nice people I had encountered on my journey back
home. I had one guy even offer to carry my bags. I told
him I would carry my duffle bag, but if he could carry
my rifle I would appreciate it. He smiled from ear to ear.
He was a young man about my age and I could tell he
sure wanted a close view of that rifle.

I had to catch a taxi down to Slaton. I had no one
to pick me up at the airport. My parents now lived in
Emporia, Kansas. My dad worked for Santa Fe Railroad
and they had moved him, my mother and brother to
Kansas. They were on a trip down to the Gulf of Mexico,
at Freeport, to see my mother's sister and to see about a
cabin on the beach for Roni and me to go to on our
honeymoon. They had stopped by Slaton and picked up
Roni, so Roni was gone. I had arrived home one day
early and was going to surprise everyone. No one
expected me until the next day. I called Mrs. Kitten
(Roni's mother) and told her I was coming and not to tell
anyone if they called. I was going to hang out on the
Kitten farm until my parents brought Roni home. They
were due back that afternoon.

So the taxi would have to take me all the way to
Slaton from Lubbock. The ride to Slaton was great, I
hadn't ridden in a car for a long time and I watched the
countryside pass by. In the plains of Texas you can see

forever and it was nice to see open country again. There was no jungle and the big skies of West Texas welcomed me home.

When the taxi turned into the long driveway of the farm tears poured out of my eyes. It was embarrassing in front of the driver, but I couldn't stop those tears of happiness, I was home, home at last. The emotions hit me all at once. This was what I had dreamed about and hoped for, for so long.

I made it.

When the taxi came to a stop I put my head on the back of the front seat and asked the driver to give me a minute.

"Sure, buddy," he replied, "take your time. I am in no hurry no hurry at all." The driver got out of the car and opened the trunk to get my things. I sat there for a minute or two, crawled out of the car, reached for my billfold. The driver stopped me. "No way, my friend. This ride is on me."

"No, let me pay you."

"No, my friend," he repeated, "this is my pleasure, trust me." He shook my hand and told me he had a cousin killed in Vietnam. "No Vet will ever pay for a ride in my taxi."

"Thank you," I replied as he nodded his head.

I gathered up my duffle bag and rifle and walked across the lawn to the front door of the farm house. Mrs. Kitten met me at the door with a big smile on her face and open arms as well as a kiss. She told me Roni wouldn't be home until afternoon.

"Could I lie down for awhile? I am so tired."

She told me to go to Roni's room and lay on her bed.

When I entered Roni's room the picture I sent her from 'Nam was on the mirror. I crawled upon her bed face down and buried my face into her pillow. Her smell flooded my senses and I took it all in. I was home. I was home at last. I closed my eyes to sleep but sleep did not come. I couldn't sleep, it was too quiet. No helicopters were running up or flying, no tanks were moving about, no outgoing fire. It was strange and felt weird. I was too excited anyway and laid there thinking. I would be marred in a couple of days. It was June 28th and our wedding was set for July 3rd.

A couple of hours passed and I heard a car drive up. Mrs. Kitten yelled out "They're here!" and I jumped out of bed. I told her not to say anything and I watched as my parents' car came to a stop and everyone got out. Finally Roni emerged. She was beautiful. I waited until everyone was getting her luggage out of the trunk and had their backs to me. I opened the door and ran up to her from behind. My brother saw me first and started to say something but I motioned for him to be quiet, then my parents saw me and I motioned also for them to be quiet. I stepped up behind Roni and put my arms around her. She tried to see who it was but I would move my head with hers so she could not focus her eyes on me. Finally I loosened my arms and grip and she spun around to see it was me.

When she saw it was me she screamed my name and fell to the ground. She did not pass out but her legs went limp and she could not stand up. I was going to reach down and pick her off the ground but Vodie, my brother, and Mom and Dad started hugging me. I looked down to where she was sitting and she was looking up at me. Finally, with help from me or one of my family members, she picked herself off the ground, slung her arms around my neck and gave me a kiss and then hugged my neck hard. It felt so good to be wrapped up in her arms with her body so close to mine. Even though she could not feel it my body trembled. We held onto each other for the longest time. Tears of joy fell down her face. We were at last in each other's arms again.

That night everyone wanted to visit with me and we could not get a moment alone. She was as frustrated as I was. But we bided our time and knew we would be alone together soon. About nine o-clock we finally got off to ourselves. We didn't get far. Down the road a ways we pulled off into a cotton field, jumped in the back seat and made love. It had been so long since we had been in each other's arms. We savored our moment together. Even though it was in the back seat of a car, it is a time we would never forget. Our love for each other had grown. Even though we were so young we knew we had a love that would stand the span of time. I wanted to spend my life with her and she did me. I saw us living together forever. If I ever had any doubts about love they were put to rest that night.

I hoped I could live up to her expectations. I never had someone love me for who I was. But who was I now? I hated to think of what I was bringing to our new life together. I knew I had issues but I didn't want to think of anything but her right then, because nothing else mattered, only us together in that moment of time. It was such a relief to hold her in my arms and let my mind soak in the peace and security as she held me tight in hers.

Now my best friend Johnny Outlaw, he was going to be my best man. We knew each other about as well as two buddies could. There was nothing I couldn't and wouldn't tell him about 'Nam, but he didn't ask. He could tell I had changed by our first get-together. He wasn't a protester but he hated the war. He didn't like protesters either so he was kind of stuck in the middle. It was the Hippie era and Outlaw dug the scene. He wasn't a hippie but he smoked dope and knew everyone that was anyone. He had a whole new set of friends since I had been gone. In some ways I felt I didn't fit. I had been out of touch with all the people I used to know for quite some time and in a lot of ways I was from the other side of the fence and was more of the cowboy type than hippie.

It was a time in my life I wanted to fit in. I felt rejected and that life had moved on without me while I was in Vietnam. Outlaw noted the awkwardness and made it his duty to catch me up on all the new styles of dress. Long sideburns and bell bottoms were in, but still being in the Army the sideburns were definitely out. While he brought me up to speed on the life around Lubbock, I brought up the subject of motorcycles. He, Mike Mason, and his cousin Joey (we all were good friends) all rode Harleys when I left for Vietnam. I asked Outlaw where his old bike was. He had a bike I had never seen before. There was a long pause and then he commenced to tell me how the three of them started riding with this cycle gang as prospects. After riding with them for awhile and thinking they would soon be full-fledged members they had a rude awakening. The cycle gang took Outlaw's and Mike's bikes from them. Joey got away with his but wouldn't ride it for fear they would take his also. Mike Mason was beat up and I think he even had his arm broken. Outlaw got away with just a few bruises.

The leader of the gang was the asshole that had my friends beaten. I can't seem to remember the whole story. I believe he had chapter members hold them down as he beat them. Mike must have done or said something that pissed him off because he ended up with the most damage.

I was infuriated and wanted to go and even the score and in a way I expected Outlaw to want to do the same. But to my surprise Outlaw was willing to forget about it and encouraged me to do the same. "These are bad dudes, Dennis. You don't want to mess with them."

For the first time ever I saw fear, real fear in my friend's eyes. I tried to talk him into settling the score but it was no use. He didn't even go to the law. They had all my friends scared to death and told them if they went to the law that someone in the organization would even the score. I never brought the subject up again, but I would never forget and in another time in my life, I did even the score.

I made it my business to learn all I could about this so-called biker gang and got to know their regular hangouts, when they went on runs and so on. I found out they were into drugs and the police hated them almost as much as me. Drugs are how they made their money, that and ripping off people like my friends who thought it was cool to belong to a biker gang. We all grew up riding motorcycles and thought the whole concept of a biker gang was cool. Sure, we knew they lived outside the law and as a kid this was exciting to us. But my friends had no idea and either did I, what was really involved in belonging to such a gang.

We had all seen the movies back in '67 and '68 or so. You know, Hell's Angels on Wheels and Hells Angels Unchained. I remember one time we rode our bikes from Slaton to Lubbock to go see the Hells Angels Unchained. We parked our bikes in front of the Arnett

Benson Theater. There were about twelve of us. People walked by our bikes and checked us out. We thought we were so cool, but we were nothing but kids trying to act like <u>Rebels without a Cause</u>, in a James Dean movie. We must have looked like a bunch of dorks, but it makes me smile to look back on it all. We didn't mean any harm. We were just trying to be cool and didn't know how.

Even though now it was 1970 and it had only been four years since we thought we were so bad, things had changed. Back then I had no idea what bad was, but now it was different for me. The war had turned me into a Dr. Jekyll & Mr. Hyde and I had come to know the true meaning of bad. I didn't think of myself as some bad ass, I had come to know the real difference between what was bad and what were childhood rivalries and bullshit.

Those bikers had done nothing to me, but I couldn't let it go. I had lived with a military code of 'Don't Tread on Me' and if you tread on my brothers or family then you have tread on me. But it was not the time. I knew I would never forget what happened to my friends and vowed if the chance ever arose, I would settle the score in my own way. (The score *was* settled, but this event in my life has to remain unspoken. I revealed what I did to one of my friends and it almost turned out to be a big mistake. I have learned the hard way to keep my mouth shut.)

As I said, I arrived home on the 28th of June and the date of our wedding was July 3rd. I had five days and I was nervous, but not about marrying Roni. There was never any doubt on how I felt about her. I was uneasy not knowing our future. I still had no education, but then I had a couple of years left in the Army to figure it out.

Since we had five days before the wedding, Outlaw felt like it was his duty to try and catch me up on all I had missed while I had been gone. He took me several big parties that were attended by only people I had known for a long time. The parties were appreciated but I felt out of place and didn't enjoy myself that much. I had a hard time fitting in, everyone had moved on in their lives and their heads were in an entirely different dimension than mine. They asked me questions for which I had no answers. Like, 'what are you going to do now are back?' I would shrug my shoulder and say, "I don't know." I know they probably felt sorry for Roni and wondered what kind of future was in store for her. I know I did.

Most of all they wanted to know about Vietnam and I didn't want to talk about 'Nam. I was having enough problems dealing with the party itself. After awhile my closest friends and I got off to ourselves and after a few joints and drinking more whiskey than I should have, I started to talk. I think what got me started was the scotch I was drinking. It wasn't Johnny Walker Black, but it was scotch. I never drank scotch with these guys before. Hell, I never even liked it until I went to 'Nam. "When did you start drinking scotch?" Outlaw asked.

I told them about West and how he got me started drinking scotch and the next thing you know, I was telling them about West, his brother and I. I told them about his brother's death and how it changed West. I told them how he segregated himself and how he wanted to do nothing but kill gooks afterward. How I eventually separated myself from people too and why one does such a thing.

I paused and looked up. Everyone was silent. The girls had tears in their eyes and guys that I had known a good deal of my life would not look directly at me. I had put everyone in an embarrassing situation. My voice cracked once when I was trying to open up to Outlaw. He was feeling my pain but it obviously made him uneasy. I sensed he wanted to give me words of encouragement, but it is hard to console someone when you can do nothing but imagine how they feel.

By their silence I determined they were embarrassed for me more than anything else. Their silence and the reactions from the girls made me uncomfortable. I stood and apologized then asked Outlaw if he would mind loaning me his Harley. I wanted to ride and free my mind. Without hesitation Outlaw gave me his bike and told me what was his was mine. He gave me a bear hug.

"I love you, brother, you know that don't you?" he whispered into my ear.

"I do," I replied.

As I turned to leave, my friends asked me not to go. But I needed to. I put them all in an awkward situation and I embarrassed myself. I needed to free my mind for awhile. I planned to return when my mood was better and my thoughts were back on track. I could not get out of there fast enough. My emotions were starting to surface and I wanted to be alone. *Wish I had Tiger*, I thought. The ride would help. I used to ride at night all the time. I knew all the back roads, especially the ones that ran through the canyons. Solitude and speed was a good antidote for me.

Although the bike was not a brand new Harley, it was new to Outlaw. It was a hand built hard-tail frame, the forks were raked six inches or so. I think it was a 1200 shovelhead engine with a stoke kit, with high compression heads and magneto ignition. The exact bike does not come to mind, after thirty-five years. Any bike would have been okay with me. I wanted to free my spirit. The hardest thing about the bike was starting it. I had lost so much weight in Vietnam it was all I could do to get it through compression stroke. My friends were concerned about me leaving on the bike. They were worried I had had too much to drink and smoke and tried to encourage me not to go. I assured them I was fine. I turned to Outlaw and told him if he didn't want me to take his bike I understood.

"No," he said, "I don't give a rat's ass about that bike if it will help you clear your mind. I do it all the time." Outlaw's girl asked him not to let me go. He laughed. "I have seen him a lot messed up than this and ride.

Nothing else was said. I turned the bike around and drove off.

As I got the bike up on a nice stretch of back road, I opened it up and was down the highway like a bullet. The wind blowing against my face took me back to 'Nam. In my mind I stood out on the skids of the aircraft with the wind flowing over my body and slapping against my face. While I rode through the back roads around Slaton, I realized this 'Nam thing was something I wouldn't be able to put behind me easily.

I decided to take the bike into town and cruise up and down the strip a few times. I'd spent many hours and miles on this drag. It was a two mile run from the courthouse square to the other end of the strip. Lots of good times. I reminisced about those and it eased my spirit. Nothing frees your mind like a good scoot. After a few drags I pulled up onto the square to watch the cars drive by. I saw very few of my old classmates. There were a lot of the underclassmen still riding the strip and once in awhile, some of the ones I knew would pull up and talk to me. It was all small talk but it made me feel good to know so many of my underclassmen wanted to welcome me back home. It was good therapy and I spent a good portion of that night visiting with some of my friends. But soon the road and the night beckoned me and I hit the highway. I decided to make a run to Lubbock by the way of Buffalo Spring Lake, the long way. I used to love that run.

That night I put about 150 miles on the bike. I was staying at Outlaw's house and when I pulled up I remembered I told them I would return to the party. It was two in the morning, but I knew I better show my face since some of them would freak out if I didn't. The party was at Joey's family cabin down in the Southland canyon, about twenty-five miles from where I was. I hoped they were all still there. If I knew them they had a big bonfire going and I figured at least my diehard friends would still be there.

Sure enough, Outlaw, Joey, and Mike were still getting down when I arrived. They looked like hammered shit but their spirits were high and some were having a good time taking turns jumping across the fire. It wasn't long before we decided to go ahead and stay at the cabin. They were too messed up to go anywhere and I was tired. I slept outside by the fire under the stars. It was a good night. I fell asleep thinking of Roni and the wedding.

After getting that initial reunion with my friends out of the way, I spent the rest my spare time with Roni. The only time we were apart after my party was the day before our wedding. Outlaw wanted to take me to Lubbock to rent a tux and buy me some new shoes. We visited some head shops that were located around the college, Texas Tech. He had some friends that worked in a shop called the Hole in the Wall. It was a place for hip clothes and Outlaw wanted to introduce me to a different way of dress. The new clothes were fun, but I knew the fashion wouldn't last long with me. I was a cowboy at heart and the clothes combined with my military haircut looked stupid.

Then we went to visit some new friends of his I didn't know, some people he met after I had gone to 'Nam. They were all bikers but didn't belong to a gang. They were all independent riders, which have always been my favorite type of people. We hit it off, right off the bat. This guy named Bear I clicked right away. His hair was down below his shoulders and he was as broad as a car at about 6 feet tall. A guy his size was intimidating, but he was as kind and well-mannered as anyone I ever knew. It was no wonder Outlaw liked him so much.

Bikers have always been my favorite people, most of them anyway. They accept you for who and what you are and the bottom line between us was the ride. Someone loaned me a spare bike and we drove around Lubbock from one custom bike shop to the next, mingling and hanging out with other bikers and good people. This was my first experience of being with people and feeling comfortable with it, almost like with my army buddies.

Outlaw made it a good day for me and put me with the type of people he knew I would enjoy. He was a good friend. He was taking care of me. I will remember what he did for me that day for the rest of my life. Thinking about that day still makes me smile. No wonder I chose Outlaw for my best man.

The first time I met Outlaw was our junior year in high school. He was walking to school in one of those West Texas wind blowing winters, the temperature was well into the teens. I had a '68 GMC pickup truck and pulled over and asked him if he wanted a ride. He jumped in and the rest is history. Outlaw told me later on that year that he never liked me until that day. Then he knew I was a good guy. I asked him why he never liked me. He said he thought I was stuck up. It is funny how people perceive each other. Who would have known we would have been best friends? I wished he and I could have been friends much sooner. He was new in Slaton.

Several years after my wedding, life for me became unbearable. At any given time Vietnam played in my mind like some movie. During this low point in my life I could not bring myself to turn to my friend for help. I did not want to share my burden. Outlaw was going through some hard times himself. He had his own burdens to deal with. For awhile he dropped off the edge of the earth and no one really knew where to find him. I knew the reason he took off and I have always felt bad that I could not be there for my friend in his time of need, as he was for me. It does no good to bring up old injuries. Outlaw has forgiven the ones that brought grief to his life and has moved on with living his. His word is his bond, what he says to you he means. He shares his love with the people he loves and he is not afraid to show it. He is confident, is his own man and lives life his way and to the fullest. One is fortunate when he can find a friend like Outlaw. I know of no one that has a relationship with a friend like I do with him. He will always remain my friend & brother.

Chapter 25
Wedding Day

My wedding day was a big event. Roni had spent a lot of time planning it. She had made her own dress and to make it special for me she sewed some pearls onto it that came from a necklace my grandmother used to wear. My grandmother was a special person in my life; she helped raise me and was my best friend. She passed away on my eighteenth birthday and Roni knew how much I loved her. Only Roni knew how much her gesture would mean to me, going of her way to make her wedding dress special for me as well as herself.

I branded that day into my memory. Without a doubt it was one of the most important days of my life.

Weddings, I know, should not be funny. But one of the humorous things to me was Outlaw. He and I waited up front, off in a little room. I was so nervous. Outlaw opened the side door. He'd parked his Harley outside, right on the grass. "See that bike?" he commented, "you walk right now and it is yours."

I laughed. "No way."

"See? You're already hen-pecked."

"No, Outlaw, I am in love."

"I know, brother. "I just wouldn't feel right if I didn't test you somehow."

We both laughed and the then the music started.

We walked out and waited up front for Roni to make her grand entrance. My knees shook. There were over two hundred people there and I didn't know half of them. Outlaw leaned over and told me to take a breath; it might help and then pinched me on the ass. It worked, I started breathing again.

Then came her cue. We turned and there she was. I had never seen such a glow on her face. I watched her every move. She slightly turned her head side to side, to acknowledge everyone that was present. Then her eyes caught mine and that was it. My heart melted right then and there. To think this beautiful woman was going to be my wife. It all hit me at that moment and it was hard to contain my joy. I was hypnotized by her gaze and as she drew closer our eyes locked onto each other and I don't remember much after that. I was cast in her spell and it put me at ease. I don't even remember the 'I do's.'

Afterward we walked down the aisle and as we reached the outdoors everyone threw rice at us. Roni had these little packages of rice tied up in lace of some sort. Outlaw didn't even un-wrap his and when he threw it he hit me upside the head. When I looked to see what the heck hit me Outlaw had a big grin on his face. "Just wanted you to remember the moment," he said." And I have.

Outlaw is one of those people that came into my life and has over the years remained a true friend. There is no doubt in my mind that there is nothing Outlaw wouldn't do for me, and I for him. Outlaw, to this day has remained my best friend. We have watched each other grow old and it is nice to know, just like in Vietnam, there is someone that will always have my back.

The reception was something else. There were a lot of people present, most were Roni's kin. She came from a huge family. They and a few other families around Slaton helped settle the town at the turn of the 20th century, so you can imagine the people that were there. When we cut the cake it was a very serious event for us both. We didn't shove cake into each other's faces. We held to much respect for each other to do that. To us, cutting the cake was part of our wedding ceremony and we took it seriously. I loved the reception but it was not good for me at this time. There were too many people and I was not ready for it. I wanted to leave and start our honeymoon. I ate, visited a little and was ready to go.

Roni wanted to stay, but knew my mood was changing and gave in. If I could do it again, I would have stayed until the sun dropped or even later. But I didn't mingle well with people back then and it has bothered me that I was the one that cut our reception short. Heck, I don't really mingle with people very well today. Roni had put so much work into this special event in our lives and even though she has never mentioned it, I know in a way I ruined it for her that day. But Roni is Roni and because she doesn't have one selfish bone in her body, took it with a grain of salt.

The third day home from 'Nam I bought a brand new 1970 Camaro, our first car together. Her brothers had got a hold of the car and painted it all up. It had a lot of funny stuff on it but the one I remember the most was 'She got him today, he will get her tonight.' We took that car down to the Gulf of Mexico to stay in Freeport in a beach cabin. It was now the fourth of July and I had no idea how much the fireworks would affect me. That night I freaked out, every time a fire cracker would go off I would jump, every time a rocket would scream across the sky I wanted to hit the floor. Roni saw the discontent and after three days we had enough of the Gulf and headed back home. We were with each other and that was all that counted. Hell, we hardly got out of the cabin anyway.

Leave from the Army is never long enough and soon I had to report to Fort Sill, Oklahoma. Outlaw and I had driven from Slaton to Fort Sill during my leave and found Roni and I a little apartment in Lawton to rent for eighty-five dollars a month. That was all I could afford. I was a specialist fourth class (corporal) and my pay was only about $290.00 a month. Rent was eighty-five dollars, car payment was ninety dollars and that left us with about $117.00 dollars a month to buy gas and food. We ate a lot of beans and popcorn at the end of the month. But we were happy. Things got better for us eventually. I was awarded flight status pay in Vietnam and when the money caught up with us, it was well appreciated. I got several pay increases and eventually we had a little money to get by on.

Fort Sill, Oklahoma was initially an artillery base. The hardest thing to overcome at Ft. Sill was the artillery fire. The outgoing or the initial firing of the cannons didn't bother me, over in'Nam I had a gun battery behind my hooch and I got used to the outgoing artillery, but we never heard the impact of the rounds. If we ever heard impact it was usually us receiving rocket fire or mortar attacks from Charlie. I really never overcame or got used to the impact of the artillery shells the whole six years I was stationed at Ft. Sill, but I learned to eventually co-exist with this problem. I jumped or flinched every time I heard the impact like someone that gets used to having the hiccups.

Another habit I had to overcome was sleeping with a weapon. In Vietnam I slept with my .45 under my pillow and my CAR-16 by my bed and my M-60 under it. They were like a security blanket to me and without a weapon within reach I could not sleep. I forced myself to not sleep with a gun under my pillow, knowing sleeping with Roni in the same bed may have dire consequences. I learned to sleep with a knife under my pillow instead.

One night Roni and I were lying in bed and she was talking to me and I drifted off to sleep. She continued talking and eventually nudged me get my attention. It was one of those nights when it was hot and heat makes me dream of Vietnam more often than not. When she nudged me I grabbed my knife and jumped onto her as if to lunge the knife into her throat. She screamed and called my name and jerked me back into reality. I was shocked by my act and from that day on I never slept with a weapon again.

The dreams of Vietnam never stop. Back then it was almost an everyday event and it made life hard for us. I wasn't dealing with it very well and turned to drugs and isolation. Life outside the military at this time would be impossible, so I reenlisted for six years and received $10,000.00 dollars for doing so. The money went toward a new trailer home and eventually Roni and I moved the trailer out to the country.

I felt (and still do today) most comfortable around military personnel. So at the time the military seemed to be the best place for me to hide out. Because of my combat record in Vietnam I made rank fast back in the States. I made SP/5 (sergeant) the first year I was back from Vietnam and my pay was increased to about $1,700.00 dollars a month. I was stationed with Knight and Ryan and Colonel Young, who eventually became our company CO I was the Flight Line Sergeant in charge of four Bell UH-1D models helicopters and four AH-1G Cobras. I had my own bird to crew and as long as I played the military game, life seemed good.

Here in the States officers and enlisted men didn't hang out. Once in awhile Knight, Ryan and I would meet at a local bar down on the strip and have a few drinks together and hash over old times and Army life. Ryan was going to get out when his time was up, but Knight decided to be a lifer. He liked the Army and this was it for him. At this time I thought about it the same way he did. The Army treated me good and I was respected by the enlisted men as well as the officers.

Although Ryan and Knight had to give up the dope here in the States, I did not. Marijuana was a relief for me and without it I would have turned into a drunk. It helped me cope with life in general and to keep an open mind. It was something you didn't want to advertise, but if you kept you shit wired tight and played the part the military left you alone. The CO knew I smoked dope. Hell, we were in 'Nam together, he knew. But as long as it didn't reflect on him or his company, he turned a blind eye.

There were heads in the army that grew their hair and mustache beyond military regulations and the CO and Top had them pegged and would dish out extra duties for them. Mostly because these men hated the Army and they bucked the system. They wouldn't do their job to the best of their ability and their military conduct was a reflection on the Old Man. So they clashed. But this was okay for me. It kept the attention on them and off of me. I was as big or even a bigger head than most of the men I knew, but I looked and acted military and by doing so I was ED (Exempt from Duties.) I had no extra duties. I didn't even pull CQ which was expected of all the E-5s and above to do. I was even the Old Man's Crew Chief. He had what he considered was his special Huey. He assigned me this aircraft to maintain and keep in tip top shape. Heck, I even kept it waxed. He told me once that it made him feel proud to be flying such a fine looking aircraft. Several times I was rewarded with extra time off for my conduct and job performance. For me, at this time in my life, the military was great.

My wife and I took up scuba diving and we became good friends with Ray and Delana Anderson who owned a place called the Dive Shop. Eventually I helped with instructing the classes and diving became a good past time for all the endless stream of energy I had. Ray and I became good friends and it was as easy to talk to him as anyone I had ever met. He got to know me about as well as anyone in my life. I opened up to him about things I had done in Vietnam, secrets that I had not told anyone at the time. Ray knew I was about one bubble shy a level, but this didn't bother him. He seemed to agree with some of the things I had done and what surprised me more than anything didn't pass judgment on me. He seemed to enjoy my company. He was eight years older than me and I kind of looked up to him like a big brother. We developed a strong bond and there wasn't anything we couldn't talk about.

Ray was also with the Sheriff's department and through the department had come in contact with the criminal element around Lawton. He had an associate, Frank Valatie that was connected with the organized crime in the area. Frank was in the scuba class and when I first met him I had no idea he was connected with organized crime. He didn't stand out in any noticeable way and to meet the guy you would never tag him as a criminal.

One night while Roni and Delana were at the pool, Frank reached over and gave my wife a hand out of the pool and when he raised her up out of the water her top opened up and Frank got a bird's eye view of my wife's breast. Later that night he made the comment to Ray what he would like to do with my wife. Ray figured if Frank didn't keep his mouth shut and his remark got around to me I might do something stupid. Well, Frank couldn't keep his mouth shut and Ray, being a friend to us both, wanted to put an end to it. Ray told me what happened and about Frank's comment. Ray saw I wasn't taking it too well, so he figured if he told me who Frank was I might back down a notch.

After Vietnam I didn't give a second thought to people like Frank. If people like Frank crossed me I would screw up their world and didn't think twice about the outcome. Not the smartest way to think but for the year I was in 'Nam it worked for me and in those days violence, for me, was the answer for every confrontation where I felt threatened or violated. The only thing that stuck in my craw was that he disrespected my wife. Things were not okay with me and the more I thought about it the madder I got. Since Ray had told me who this guy was I watched him closer. People bowed to his every comment and he was used to having his way. So I decided something had to be done. If I overlooked it, he would be encouraged to make more smart remarks or even flirt with Roni.

Roni was not only my wife, she was my best friend and we had been together since we were kids. If anything in my life was good and pure and sweet, it was Roni. She was my only refuge in what seemed to be a sea of madness and I'd be damned if I would stand idle and let this issue go unchecked. I let a little time pass to gather my thoughts. I didn't want to go into this situation not prepared or without thinking it through first. Roni had no idea what was going on or even knew that Frank had seen her breast and she sure didn't know about his comments. I didn't let Roni know anything about the incident and since Ray's wife and Roni were friends I told Ray, if Delana knew about it to keep it to herself. Ray assured me he didn't tell her anything but this made him want to know what was brewing in my mind. I told him I didn't want Roni to know and that seemed to satisfy him.

Frank was a guy that hit on all the women and considered himself a real ladies' man, but to me he was a short, hairy guy with a pot belly and nothing more. I couldn't see how any woman found him the least bit attractive, but Frank did have a certain way about him. He was a nice guy in a lot of ways and if he hadn't of stepped over the line with me, I we could have gotten along and been friends.

It wasn't long before I found my opportunity to address the situation. He had set up a date at his home with this woman that was taking the scuba class. She was married and the meeting should have been kept under wraps, but Frank being Frank had to brag about it to all of us guys.

What an idiot, I thought. *This guy is asking for trouble or hasn't he ever heard of a jealous husband.* His alligator mouth was over loading his common sense and in another situation it might have been Roni that was the topic of his discussion and for me there was no other solution but to shut his mouth permanently. He had given me the perfect opportunity to kill him and the police would just think a jealous husband shot his ass. Plus, this guy is connected with organized crime. To top it off, he had done thirteen years in prison for shooting a police officer so the cops would probably laugh and sweep the case under the rug. That's what I would do if I were them. There would never be such an opportunity laid before me again. It was now or never.

It was a Friday night and I told Roni I had something to do at the scuba shop. I had already loaded my shotgun with six rounds of double 00 and stowed it in the trunk of my car. I drove over to Frank's house. His car was in the driveway so I knew he and the woman was already there. I gave them a few minutes then grabbed my shotgun out of the trunk and went to the door. My shotgun was a Remington 1100 automatic, I pulled the bolt back to chamber a load but locked the breach open with the round resting in the chamber. I opened the outer storm door and rang the door bell.

When Frank opened the door I shoved the gun in his face and backed him up against the hallway wall. His eyes were as big as silver dollars and his hands went straight into the air. "What the Hell?" he screamed.

"Frank, I heard you were talking about how you wanted screw my wife and you are telling everyone how you saw her tits. Is that right Frank?"

He didn't know what to say except that it was blown out of proportion and he meant nothing by it. "It was just bullshit talk." His voice shook and he apologized and begged me not to pull the trigger.

"I know you're connected. I know you've done prison time. If I have to worry about looking over my shoulder all the time, I'd just as soon end it now." I released the locked-back bolt on the gun and let it slam forward, sliding a shell up through the breach and loading it into the barrel. He thought I'd pulled the trigger and screamed like a girl.

He now shook all over. "Don't kill me! We'll just forget this ever happened! Please!"

I guess the woman he was with thought I was her husband. She had heard loud voices and came into the hallway. When she saw the gun shoved into Frank's neck she put her hands up and screamed. Frank told her everything was okay but her legs gave out and her butt hit the floor. She just sat there with her hands over her mouth.

I backed up a couple of steps, which put me almost out the door. I lowered my gun, but at the same time kept it pointed at his mid mass. "Listen to me, Frank. If anything happens to me or my family there will be ten others to take my place and there is no doubt in my mind they will carry out what I started tonight."

"No, Dennis! No! I give you my word there will be noting said or done, it will be forgotten." He stuck out his hand.

I shook his hand but kept my gun pointed at his chest. I backed away and he shut the door and that was that. When I got to my car I was still pumped and wondered if I screwed up by letting Frank go. I had almost taken this man's life and as I sat there contemplating what just happened, I felt no remorse. Nothing at all. I wondered if I pulled the trigger it would have bothered me. This played on my mind. I had a serious problem and needed to make drastic changes if I wanted to live a somewhat normal life.

I let some time pass before I told Roni what had happened. I didn't want her to hear it from someone else. I told Ray what I had done and it blew him away. I told him not to let Frank know he knew what happened, because it may embarrass him to the point he felt like he had to retaliate to gain back his pride. I figured if Ray told his wife and she said something to Roni, Roni would be upset. Most of all she would worry, so I figured it would be best if I told her myself. I don't remember Roni's reaction, but then she can hold back her feelings. She had heard about my experiences in Vietnam and compared to that, this probably seemed like nothing to her.

Chapter 26
My First Born: Brandy

Roni became pregnant shortly after I reenlisted. I remember the day she got the results from her pregnancy test. I drove her to the hospital that day on base and I waited in the car. I stayed behind to prepare myself for what I knew was going to be a shock. We weren't ready for kids. Roni knew I had issues about having kids and she didn't know how I would handle the news if she was pregnant.   Roni, on the other hand was solid. She could handle anything as long as she knew I stood with her. I knew my reaction to the news would set the precedent for her whole pregnancy. When she opened the door to give me the news I wasn't ready for it. I needed more time. Then she laid it on me.

"I'm pregnant" she said. Her tone of voice said she was not sure how I would react.

As soon as I heard those words my mind was made up. I was unsure of how it would all turn out, but I felt real joy in my heart. We hugged each other. "Okay. Things are going to be okay. It's great news." We started dealing with having a child at that very moment in time.

My wife's pregnancy was a highlight of my life. She was beautiful, I couldn't keep my hands off of her, and I was always putting my hands on her stomach. Sometimes in public I would point to her stomach and say something like, 'I did that' or 'that's my kid Brandy in there.' This would embarrass Roni, but I was so proud to be a father and I wanted everyone to know. The best part was how my feelings for Roni grew. I was bonding tighter with the woman I loved while making a life with her. The day Brandy was born were the happiest days of my life so far. These were the good times and it seemed I had life by the tail and I was just going along for the ride.

As happy as I was then, the flashbacks of Vietnam were forever present. Anything could trigger them. The sound of a gun while hunting, the rotors on a helicopter on certain occasions, certain smells even played with my head and took me back. The flashbacks weren't some psychedelic blackouts, they were just quick flashbacks of certain events. Sometimes they made me think of Vietnam and random memories flooded my mind. I hated it. Mostly it was the same dreams repeatedly. They always hit me like a ton of bricks and my heart felt like it would burst. I often woke screaming and Roni would put her hand on my chest or talk to me to bring me back. The dreams were so vivid and I wondered if they would ever stop.

The birth of my child helped me deal with the pain of Vietnam. My thoughts were focused on the family and even though I thought of Vietnam every day, my dreams didn't come as often. The flashbacks would occur, I couldn't stop that, but my new family helped me stay steady and kept me from pondering on it for any amount of time. It wasn't long and Roni became pregnant again. We didn't care. We decided we wanted two kids anyway, so the first one would have a brother or a sister. I was happy, and hiding out in the army wasn't all that bad for me.

Chapter 26
Korea Bound

Just when I found peace in my life, I got orders to go back to Vietnam. My first reaction was anger. I couldn't believe they wanted to send me back. When my friends found out they also couldn't believe I was headed back to Vietnam.

Roni and I talked about it and after giving it a great deal of thought, I decided I was not going. I knew there would be consequences to pay, but I couldn't do another tour in Vietnam. So I went down to S-2 and told them I was not going back. They informed me if I refused I would be put in Leavenworth Prison. My response to them was I didn't care, that would be better than Vietnam and they could do whatever they wanted.

When I got back to the company everyone knew. No one tried to change my mind. They knew as well as I did that I couldn't do another tour. We had a new CO, Major Peters, and although he had known me for a short time we had become good friends. He tried to sway me from my decision to disobey orders for overseas duty. After some time he knew he was talking to a wall. I wasn't going back and that was that. Major Peters was a good company commander. He had a certain sense of humor you don't find in many commanders and even though he did not agree with my tactics, he understood my reasons.

A couple of days passed and I was out on the flight line checking the flight log book entries on the aircraft when my old company commander Colonel Young drove up in his staff car. He was now General Young . At first I had no idea what he was doing down on the flight line because he didn't schedule a flight, but then the post commander doesn't have to schedule anything. Whatever he wants he gets.

When he got out of his car he headed straight for me. I knew I was in deep shit. He shook his head and said, "What am I going to do with you?"

I came to attention and popped a salute. He returned my salute and told me to be at ease. He put his arm over my shoulder and told me to walk with him down the flight line. By the tone of his voice I knew he was not mad or upset. We took several steps without him saying anything at all. When we had got away from everyone he told me I was not going to Vietnam.

"Good," I replied.

"I got your orders changed and you are going to South Korea instead. I had your orders exchanged with a soldier that was headed there."

"Bullshit," I said, "I'm not going there either. I'm not going to live in a damned tent for a year."

He then put his arm around me. "Do you trust me?"

"Of course I do, sir. I trust you with my life and have on several occasions."

"Then trust me on this. You need a vacation, Brooks. You will like this assignment, I promise. You and Knight are going to Korea together. You are going to be personal bodyguards and flight crew for a General

Knowles. He is a four star general and a personal friend of mine. He also has a brand new UH-1H helicopter and you and Knight will be flying him whenever and wherever he wants to go. Trust me, Dennis. You will love this assignment."

I didn't know what to say after that. I still didn't want to go, but it was better than prison. What made me feel better about the whole deal was that I would be going overseas with Knight. At least I would be with a good friend. I would leave in about two months and that would make it June. It was a thirteen month unaccompanied tour and that meant Roni couldn't go with me. At least it wasn't Vietnam, I kept telling myself. But the separation from my wife would be hard and she would give birth while I was overseas.

Even though Korea was considered a hardship tour, the Old Man was right. For the most part it was a good assignment. When I first got in country my orders got screwed up and I ended up in The Second Division. My MOS was 67N20 and because I was awarded flight status that made my MOS a 67N2F. But I had mistakenly been assigned to a tank and grunt unit and there wasn't a helicopter within fifty miles of the place. I believe the name of the place was Taedunsan. Rule has it if you are a sergeant and above they have to put you in your MOS or send you back home. So they sent me to a place called Camp Stanley by Uijeongbu, but the Second Division didn't have any helicopters so I went down to the Eighth Army who did have them and landed myself a job.

General Knowles was the commander of I-Core and I had no idea how to approach a four star general and tell him I'm his new crew chief and body guard. Thank God Knight was on my orders of assignment and when it was all said and done I was only fifteen miles from them.

They were at a base called Camp Campo. Instead of going through all of the red tape in getting me assigned to I-Core, Knowles pulled some strings and I ended up with a whole bunch of paperwork telling me how I was assigned. I was assigned to Second Division, attached to Eighth Army, and working for I-Core. Clearing country would be a mess.

Korea was great, and like Vietnam, pot was cheap. Five dollars a pound and it was the best marijuana I have ever had in my life. The first time I tried it over there I thought someone had laced it with something and I almost whipped the guy's ass that I smoked the joint with. I thought he was the culprit. He laughed and told me all the dope was that good.

I got heavily into drugs in Korea. Cocaine, opium, window pane (a type of acid.) I did heroine once and some stuff we called B-29, which was a diluted version of LSD. To top it off, Knight and I could not wear rank or a name tags. We grew our hair long for military standards and had big handle bar mustaches.

The General, who we now called the Old Man, was the coolest officer I had ever met. He let us get by with our appearance but expected us to hold the highest standards of military discipline and courtesy toward any officer, Korean or American. In the next year we would meet and mingle with the highest ranking officers in the Korean Army and he expected us to be very solicitous toward them. We brown-nosed the hell out of them, but no one, and I mean no one, except the Old Man could even approach us. It was great and Knight and I took full advantage of the situation. Plus, when the Old Man was not using his aircraft Knight and I had it at our disposal. We took full advantage of this perk and we had a ball.

We accompanied the Old Man to banquets, top brass meetings, and hundreds of dog and pony shows. Political bullshit. Knight and I usually didn't sit in on meetings or join everyone in the banquet area. We were usually isolated from mingling with the populous at any of these parties, but we never wanted for anything. We were fed well and were always treated with the highest respect. Heck, for me it was like being an officer. Everyone knew we were part of the Old Man's staff and knew we were always armed with .45s and except for secured areas we never let the Old Man out of our sight. Even though no one knew our rank or names, they knew what our job was and accepted our presence.

I was told later that to qualify for being the Old Man's crew and body guard you had to have had combat experience and a high proficiency score. Out of 160 points my score was 138. It was a good thing the test was given based on your job scope.

Korea was a good tour for me, but I missed the birth of my second child, Jenifer Ebony. I was away from Roni. When I received the word from Roni that she delivered a girl I admit I was a little disappointed. I wanted a son. Now that I have raised girls, I would throw boys back. My kids and my wife are the three best things I have ever attained in my lifetime. But raising kids is a huge responsibility and in a lot of ways, I was a kid myself. I swore no matter whatever I wanted in life, or whatever I did, my family would come first. I knew I still had issues. I hoped I could be a good father and husband.

I had many adventures in Korea, but to write about them would probably be boring and plays no significant purpose in my life. When I got back to the States, things changed for me. I looked at life differently. I was restless, but somewhat happy.

When my thirteen month tour ended in Korea, the Old man's tour was ending as well. He asked Knight and me if we wanted to go with him to his next duty assignment which was going to be Hawaii. We declined. We wanted to go home. General Knowles gave us a choice of our duty assignment and we felt privileged to have it, so we went back to Ft. Sill and our old buddies.

Chapter 27
Red Mic Down

When I got home Jenny was already walking and Brandy barely remembered me. Roni had pointed to a portrait every night and had Brandy kiss it and say my name. Brandy accepted me on my return home, but Jenny was shy and wanted nothing to do with this stranger in her life. It upset me to some degree but it was to be expected. I knew in time she would come around. Jenny was a mother's girl for sure and every time I tried to correct her she ran to Roni for consolation, but it didn't take long for her to warm up to me. For awhile, life was good again.

After returning from Korea, Knight and I resumed our roles at Ft. Sill. I was given my flight line section chief job back and military life for Knight and I picked up where it left off. Having been part of General Knowles' staff was good for our records and we knew from this time on the rest of our time in the service would be gravy. We were both given top secret clearance and were told we would be going on a special assignment flying gunship escort for a couple of Chinooks hauling nuclear warheads out of Ohio and into Wisconsin and Illinois. The job took us four months and was a good assignment. But I only saw my family twice. But compared to Vietnam and Korea it was a walk in the park and we again resumed our life in Ft. Sill afterward.

On that mission, Knight used the radio call sign Red Mic to identify himself. Red mic in Vietnam was a term we used many times in combat. It was a mode we put the radios so we didn't have to use the switch to talk to each other on the intercom. Hot mic is another term, but red mic meant you were going into combat mode. So Knight kept this call sign and everyone called him Red Mic when they flew. Knight had transitioned into Cobras and he did a lot of training with new pilots that had not been to Vietnam yet, or that had been in Vietnam but hadn't flown Cobras. Ryan and I stayed in Slicks and made sure everyone stayed current on their flight time.

Life for me then wasn't that bad, and even if I got another overseas assignment it would be an accompanied tour and my family could go with me. I have had two hardship tours so from then on if I went anywhere I would be accompanied with my wife and kids and if I went anywhere it would be to Germany. I have always been suspicious of when things are going good. There is something always waiting around the corner to kick you in the teeth and that day wasn't long in coming.

One day while I was out taking care of the work on the flight line Knight asked me if I could pull a Cobra out of the hanger. He had to make an orientation flight with a new guy and he and two other Cobras were going to go out and have a little fun. I wasn't in charge of the Cobras, but I told him it was no problem. I checked the books and found an aircraft that was ready to go. I picked one that he and I had flown in many times, it was one of his favorites. I had it pulled out of the hanger and put on the flight line. Knight and another pilot gave it a good pre-flight and soon afterward they were airborne with a couple of other Cobras. I envied them. It was a good day to fly.

I went to my office and worked up a status report. About an hour had passed when Ryan ran into the office. "Brooks, Knight's Cobra is down."

"Is he okay?" I replied.

"I don't know, it doesn't sound good. He didn't call in a MAY-DAY, his wing man did." He asked me what aircraft we could take to go out to the crash site. The only bird I had out on the flight line was the Old Man's bird. "Let's take it," he said and I jumped up from behind my desk, grabbed my flight helmet and we were out the door.

When we were in the aircraft, I asked Ryan how long had it been since the aircraft had been reported down. He told me about forty-five minutes. He had returned from a late lunch and everyone was over in operations talking about it and that an investigating team was already on sight. I knew it wasn't good, but sometimes you choose to cling onto the hope that things will be okay. Well, that was me. I hoped everything was fine and Knight was okay. When we arrived at the crash site we knew the news was bad. Knight's aircraft was scattered all over the field. Ryan and I just looked at each other and it was like we were both back in 'Nam. We radioed back to base and everyone knew then that Knight did not survive the crash.

When we landed the aircraft there was a team already on the ground. We landed far enough way so the rotor wash would not blast the area. Ryan and I jumped out, neither one of us wanted to approach the crash site for fear of what awaited.

As we approached I saw my friend's mangled body. Even though his body was badly damaged I knew it was Knight. We were stopped by a member of the investigating team. He told us we were not allowed on the site. We pretty much told him to piss off.

Ryan is a big, tall man and as he looked down on this pompous ass, he pointed to Knight's body. "See that man that you are allowing to lay face down in the dirt? He is our friend and brother, so don't tell us we don't belong, or aren't allowed here." After that the man turned and walked away.

We stood around in the hot sun watching our friend's blood turn black from the heat. I went to my aircraft and pulled off a blanket of sound proofing from around the transmission wall and went over to put it over Knight. I was stopped by the same guy, telling me we could not enter. I pushed him aside, told him to take a flying leap and then I went over and put the blanket over Knight.

The worm I pushed out of the way got his boss and he came over with this look of authority on his face and told us we would have to leave. I'd had enough of that bullshit and asked him what part friend's body had to do with the cause or investigation of this crash. His answer was stupid and Ryan and I reached down and took the blanket off of Knight, rolled his body over onto it and carried him to the aircraft. We were taking Knight's body with us and that was that. The main guy of the three-man investigating team got on the radio and called someone, but Ryan and I didn't care. We loaded Knight's body into our aircraft.

When we took off, this guy was still on the radio. When we got a little altitude we radioed our company and told them we were bringing in Knight's body and would require transportation. The radio was silent for the longest time before a 'Roger' came back to us. We were about fifty miles from Ft. Sill and the flight back was a hard one. Nothing was said between Ryan and I, we put down our sun visors on our helmets to hide the pain and tears. Knight was a good friend and we had been through too much together for it to end up like this. Although we did not talk, I knew we both thought of the history the three of us shared. Knight and I were good friends, but Knight and Ryan were best friends and I know his grief was unbearable. He would never be the same. Ryan asked me to fly the aircraft for a minute. I took the controls while he wiped the tears from his eyes and cleared his head. The smell of the blood circulated throughout the aircraft and gave us both flashbacks, recalling the smell and drama of war.

When I got home that night I told Roni of Knight's death. I didn't talk too much about it. She knew I didn't want talk about it and I never mentioned the subject again. I didn't want her to be concerned. She knew I was having issues and I didn't want her to think I couldn't handle it. I had told her more about the war than I should have and probably more than she really wanted to know.

It was about this time in my life I kept my feelings to myself and drew up into a tight little ball, but acted like I was fine. I turned to drugs more, but was careful not to become dependent on them. I never got a craving for drugs but I did long for the relief they gave me, and they helped me pretend life was good and I would heal, in time, *I just needed more time*, I thought.

Chapter 28
The Set Up

I grew my own pot and traded it for other drugs that were available. Roni didn't care for pot that much, but she did like speed, so that was the drug of choice for her. Me, I liked just about everything. The drugs that did me the most good and freed my mind were Mescaline and Quaaludes. Mescaline was good by itself and changed my moods from a state of depression to one of well-being. Quaaludes worked better with alcohol. The police knew I was doing drugs and selling them, but they could never catch me. So with the help from a hardcore druggie, the police set me up. One time, while giving this guy a lift, he placed a couple of joints in my car and soon after I was pulled over and arrested.

It was a Friday night and I was going to Texas to work the oil fields. I was going to hook up with my brother in Pampa we would work the oil fields to make a little extra cash. This was something I did often for that extra money and to help keep my body in good shape. The only thing that freed my mind other than drugs was hard, physical labor and the oil fields did that. I was seven years older than my brother and while I lived at home, like all little brothers, he was a pain in the ass. But when I came back from Vietnam he had grown up and we eventually became best friends. His regular job was working the oil fields around Pampa and he got me hired on for the part time work.

Anyway, I picked up this guy who told me he needed a lift to the Texas border and because my trip to Pampa was about a four hour drive, I figured the company would be welcome. We didn't get far into our trip when in the middle of nowhere he wanted me to drop him off. I thought it was odd, but obliged and pulled over to let him out. As he got out he told me he would hitchhike back to Medicine Park, an area where we both lived. Back then, if you lived in Medicine Park you were most likely into drugs. It was out in the country from Lawton and actually a beautiful area to live. Especially if you were a head.

Shortly after dropping him off, I was pulled over by the state police and busted for possession of marijuana. The guy I gave the ride to put two joints in my console and the police officer knew just were to look. It's not that I was innocent. I had a half pound of home-grown under the back seat floor mat and after a search it was found. I was taking this dope to my brother. Back then, in Oklahoma, having a joint was a felony so I was pretty much up a shit creek without a paddle. The cop was a real asshole and enjoyed every minute of arresting me. He squeezed the handcuffs into my wrist as he put them on and asked me if they were tight enough.

I was taken to the county jail in Lawton, Oklahoma and booked for possession with intent to sell. The cop said carrying around that much dope would get me jail time for sure and laughed about it. I didn't say much. I asked him for a phone call and he gave it to me. I called Roni and let her know I was in jail. I hated telling her I was busted but asked her to call Ray. He was connected with the police department and I figured if anyone knew a good lawyer he would. I knew the police department was crooked. Ray told me of some of the deals they were involved in and I kind of figured there may be a pay off. If anyone could arrange it, it would be Ray. But my biggest concern was the military. I figured this would pretty much screw my career. I already regretted having to face the Old Man.

Soon after being booked I was put into the tank with about thirty prisoners. Some were doing county time up to six months and some, like me, were waiting that Friday night to have our day in court on Monday. When I was put into the holding cell it was so dark I could hardly see. I stood for awhile, until my eyes adjusted. I saw an empty bunk and walked over to sit on it. It was nothing more than a flat sheet of metal extending from a wall, no mattress. People had been putting out cigarettes on it and it was nasty. Monday couldn't come soon enough. A voice from the bunk above asked me why I was busted. When I told him, this skinny, red-headed boy jumped down and said 'me too.' I wasn't in the mood, but this guy wanted to strike up a conversation. I sat there hearing this guy move his mouth without really listening. My mind was not on socializing.

After some time, my back began to hurt. My injury from Vietnam wasn't going to take much of that cold slab of steel. I interrupted the guy and asked him where I could get a mattress and a pillow. He told me he didn't have one either and if I wanted one I would have to ask the guys in the back cell for one. He told me they were doing time and had horded all the extra mattresses. Some had two or three. I sat until my back could take no more, and then got up, walked across the bay and through the door. In that cell there were bunks bunched up close together blankets hung off the top bunks, to close in the bottom bunk so its occupant could have privacy. I smelled the faint, sweet scent of marijuana and knew these guys had to be in cahoots with the jailer.

I asked the first guy that I saw had more than one mattress if I could borrow one. He looked up at me. "Say what, mother fucker?"

I knew then I was considered an outsider. The guy was black and didn't give a shit about a white boy that wanted a mattress. I repeated myself and told him I would make sure come Monday he would get his mattress back. He then stood up and told me if I wanted a mattress I would have to take it. This guy was well over six feet and weighed over two hundred pounds.

"Screw that," I replied and turned to walk out of the cell block and back into the bay area. As I turned away the guy laughed and triggered a chain reaction from the rest of his cellmates. In a matter of seconds I was the center of amusement.

The hair on the back of my neck stood up and in a split-second my anger erupted. I turned and with all my might and body weight I hit this guy square on his nose. It exploded like a ripe tomato and his head thrust backward and struck the brick wall. He fell to ground and didn't move. I reached down and took a mattress from his bunk and went toward the bay area.

Before I could get back to my bunk, people came at me from behind. His friends. I ran over to the corner of the cell where there was a mop in a bucket. I grabbed it and broke it over my knee to make a club. I would rather have an ax handle, but this small club on some ones face or nose would do the trick. There were three of them and I knew I better make my strikes count.

I noticed one guy held a piece of steel of some sort that was sharpened to a sharp point. He held this shank in front of him like he was going to lunge. I slammed my makeshift club onto the hand that held this shank. His knuckles cracked. Then I backed into a corner and waited for them to make the next move while screaming at the top of my voice to bring it on, hoping the jailer would hear all the commotion and come running to my aid.

The guy I busted across the knuckles had backed off several feet holding his hand, but another guy picked up the shank and started toward me. This time not only was I going to crack this guy across the knuckles the next blow would be across his nose. Then I heard the jailer or what I thought was the jailer opening the door. It was not the jailer but the guy that had arrested me. He was still there and as soon as he opened the door he told me to drop my weapon.

"Weapon?" I responded, "This guy has the weapon." I pointed to the guy holding the shank.

This cop then told me he was not going to tell me again to drop my weapon.

"To hell with you! Make this asshole drop his weapon." The door to the cell opened and as I kept my back to the bars I moved toward the cell door.

The next thing I know I felt this pain run up the back of my neck and I blacked out. The officer had cracked me across my lower back and kidneys. The pain from my old injuries was unbearable as I fell to my knees. The intensity knocked the breath out of me to the point I couldn't catch a breath. Every time I tried to breathe, pain shot up my back and into the base of my head.

The police officer and the jailer dragged my limp ass body down the corridor and threw me into a small cell. I was told later that the small cells were for trouble makers. I was the only one in there and that suited me fine. At least I had a bunk with a mattress. I stayed in this cell for three nights and two days, until Monday rolled around. I was awakened several times a night and asked by a trustee if I wanted coffee. Coffee would have been nice, but it was always two in the morning or so when they asked me. It was a means of harassing me that I'm sure was encouraged by the officers. Other than that, no one said a word to me. I didn't know how my case was going, or even if I would appear in court Monday morning to get my bail set. Other than the aforementioned harassment, no one said a word to me.

My back was killing me and I had a headache that wouldn't stop. I asked for aspirin several times but they would just grin and turn their backs. The last morning there I accepted the coffee and when the trustee handed it to me I threw coffee on him. He cussed and told me I would have to beg him for my dinner. But I knew it was Monday morning and figured at least the military would come and get me.

My time for court finally came and I was taken from my isolation cell and walked down the hall corridor and past the cell where I clobbered that guy. He stood at the cell bars. He had a huge bandage over his nose and both his eyes were almost swollen shut. As I passed the cell he told me I would be seeing him again and threatened me. I reached through the cell and grabbed his nose, he did nothing but scream. The officers then put me in cuffs and walked me to an elevator and took me, along with several other prisoners, down to the first floor where the court room was located.

On the way down the cuffs were removed and as I stepped out of the elevator I saw Ray and my wife. Ray had gotten me a lawyer, my bail was soon set and I was released to the custody of two MPs from Ft. Sill. They took me out of the court room and turned me loose. The two MPs were good guys. They patted me on the back and wished me good luck. I went home and crawled into my bed and stared up at the ceiling. My God, what a hell of two days it had been. *God. Now there is a subject,* I thought. I hadn't said a prayer since 'Nam. But when people are down they always turn to God.

God. What a joke, I thought. I had seen nothing but death and destruction on this earth. Then for some reason I started talking to Him. *God, if you are real prove it to me. I haven't seen your presence in any form or fashion my whole life. I have seen what man can do to man and you sit by and let it happen. If you are real, or there is a God, prove it to me and I will take my family down that path. But if not, back off. You haven't proven crap to me.* I left it at that.

I caught myself blaming God for everything that had happened in my life that was bad. It was easy to shift the blame to someone besides myself and that is just what I did. I blamed God for everything. It was His fault and I festered in self pity and became bitter toward any religion or anyone who claimed they knew God. *Bullshit,* I thought. For what I had seen and done, I knew there could be no God.

Atonement

I knew I would soon face my company commander, Major Peters and I was not looking forward to it. He had no idea that I used drugs and I knew he would be shocked. Even though I had not served in combat with Major Peters, I felt like I had known him forever. He pinned my SP-5 stripes on me and he is the one that had promoted me to section chief. I hated that he would have to be the one to dish out my reprimand, but I would rather have it dealt out to me by a friend than someone I didn't know or respect. I hated disappointing him more than anything else.

The next day I reported to the Old Man and he made me sit outside his office as he reviewed the police report of my arrest and the trouble I caused in the jail. I saw his orderly bring him my military records and I thought the trouble I had gotten myself into was not going to go away. It would probably follow me around for awhile.

The Old Man let me sit out there long enough to let it simmer in my mind, but I wasn't thinking of my military carrier. I was thinking of my life in general and that I had two kids and as a parent I had to do what was best for them. But hell, I didn't even know what was best for me. I began to think I was turning out to be like my real father and that played on my mind to no end. I had reached a crossroad but was confused as to what my next step needed to be. For most people, the choice might have been easy. But not for me. A lot of people had come into my life and out again in the blink of an eye.

Even though I tried my best to put Vietnam behind me, it haunted my spirit and the faces of the ones I had seen die in battle visited my dreams almost every night. I wished Knight was still around so I could talk to him. In a lot of ways I was still a kid and needed someone to talk to. But I felt alone. Ryan was the only person around that I'd served with in combat, other than General Young, the post commander. Ryan and I understood each other but had never been real close. Not like Knight and me. I closed my eyes and saw his smiling face. I got caught up in the moment and my eyes teared up. At that moment the door to the Major Peter's office opened. He told me to come into his office.

He noticed I was upset and I knew he thought it was because of the trouble I had gotten myself into. But it had nothing to do with my arrest. Sure, that weighed heavily on my mind, but it had nothing to do with the military and my feelings about it. I knew I was simply hiding out in the military because I did not feel comfortable around civilians. The Old Man gave me the courtesy to compose myself and went back into his office. I took a minute then walked up to his desk, saluted, reported, and came to attention. He told me to feel at ease, and have a seat.

As I sat down and watched him thumb through my records, I noticed he didn't want to make eye contact with me. He was embarrassed for me and in some way that made me feel more at ease. I knew then there was a man with compassion sitting behind that desk. I sat there for what felt like was forever. But he read through every detail of my military carrier up to then. Quite some time passed before he closed my records and sat back in his large easy chair. He then looked me straight in the eye and asked me what I thought he should do about my situation. I told him I didn't know.

He let me know what his thoughts were on the subject and his words have remained in my mind all these years. He told me that he hadn't served in combat with me, but he knew people that had and had nothing but good things to say. "Brooks, we are not going to burn our heroes and son, weather you admit or not, you are a hero. Your career, up to this point, is spotless and it is up to me to keep it that way. Nothing is going into your records. The military is not going to ruin what I consider a good soldier's career. You have served your country

Brooks, and you have put your life on the line more than once for your country and fellow soldiers. Your record reflects that and I am not going to be a part of discrediting, or blemishing your military record."

He then dismissed me, and as I started to leave he came from around his desk and shook my hand and thanked me for my combat service. A lump lodged in my throat and I could not say a word. My eyes were full of water and I was doing my best not to shed one tear. Peters knew this and opened the door for me to make an exit without embarrassing myself. As I walked down the hall I could tell by people's faces they knew the outcome of the Old Man's decision, I'm sure he discussed it with several members of his staff. Everyone I ran into had this shit-eating grin on their face and some gave me a pat on the back as I passed. The pat was one of those gestures to encourage me.

At this point I really didn't care one way or another. Oh sure, I was happy nothing came of my arrest but it didn't really have an impact on the way I lived my life. I was still going to smoke dope. It was the only thing that calmed the beast in me.

The first thing I did was go to Frank and put a contract on that asshole of a police officer that set me up. Frank owed me big time for a favor and he had no problems returning it. I made a mistake by telling Roni about the contract and it bothered her to no end. She asked me not to do it, knowing it would be something that would haunt me later, and besides, to her it was the same as murder. I believe it scared her that I would even consider doing such a thing. I think it scared her the most because I didn't even blink an eye or show the least amount of concern when I told her.

I didn't debate the subject any further with her. I told her I would have Frank back off. I also didn't want her to know how connected I had become with Frank. I had done some things for him that can't be discussed or mentioned for fear that I could still be held accountable. But it had been nothing I hadn't done in Vietnam and at the time I had no conscience when it came to certain matters. I felt no remorse for what I had done for Frank and that I felt justice was served for doing what I did for him. But to put Roni at ease I broke off my ties with Frank. We were still friends but Roni didn't care for him and she knew before I did that he wasn't good for me. Frank was a user and now that I look back, I was nothing but a pawn in a game of chess. Deep down, I believe I knew this.

Like I mentioned before, when I was in Korea, drugs played a bigger part in my life than ever before. I was out there running and didn't even know what I was running from. I know now that I was running from myself. I didn't like what I had become. Life was not supposed to be this complicated and the drugs twisted things even more. I expected things to fall into place. Vietnam was supposed to fade away and life was supposed to be gravy when I came home from the war. This wasn't the case. My dreams haunted me and the drugs magnified my depression.

I felt guilty for not keeping in touch with my brothers that were still in Vietnam and with the ones that had come home. The war was the only thing that bonded us. I was trying to put Vietnam behind me and in doing so I forgot about my brothers. This put additional strain on my crippled state of mind.

One Saturday I climbed atop a hillside on the refuge at Fort Sill. I didn't sleep very well the night before and I wanted some time to myself. I had partied with some of my military friends but it didn't bring me much comfort. None of those guys were ever in Vietnam and in a way I was glad. On the other hand no one understood my mood swings and sometimes I was a loaner even when we all got together. After awhile I drifted off into my own little world and after that I might as well go home.

I sat there on top of that mountain watching the morning come to life. I thought that day would be a good day to die and with no hesitation I pulled my gun from my jacket pocket placed it on rock beside me and stared at it for the longest time. After a while I decided death was a better way for me. I placed the gun to right side of my head and closed my eyes. I wanted my last thought in this world to be of the best of things in it, so I thought of my wife and kids. About the first time I held each of them in my arms. About Roni and how we had grown up together and how much I loved her and she loved me. I thought of our kids again and how they would grow up without their dad. One thought like this led to another and I knew death was not the answer.

I needed to get a grip on things and I caught myself cursing God, if there was one, and blamed Him again. It made me feel better. After a while I pulled a joint out of my shirt pocket, lit it and let my mind drift into nothing but the good things in life. My spirits lifted and I felt better about myself. Pot always did that to me. I knew I had to give up all drugs, but not pot. It was the only drug that never took my mind to bad places. It eased my soul comforted my spirit. Opened my mind. I considered it a good friend.

But Roni was my island. She was who I turned to when the depression crept into my mind. She always listened and tried to understand my pain. Sometimes I told her too much. Her mood would change and I could tell she'd had enough. It wasn't fair to keep dumping my problems on her so I got to the point I didn't bring up Vietnam. I made sure not to get too detailed in the descriptions of what haunted my soul and I never told her about that day on the mountain.

Roni and I smoked pot together and she took a little speed once in a while. She never got into drugs like I did. I guess she knew one of us had to be an adult. She was that alright. She was and still is my rock and she saved my live more than once. Without Roni I wouldn't have survived what I consider my most difficult years. I know she considers those years her hardest too.

Chapter 29
The Truth at My Door

There are things in everyone's life that change them forever. Of all the things I have written about, this chapter is the most meaningful and important for me. After being off hard drugs for awhile and my life returning to some normalcy, I felt guilty for some of the things I blamed on God. Roni was brought up Catholic and I was raised a Baptist. We both saw the hypocrisy in our churches and I chose not to have anything to do with religion.

Roni, on the other hand, never lost her faith in God and because we were a family, she wanted us to worship together. I tried going to a Catholic church with her, but I couldn't accept it as the true word of God. The church I was raised wasn't any better and couldn't prove anything to me either. There were no real answers to my questions no matter what authority figure I went to. Questions like, why does God allow wars, pain, suffering when he has the power to stop it? Why do infants, who are innocent of any sin, die such horrible deaths? Why did people in Biblical days live for hundreds of years? Hellfire, tortures mentioned in the place of the cross, the second death, the thousand year reign, Satan put into the abyss and let out again, the great crowd, the anointed and so on.

I had lots of questions but no real answers. Oh sure, there were lots of so-called clergy that could give me what they considered answers, but the trouble was every preacher had a different explanation for the same question and they couldn't prove things to my satisfaction. After making fun of the clergy figures and getting nowhere, I decided if I was going to find answers to these questions I would do it myself. Yeah right. I with no education find these answers. But it was fun getting high and trying to understand the book of Revelation. At most it was entertaining, especially when a bunch of my friends came over and we would sit around get high and each gave his interpretation of Revelation.

One Saturday morning Roni and I were hanging out around the house. She and I were about finished smoking a joint when we heard the dog bark. A couple of people were at our gate. I looked out the window and saw a young girl with her mother wanting to come into our yard but they weren't too sure of the dog. Not wanting them to come to the door in fear they would smell the smoke from the joint, I rushed out the door to greet them.

As soon as I stepped out of the door I asked them if I could help them. They identified themselves as Jehovah Witnesses. I had heard of these Witnesses but never knew much about them. My mother used to call them a cult and I had heard people tell me to watch out for these people. But to me these two looked very nice and their manner of speaking was pleasant. It was good to hear people talk in such a nice manner so I decided to listen to them. I considered myself pretty knowledgeable concerning the Bible, plus I wanted to throw some of my theories of Revelation on them. I liked the idea they showed no fear of talking to a total stranger. I saw kindness in their eyes. Besides, I never liked putting titles on people until I could make up my own mind.

These two were a mother and daughter working together in what they called the Field Service. I had talked to Mormons doing something similar but these two actually knew what they were doing. What attracted me most about them was they weren't intimidated by my comments and they were sincere in what they were doing. I threw a couple of my theories at them and they used their Bibles to show where I was wrong in my interpretation of particular scriptures, using common sense and understanding of what Jesus was saying. They explained how Jesus talked in parables and illustrations so the disciples could understand and that everything is not to be taken literally, there is usually a point Jesus was trying to get across. They told me many things and the way they were explaining it to me did make sense.

Then I thought I would throw them a curve and asked them why in one book of the Bible you read where Jesus was put on a limb of a tree when we all know he was put on a cross. They looked at each other as if debating what to say. I knew I had them then and at last I could take control of this discussion. They not only knew about it, they showed me the scripture and where it was to be found in the Bible.

"But isn't the Bible being contradictive?" I asked.

Then they did something that totally blew me away. They asked me to go and get a copy of my Bible. I was hesitant because I didn't want to open the door for fear they would smell the marijuana. But they were still at my gate and it was fifty feet from the door of my house so I decided to go ahead and take a chance and retrieve a Bible that I'd had since I was a kid. When I returned they took my Bible and showed me where the scripture about the limb of a tree was located. Then they showed me their Bible, which said pretty much the same thing. But then they showed me where their Bible didn't have the word 'cross'in it. They knew I was confused so they pointed out how the original scriptures were written in the two languages of Hebrew and Greek, Hebrew being the Old Testament and Greek being the New Testament.

They then told me their Bible was a direct translation from the Greek and Hebrew scripture and in this direct translation there is no mention of the word 'cross.' A 'torture stake' is what they put Christ on, not a cross. They told me the Romans didn't put people on the cross until three hundred years after Christ died. Then in great detail they explained how the Romans killed the people they put on these so called torture stakes. They would stake their hands together over their heads and then stake their feet together in the same fashion. Then when they were raised into the air the weight of their body along with their arms raised above their head would cut off their air, so in order to breathe they would have to try and take the weight off by their legs, which would be very painful. That person would have to do that all day long to breathe, until they died. And if for some reason they didn't die, a Roman soldier would take an iron scepter and break their legs, which would keep them from getting air and suffocate them.

Well, I guess they could tell by the look on my face I had received more information on that one subject in about twenty minutes than I had heard in my whole life. As I stood there with my mouth open the mother asked me if I would like to start a study with her and her husband and learn about all the subjects I had brought up. Then she told me that she and her husband didn't want me to believe anything they said, but only what they could prove and what I learned myself. Then she told me I could go to a public library and find what we had talked about so far in the biblical history cross references and books on the Roman Empire. So this is what I did and I was amazed at what I learned.

I learned that the cross was a pagan symbol and at first I had a hard time accepting this fact. I wore a cross around my neck that was given to me by that Vietnamese girl and it has never been off in the five years since it was given to me. I thought of it brought me good luck, but as I looked back I realized my luck wasn't all that great. Even though the cross was twenty-four carat gold I took from around my neck and threw it away. I came to this decision not in haste but by reasoning.

First I learned Christ was not put on a cross, which was reason enough not to wear it anymore, but then I was helped to understand that Christ didn't love the tool that took his life. If an intruder came into your home and shot your loved one in the head and killed them, would you take a replica of that gun and wear it around your neck in remembrance of that loved one? Do you think the person that was shot with that gun would hold that gun in high regard, or wear it around his or her neck? Would the parent of any loved one wear a replica of that gun around their neck? My reasoning would always come up 'no,' so I rid myself of that cross and never thought anymore about it having some religious meaning. It became just a symbol to me.

Roni and I started a study. Frank and Leona Stauffer were the two we studied with and no one could have been better for us. Frank was a rancher who raised feeder cattle. He had a small operation but was very good at ranching and made a good modest life for him and Leona and their four children. When we first started our studies I would smoke a joint and get into talking and studying the Bible. Roni couldn't smoke marijuana and study so she gave it up. Me, I was a diehard and continued getting high and studying.

It wasn't long before Roni got baptized and became a Witness. I on the other hand put up a fight hashing things over. During one of our studies I went over things we had covered at least three times over the a two year period when Frank closed the book in the middle of one of my debates and told me I knew the truth when it came to God's word. "But you know what you don't have?" he asked.

"What?" I replied.

"You don't have the appreciation for the things you have learned."

That hit me like a ton of bricks. He was right. So I started appreciating what I had learned over the past two years.

I'm not here to tell anyone how to worship their God. Most people are not interested in the truth when it comes to religion. They have been brought up in their faith and feel their religion is the right one. If you try and tell anyone about the truths you have found in the Bible, they will ask what gives you the right to tell them you have the right religion. My answer is to ask them if they think their religion is the right one. They will say to you that they know their religion is the right one. Then my response to them is to ask what gives *them* the right to tell *me* their religion is the right one? If anyone wants to learn the truth they can. It is a free gift given to God's people. It has been handed down through the centuries from the ones that had it in the first place: the Disciples. He was the Great Teacher and the Disciples were his students and they passed it on. It is as simple as that.

Who has the truth? Well, that is up to you to find out. You will know the truth when you hear it. It is simple, not complicated as the clergy would lead you to believe. Clergy have the tendency to make you think they know the word of God and in return you pay them to teach it to you. I will tell you, the word of the true God is free. The ones that have it got it free and they will give it to anyone who wants it, free.

The clergy are going to take you to the old Hebrew laws and show you where you should give ten percent of your earnings to the church, from which their salary is taken. But they forget to tell you those old Hebrew laws were done away with by God's son, Jesus. If we were still under those laws then we wouldn't be able to work, or walk a mile, or do anything on the Sabbath. The High Priest started adding to God's laws and those laws were getting to the point where they were burdensome on the people, so when Jesus came into the picture he did away with those laws.

The only reason I am covering religion is to let you know I found the answers to all my questions concerning God Jehovah and it lifted the burden of guilt from my spirit and allowed me to somewhat heal the mental scars I brought back from Vietnam. It helped me get on with life and come to understand why the things in this system are like they are. I am not a Bible thumper with 'praise the Lord' coming out of my mouth after every sentence. I found answers for me and by doing so I came to a better understanding of myself and mankind's purpose.

Chapter 30
Choosing a Side

After studying the Bible I came to appreciate that God never intended for man to kill man, especially for political or government gain. So I decided to end my military career and submit my paperwork for conscientious objector. You can imagine the debate and arguments that were generated by me doing so. People that I had been in combat with, like Ryan & General Young were confused. They knew I had killed and they even knew of the ears I had taken for trophies, so this threw them for a loop.

My first hurdle to get over was our First Sergeant. Even though I hadn't been in combat with him and he hadn't seen any combat, he thought he would punish and humble me by grounding me, relieving me of Section Chief and putting me in charge of the latrines. I didn't give this man the satisfaction of thinking he got to me. I cleaned the latrines and even took it upon myself to go down to supply check out some white paint and painted them. He was shocked when he came in the one day and found all the latrines in the barracks had been painted bright white. He was really floored when he got a letter from General Young telling him he could not strip me of my flight status. It was awarded to me in combat and only a full bird colonel could strip me of it. So he had to give it back to me, which meant an extra seventy-five dollars on my paycheck.

My next obstacle was Major Peters. He was so disappointed in my decision that he didn't want to talk to me. Next was the post commander, my old friend General Young. Even though there was nothing in the procedure about talking to General Young, he wanted to talk to me. I wasn't looking forward to talking to him but he was a friend and if anyone understood me it was him and Ryan. They both knew my history and thought maybe I was off my rocker a little and that I may be turning into some Jesus Freak or something like that. If anything, I knew these two were my friends and if they were upset with me it was because they were interested in my welfare.

The day I walked into the Old Man's office he had a confused expression. Even though we were in a building and I was not in uniform, I approached his desk and reported to him with a salute and a firm stance of attention. I did this out of respect and he knew that. He returned my salute and asked me to take a seat.

"Brooks, Brooks, Brooks, Brooks. What am I going to do with you? Conscientious Objector. Do you expect me to swallow that?"

I grinned. "I know, sir. I wouldn't have thought so myself, but it is true and I wish I could explain it to you in one sentence, but that's not possible."

He told me I wasn't leaving until I explained enough so he could come to some understanding. I told him about my studies of the Scripture for the last two years. After talking for thirty minutes he knew I was serious in my belief, and then it was his turn.

"Brooks, if everyone thought like you we would all be Communist."

"Sir, if everyone thought like me there wouldn't be any wars."

"You have a point. I have to say you do have a point." He told me he wasn't going to ask any more questions. He knew I would be going to a board review and if they thought I was full of bullshit then they would probably shoot my conscientious objector paperwork down. Then he asked why I couldn't wait until my ETS (End Term Service.) I only had eight months to go.

"Sir, I believe with no doubt I have found the Truth and in my mind I know what I should do. I have to take a stand. If I don't, I am compromising what I am supposed to believe. God knows I know the truth and if I don't take a stand on this matter, then I will give into opposition every time I am faced with it. I believe in what I am doing, sir, and it is right for me. My heart is not into killing anymore. It is not in me, sir, and in the eyes of any commander, I would be a poor soldier to have in his command."

He stuck out his hand to shake mine and told me he was proud to have served in combat with me and even though I may not hold my medals for bravery in high esteem any longer, it was his honor to have pinned two of them on me. He grasping my hand with both of his and told me he wished me all the happiness in the world. "You deserve it, Brooks and I pray you find it."

"Thank you, sir." I turned and walked out the door. He had given back my respect and I appreciated those words from such an honorable man.

I don't know for sure if the General called Major Peters or not, but I was never put on latrine duty again. In fact, all I did was sit in the recreation room and read or play pool. This did not go over too well with the First Sergeant, but there was nothing he could do about it and

I made it a point to have a big smile on my face every time I ran into him in the halls.

My day to go before the board came and I was pretty scared. There were a couple of other soldiers that were applying for conscientious objector, but theirs didn't have to do with being a conscientious objector, they were on orders to Vietnam and they figured this would keep them from it. The board viewed their cases first and neither one was in there more than ten minutes before they walked back through the door with their heads held low. They were disapproved and were headed back to their units. As one of them passed me he told me, "Good luck, you will need it." Luck had nothing to do with what I knew in my heart and mind. If I wasn't approved for conscientious objector status it would be because I didn't explain myself well enough. The only thing I was allowed to take into the hearing was my Bible. I bowed my head and asked Jehovah to help me find the words so the review board would understand my new convictions and to help me word it properly. My vocabulary was limited and I always had a hard time explaining myself.

Soon the door opened and I was asked to come in. As I walked through the big doors I saw a chair in the middle of the room facing a panel of nine officers and two Master Sergeants. I recognized one of the officers, but I didn't know him very well. The rest of the panel was strangers to me. I took my seat and a Major who was ahead of the panel explained how each member of the board would be asking me a question and it would be in my best interest if I answered as honestly as I could. I acknowledged that I understood and took my seat.

The first question was from the Major. He had a serious look on his face, as if to intimidate me. He brought up my military record and how I had served in combat and that I was a highly decorated soldier and he couldn't see how it was possible for someone like me to seemingly overnight decide I was a conscientious objector. I told him it wasn't overnight that I had made this decision. I explained how I had been studying for over two years and only after intense studying of the Scripture had I come to an accurate knowledge of God's Word and upon that I made my decision.

"Sir, I didn't make this decision because I want out of the Army. I love the Army, sir, but I feel the Army collides with God's laws and therefore I feel I need to choose a side and this is why I am here today, I have chosen that side. Do you think it is easy for me to come here today and face this board? I tell all of you, it is not. I feel I am taking a stand against a family member and it does not bring me any pleasure standing here before all of you today and explaining something you won't understand. After all, Sir, it took me two years. I can only hope you will see I am sincere in my belief and that I know in my heart and mind this is right for me."

He then made the said for anyone on the board to feel free to ask me any question. A chaplain who was a Captain was the next to put in his two cents. With an arrogant attitude and a confident voice, he asked me why I couldn't seek a non-combatant role in the Army.

"Sir," I replied. "What do you mean by non combatant?"

"We see in your records where you have had some medical combat training. Why don't we change your job to the medical field and remove you from a combatant role in the Army?"

"Sir," I replied. "Wouldn't that make me a hypocrite?"

"What do you mean, Specialist Brooks?"

"Well sir, let me see if I understand what you are telling me. You want me to help a fellow soldier recover from his wounds that he received in combat, so he can go back out into combat and kill someone else or get himself killed. Wouldn't that be the same as me pulling the trigger myself?"

He didn't say a word and his cocky attitude and arrogance ceased to exist.

The next question came from a Captain. His voice was not intimidating, but it was firm in definition and to the point. "Do you believe in paying taxes, Specialist Brooks?"

"Yes sir," I replied.

"Then how does it make you feel to know that your tax dollars go toward building bombs and munitions that are used for killing people? Aren't you taking part in killing what you consider fellow human beings?"

I asked him if I could use my Bible to answer that question. He told me to feel free to use any method I wanted to explain the question. I turned to the book of Matthew were Jesus was being put on trial and where the governor of that sector threw a coin to Jesus and asked him this very question. Jesus turned to the picture of Caesar on the coin and replied, 'Give unto Caesar what is Caesar's and give unto God what is God's.' So therefore sir, I have to obey the laws of the land of our government according to God's law. I have to pay my taxes, but if the government uses that money to fund its army like Caesar, or to build a tank, or a bomb like today, the blood quilt in the eyes of God will be on their hands not mine. Sir, I can't make that money turn into a weapon; the government does that, not me.

The answer I gave him seemed to satisfy him, he did not ask another one.

A Sergeant Major was the next to ask me a question. He was a fine looking older guy with gray hair. He looked to me if he was about ready to be retired. The whole time the rest of the panel was asking me questions, I noticed he kept his nose buried in my records. He was reading everything; I couldn't help but wonder what his question would be. Whatever it was I knew it would probably be the hardest one to answer.

The Sergeant Major looked at me and never cracked a smile. The medals on his chest dwarfed the other panel members and even they had to feel a little intimidated by his presence. I was honored by having such a person reviewing my record. I noticed he was awarded a Distinguished Service Cross. He caught me looking at it and paused to give me time to survey his accomplishments and awards. If anyone disserved respect, he indeed was one. I knew his question would be well thought out and if anyone knows how an enlisted man thinks it would be someone like him.

"Mr. Brooks," he said. He was interrupted by the Major bending over and whispering something to him. The Sergeant Major, with a voice loud enough so everyone could hear, responded by saying "No Sir, this man is not Specialist Brooks. He is a Mr. Brooks until this board decides whether he will stay in the Army or not."

The Major was embarrassed by the whole ordeal and told the Sergeant Major to proceed, to let everyone know even though he might have been corrected by a Sergeant Major, he was still in charge of the proceedings.

The Sergeant Major was red in the face and I was glad he was focused on confronting the Major rather than me. When things cooled down the Sergeant looked over at me and said, "Mr.. Brooks, I apologize to you for this interruption and if we now can resume our questioning," as he looked over at the Major, "I have two questions for you."

"Yes, Sergeant Major," I replied.

"Mr. Brooks, it is my understanding you will no longer pledge your allegiance to the flag. Is this true? Will you please explain to me how you have come to this decision not to salute or pledge your allegiance to your country's flag, how can you disrespect your flag after serving under it so gallantly?"

"Sir, I do not think any less of my country's flag. You are right though, I will not pledge my allegiance to any country or its flag. I will only from this day forth pledge my allegiance to God and Him alone. Now if I can elaborate on what I just said, I would appreciate it."

"Sure, Mr. Brooks. This is your moment to help us understand, please continue."

"I would never dishonor my country's flag. It would even be against God's will if I did. I have respected it all my life and I always will. I will obey my countries laws. I will be a better citizen now that I have learned the truth than before when I did not have the truth. The only difference is I will not kill another human for my country, under its or any other flag and I will not pledge my life or allegiance to either. I will honor my country's laws until it collides with God's law and if it does, then I will obey God and make my stand, just like I feel I am doing today."

"So, Mr. Brooks, you would never burn your countries flag?"

"No sir, and I would look down upon anyone or any organization that would."

"Mr. Brooks, is there any circumstance in which you would take a human life?"

I knew he was digging for something, so I asked him, to explain, for I did not want to answer what I knew would be his next question.

"Mr. Brooks, I am going to give you a situation and I want you answer it truthfully."

"Okay," I replied.

"I see in your records you have been scored as an expert marksman with a Colt .45 ACP" pistol."

"Yes, sir."

"You come home one night and you have your gun on you, you walk into the house and a man you do not know has a knife held at your wife's throat. You know he is going to kill her and possibly you. You know your ability and you know without a doubt in your mind you can take your gun and deliver a round to this man's head and kill him before he knows what you have done. Would you do so or would you let him take your and your wife's life?"

I knew the answer, but I did not want to tell him. I closed my eyes. I had to be truthful but I figured the answer would bury me. "Yes sir, I would indeed kill the man and not think twice about it. I have the right to defend myself and my family's life. God gives me the right to protect myself if my life or anyone's life is threatened and I have the right to do so with deadly force if there is no other means possible. The only catch is that I must not have put myself in a situation where deadly force may be my job, like law enforcement or military service. I know I would kill this man if there was no other alternative, I know for a fact I would do this, but sir, for my wife, even though I may be held blood guilty for the act, I would still do it. On the other hand, sir, I also know for a fact that I will never bear arms against another human being for political and government gain. This I know I will never do again."

When I finished my statement the sergeant nodded his head and I believe he cracked a little smile.

"I thank you, Mr. Brooks, for you honest answer. I have no further questions."

The major asked if anyone else had any further questions and when no one responded he drew the hearing to a close and I was dismissed. Because my case was more in-depth than the other two soldiers that had seen the board before me, I wouldn't know the outcome of my case for a couple of days. I went back to my unit not knowing where I stood. A few days went by and after about a week I was told by Major Peters that the Army had granted me my conscientious objector request and I could start clearing post as soon as I wanted.

Chapter 31
Branded a Coward

Thinking that clearing post would be easy, I told Roni and my friends I would be out of the Army in a couple of days. But this was not the case. Everywhere I tried to clear, from turning in my gear and clearing various facilities and records, I was harassed. I was looked upon as a coward and I was treated badly. They gave me the run around and delayed the process by all means available. I sucked it up and took all the harassment and one by one I cleared everything except records. When I went to records at S-2, they told me my records where not there yet. I went back several times and before long over a month had passed.

I had one guy working on my DD form 214 (Military Background and Accomplishments) tell me I didn't deserve to have two Bronze Stars in my record and I sure didn't deserve to have been awarded one for Valor. I asked the guy if he had been in combat and he told me he hadn't. I told him if he was a real combat trooper instead of a pencil-pusher he might have a different opinion of who deserved what. He didn't like the comment and later I discovered that he left out the information of me receiving one of my Bronze Star's for Valor on my DD form, but I didn't care. I had the citation at home and later on the VA had it put back into my records.

Clearing my last station was the straw that broke the camel's back. I had been over to S-2 to get my final records. I hadn't turned in my field gear because that would be my last stop, but to do so I would need all of the information that S-2 kept from me. One morning a friend of mine who worked in the orderly room at my unit told me my records were at S-2 and they were simply not giving them to me. He told me to head on over and he would tell a friend of his to hold them for me until I got there. I jumped into my truck and drove across post to retrieve my records. Maybe I could clear post today and finally be out of the Army.

When I entered the office everyone there, about twenty people, knew me. They had seen me come through those doors at least ten times in the last ten days. Some of them had stupid grins on their faces as if to say, 'Here comes that coward again' and some were merely embarrassed for me or compassionate toward my situation and dilemma. All of them knew I was getting the run around and I knew I had been the topic of some of their discussions. It got to the point I was embarrassed and I hated walking through those doors. I despised more than anything being called a coward. Hate crept back into my soul and I tried my best to ignore them even though this was hard for me to do.

My friend's buddy held up his hand and motioned for me to come over to his desk. When I got there he told me that the lieutenant had taken my records from him and had them in his office. I turned just as the lieutenant walked out. Someone had told him I was there because he gave me that go to hell stare and never bothered to look anywhere else but at me. He motioned to come over and when I stood in front of him he told me that he didn't have my records. He knew what I was there for; I had been coming here every day for the past ten days.

"I was informed that my records were here and I came to get them," I told him.

"Who in the hell told you that?" He glared at the clerk I had spoken to.

"My company, sir. My company told me."

"Who in the hell told them your records were here?"

"That, I don't know sir and neither do I care. I just want my records." I hated calling him 'sir.' I had served with real men and officers in combat, people who earned the respect to be called sir. This guy did not deserve this courtesy and I decided not to extend it to him again. Then he said something to me that really put me to the test.

"Let me tell you something you little coward son-of-a bitch," he yelled at the top of his voice, "I have your records and I will give them to you when I get goddamn ready to. Until then, you get your cowardly ass out of my office."

I cannot describe the anger that rose up the back of my neck. I was so mad tears formed in my eyes. In my whole life I never let anyone call my mother a bitch and it took all I had not to rip this man's head off. If he knew what lurked within my soul and was embedded into my spirit he would think twice about what he said. Old feelings that I had put to rest were now awake and the thought of taking this man's life flashed. I clinched my fist so tight that my nails cut into the palms of my hands, to the point blood formed in the crevasse of my right palm. I tried to come back with something witty but my throat had a lump in it. He knew he had gotten to me and wanted me to hit him. He would love to see me put in the stockade. I turned and walked toward the door.

"That's it, you little son-of-a-bitch," he said to my back, "Get the hell out of my sight." I heard a few of the clerks laugh as I walked through the door.

By the time I got to my truck, tears streamed down my face. My anger was out of control and inside the solitude of my vehicle I screamed at the top of my lungs and hit the dash of my truck so hard it popped the knobs off the radio. I spun out of the parking lot and headed back toward my unit. My thoughts focused on what I should do next. I thought of the Old Man, General Young. I had never used his office or his friendship to speed up my processing out of the Army. In fact, I never asked him to help me in anyway whatsoever. I wondered if he could help my situation, so I turned the truck around and headed for the Post Commander's office. I knew I would be breaking the chain of command by going to see him on my own, but I didn't care. The way I looked at it, I was wronged and professional edict was just what I needed to tie a knot in that lieutenant's ass. I took into consideration that the Old Man may not see it the same way I do, but I was mad, hurt and desperate and thought it couldn't hurt. That is the way I perceived it, anyway.

When I got to the Old Man's office his secretary, an E-6 Sergeant, was shocked when I barged in. "Can I help you", he asked.

"I need to see the Old Man, ah, I mean General Young."

"Who are you?"He didn't like me calling his Boss the Old Man. No one referred to the Post Commander, a Brigadier General, as simply, the Old Man. But it was an old habit and old habits die hard.

"I am Specialist 5th Class Dennis Brooks and I need to talk to General Young."

"Oh you do, do you? Well, Specialist Brooks, you will need to go through your chain of command and make an appointment to see General Young. Maybe then you might get an appointment."

"Look, my name is Dennis Brooks and I am a personal friend of General Young's. If you don't tell him I am here and he finds out that, I wouldn't want to be in your shoes."

He looked at me in disbelief, but he didn't want to take that chance. He cracked open the door of the Old Man's office, and asked if he knew a Dennis Brooks and that I was here and wanted to see him. Right away the Old Man described me to his secretary and told him to send me in. The sergeant turned to me, shocked, to just go right in.

When I opened the door the General was already up from behind his desk and walking toward me. He reached out and gave me a bear hug which surprised me at first, but then I thought he probably thought I was out of the Army and a civilian. Sure enough he did, because the next words out of his mouth were to ask how I got on post, being a civilian.

"Sir, I'm still in the Army."

"What? I thought you would be enjoying your civilian life by now. What happened?"

I told him we better sit down. His expression said he was eager for me to explain. I told him about all the trouble I had encountered since I began my procedure. About how people were calling me a coward, but it was no big deal until today. As I told my story he moved around, arranging things on his desk and scrumming around in his seat. He was upset to the point he couldn't contain himself any longer. Anger flashed in his eyes and then on his face. He picked up the phone and called Major Peters at my unit and told him to come to his headquarters as fast as he could. He then called his secretary and told him to get his car pulled around, notify his driver and get all the paperwork together to process someone out of this man's Army.

After he got off the phone he was mad and didn't want conversation at that moment. After he sat there for awhile he asked me again to explain exactly what this lieutenant said. I told him again and he asked me for the man's name. I told him I did not know, his name wasn't important to me and after I got mad I wasn't thinking straight enough to get it.

"Hell, sir, it was at the spur of the moment that I came here to you. I hate to involve you sir, but I didn't know who else to turn to. I know I broke the chain of command and I'm sorry I didn't give Major Peters a chance to settle this matter."

The Old Man stopped me right there and told me I had nothing, nothing to be sorry for and Major Peters would understand. "He knows of our relationship and if he doesn't, he will." The general became impatient and hit the intercom and asked what was taking so long.

"Nothing sir, your car and Major Peters are here."

He jumped up. "Let's go."

When we ran into Major Peters he had a look of concern on his face, wondering what I was doing there. He knew I sure didn't go through him to see the General. The General set Major Peters at ease and told him he would explain on the way to S-2. Walking to the Old Man's car I was stunned that I received this kind of response from him. I thought at most he would make a phone call. Then I thought about how that lieutenant was going to mess his britches when he saw the post commander walk into his little part of the world. I smiled. This was going to be interesting, more than that it was going to be sweet. This pompous ass of a lieutenant was going to have his world rocked, but the best thing about it all, I was going to see it firsthand.

The whole way over to S-2 the Old Man and Major Peters didn't do much talking. Major Peters tried to make conversation with the general but the Old Man didn't want to talk. He would say enough to be polite, but wouldn't carry the conversation. The car hurried across post and all traffic was stopped. As we flew by each intersection there would be an MP there to salute the general's car. It didn't matter if he was in it or not, when the flags were uncovered on his car the MPs or any other soldier didn't take a chance and saluted the vehicle anyway.

It reminded me of when Knight and I worked for General Knowles. I have to admit it felt good to know all I had to do was let General Young handle the situation and it felt good to be associated with someone who had this kind of authority. When we arrived, no one in the building knew the general was coming. He was arriving unannounced and I could hardly contain myself.

The Old Man looked over at me and told me not to say a word when we got inside. "I know you, Dennis. You get mad and you react. I promise, you will be vindicated today and I will say and do enough for the both of us."

"Don't worry, sir," I replied, "you won't even know I'm there."

When we got to the door the general opened yanked it open and stepped inside. Some of the clerks sat at their desk with their shirts half unbuttoned and some even had their feet propped up. When the Old Man stepped in their eyes grew as big as saucers and someone yelled out 'Attention!' Everyone scrambled to their feet, came to attention and popped a salute. Chairs fell over and one guy even spilled his coffee. The whole room looked like popcorn exploding in a popper. It struck me as funny but I didn't even think about cracking a smile.

The Old Man did not return their salute, therefore they had to stand there like frozen toy soldiers. Then the Old Man walked toward the lieutenant's office, but before he got there the lieutenant swung open the door, probably wondering what all the noise was about. When he saw the Old Man in front of him, he came to attention and popped the general a salute. The Old Man did not return his salute either and everyone in the room stood stock still. Finally the General turned his back to the lieutenant and faced the office staff. He gave them a salute and told them to stand at ease. Then the general turned to the lieutenant and stared at him. He made him stand there long enough so the lieutenant had time to see that I was present. The general motioned for me to come forward and stand by his side. When I reached the general's side he put his hand on my shoulder and asked the lieutenant if he was the one that called me a son-of-a-bitch.

At that moment the lieutenant knew his ass was going to suck buttermilk and I stood there with a big grin and waited for him to get his color back. He didn't know what to say.

Finally, the general asked him again, louder. "*Did* you call this man a *coward* and a *son of a bitch*?"

The lieutenant looked back at the Old Man. "Yes, sir."

The Old Man stood there for some time and finally returned the lieutenant's salute. He then ordered him to retrieve all of my records and while he was at it, bring out all of his own. When the lieutenant returned with his and my records the Old Man took his arm and cleaned off a desk with one sweep. Things flew everywhere. Then he had this lieutenant read aloud to everyone my military record. He made him read about every medal I had received, from my Bronze Stars and Purple Hearts to my Air Medals. My time with General Knowles to my Top Secret status. It took the guy about forty-five minutes to read all of my commendations and letters of commendations. Then the Old Man made the lieutenant read aloud his own achievements in the military. He read about he was in OCS in college and then went into the military to pursue a career and was awarded a Good Conduct Medal. That was it. It took him about two minutes.

Then the Old Man got up in the lieutenant's face. "And you have audacity to call this man a *cowardly son of a bitch?*" He ripped the butter bars (his rank) off the lieutenant's collars and field dress, busted him to an enlisted man. You could have heard a pin drop. Even Major Peters looked shocked. The Old Man was mad but he did not say another word to the lieutenant. He turned to Major Peters and told him to take care of my paperwork. Major Peters stepped forward, put his briefcase on the desk, opened it, pulled out a rubber stamp and stamped all my paper work as 'cleared.' He then handed it to the General then the General signed it and handed to me. He told me to drop by his office for my discharge papers. Then the Old Man turned to all the personnel in the office and told them he had served in combat with me in Vietnam and that he can assure everyone in that office that I was not a coward. He then turned toward me, shook my hand and said, "Thank you, Dennis, for your outstanding service to your country."

I told him I had not turned in my gear yet and he told me to consider it a gift from the U. S. Army and in the matter of a few minutes it was a done deal. I was a civilian.

I thanked him and he stopped me. "No, I thank you, Dennis. You seem to forget there are several of us that owe you for that day we were pinned down and you came to our rescue.

I looked over at the used-to-be-a-lieutenant and hoped he heard what the Old Man had said. He had and his head was hanging low. His military career ended that day. In the matter of a few minutes the Old Man gave me back the pride and dignity that had been taken from me by this so-called butter bar lieutenant. Even though my views had changed concerning the military, I did not want to leave it on bad terms. I had served with some of this country's bravest men. I wanted to count as one of those that stepped up to plate when my fellow brothers needed me.

I cleared post that day with twenty dollars in my pocket. I left the Army owing some of my reenlistment money, because I got out eight mon
ths early on a six year reenlistment. The Army took it out of my last paycheck. But at least the Old Man gave me back my pride and I'd had my retribution.

To me, the military brought some of the happiest and some of the saddest moments in my life. I was a boy when I went into the military and I was forced to become a man under great duress. Through the military I learned to face my fears, stand my ground when I know I'm right, to compromise when it is important to do so, and there is no such thing as a coward in combat. Some situations put before you may cause others to think of you as a hero. I never, ever considered myself as a hero. To think of myself in that way would be arrogant, considering some of the men I served with.

Note: Yes a general can bust an officer as high up as he can promote, and he can take the rank from him as well. But for an enlisted man he can only take away no more than two ranks. I was questioned about this and some other thins when I first posted my book.

Chapter 32
Ranch Life

When I got out of the Army, I was broke. I needed to find work, and soon. I accepted a job being a cattle foreman on the Bushnell Brahma ranch near Lawton, Oklahoma. I didn't really know anything except cattle and helicopters and since the only helicopters around were the military, there was no alternative but work cattle.

When I say 'cattle foreman' you might think I had a whole crew of hands to help me out. Wrong. I was the only hand. If I needed help I could hire it, but taking care of 500 head of cattle for was a one man operation. I built six miles of fence, fed the cattle, spent at least four hours a day in the saddle, planted oats to bale for hay, baled and hauled the hay, spent lots of time on a tractor, repaired water pumps, built stock pens and the list goes on. Managed the records, artificially inseminated stock, dehorned and inoculated the animals, stitched their cuts, branded, halter broke calves, picked up 28,000 pounds of feed every two months from the co-op and unloaded it all with no help. When winter came I had added chores. Chop ice on the ponds, haul hay twice a day, seventy five bales in the morning and seventy five in the evening.

Then there were my chores, I had to milk and feed our cow, take care of the horse, chop fire wood to sell and for home use. Our only source of heat was wood. We had a big garden and Roni used her skills from when she was on the farm and canned our food. We kept potatoes and things we canned from the garden in the cellar. We had fresh milk, butter, all the beef we could eat plus all the wild game like quail, frog legs and fish from the pond, deer, and once in awhile goat meat. The work was hard, but I was young, twenty-eight, and I in my best shape. We always had plenty to eat and I was never as happy as I was on that ranch. I managed 6000 acres and knew it would be the closest thing to ever owning a ranch.

One time we kept records on our food bill. You know, things we had to get from the store, like flour, sugar, coffee and so on, but for the most part we were self-sufficient. One year we figured up we spent around 400 dollars on groceries. The work was hard but there is not a more rewarding work than ranching and farming. I was in my element and it was great teaching my kids the country life. They loved it and today they still talk about those good times on the ranch. Even though the pain of Vietnam was still ever-present, the ranch life allowed me to dream again. It freed my mind of the war and along with keeping up with the study of the Bible, my mind and spirit healed and I found myself truly happy.

But nothing is forever. One day I turned around and my girls were growing up. Getting to the age where I felt I needed to provide for them better in a material way. Of course they were happy wearing blue jeans, but I knew they needed more and I knew hiding out on the ranch would have to end someday. I had to move on and try and seek a better way of life for my family. I was content, but needed a better paying job.

The owner of the ranch and I had a falling out and he called me a liar. The falling out was over some liquid feed I had called to have delivered and it never got delivered. He said I never called the guy. When I tried to explain to him I talked to the guy's wife, he cut me short and called me a liar. I quit right then and there on the phone. A few days later he found out I was telling the truth. The man's wife never told her husband about the order. When the truth finally came out it was too late. The damage to our relationship had been done. He asked if I could find him another cowboy to take my place and I told him I would try. I told him he would not find someone to do what I had done for the wages I made. He found this to be true and he ended up losing 18,000 dollar's worth of cattle. The guy he hired did not keep the ice chopped on the ponds. The cattle got out onto a large pond to find water and some of his prized stock that I had helped deliver and train fell through the ice and drowned.

The owner called and wanted me to come back, but I had put that job behind me and moved on.

Chapter 33
Desperate

I had nothing to offer an employer. I was uneducated, a drop out, and war damaged to some degree. My brother-in-law, Vernon Singleton, took a gamble and hired me to work on one of his drilling rigs down in South Texas near the Gulf. He told me I was a good worker and the oil field would be a breeze for me. He put up the money to have my family moved down to Victoria, Texas to work for him as a roughneck. I had done this type of work before to make a little extra money. It doesn't take much talent to throw iron tongs around and work on a drilling rig. But the money was good and it is an honest way to make a living. After working on the ranch, I found being a roughneck was easy.

The hard part about rough necking was the association. There is so much testosterone flowing in the oil field you find yourself standing your ground every time you turn around. If you don't, the roughnecks will put you at the bottom of the pecking order doing every little job they don't want to do. I had no problem of setting matters straight, I even enjoyed it. It bothered my conscience though, having to stand my ground all the time.

My brother, Vodie, already worked for Vernon and we would work together. We watched each other's back and became known as the Brooks Brothers and were pretty much left alone. Vodie had become a good friend over the years and his wife Becky and Roni were like sisters. So the move was a good and happy one for us all, but life has a way of humbling you and it was only a matter of time it knocked on our front door.

My brother and I threw iron around for a couple of years then Becky died from complications from an appendix bursting and Vodie and I ended up going separate directions. Vodie hated the oil field and blamed the oil field and himself for Becky's death. Vodie and I were working on an oil rig on a location close to the border of Old Mexico when Becky took ill. By the time we got home she was already in the hospital and it wasn't long afterward she passed away. Her death crushed my brother's spirit and it saddened my heart to see him and my wife grieve over Becky's death. I loved Becky and I knew we all would miss her splendid nature.

Becky was my brother's first real love and it broke his heart when she was gone. Vodie and Becky had a boy at the time of her death and they named him Nicklaus. He was eight months old and Roni and I took Vodie and Nick into our home and we tried to be a family. But Becky's death was that link in the chain that kept us a foursome. It wasn't long after Becky's death Vodie and I drifted apart little by little. Vodie had found a wonderful girl and they dated for some time and then they married. Her name was Linda and she was a rock and heaven sent to our family. She took Nicklaus in as her own child and we knew then and there Linda was good for us all.

When Vodie married Linda I wasn't asked to be best man like I was with him and Becky. I knew then that Vodie and I had drifted apart in some way and it bothered me to know we would most likely drift apart even more over time. I'm sure Vodie was tired of me being a big brother figure in his life. Vodie was his own man and I guess to me he would always be my little brother. Heck, I'm in my sixties now and my brother is in his fifties and I still think of him as my little brother. As long as he and I were together I felt like I had family around me and I felt a little safer in the world. In a lot of ways he was the big brother and I looked up to him more than I ever let on. I always felt like I had to be the big brother but in reality I was the mentally younger sibling. My dreams of Vietnam visited me every night after Becky's death. She was the closest person I had lost in my life after Vietnam, and I guess it triggered old events in my head.

Even if it was not true I began to think Vodie didn't want to associate with me anymore and I decided I had to do something to distance myself from him and pursue a better way of life for my family. I was restless and didn't know what I wanted to do for a career. I was limited in my knowledge, but I didn't want to roughneck the rest of my life.

One day I was working on a drilling rig near Port O'Conner and I saw helicopters flying over, taking workers off shore to oil production and natural gas platforms. After work one day I followed one to a base at Port O'Connor and approached some mechanics to ask them if their company was hiring. They asked me if I had my A&P (Airframe & Power plant) license. I told them no but I had ten years experience working on them. They gave me an address to write to in Lafayette,

Louisiana, a company called PHI (Petroleum Helicopters Inc.) I wrote the company, they called me back and paid my way out to Louisiana for an interview.

PHI liked the experience I had and hired me. I made less than working as a roughneck but there was room for advancement and I accepted the job. My experience was in large helicopters, so they put me in what they called the large ship section. I honed my skills with PHI by working on aircraft that had been upgraded sense I worked on them. I went to the Bell Helicopter Technical schools that PHI paid for and got certified on the Bell 212, 206 and 412 aircraft.

PHI told me if I would go to school and get my A&P license they would up my pay. Because of my experience and background in the Army I qualified to only take the test, so I did and I quickly received my license.

I felt a great sense of accomplishment when I received that license. It was the equivalent of two years of college and if I wanted to pursue a career in air atomic engineering it was a good start. But I only wanted to work on aircraft. Besides, I never finished high school. Nevertheless, -t was a self image booster for me and I was proud of myself. Roni and I lay in bed and she would help me study for my test. We had over two thousand questions to prepare for and before it was all said and done she probably could have passed the test.

After receiving my A&P I worked for PHI for about three years. Then my restless spirit kicked in and I took a job overseas in Saudi Arabia working for a company called Augusta Bell as a platform instructor and mechanic, teaching the Saudi military how to work on and fly helicopters. I needed to get ahead and make up for lost time so I went overseas on a contract for about

$90,000.00 That got us out of debt, but the time apart from my family was hard.

Saudi was something else. You could spend a lifetime trying to teach those people something and they would still know nothing. Sorry, but it's the truth. They have the ability to learn but everything is given to these people and they know they don't have to learn a thing; they will still get a check from their government. They have no initiative.

Roni came over to Saudi Arabia for a couple of months to break up my eleven month contract. If she hadn't I don't know if I could have done the time. The time we spent together in Saudi was great. We did everything together and even took a trip down to South Yemen with one of my students and his family. His name was Calieg and he was my best student, but only because he took the class seriously. I was offered a good retirement to stay in Saudi Arabia for ten years, but there was no way I would even consider it. I have never seen more self-centered, haughty, egotistical, and downright stupid people.

While I was in Saudi I witnessed a beheading execution. Because I was an American the crowd made sure I had a front row viewing of the event. The man was executed because he had an affair with an Arabic woman and was caught by her husband. The husband pulled a knife on her lover, who happened to be Japanese. The Japanese guy took the knife away from the Saudi man and instead of letting it go at that, he killed the guy and he did so in front of witnesses. He was executed and the woman was bound and thrown from top of a high building to her death. When the man was executed and his head was severed from his body. The crowd looked at me for some kind of response. It was not what they expected and it disappointed them.

I had a flashback of Vietnam and removing ears after a kill. I turned around, caught up in my own past and thought times that were long gone. I walked away eating a peach and watched the crowd's faces as they observed my unconcerned attitude. *If only they knew*, I thought and grinned as I walked passed them.

My last two months in Saudi Arabia was the best for me. Because of my background with horses I was sought out by one of the king's nephews to take care of some Arabian horses his grandfather had left him when he died. They shoed their horses with a solid plate horseshoe and because the horses stood in wet pens that didn't drain all the time, they developed thrush. Plus the horses' frogs grew out of control and needed to be trimmed back. The natural dish on the bottom of the horses' feet had filled in and after I removed these hoof plates I had to dig out each hoof so it had a natural cup for the frog fit in. If this was not done the horses would step on their frogs all the time and this was uncomfortable. There were over twenty horses I had to care for and it took me a couple of weeks to complete the job. After I had taken care of these fine animals I was asked if I wanted a job running the stables. I didn't hesitate in accepting and was given a nice place to live at the stables. Several Turks worked for me for all the manual labor and I made sure the horses were fed and cared for correctly.

Before I got there they were feeding the horses a whole corn that was soaked in water as not to give them bloat (colic) and founder them. The trouble with that was the corn was not being used fast enough and the corn it fermented and gave the horses colic anyway. After saving one of the prince's favorite horses by shoving a water hose down its throat and reliving the built up gas, I became somewhat of a hero in the eyes of this prince and was given the run of the place.

The stables had every kind of riding gear you could imagine, from Western pleasure to English style riding and every kind of saddle and bit that was made. I used to saddle up a horse and ride into the mountains and out into the desert. I took a pack horse with me and loaded it down with plenty of food and water. I visited some old ruins of market places that were around in Biblical times and spent my time wandering in the desert and in the mountains around Tiaf. I followed the baboon herds around and even befriended some of the baboons by giving them fruit. I spent many nights in the desert camping under the stars. It had its own beauty and it was a good way to spend my last days in country.

I was so anxious to go home. It had been four months since I had seen my wife, but it had been eleven months sense I had seen my girls. When I got home they had both grown a foot and were starting to look like young women. The time I had spent away from them taught me a valuable lesson and I decided to never go overseas again without my family.

Chapter 34
Back to the Gulf of Mexico

When I got home I took a job working for a company called Evergreen Helicopters. They were a small company on the Gulf, but aviation-wise they were huge. Through Evergreen I traveled to other countries working on helicopters and worked a lot of contracts through Evergreen that were exciting.

A pilot friend of mine (Eastman) and I flew a Bell 212 on the Yellowstone Fires. We started working on the fires in Idaho and ended up in Mammoth Yellowstone and Cook City Montana. We ended our fire season in Cody, Wyoming and had some narrow escapes and exciting times. We met some very brave firefighters and came away from there with a whole new respect for them and six hundred thousand dollars of income for our company.

During the process I caught pneumonia to the point I coughed up blood and had to go to the hospital for a couple of days. Breathing the smoke continually for three months along with the cold weather allowed pneumonia to creep into my lungs. Eastman was in the air more than I was and didn't get exposed to the smoke from the fire as much. Plus, I worked a lot at night keeping the aircraft airworthy for the next day.

Once I had to pull out the drive train to replace my lower lord mounts. I rented a crane in Cody and had it driven over the Continental Divide to a place in Montana called Crandall. Pulled the transmission and rotor head and blades off the aircraft, replaced the mounts and had it back on line in eight hours. We lost no flight time and Evergreen was glad, no one had ever done such a job by themselves in the field. They were so amazed they sent a guy from McMinnville, Oregon to see who Dennis Brooks was. I was commended by the Director of Maintenance for the major work I had completed in the field.

Evergreen had several helicopters working the fires and when they were all done we flew the aircraft back to McMinnville, Oregon. They told us they wanted to look them over for the next season but the real reason was they wanted to throw some of us guys a party and I have to say I had a blast. Evergreen was good like that. When you did a good job for them Delbert liked to show his appreciation and do something special. Evergreen gave me as much responsibility as I thought I could handle and I felt like I had at last found a home in a company I could work for and be happy.

After the fires, Evergreen landed a contract with the Department of Defense and I was asked if I would mind maintaining and flying a Bell 212 in Huntsville, Alabama at Red Stone Arsenal. Evergreen explained that it would require a top secret clearance. I knew I would have to let them know I had been arrested for drugs when I was at Ft. Sill, Oklahoma. I told my superiors at Evergreen I wouldn't be able to pass a clearance check. Of course, they asked me why and I had to tell everyone the trouble I had gotten into with the law.

Evergreen understood my situation and did not show any animosity toward me. Being in aviation and working on aircraft you are drug tested frequently so they knew I was clean, but getting a clearance might be a problem. Evergreen asked if I could buy them some time and start the project, that it would take the government at least a couple of weeks to process my clearance and in the meantime they would find someone to take my place. I agreed and to buy Evergreen as much time as I could, I would not mention the arrest on the background investigation questionnaire the DOD gave me to fill out.

TRW was the subcontractor for the government and they were the people we would work with. When I first started I didn't have a clue what we would be doing. But after a couple of weeks I came to understand more about the project than I should have without a clearance. We were slinging an object 200 ft. below our aircraft that the engineers on the project called Albee. It looked like a huge dart and different companies like Motorola, GE, Panasonic, would come in and install their equipment and we would fly it below our helicopter while they ran tests on it. There were several computers installed in my aircraft and there was, what we called a- billycan cord running from Albee to the computers inside the aircraft.

My contribution to the project was designing a way to lower an antenna below the skids of the aircraft once it was airborne. I designed a device we called a guillotine to cut the billycan cord in case the aircraft lost an engine and we had to jettison our load. The engineers I worked with thought my ideas were great and complimented me for incorporating the scope antenna and guillotine jettison device into the aircraft. I had to get a FAR-337 approval for the guillotine, since it was attached to the aircraft, but for the antenna I used a pipe in a pipe that would slide within its self, attached it to the gun mount hard points to lower it when the aircraft was airborne and retract it when the aircraft landed again. It was a simple idea but saved time getting the project on its way and saved money by not hiring an engineer to come up with a complicated means of doing the same job.

I was proud that highly educated engineers thought my ideas were good ones. I think it was their way of making me feel like I was a part of it all. I did impress the Army, though, by how I kept my aircraft flight ready every day, even after changing out components like hydraulic servos and such. Evergreen took this contract away from the Army because they couldn't handle the 200 ft long line and keep the aircraft on continuous flight ready. The post commander of the base bucked us all the way and tried to quote FAA regulations. But I was an extension of the FAA with my A&P and this allowed us to operate totally different than the military was used to.

It finally came time for me to get interviewed for my top secret clearance. Evergreen could not find anyone to take my place. I had so much experience on this type of aircraft that it was hard to find someone to replace me, plus the fact the TRW personnel wanted me and didn't want a replacement. I confided in some of the TRW people and told them why I might not pass my clearance. They were kind of surprised to hear of the trouble I had gotten into twenty years ago, but understood and told me they still wanted me on the project. "Who hasn't smoked dope?" they commented and laughed it off.

Soon after this conversation with TRW my interview came up and I had to go sit in front of a couple of CIA agents and have them rake me over the coals. Right off the bat they asked me why I hadn't listed all of my past and I played dumb. Then they brought up my arrest and asked why I didn't mention it in my questionnaire. I told them I was trying to buy time for my company to replace me. I told them they were having a hard time finding someone with my experience and it was taking them longer than they originally thought it would.

They sat there a minute or two to let me sweat, but I they weren't getting the response they expected from me. Finally one of them spoke up. "Mr. Brooks, we know you have been in trouble with the law, but we don't consider you a security threat."

That wasn't the answer I expected. I was shocked. They told me they knew about my military career and how I was a highly decorated soldier. They told me my record of service to my country was sufficient enough to give me a clearance. Then they told me from then on no local law enforcement would be able to pull up my arrest record and that only a government operation would be able to view my arrest. This was something that had haunted me forever and to have it taken off my record was great. I had been stopped by law enforcement before that treated me like a criminal because of that record and now it would be clean.

"Great!" I was embarrassed I said it so loudly.

The two CIA agents grinned and told me my top secret clearance had been reactivated. Then they explained how having a civilian Top Secret was different than a military. I would now be in a position to sell information. If I was caught passing secret information from one contractor to another or to a foreign power, I would do prison time. To top it off, I took an oath not to mention any particulars of this project for the next ten years. It's been way over ten years, so I am free to say what I want about the project. It had to do with smart weapons and low frequency tracking. You know being able to track a hand-held low frequency radio and take it out. Take away the communication to and from headquarters to your men in the field and you win the war.

This contract lasted fourteen months and I spent some of my time in Florida. It was one of the best jobs I had been on. I met some great people they were very intelligent and educated and treated me like an equal. This gave me more confidence in myself in what I might accomplish, if I set my mind to it.

After this contract was over I was offered the job of Gulf Coast Field Supervisor. I never had a job that carried a title, other than mechanic. Of course it came with a pay raise and a new truck to drive up and down the coast to all the field bases.

Chapter 35
Northumberland

Being Gulf Coast supervisor was a good position, but I had to do a lot of traveling to check out our field basis every other week. The company at the time had field basis from Port Mansfield way down south near Brownsville, to Venice, Louisiana. It was my job to make sure everything ran smoothly at all the bases, so it took a lot of travel time. I enjoyed it and Evergreen treated me well. I had company credit cards and I would stay in New Orleans every time I passed through going down to Venice. I did not abuse my new privileges and Evergreen was fine with me even buying the guys Pizza and beer when I passed through each base. I used some of my allotted expense to do this and the guys appreciated it. I had worked the trenches and knew it was the mechanic that was the backbone of any company. The company was only as good as its people and Evergreen Helicopter division had some very good people working for them.

One day, when I was at one of our field bases in Sabine Pass, Texas, a pilot and I were talking on the front deck of one of the living quarters when we saw a large explosion off shore. Allen (the pilot) asked me if I wanted to go and check it out.

"Sure!" I replied. It was my last day and I was only seventy miles from the home base at Galveston and we were curious about what caused that explosion. The first thing that came to our minds was that a gas well head must have blown. We jumped into a Bell 206-B Jet Ranger and headed out to the where the explosion had happened. It was only about a mile offshore and it wouldn't take us long to get out there. There were flames over 300 feet in the air and at least that wide.

When we first arrived on the scene all we could see was a large flame. Our altitude was 500 feet and the flames were at least 300 feet into the air. The flames were so intense you felt the heat from within the helicopter. The flames weren't coming from a well head; they looked like they were coming right out of the ocean. As we circled around from the southwest we noticed there was a large ship right in the middle of the flames. Allen and I knew there would most likely be people that needed help. So we circled around the flames and ship and right off we saw three people in the water. Two were swimming and had life vest on and seemed to be doing fine. But we both noticed that there was a man having a hard time staying afloat.

The altitude at this time was 200 feet. We had no time to waste so I kicked off my boots, opened the door of the aircraft and stood outside on the skids. I had to get to the six man raft that was located in the back of the aircraft. I had walked the skids many times in Vietnam for fun and for a brief second I had a flashback of doing so, but was snapped back to the present by the intense heat. The flames towered over us as we drifted downward, with Allen never taking his eyes off the victim. I reached the raft and pulled it outside the aircraft and positioning myself I grabbed a hold of the eight foot lanyard that was tucked inside the float pocket and flung the raft outward. When the raft came to the end of the lanyard it inflated, but I held onto it. I knew I had only one chance to make sure this raft got to the man, who kept going under and struggling to surface again.

We were going to use the rotor wash to blow the raft to the victim, but flames encircled the drowning man and every time Allen tried to get the aircraft closer to the victim the rotor wash would push the flames toward him. I aimed the raft as good as I could and I let it go. The raft came as close as three feet from the guy, but he hadn't the strength to even reach out and grab it. I had to go in after him, as I looked into this man's eyes I saw the desperation on his face. He was burned badly and his eyes begged for help. I had no time to think. I had to go for him now or he would go under.

This man's death was not going to be on my hands, his face was not going to haunt my dreams. I turned to Allen.

He yelled to me above the noise. "You're going in, aren't you?"

I didn't have to say a thing he read the expression on my face.

"I hate this shit!" he screamed.

I felt bad for Allen. He would now have two people in the water and no means to help them. But he knew I had to do it. Allen flew dust offs in Vietnam (medical evacuations) and had been in my shoes many times.

"Just do it," he yelled. "Just do it."

I told Allen to pull up to thirty feet or so and when he did, I dove into the water. The momentum I gained from the height got me half way under the flames and I swam with all my might toward the drowning man. I looked up and saw there were no flames above me. I surfaced and came up in front of the victim. He reached for me and I told him to turn around. He did and when I grabbed him he fell limp in my arms. I got him over to the raft and had him hold on until I got myself inside, then I grabbed his arms and pulled on them. The skin from his arms peeled all the way to his wrists. He was in great pain. I tucked his head and grabbed him by his belt then pulled him into the raft.

When I got him into the raft I saw he was burnt very badly. The salt water that came into the raft burned his skin so I placed the man on top of me to get him out of the salt water. He was trying to go into shock so I kept talking to him. I asked him for his name and he told me it was Mac. Mac kept asking me how bad was he burned and my reply would always be 'not bad, you will be okay.' The truth was he was burned over sixty percent of his body and his ears were almost gone. His hands were also burned and I knew he was in great pain and in great danger of going into shock and dying.

Mac told me there was a crew of fourteen on the ship and asked me how many got away. I had only seen two others. I didn't want to tell him that so I told him I had no idea. I saw at least two bodies floating in the water but did not want Mac to see them. I kept him talking but he was going into shock. I had seen this many times in Vietnam and knew if the Coast Guard did not get to us soon, his burns were the least of my worries. Soon the Coast Guard showed up in a cutter and worked their way over to us. We hoisted Mac up first and then I came aboard. I asked them if the helicopter was on its way, they told me it had to come from Lake Charles, over ninety miles away. I looked onshore and there was one of my company's helicopters sitting on shore less than a half a mile from us. I told the captain of the cutter to get us to shore and I would have one of Evergreen helicopters get him to the burn center in Galveston within thirty minutes. He told me he couldn't do that, once on board it was now in their hands and we had to wait for the Coast Guard helicopter.

As we stood around waiting for the helicopter to show up I noticed there was no litter on which to put Mac. I asked the captain how he was going to get Mac into the helicopter.

"On a hoist from the aircraft," he replied.

I told him he needed a litter because Mac could not take the pain from the harness strapped around him.

"I didn't think about that," he shouted. "We have a large basket." He sent two guys to retrieve it.

This basket would do but it was small and we would have to crunch Mac into it. I knew this would cause him ever greater pain. They were not tending to Mac at all. I told them that Mac needed blankets and I asked them if they had any Vaseline to smear on Mac to help hold in his body heat. The captain told me no but they had a first aid kit. The kit, I told them was worthless and asked them if they had any axle grease or anything of that nature. They brought up a bucket of grease. I knew this would probably give Mac an infection but we had to do something. Mac now shook uncontrollably. I took the grease and smeared it all over his body and wrapped him up in a couple of blankets. Mac screamed in pain as we tucked him into the basket. The helicopter finally got there and I rigged up a drag for the basket so it would not spin around once he was in the air. They lifted Mac up and at the same time started pulling away. I was glad I had rigged up that drag on the basket. It was all up to Mac now; even though I did not know the man, I could tell he was a fighter. I said a prayer for the man and hoped he would make it.

The Coast Guard told me I would have to stay onboard because they had to recover bodies and search for survivors. I didn't care one way or the other. I was tired and cold. All I wanted was a blanket and something hot to drink. It was December and the water had chilled me to the point I shook a little. One of the crew members brought me a cup of coffee and it was the best cup of coffee in the world.

Night fell and the fire lit up the night with an orange glow. The ship's prop had cut into a huge natural gas line and when the pumps offshore indicated a pressure loss in the line it stepped up production and forced the gas out of the ruptured line with great pressure. The fire was so big it warmed the night and it wasn't long before I warmed up and shed myself of the blanket.

It wasn't long before we spotted our first body. The captain told us he would be coming up on the starboard side of the boat. I looked off the side of the boat and saw the body getting closer but no one made any effort to grab it. I reached down grabbed the body. The man was big, at least 300 pounds. Because of his weight and the forward momentum of the boat, the body was slipping out of my grip. I looked around and everyone was just watching me. "If you want this body you better give me a hand," I yelled. "I'm about to lose him." One of the crew members reached down and grabbed a hold of the shirt, he obviously did not want to grab the man's body. I told the young man to take hold of his belt and directed the other crew member to grab the other hand. Reluctantly, he did. I gave him the hand I held and latched onto the man's belt. Together we lifted the man out of the water. We had to bring him out about three feet and over the railing. The crew member that held the dead man's hands had positioned himself directly in front of his head. I told him he stood in a bad area, but he did not want to touch the body anywhere but on the hands. When we hoisted the man over the railing and had him upside down everything in this man's stomach would fly out all over the deck. I had seen it before and decided it was time to let this pup get a taste of reality. Heck, he wouldn't listen to me even if I bothered to tell him.

Sure enough, it happened. The dead man spewed all over this young pup and then he started vomited all over the place. The body hit the deck and everyone let go. The guy that opposite of me turned his back and the other one kept throwing up all over the place. Every time he stopped he got a whiff of the dead man's vomit on his clothes and started up again. I took him by the back of the neck and walked him over the side and into the water. When we got him out of the water he was as white as a ghost but he'd stopped vomiting. He went down below to get a blanket and came up on deck and stood beside me with a cup of coffee. After awhile he looked over at me and asked how I could do that shit. They were trained and should be prepare, but how could I handle it all so calmly? I smiled and told him it was not my first rodeo and that I had seen this many times in Vietnam. He stuck out his hand to shake mine and thanked me for my help.

A little while later the captain told me he was going to put me in for a Silver Star. I laughed and asked for what? He started to say something but was interrupted by another body sighting.

We recovered three bodies that night and I could not help but think about Vietnam. I was having so many flashbacks it was hard to even stay focused on what we were doing.

It was now one o-clock in the morning and we could find no more bodies. The Captain told me we were headed back, but there were a lot of newspeople at the docks that wanted to talk to me and when we docked I was flooded by reporters. I made a short comment and Allen came up and gave me a hug.

"Good job, Brooks. Let's get a drink."

That's what I wanted, a good stiff drink and to be with someone like Allen who knew where my head would be right now.

When it was all said and done I was awarded a Congressional Life Saving Medal and was treated like a hero by the Coast Guard, by my company Evergreen Helicopters, and the Texas Legislature. It was nice being congratulated by everyone, including Mac, the captain of the Northumberland. He survived the ordeal and we have stayed in touch over the years. His gratitude has been expressed to me many times and I am glad to have had the experience that was needed that day to save his life.

I was also awarded a proclamation from the House of Representatives in the Texas Legislature in Austin, Texas in 1990. The embarrassment of it all is still present. But my family, along with Allen's, got to eat where the governor and the president eat when he is in town. My family was treated like royalty. My two girls loved the limousine provided for us, but it was the cute limo driver that was the hit. They had a great time, so the acceptance of the proclamation was worth the discomfort and little embarrassment of the event.

To be honest, it was for selfish reasons I jumped out of that helicopter that day. I knew without a doubt in my mind I could have saved Mac, and if I didn't, than I would have had to live with his death on my conscience for the rest of my life. I didn't want that for myself, so I jumped out and saved the guy. After Vietnam, this was nothing to me but a swim in the Gulf and that is all. To be honored for such a deed was nice, but mostly embarrassing.

I thought of it as vindication for my return from Vietnam when I was spit upon. I wished I could have been honored back when it was really important to me. It was nice people wanted to do this, but it brings me greater joy when my girls look at me as their hero. It is important to me how they view my life. I have not always been the father I could have been and despite my shortcomings they have turned out to be great adults. Both of them are more mature in their thinking than I am now. They take after their mother, who has always considered me her hero.

This is the Citation for the Congressional Life Saving Medal.

On behalf of the Secretary of Transportation, the Commandant takes great pleasure in presenting the SILVER LIFESAVING MEDAL to

MR. DENNIS BROOKS

for acts as set forth in the following

CITATION:

"For heroic action on the afternoon of 3 October 1989 when he rescued an injured, drowning crewman from a fishing vessel in the Gulf of Mexico. The fishing vessel NORTHUMBERLAND had struck a submerged natural gas pipeline offshore from Sabine, Texas, rupturing the line and causing an explosion of epic proportion. Flames, projecting hundreds of feet into the air, suddenly turned the NORTHUMBERLAND into a fiery inferno. The blast threw many of the stunned crewmen into the cold waters of the Gulf of Mexico. Mr. BROOKS, a field supervisor for a helicopter company, immediately went to the scene. Aboard the first helicopter to arrive, he witnessed a frightening spectacle. Despite the intense heat, the helicopter maneuvered within yards of the wall of flames. When several badly injured men were spotted in the seas below, the helicopter approached one who appeared to be in dire need, floating face down. Mr. BROOKS inflated a small life raft and threw it to the injured man. Unfortunately, the raft drifted out of his reach. Mr. BROOKS, with little regard for his own personal safety, plunged from the helicopter into the oily waters. He swam to the injured man, keeping him afloat until the pilot maneuvered the helicopter so that its rotor down draft blew the drifting life raft back to them. Mr. BROOKS then labored to assist the fatigued, injured man, later determined to be the NORTHUMBERLAND's captain, into the raft. Shortly thereafter, a Coast Guard helicopter arrived, hoisted the severely injured captain aboard, and flew him to a hospital for emergency treatment. Mr. BROOKS remained aboard a Coast Guard patrol boat and assisted in further search efforts. Mr. BROOKS determined efforts, outstanding initiative and fortitude during this rescue resulted in the saving of a man's life. His unselfish actions and valiant service reflect great credit upon himself and are in keeping with the highest traditions of humanitarian service."

This is the Congressional Life Saving Medal I was awarded while I was Gulf Coast Field Supervisor for Evergreen Helicopters.

Chapter 36
My Corner Stone

This brings me to my wife, who is my rock and the cornerstone of my foundation. I have never known such a wonderful person upon the face of this earth and I only wish I were a real wordsmith so I better record how I feel about this extraordinary woman.

She overlooks my faults with such ease it makes me want to be a better person. We both hate arguments and if we ever get into a dispute it is usually my fault and after awhile she knows I will come to my senses and get back on track. She makes me laugh and she is my best friend. Without this beautiful person in my life I would have become a bitter man a long time ago. I owe everything to her and when she reads this she will be embarrassed that someone besides family may read it. She is humble in every aspect of the word, but strong-willed at the same time. Her faults are so few I can't even think of one. I am so fortunate to have her in my life.

Time with you is life to me. She wrote these words on the back of a gold watch she bought me when I returned home from Saudi Arabia. How true those words are for the both of us today. We love each other with all our hearts and time with one another has been life for us both.

Chapter 37
Full Circle

My wife and I are living where it all began for us, West Texas. We are living 120 miles north of where we first fell in love. We have come back home to the area we love and where we were brought up.

I am employed at Bell Helicopter in Amarillo, Texas, working on and flying a forty one year old aircraft, an aircraft where it all started for me. I maintain the Rescue Helicopter here at Bell. It is a hybrid aircraft made up of three of the aircraft I have worked on all of my life. The Bell 212, Bell 205 and the engine is out of a Cobra, a T-53 L-17 series. So in a sense I have come full circle.

I started working on the 205 (Huey) and the AH-1G Cobra when I was nineteen-years-old. I began working on the Bell 212 when I was thirty-nine and now I am in my sixties. I have seen helicopters come a long way and have been fortunate to be a part of the V-22 Osprey as it came onto the scene. What a fine aircraft this has proven to be. Sure, it had it's hard times, but what new aircraft coming out of production doesn't? The faults of the aircraft had nothing to do with its design. It was the customer that pushed it past what is was capable of doing. But Bell took the brunt of all the V-22's criticism and in return has gotten the appreciation from its customer.

Here are a few pictures of me today, working and maintaining that forty year old aircraft. I still love helicopters and to some degree I miss the action. Most of all I miss my buddies. We are all old now and have had our time in the sun.

This is me today at Bell Helicopter, flying and maintaining a type of aircraft where it all started for me forty two years ago.

This is my aircraft responding to a downed V-22 that made a precautionary landing.

I will retire soon and life for me has been quite a ride. This book has been a bitter sweet undertaking. It brought back things I tried to forget. But forgetting parts of your life, no matter how hard it gets, cheats you out of life itself. You learn from every event. Some may not be pleasant, but all of it is important. How can we learn from our mistakes if we don't remember our past? I've heard this all my life, but never put it into play until now.

No matter how painful it has been for me to write this book, I am glad I took the time to do so. Everyone that has read it has told me they were glad I did. At the time of this writing, only my friends and family have read it and maybe they are just being kind. In some ways it has been therapeutic for me and I am glad I took the time to document these snippets of my life.

'If only I could turn back the hands of time.' This has been said or thought by everyone, but it is only when you are getting old you come to appreciate the meaning of the phrase. No matter how long I may walk the face of this earth, I will never forget my fallen brothers in combat. Life for them was short-lived. I often think of each one and their personalities. In my memory I keep their spirits alive, for I believe there will come a time when they will live again on an earthen paradise and I hope I will be there to welcome them back and watch their lives come full circle too.

LAY YOUR BODIES DOWN

The battlefields are quiet now, a moment of relief.
No matter how long the quiet lasts, it's all but too brief.

With hesitating eyes we looked around to see who is no longer there. And you wonder if back home does anyone really care?

Back home we are called baby killers, that is their chant and cry. It is something we don't talk about but sit and wonder why?
I say to them, come find the cost of freedom and lay your body down. Then, you will find the cost of freedom, for it is lying in the ground.

So chant your cries and call us names, for that is your freedom of speech, I guess. But respect the ones who gave you that right and defended it to their death.

Freedom is not cheap my friend, wherever you may be sent. But to me it was my duty to do so, for you see, I was just paying rent.
Dennis Brooks, 1969

Afterword

All the things I have written about have flooded my mind for years. Sometimes events come together all at once and it gets to the point I have to stop and put it into perspective again. It has been over forty years now and my mind still gets lost in time. A time that has long since passed, but was never forgotten, a time gone but refuses fade. A melancholy feeling that sometimes haunts my very soul and from time to time creeps into my mind to influence my true spirit.

I have never, completely been able to put the war behind me. I would like to fall asleep and wake up with no memory of Vietnam but that is never going to happen. If that happened there would be no lessons learned. I often wonder how I would have turned out if I had never gone to war and lived without the memories that sometimes haunt me.

Now I look back on my memories of Vietnam and try to make sense of it all. There is no sense to war. War may have some great objective or it may not, as the case in Vietnam. But one thing is for certain. The ones that actually fought in a combat roll will forever remember its horror. It will for a fact warp your true spirit and callous your heart. Some will spend their life never letting the war rest and never feeling completely at ease with themselves or people around them.

I sometimes want to tell everyone how I feel but the words don't come. If they did come, what parts would you want to tell them and what would you keep to yourself? There are things in all of us who have served in front line combat that should just as soon be left unspoken.

My family has been my refuge. I know in the beginning I made it hard on them. My wife has stayed by my side and has listened with complete understanding and compassion. She has saved my life more than once.

Years ago I thought about ending it all. I wasn't handling life very well I was hiding out in the military. The world seemed to be closing in on me and I wasn't adapting to it. I was running in every direction and not escaping at all. The nights would come and the dreams seemed endless. I just wanted rest and an end to it all. Death became a part of my life at a young age and I had learned not to fear it, but the thought of losing my wife and never seeing Roni or my kids again put a fear in me that kept me from doing this selfish act.

Eventually, with help from friends and family, I came back to a good life. I see my kids and grandkids grow and think of all I would have given up and missed if I would have followed through with ending my life. It scares me to think what the mind is capable of doing. When you live with death day in and day out, you become accustomed to its presence. You have a slight fear of it, but only of the unknown and not death itself. Death became just another option for me.

As I eventually started to obtain some normalcy in my life, I never thought of death as an option again and it scares me that I even had considered it as such. The things man can do to one another can make them completely lose their good conscience. It is at these moments mankind does the most harm to one another. I have witnessed it first-hand. Still, after all these years, it comes back to haunt me, because I have taken such a physical part in such acts and I still feel guilt. Because of the things I have done it has made me a loner in a lot of ways. Other than my family, I don't really like to associate with people. I let certain people into my small circle that I am comfortable with and that is it. Even when my family is around, after awhile I seek solitude. If I can get off to myself for awhile I then can re-circulate back into the crowd.

My wife seems to understand, but after a couple of days of her visiting her mother I am yearning for her return. It is during her absence from me when I fully understand how much she is a part of my life and I would be so lost without her. She has a much stronger will than I do. I have told her many times that when it comes our time to pass, I need to go first. She doesn't agree, but it is true.

My wife tells me I am a compassionate man, but on the other hand she knows the other me and I believe she tells me these things because I need the reassurance that I am not what I used to be.

One time I asked her why she married me. She told me she knew I was not the same person when I returned from Vietnam. She told me I had changed, but the person that I was when we were young was still present and it was that person she was in love with. Those words took my breath away. My love for her has grown so deep over the years, I depend on her more than she could ever imagine. I make it a point everyday to kiss her as often as I can without being a nuisance and to tell her I love her with each kiss.

I have no problem of showing affection toward people I love, whether it is man or woman. On the other hand I have no problem distancing myself from those who are only interested in themselves and don't take the time to understand issues that may be important to everyone. I hate unruly behavior and have a bad habit of getting up in someone's face to see how far someone wants to push it. I don't try that hard to make friends with people. I don't try to live up to any ones expectations. I do good to try and live up to my own, which aren't all that high.

I have no animosity toward the Vietnamese people. I respect my old enemy. I respect him more so than I do the people that threw bags of shit at us and called us baby killers on returning from combat back to the States. I believe this crippled me mentally as much as anything. Today I still carry a hate for those people. Not just for me. To some point I have put it behind me. But I have friends that to this day that are mentally damaged and bitter because of what they went through upon their returning home from the war. It forces them to continue to evaluate their lives and to try and deal with the guilt this country has bestowed upon them.

As for myself, I have a bitter taste of it all. And for these people I find it hard to forgive. The friends I lost in 'Nam in their eyes was nothing. Maybe the war was stupid and we should have never gotten into it. But do you condemn the ones that laid their bodies down for you? The point was, our country thought we should go to war. And I, for one, and others, were more than willing at the time to pay back to our country for all the freedom this great nation had given us.

If war was what was expected of us, then so be it. That is all there was to it. My brothers and I were soldiers, not politicians. Sure, when we got to Vietnam and saw what was going on, we knew the war had to do with politics, but what war doesn't? For us it was not about politics, it was about taking an oath and living up to it. When our country asked us to serve we weren't sought to be found. Then in the middle of it all it became a personal vendetta. Our friends were killed and we wanted revenge and of course the Army gave us the legal right and means to do just that. We no longer cared if the war had some objective. We wanted payback. It became a matter of revenge and survival. You tell me, what war doesn't? That is what war truly is for the combatant: hate, revenge and survival.

The military knows how a solder will react to any given situation when it comes to warfare, or if it comes down to kill or get killed. We have had two hundred years plus perfecting it. But I don't sit around blaming my country for what happened in Vietnam. I, along with a lot of us, volunteered for service. We felt an obligation to our families and country to do so. I am the one that stepped outside the boundaries of war. I am the one that brought the guilt upon me by ignoring my conscience. I blame no one but myself for the things I have done in my lifetime. I have done all I can do to put Vietnam behind me and get on with life. Over the years people have told me I have to forgive myself. I don't choose to forgive myself for the things I have done. Only God Jehovah has the power to forgive me totally and I pray that he has.

I carry my guilt to help me stay on track, to remind me of how cruel one can become in combat. How can one put behind the guilt when one is guilty? You live with it, try to put it in perspective and do the best you can. Harder yet is to keep what you know you are capable of doing in check. In the back of my consciousness lays a sleeping demon. To him combat, death, and destruction should never sleep. I have come to believe every man possess this demon. I think this is why we have wars. Once this demon is activated and is put into play, it is hard for him to deactivate. It doesn't work that way. It is not like a light switch you can turn off at will.

I still get emotional on certain subjects and events and writing this so-called book has not been an easy task.

It has taken me years to write. But I never felt like I had some deadline to meet. I didn't write the book on the intention that it would ever go public. I didn't write this all down for some type a profit, it is for the eyes of my family and friends, and if anyone can learn something from it, then good. This book was not written for entertainment, it is a contribution to my fallen brothers and where maybe someone can come to understand what we went through in Vietnam as well as any war.

Hate the acts we committed in Vietnam, we do, but don't hate the soldier that has seen combat first hand. For it is a sacrifice he has made for you and it is a sacrifice he will carry for the rest of his life. It is a sacrifice he has made beyond your imagination. So when a combat soldier that has seen action gets a little out there in left field, be patient and understanding. Give him respect for the things he sacrificed. He may or may not come around. If he has been consumed by the things he has seen or done, remember this is another type of casualty, as well as a byproduct of war.

I don't claim to have all the answers. I only have some of the answers for me and what has affected my life. But I do know one thing and that is you have to be truthful with yourself before you can be truthful to others and put such things in its proper perspective. Lie to yourself and you will never learn The Truth when it comes knocking at your door. 'Learn the truth and the truth will set you free,' so reads the Bible, but with truth comes responsibility and that responsibility sometimes becomes a fight within its self.

That's the way it is in this race of life, it's easy to go along with the rest of the world and accept that the times we live in now are just the way they are. That is the easy way to live your life. But you run a race to win, not to sit back and accept things as the way they are. Possessing truth isn't hard. It's maintaining its values and holding on to its principals that sometimes feels impossible. I fight this battle every day of my life in a world that has gotten out of control.

Sometimes I fall behind in this race and sometimes I feel that I gain a little, but if you don't feel that battle raging inside your soul, then you have already lost. I may lose this race myself, nothing in life is guaranteed, or owed you. But it won't be because I wasn't given an opportunity to participate. Even though you may not know it, mankind, too is in this race. Where do you stand and what is your position in this great race? How far and how long will you, along with mankind, have to run before the race is over and you receive your justified reward? Did you finish? Did you even place? I feel sometimes I have veered poorly.

*These pages are dedicated and in memory of my friends, that have missed out on so much life and of course, to their families who also made their sacrifice.

KIA LIST
Gone but Never Forgotten

James, Michael Jones, Rupert Funderburk, *Jerry Lofton, *John Sharp, James Westland Sharp, *James Dunn III , Samuel Bosenbark, Bruce Churan, Paul Erland, Babcock, I
Peldago, Hardbottle.

Must end that work that the ides of March begun; and whether we shall meet again I know not. Therefore our everlasting farewell takes: Forever, and forever farewell, Cassius!

If we do meet again, why, then we shall smile; if not, why then, this parting was well made."

---William Shakespeare, *Julius Caesar, Act V, Scene 1*---

ABOUT THE AUTHOR

I was a typical Midwestern boy that grew up in West Texas. (Slaton) I don't consider myself an educated man and I don't have the credentials and other impressive titles to even consider myself an author. I have no great honors or accomplishments in life except, my children and my grandchildren and in the fact I have only truly loved one woman.

But what I do know about is my life and the life that my brothers in combat experienced in Vietnam. Some people have told me that the medals I have been awarded in combat are some of my honors and accomplishments, but the medals given to me in combat only legitimize and give me authority to write about this subject.

There have been many stories written about Vietnam and this one has come late for the greater populous to even be interested in its contents. But the book took me many years to complete and in the beginning it wasn't written for the general public.

It has been painful for me to sit down and go back in time and bring back to memory the things I have fought so hard to put behind me. But I felt this story had to be told, so maybe it's a lesson my kids and grandkids can learn from. Many times I have had to put this book aside, for at times I felt like it was overflowing into my marriage and my wife would start to see the changes in my mood that the book would bring about.

Most of my friends have encouraged me to write this book, so I have. But mostly I wrote this book because I didn't want our efforts, for those of us who fought in Vietnam to be forgotten. Some of my friends paid the ultimate sacrifice and it is in their memory I honor them within these pages. Some honor our brothers by riding to the Memorial Wall for the Vietnam Veterans in Washington, D. C. Some honor them by placing flowers on graves each Memorial Day or thinking of them on Independence Day. I chose words, for words can tell the story and may bring to life some type of understanding to a subject that has met so much controversy over the years.

My time in Vietnam is one story among many. Vietnam affected different people in different ways, some can talk about their experiences in Vietnam and some cannot. So in the pages of this book I try to speak out for those vets who cannot and will not talk about the war they fought and the war they are fighting within themselves, even today. There was no Post War Syndrome Program for us who returned from combat roles in Vietnam. We dealt and still deal with it every day, each in our own way.

It is the veteran who honors and salutes the Flag and it is the veteran who serves under it.

"You have never lived to you have almost died, and for those who fight for it, life has a flavor that the protected will never come to know."

This quote was written on the wall of the Hanoi Hilton prison in North Vietnam. Powerful words that are totally understood by combat vets, so powerful they are written on the headstones of some who experienced front line combat. They will be inscribed on mine. For there are many ways to fight for life in this world. The world seems to be consumed with its own interests and along the way people take for granted the gift of life. I can only have faith that I will be granted a second chance to correct the wrong that I have committed during mine.

DENNIS BROOKS, MILITERY SERVICE U. S. ARMY, 1968-1976

SABER SIR

Left to right, Bronze Star V-Device stands for valor the oak leaf cluster means I was awarded this medal twice. Next is the Air Medal, V-for valor and the number 28 stands for how many times awarded. To receive one of these medals you have to spend 25 hours in Air Combat. I was awarded this medal 28 times. The Purple Heart is for wounds received in combat, awarded twice.
I only list them to legitimize the authority for me to write about such things....

I know brothers that have seen & been through a lot more than I. Some that had lost limbs, but I cannot tell their story just like no one can tell mine, we are all different. One thing is for sure, people can still be cruel. This in part is pretty much why I keep to myself. I fear that I have failed to reach the hearts of some.

You may reach me via email at redmic69@hotmail.com